FOUNDATIONS OF CORPORATE HERITAGE

Heritage is increasingly recognised as a significant corporate concern, with corporate heritage brands and identities often forming an important part of a nation's patrimony. *Foundations of Corporate Heritage* explains the principles, processes, strategic significance – and challenges – of corporate heritage formation and management. This scholarly but accessible anthology includes seminal articles on the territory and also includes five new contributions with questions for study and reflection with students on executive/taught courses in mind.

With contributions from the leading international experts in corporate heritage, this book examines the research foundations of the area and applications in practice. It will be important supplementary reading for students, practitioners and specialists in corporate marketing brand management and marketing communications, as well as tourism, hospitality and heritage studies.

John M. T. Balmer is Professor of Corporate Marketing at Brunel University Business School London; quondam Professor of Corporate Brand/Identity Management at Bradford University School of Management. He is credited with formally introducing the corporate brand and corporate marketing concepts and co-created the corporate heritage brand concept with Professors Greyser and Urde. His work has been published in leading academic journals. He took his PhD from Strathclyde University in 1996 and his first professorial appointment dates back to 1999 when he was elected to a named chair as Professor of Corporate Identity at Bradford School of Management. Subsequently, he was conferred the title of Professor of Corporate Brand/Identity Management in the same institution in recognition of his pioneering scholarship in these fields. In 2007, he was appointed to a personal chair at Brunel University London where he was bestowed the title Professor of Corporate Marketing. These professorial appointments are understood to be the first of their kind. In 2011 he established the International Corporate Heritage Symposium and is its Chairman and Conference Organiser. In 1994 he founded the International Corporate Identity Group (ICIG) and is its Chairman. He is the Director of the Marketing and Corporate Brand Research Group at Brunel University London.

This pioneering volume explores the corporate heritage brand concept from its inception. The articles and Balmer's penetrating commentary provide insights for both managerial and academic audiences interested in advancing their knowledge and understanding of corporate heritage brands. It treats the identification of an organisation's brand heritage, how to harness and apply it, and its continued stewardship. The contents encompass heritage in corporate and non-profit entities across different cultures, eras, and industry settings – from monarchies to hotels, from breweries to medicine shops. Balmer, himself a co-creator of "corporate heritage brands", is the most appropriate guide to offer these collected foundations on the nature, value, and use of the concept.

Stephen A. Greyser, *Richard P. Chapman Professor Emeritus,*
Harvard Business School (co-creator, "corporate heritage brands"), USA

Undoubtedly some of the richest and most meaningful brands around, corporate heritage brands can also be the most challenging to fully understand and manage. In this scholarly tour de force, John Balmer assembles a fascinating collection of readings notable for their deep insight and sharp practical value.

Kevin Lane Keller, *Tuck School of Business, Dartmouth College, USA*

Corporate heritage plays an increasingly significant role in contemporary marketing brandscapes. Representing a type of "living history", heritage brands symbolise continuity as well as awakening nostalgia for times past. This compendium pulls together the most important international scholarship on corporate brand heritage and is a must-read for all those researching and working in this area.

Pauline MacLaran, *Professor of Marketing and*
Consumer Research, Royal Holloway, University of London, UK

FOUNDATIONS OF CORPORATE HERITAGE

Edited by John M. T. Balmer

Routledge
Taylor & Francis Group

LONDON AND NEW YORK

First published 2017
by Routledge
2 Park Square, Milton Park, Abingdon, Oxon OX14 4RN

and by Routledge
711 Third Avenue, New York, NY 10017

Routledge is an imprint of the Taylor & Francis Group, an informa business

British Library Cataloguing-in-Publication Data
A catalogue record for this book is available from the British Library

Library of Congress Cataloging-in-Publication Data
Names: Balmer, John M. T., editor.
Title: Foundations of corporate heritage / [edited by] John Balmer.
Description: Abingdon, Oxon ; New York, NY : Routledge, 2017. |
    Includes bibliographical references and index.
Identifiers: LCCN 2016042263 (print) | LCCN 2016057151 (ebook) |
    ISBN 9781138833555 (hardback : alk. paper) | ISBN 9781138833579
    (pbk. : alk. paper) | ISBN 9781315735436 (ebook)
Subjects: LCSH: Corporations. | Corporate image. | Corporate culture. |
    Branding (Marketing)
Classification: LCC HD2731 .F68 2017 (print) | LCC HD2731 (ebook) |
    DDC 659.2—dc23
LC record available at https://lccn.loc.gov/2016042263

ISBN: 978-1-138-83355-5 (hbk)
ISBN: 978-1-138-83357-9 (pbk)
ISBN: 978-1-315-73543-6 (ebk)

Typeset in Bembo
by Apex CoVantage, LLC

IN MEMORIAM
Anna Balmer (1927–2016)

CONTENTS

List of figures   *xii*
List of tables   *xiv*
List of contributors   *xvi*
List of sources   *xx*

Introduction to corporate heritage: foundations
and principles   1
John M.T. Balmer

SECTION 1
Corporate heritage and corporate heritage
identities: insights from monarchies   **19**

1   Corporate heritage identities, corporate heritage
    brands and the multiple heritage identities of the
    British Monarchy   21
    John M.T. Balmer

2   Scrutinising the British Monarchy: the corporate
    brand that was shaken, stirred and survived   44
    John M.T. Balmer

SECTION 2
Corporate heritage connoisseurship:
key concepts and theories   87

3   Corporate heritage, corporate heritage marketing, and
    total corporate heritage communications: what are they?
    What of them?   89
    John M.T. Balmer

4   Repertoires of the corporate past: explanation and
    framework: introducing an integrated and dynamic
    perspective   130
    Mario Burghausen and John M.T. Balmer

5   Corporate heritage brands: Mead's theory of the past   151
    Bradford T. Hudson and John M.T. Balmer

SECTION 3
Corporate heritage identity stewardship and
corporate heritage tourism brand attractiveness   167

6   Corporate heritage identity stewardship: a corporate
    marketing perspective   169
    Mario Burghausen and John M.T. Balmer

7   Corporate heritage tourism brand attractiveness
    and national identity   214
    John M.T. Balmer and Weifeng Chen

SECTION 4
Corporate heritage and family businesses   245

8   Contrasting cases of corporate heritage-in-use:
    vibrant versus latent approaches   247
    Dale Miller, Bill Merrilees and Holly Cooper

9   Family heritage in corporate heritage branding:
    opportunities and risks   259
    Olof Brunninge

SECTION 5
**Corporate heritage image, management
and inheritance** **273**

10 Corporate image heritage: a customer view
    of corporate heritage   275
    Anne Rindell

11 Approaches to corporate heritage brand management:
    the cases of Cunard and Ritz-Carlton   288
    Bradford T. Hudson

12 Corporate heritage or corporate inheritance:
    a French perspective   302
    Fabien Pecot and Virginie de Barnier

Index   *315*

FIGURES

1.1 The importance of bilateral trust, authenticity and affinity
     vis-à-vis corporate heritage identities   30
1.2 A revised heritage identity framework vis-à-vis the
     British Monarchy   31
2.1 Balmer's corporate marketing mix   70
3.1 Key institutional trait constancy types   109
3.2 External/internal tri-generational heredity criterion   113
3.3 Augmented role identities – indicative example of the BBC   115
3.4 Multigenerational stakeholder dimensions vis-à-vis corporate
     heritage institution trust   116
3.5 The corporate heritage marketing mix   119
3.6 Total corporate heritage corporate communications: focus,
     nexus and effect   121
3.7 Quadripartite dimensions of total corporate heritage corporate
     communications   122
4.1 The repertoires of the corporate past, schematic framework   143
5.1 A framework for brand heritage   157
6.1 The process of data analysis   183
6.2 From open coding to conceptual categories   184
6.3 The corporate heritage identity stewardship theory
     (theoretical framework)   189
7.1 Defining characteristics of corporate heritage   222
7.2 Significance of indigenous Chinese philosophies/religions
     to TRT and to Chinese approaches to the past/heritage   225
7.3 Conceptual framework of corporate heritage as heritage
     tourism brand attraction in China   231

8.1   Model of sustainable corporate heritage   253
10.1 A three-dimensional tool for mapping customers'
      corporate image heritage   282
12.1 From legacy to heritage in four steps
      (Ferrero France example)   310

TABLES

1.1 Succinct explanations of the principal corporate-level constructs which draw on the past or which are linked to the past   24

1.2 Scrutinising the principal corporate-level constructs which draw on the past   24

3.1 Scrutinising the principal corporate-level constructs which draw on the past   92

3.2 Insights (empirical and conceptual) from foundational articles on corporate heritage brands   99

3.3 Delineating the significance of heritage: sociological, national/ national cultural, institutional and corporate marketing, stakeholder and postmodern perspectives   104

3.4 Institutional trait constancy modes: explanations and examples   110

3.5 Dimensions and explanations of the corporate heritage marketing mix   120

4.1 Towards repertories of the corporate past, development stages in the literature   135

4.2 Balmer's (2011c, p. 1383) tentative categorisation of past-related corporate-level concepts   136

4.3 The repertoires of the corporate past, foundational past-related corporate-level concepts   137

6.1 Overview of interviews conducted   182

6.2 Corporate heritage identity stewardship awareness dimensions and dispositions   185

A6.1 Sense of continuance   205

A6.2 Sense of belongingness   207

A6.3 Sense of self   209

A6.4 Sense of heritage   209

A6.5	Sense of responsibility	211
A6.6	Sense of potency	212
7.1	Descriptive statistics, correlations and average variances extracted (AVE)	232
7.2	Construct measures	233
7.3	Research hypotheses test results	235
9.1	Key characteristics and trait constancy of cases addressed in the chapter	268
12.1	Latin and French roots of heritage/inheritance	304
12.2	The four distinctions between inheritance/*héritage* and heritage/*patrimoine*	307

CONTRIBUTORS

John M.T. Balmer, PhD (Strathclyde University, Scotland), MBA (Dunelm-Durham University)., BA (Hons) (University of Reading, England), PGCE (Durham University), Dip.M., A.Mus.TCL., is Professor of Corporate Marketing at Brunel University Business School London; quondam Professor of Corporate Brand/Identity Management at Bradford University School of Management and Director of the Marketing and Corporate Brand Research Group at Brunel University. He established the International Corporate Heritage Symposium in 2011 and is its Chairman and Conference Organiser. In 1994 he established the International Corporate Identity Group (ICIG). Launched in the House of Lords (*Palace of Westminster, London*) he is the Chairman and Conference Organiser of the ICIG: symposia have been held in Denmark, Malaysia, South African, Spain, Switzerland as well as at the Universities of Oxford, Strathclyde, Brunel, Essex, and at the Queen Elizabeth II Conference Centre in London. He took his PhD at Strathclyde University in 2006 and within 3 years was elected to a personal (full) chair as Professor of Corporate Identity at Bradford University School of Management. Subsequently, he was conferred the title of Professor of Corporate Brand/Identity Management at the same institution in recognition of his pioneering scholarship in these fields. In 2007 he was appointed to a personal chair at Brunel University London where and was conferred the title Professor of Corporate Marketing. All three professorial appointments are understood to be the first of their kind. He is credited with writing the first articles on corporate brands (1995) and corporate marketing (1998) and co-developed (with Professor Greyser and Dr Urde) the corporate heritage notion (2006). He is the Chairman of the Board of Senior Consultant Editors of the *Journal of Brand Management* and a member of the senior advisory board of the *Journal of Product and Brand Management*. He has edited, co-edited well over 20 special editions of academic journals. His articles have been published in *California Management Review, British Journal of Management, European Journal of Marketing, Journal of Business Research, Long*

Range Planning, Industrial Marketing Management, International Studies of Management and Organizations, Journal of Brand Management, Journal of General Management among other journals.

Virginie de Barnier, PhD (University of Montpellier, France), MBA (University of Wisconsin, USA), MSc Psychology (University of Nice, France), is the dean of Aix-Marseille Graduate School of Management IAE, France. She is a full professor of marketing and holds degrees in both marketing and psychology. Her research interests include branding, consumer behaviour and advertising (persuasion techniques and advertising effectiveness). Her work has been presented at conferences such as the Conference of the Academy of Marketing Science, the European Marketing Academy and the Annual Conference of the French Marketing Association. She has written several books and published articles in academic reviews such as *Recherches et Applications Marketing, Advances in Consumer Research,* the *Journal of Business Research* and the *Journal of Brand Management.*

Olof Brunninge, PhD (Jönköping International Business School, Sweden) is an associate professor of business administration at Jönköping International Business School (JIBS) in Sweden. He is a member of the school's Centre for Family Enterprise and Ownership (CeFEO). Brunninge defended his PhD entitled "Organizational self-understanding and the strategy process" at JIBS in 2005. His research is focusing on organisational identity and social memory in organisations, related to strategic renewal in family businesses as well as in widely held firms. Brunninge mainly teaches strategy and international management. He has published in many academic journals, including *International Studies of Management and Organizations, Corporate Communications: An International Journal, Management & Organizational History, Small Business Economics* and *International Journal of Entrepreneurial Behaviour & Research.*

Mario Burghausen, PhD (Brunel University London, England) is a lecturer in marketing at Essex Business School, University of Essex in Colchester, UK. He has extensive industry experience, having worked for Allianz of Germany (Insurance), amongst others, in different managerial and non-managerial roles before his move into academia. He holds a PhD from Brunel University London, and his general research interests are within the nascent fields of corporate marketing and corporate heritage scholarship. He has published articles in the *Journal of Business Research, European Journal of Marketing, Journal of Brand Management,* and *Corporate Communications: An International Journal.*

Weifeng Chen, PhD (Brunel University London, England) is a lecturer at Brunel University Business School London and is a member of the Marketing and Corporate Brand Research Group at Brunel Business School. Dr Chen specialises in international business and corporate branding and has a particular research interest in the management of Chinese brands, including corporate heritage brands. Dr

Chen has published in the *Journal of Brand Management, Journal of Organizational Change Management, Regional Studies, International Journal of Production Economics, Journal of Information System Management, Advances in Information Systems Management, International Journal of Knowledge Management Studies* and *Journal of Product and Brand Management*. With Professor John M. T. Balmer (2016), he has co-edited an anthology, *Advances in Chinese Brand Management* (Palgrave Macmillan). Also with John Balmer, in 2015, he co-edited a special edition of the *Journal of Brand Management* on China's brands (Volume 22, No. 3).

Holly Cooper, PhD (Griffith University, Australia) researches corporate heritage and corporate brand heritage, and how these fields can contribute to enduring corporate success. She has a deep interest in investigating how to recover and advance corporate heritage in organisations. Her research interests include sustainable corporate branding, brand heritage and heritage brands. Her branding research is published in *Psychology & Marketing* and the *Journal of Brand Management*.

Bradford T. Hudson, PhD (Boston University, USA), MPS (Cornell University, USA), is associate professor of the practice of marketing in the Carroll School of Management at Boston College, Boston, USA. He is also assistant chair of the Marketing Department at Boston College. Previously he was a faculty member at Boston University, where he held concurrent appointments as associate professor of the practice of marketing and business history in the School of Hospitality Administration, and as lecturer in marketing at the Graduate School of Management. He has written numerous articles and chapters on business history and brand heritage for publications including *European Journal of Marketing, Corporate Communications: An International Journal* and *Cornell Hospitality Quarterly*. He is a former management consultant whose clients with historic brands included AT&T, Cadbury Schweppes, Cunard, Harley-Davidson and Nestlé. He holds a PhD in business history from Boston University, a master's degree in services marketing from Cornell University, and a certificate in strategy from Harvard Business School. He is a former Fulbright Scholar to Canada.

Bill Merrilees, PhD (University of Toronto), MA (University of Toronto), BCom (Hons) (The University of Newcastle, Australia), is professor of marketing, and leader of the Branding@Griffith Research Cluster at Griffith University, Australia. His research interests encompass branding (including corporate rebranding and brand morphing) and innovation in various contexts including firms, cities, communities, retailing and franchising. His research has been published internationally including in the *European Journal of Marketing, Journal of Business Research, Industrial Marketing Management, Journal of Advertising Research* and *Journal of Strategic Marketing*. Professor Merrilees sits on the editorial boards of the *European Journal of Marketing, Journal of Brand Management, Journal of Product and Brand Management* and the *Australasian Marketing Journal*.

Dale Miller, PhD (The University of Newcastle, Australia), MBA (University of South Australia), BAppSci (OccTher) (LaTrobe University), is a senior lecturer and deputy leader of the Branding@Griffith Research Cluster at Griffith University, Australia. Her research focusses on branding, including corporate heritage brand management, city branding and retail history. She publishes extensively in the branding domain, including in the *Journal of Brand Management, Journal of Business Research, European Journal of Marketing, Journal of Product and Brand Management* and *Journal of Historical Research in Marketing.* She has also published invited book chapters in the branding discipline. Dr Miller sits on the editorial board of the *Journal of Product and Brand Management.*

Fabien Pecot, PhD (Aix-Marseille University, France), MSc (NEOMA, France), is a visiting scholar at Boston College (in the autumn of 2014). He holds degrees in history and marketing. His research interests are in brand heritage and corporate heritage, he has delivered several papers at the International Symposia on Corporate Heritage, History and Nostalgia.

Anne Rindell, PhD (Hanken School of Economics, Helsinki, Finland), is an associate professor at Hanken School of Economics, Helsinki, Finland. Her research focuses on branding, corporate heritage and image heritage. She has published on corporate and product image heritage in numerous journals including the *Journal of Brand Management, Journal of Product and Brand Management, European Business Review* and *Qualitative Market Research: An International Journal.*

SOURCES

1 Corporate heritage identities, corporate heritage brands and the multiple heritage identities of the British Monarchy

Balmer, J. M. T. (2011) "Corporate heritage identities, corporate heritage brands and the multiple heritage identities of the British Monarchy", *European Journal of Marketing*, 45(9/10): 1380–1398.

2 Scrutinising the British Monarchy: the corporate brand that was shaken, stirred and survived

Balmer, J. M. T. (2009) "Scrutinising the British Monarchy: The corporate brand that was shaken, stirred and survived", *Management Decision*, 47.4, 639–375.

3 Corporate heritage, corporate heritage marketing, and total corporate heritage communications: what are they? What of them?

Balmer, J. M. T. (2013) "Corporate heritage, corporate heritage marketing, and total corporate heritage communications", *Corporate Communications: An International Journal*, 18.3, 290–326.

4 Repertoires of the corporate past: explanation and framework: introducing an integrated and dynamic perspective

Burghausen, M. and Balmer, J. M. T. (2014) "Repertoires of the corporate past", *Corporate Communications: An International Journal*, 19.4, 384–402.

5 Corporate heritage brands: Mead's theory of the past

Hudson, B. T. and Balmer, J. M. T. (2013) "Corporate heritage brands: Mead's theory of the past", *Corporate Communications: An International Journal*, 18.3, 347–361.

6 Corporate heritage identity stewardship: a corporate marketing perspective

Burghausen, M. and Balmer, J. M. T. (2015) "Corporate heritage stewardship: A corporate marketing perspective", *European Journal of Marketing*, 49(1/2): 22–61.

7 Corporate heritage tourism brand attractiveness and national identity

Balmer, J. M. T. and Chen, W. (2016) "Corporate heritage tourism brand attractiveness and national identity", *Journal of Product and Brand Management*, 25.3, 223–238.

INTRODUCTION TO CORPORATE HERITAGE

Foundations and principles

John M. T. Balmer

The corporate heritage notion: Revolution and captivation

Increasingly, corporate marketing scholars and practitioners find the broad corporate heritage territory to be compelling and persuasive. A scrutiny of the business domain reveals the extent to which the corporate heritage notion has progressively captured our emotions and intellects. Moreover, corporate heritage is a field of scholarship which is very much in accord with the current *Zeitgeist* – a *Zeitgeist* where the past is sought, enjoyed and fêted. More particularly, this comes with a realisation that many customers find heritage institutions to be captivating, consequential and vital. Heritage institutions are prized not only in terms of what they offer but also in what they symbolise in social, cultural, ancestral and territorial terms. Consider, among others, notable heritage organisations such as the Banca Monte dei Paschi di Siena, BBC, Bentley, the British Monarchy, Coca-Cola, Hudson Bay Company, Jose Cuervo, Kikkoman, KLM Royal Dutch Airlines, McDonald's, Nestlé, Raffles, Royal Canadian Mountain Police, Royal Enfield Motorbikes, Shell, the Sorbonne, Taj Hotels, Tong Ren Tang, Taittinger Champagne and Villeroy & Boch.

The above being noted, the formal introduction, and initial articulation, of the corporate heritage notion was something as an aside – as an afterthought – by scholars who mused on the potential significance and impact of their research (Balmer, Greyser and Urde 2006). Yet, their addendum was to be far more than a fleeting excursus but, moreover, a deliberation on heritage which, as has become apparent, was to be of considerable and lasting import.

In 2006 a trio of scholars from England, the USA and Sweden, namely Professor John M. T. Balmer (Bradford University School of Management, England), Professor Stephen A. Greyser (Harvard Business School, USA) and Dr Mats Urde (Lund University, Sweden), formally introduced the corporate heritage/corporate heritage brand notion (Balmer et al. 2006). Their formal introduction of the notion came in the conclusion of a groundbreaking article in the *Journal of Brand Management* on the Swedish Monarchy (and monarchies generally) as corporate brands. The article was entitled, "The Crown as a Corporate Brand: Insights from Monarchies".

The above triumvirate identified monarchies to be part of a wider, highly significant, but hitherto but as yet unidentified, organisational genus which they termed corporate heritage institutions/corporate heritage brands. In their article, Balmer *et al.* (2006) pinpointed some of the key attributes of corporate heritage institutions, and the reader is urged to read the closing paragraphs of their article for their pioneering reflections.

There is a degree of irony that their *en passant* reference to corporate heritage, in effect, heralded a new branch of corporate marketing/management. Increasingly, it has attracted the attention of scholars and practitioners alike and marked a veritable revolution in marketing thought. It has also drawn attention from scholars working in other heritage domains which, for the main, conceptualise heritage from a more avowedly retrospective standpoint.

Traditionally, marketing scholarship focusses on the present and future apropos products and services from a consumer perspective. In contrast, the corporate heritage notion as defined by these scholars marshalled, and was informed by, a corporate marketing philosophy (which focusses on institutions and stakeholders and recognises that the past may be significant), but on institutions which are invested with a strategic advantage apropos customers and other stakeholders because they are invested with resilient and appealing omni-temporal traits. In short, corporate heritage institutions are invested with time: times past, present and future. In part, these organisations and brands are attractive because they are viewed as stable reference points in an increasingly changing world. Scholars and practitioners have found these initial insights to be both compelling and persuasive and, since 2006, this has resulted in an upsurge of interest in corporate heritage as a distinct branch of corporate marketing and management scholarship.

Subsequently, the same triumvirate particularised the corporate heritage brand concept in greater detail (Urde, Greyser and Balmer 2007) and marshalled their individual and collective field research to this end.

The inexorable rise of interest in corporate heritage

Indubitably, since 2006, the inexorable rise in interest in corporate heritage – reflected in the corporate heritage notion moving towards the centre ground in corporate marketing – has been striking. *Why is this so?*

There are many explanations. Let me proffer three.

- First, and unquestionably, and to reiterate an above point, seminal articles on the territory (Balmer *et al.* 2006; Urde *et al.* 2007; Balmer 2011) identified and classified a distinct and significant category of institution/corporate brand (corporate heritage institutions/corporate heritage brands). As noted in their first cornerstone article (Balmer *et al.* 2006), corporate heritage possesses meaningful and durable corporate brand/identity traits: traits which were not only of the past and present but also of the prospective future too.

- Second, the nascent corporate heritage perspective not only challenged marketing management orthodoxy focussed on the present and future but also (albeit obliquely) contested one conceptualisation of history which primarily focussed on the past and present. In contrast, corporate heritage – with its emphasis on omni-temporality – stressed the importance of all three time frames; made allusions to "living history"; and underscored the significance of both change and continuity.

- Third, these – and subsequent – seminal articles represented original and powerful theoretical and normative lenses via which corporate heritage institutions/ corporate brands can be characterised, comprehended and cultivated. Frequently, containing theoretical and normative insights frameworks, these contributions spoke, and continue to speak, to both academics and managers alike.

Furthermore, in the intervening period since 2006, there has been an inexorable increase of developmental scholarly articles focussing on this conspicuously distinctive genus of corporate identity/corporate brand.

Of course, since 2006, there have been a number of significant milestones in the annals of corporate heritage studies and scholarship. These include special editions on the territory and the establishment of an annual international symposium on corporate heritage. The first special edition on corporate heritage, entitled "Papers from the First International Symposium on Corporate Heritage, History and Nostalgia", appeared in *Corporate Communications: An International Journal* (Balmer 2013a). This was subsequently followed by a second special edition, entitled "Corporate Heritage, Corporate Heritage Brands, and Organisational Heritage", that was published in *The Journal of Brand Management* (Balmer and Burghausen 2015a).

Arguably, the above special editions owe much to the establishment in 2011 by John M. T. Balmer of the International Corporate Heritage Symposium (to use its shorter and now commonly used title). The first symposium – and two subsequent symposia – was hosted by the Marketing and Corporate Brand Research Centre, Brunel Business School, Brunel University, London. Since then, the symposium has been held at leading business schools in Finland (Hanken School of Economics, Helsinki), France (Aix-Marseille Université, Aix-en-Provence), and Sweden (Jönköping University, Jönköping).

A landmark book

Arguably, too, this publication also represents another noteworthy milestone in that:

- It is significant since it is the first book of its kind and therefore is timely since it complements and reinforces academic articles published in the field.

- It is valuable because the book takes cognizance of and builds on existing research and scholarship and represents a valuable addition to the canon.
- Finally, it is expedient since it provides in book form a synopsis of the field which seeks to benefit both scholars and practitioners alike.

Notably, and appealingly, this cornerstone anthology includes new contributions penned by prominent corporate heritage scholars from Australia, Finland, France, Sweden and the USA.

In addition, this book also incorporates the republication of a number of foundational articles taken from the editor's individual and collaborative endeavours with Dr Mario Burghausen (Essex University, England), Dr Weifeng Chen (Brunel University London, England) and Dr Bradford T. Hudson (Boston College, USA). These publications have variously been published in the *European Journal of Marketing*, *Management Decision*, *The Journal of Product and Brand Management*, and *Corporate Communications: An International Journal* and have been republished with the kind permission of Emerald Publishing.

Moreover, this compendium is testimony of the global interest in corporate heritage, as can be gleaned from the authors represented in this anthology, who are affiliated with prominent universities in Australasia, Europe and North America.

Formal introduction of the corporate heritage brand notion

As previously detailed above, it was in the final pages of a seminal study of monarchies as corporate brands that Balmer et al. (2006) formally introduced the corporate brand notion and some core precepts of corporate brands were identified. The article is, arguably, of seminal importance because these scholars:

- noted the significance of the temporal dimension vis-à-vis corporate heritage brands: corporate heritage brands are of the past, present and future; and
- noted the value of corporate heritage brands that are stable points of reference in a changing world and help to define peoples and places (in terms of "giving identity").

In addition, this first article on the area noted – and offered advice on – how corporate heritage brands should be managed, namely:

a. Senior managers in managing corporate heritage brands should be mindful of the past, present and future;
b. Senior managers should take care *not to* wear out brand symbols;
c. Senior managers should ensure that a corporate heritage brand's emotional bases are built on and/or refreshed (so that it remains relevant for customers and other stakeholders);
d. Senior managers should balance a corporate heritage brand's values so that they speak to the present (thus accommodating the need for change).

The particularisation of the corporate heritage brand notion detailed discussion of the corporate heritage brand notion

This second landmark article is noteworthy since it further delineated the corporate heritage notion, and this was undertaken via a number of means.

The first and most visible contribution by Urde, Greyser and Balmer (2007) was their formulation of what they called "the corporate heritage quotient". The quotient is a five-part framework detailing the dimensions of a corporate heritage brand, which were identified as:

* track record;
* longevity;
* core values;
* use of symbols; and
* the importance of an institutions' history.

The second impact of their work was their observation that *a corporate heritage brand* was differentiated from *a corporate brand with a heritage.*

A corporate heritage brand

A corporate heritage brand refers to organisations which highlight their institution's heritage as part of its corporate brand identity.

A corporate brand with a heritage

A corporate brand with a heritage relates to those firms who have decided not to formally utilise the organisation's heritage. (This can be for strategic reasons, or because they are unaware of the institution's credentials as a heritage organisation, etc.)

The third advance of these authors was their conclusion that corporate heritage brands often (but not unvaryingly) can have strategic value. Often, senior managers can utilise a corporate heritage brand to significant strategic effect. However, they issued a canard by asserting that corporate heritage brands *are not automatically valuable* but *merely offer the opportunity to bestow strategic value to an organisation* in the pursuance of an organisation's mission and purposes.

The formal introduction of the corporate heritage identity notion

The next key development in the field was the formal introduction of the corporate heritage identity notion (Balmer 2011). It examined the notion that heritage institutions have certain identity traits that are perennial. Whereas, to date, the corporate heritage notion was scrutinised via a corporate branding lens, Balmer saw the efficacy of adopting an explicit corporate identity perspective in examining the corporate identity notion.

The importance of multiple role identities, relative invariance, and authenticity, trust and affinity

The advent of the corporate heritage notion was also accompanied by some further conceptualisation of the nature of corporate heritage. The multiple role identities, the notion of relative invariance and the importance of authenticity, trust and affinity have the aim of furthering an understanding of the territory.

(i) Multiple role identities

Balmer (2011) explained that one reason that corporate heritage identities could be highly meaningful was because they were imbued with "multiple role identities". As such, corporate heritage identities are invested with additional – often powerful and meaningful – identities associated with, among others, people and places. Why is the notion of multiple role identities of significance? This is because heritage institutions, by virtue of being invested with multiple role identities, can confer identities of peoples, places, communities and cultures to peoples, places, communities and cultures.

(ii) Relative invariance

It was further explained by Balmer (2011) that corporate heritage identities remained meaningful and were valuable owing to their relative invariance. Why is the notion of relative invariance accorded such importance? This is because whilst heritage organisations might appear to be *invariant (unchanging)*, they are likely in fact to be *variant (they change)*. Sometimes this involves changes to core corporate identity traits; the acquisition of new, additional and meaningful role identities (and sometimes the tempering of extant role identities); and new meanings accorded to existing heritage activities, symbols, rituals, ceremonies, etc.

(iii) Authenticity, trust, affinity

Finally, Balmer (2011) argued that a key dimension of a relevant and meaningful corporate heritage identity is bilateral company/stakeholder trust. Therefore, there needs to be authenticity on the part of the corporate heritage institution and affinity to the heritage institution by customers and other constituencies.

Fundamental criteria of corporate heritage identities

Balmer (2013b) expounded the fundamental criteria of corporate heritage identities. These were delineated as follows:

- Omni-temporality: corporate heritage identities subsist in temporal strata of the past, present and prospective future.

- Institutional trait consistency: certain corporate heritage identities have remained meaningful and constant.
- Tri-generational heredity: a corporate heritage identity has been in existence and has been meaningful to customers/stakeholders for a minimum of three generations.
- Augmented role identities: a corporate heritage identity is infused with multiple role identities including territorial, cultural, social and ancestral identity.
- Ceaseless multigenerational stakeholder utility: a corporate heritage identity has been demonstrably salient for consecutive generations of stakeholders.
- Unremitting management tenacity: a corporate heritage identity has been underpinned by assiduous management of its corporate heritage. (Thus, a distinction can be made between a corporate heritage identity and a corporate identity with a heritage: an analogous distinction to that made earlier apropos corporate heritage – see above).

The formal introduction of organisational heritage

A key landmark in the annals of corporate heritage scholarship was the formal introduction by Balmer and Chen (2015) of the organisational heritage notion that differentiated between *organisational heritage* and *organisational heritage identification*. The organisational heritage conceptualisation was subsequently further deliberated on by Balmer and Burghausen (2015c), who substantially developed the organisational heritage notion and particularised the organisational heritage field of Balmer and Chen (2015) via the articulation of three schools of thought apropos organisational heritage (Balmer and Burghausen 2015c) which aimed to build on and advance the preliminary musings of Balmer and Chen (2015).

This led to the articulation of a further concept by Balmer and Burghausen (2015c) of *organisational heritage cultural identification*. As such, three concepts appear under the organisational heritage umbrella, namely: *organisational heritage identity, organisational heritage identification*, and *organisational heritage cultural identification*. The Balmer and Burghausen (2015c) article is notable because it defines the above concepts in considerable detail. Also of note is their review of the broad corporate heritage literature; see their *Journal of Brand Management* article "Explicating corporate heritage, corporate heritage brands and organisational heritage" (Balmer and Burghausen 2015b).

Seemingly, the exposition and elucidation of the organisational heritage notion was noteworthy since this provided a much-needed bridge between corporate marketing and organisational/management studies. At the time of the formal introduction of the organisational heritage notion (Balmer and Chen 2015), there was a paucity of scholarship/conceptual insights of past-related concepts within organisation and management studies. In short, the heritage notion had not meaningfully appeared on the radar of the aforementioned scholars.

Corporate heritage and organisational heritage: Key concepts

For the novice of corporate heritage, it is important to understand that many corporate and organisational identity constructs inform the territory. Thus, in order to more fully appreciate the field, it is imperative for scholars and managers alike to have a working knowledge of the central constructs. To this end, in this section, definitions of some of the main heritage concepts are delineated. In addition, scholars and managers are recommended to appraise themselves of foundational concepts relating to the past, of which heritage is one (Balmer 2011; Burghausen and Balmer 2014).

Corporate heritage marketing

Corporate heritage marketing is an organisational-wide philosophy which is underpinned by a multi-generational focussed, customer, stakeholder, societal and CSR/ ethically focussed ethos. It is enacted and created over successive generations and should broadly meet a tri-generational criterion.

(Balmer 2011, p. 1345)

Corporate heritage identity

Corporate heritage identities should be viewed as a distinct identity type. Corporate heritage identities refer to those institutional traits which have remained meaningful and invariant over the passage of time and, as such, a corporate heritage identity viewed as being part of the past, present and future. This said, the meanings attached to particular facets of an institution's identity can vary with the passage of time. Heritage identity traits can include corporate competencies, cultures, philosophies, activities, markets and groups etc. and may find, in addition, expression in distinctive visual identities, architecture and service offerings.

(Balmer 2011, p. 1385)

Corporate heritage brands

Corporate heritage brands refers to a distinct category of institutional brand where there is a degree of continuity in terms of the brand promise as expressed via the institution's identity, behaviour and symbolism.

(Balmer 2011, p. 1385)

Total corporate heritage marketing communications

As noted by Balmer (2013*b*, pp. 317–320), total corporate heritage marketing communications encompasses primary, secondary, tertiary and legacy corporate heritage communications (internal and external):

- *Primary corporate heritage communications:* omni-temporal effects of products, services, management and employee actions, etc.;
- *Secondary corporate heritage communications:* omni-temporal effects of controlled corporate communications (corporate advertising, corporate PR, etc.);
- *Tertiary corporate heritage communications:* omni-temporal effects of communications by third parties;
- *Legacy corporate heritage communications:* the multigenerational and omni-temporal communications. Note that corporate heritage communications can be bequeathed and inherited, and certain groups may see themselves as custodians of an institution's heritage communications.

Balmer also noted that internal heritage communications encompass multigenerational and omni-temporal internal corporate heritage communications on the part of managers and organisational managers and to families (in family-owned businesses), while external corporate heritage communications relates to customers and other stakeholder groups in a similar means to the above.

Corporate heritage culture

The perennial sense of who we are on the part of successive generations of organisational members and, where applicable, owners (family-owned businesses for example).

(Balmer 2013b, p. 321)

Organisational heritage

By means of context, it should be noted that concepts which have the prefix "organisational" largely belong to the organisational behaviour/management discipline and thus focus on employees (organisational members) and their perceptions and concerns. In contrast, concepts which have the prefix "corporate" largely belong to the corporate marketing/strategy fields and thus focus on customers and other stakeholders and on strategic perspectives. Arguably, therefore, the latter is broader than the former and may be seen to accommodate "organisational" constructs within its purview.

Organisational heritage and organisational identification were formally delineated as follows:

The significance of heritage to organisational members of the broad corporate heritage notion opens extant corporate marketing scholarship on the territory to scholars within the organisational behaviour field. As such, the extant concepts of organisational identity, organisational identification can be adapted within a corporate heritage context viz: organisational heritage/organisational heritage identities and organisational heritage identification.

(Balmer and Chen 2015, p. 202)

Balmer and Burghausen (2015c), building on the previous two definitions of organisational, further differentiated between three modes of organisational heritage which, de facto, can be designated as distinct schools of thought. These three modes can be verbalised as follows:

Organisational heritage identity

The perceived and reminisced Omni-temporal traits – both formal/utilitarian and normative/societal – of organisational members' work organisation.

(Balmer and Burghausen 2015c, p. 403)

Organisational heritage identification

Organisational members' identification/self-categorisation vis-à-vis the perceived and reminisced Omni-temporal traits – both formal/utilitarian and normative/societal – of their work organisation.

(Balmer and Burghausen 2015c, p. 403)

Organisational heritage cultural identification

Organisational members' multi-generation identification/self-categorisation vis-à-vis the perceived and reminisced Omni-temporal traits – both formal/utilitarian and normative/ societal – of their work organisation's corporate culture.

(Balmer and Burghausen 2015c, pp. 403–404)

Structure of the book

This compendium is organised as follows:

- Section 1 Corporate heritage and corporate heritage identities: Insights from monarchies
- Section 2 Corporate heritage connoisseurship: Key concepts and theories
- Section 3 Corporate heritage identity stewardship and corporate heritage tourism brand attractiveness
- Section 4 Corporate heritage and family businesses
- Section 5 Corporate heritage image, management and inheritance

In the next part of this introduction, the editor provides a brief synopsis of each chapter. This enables the reader to have a sense of the breadth of ambition of this book as well as having a foretaste of each contributory chapter.

Section 1: Corporate heritage and corporate heritage identities: Insights from monarchies

Two articles comprise this section.

The first article, entitled "Corporate heritage identities, corporate heritage brands and the multiple heritage identities of the British Monarchy" by John M. T. Balmer (2011), reprints an article which appeared in the *European Journal of Marketing*. Notably, the article includes a taxonomy of past related constructs which were later developed by Burghausen and Balmer (2014): see above. This article is notable, since its reflections on the British Monarchy not only provide insights for this institution but also aim to provide insights for corporate heritage institutions per se. Thus, this article is analogous to the foundational article on corporate heritage by Balmer *et al.* (2006) which scrutinised monarchies via a corporate branding lens. In this article John Balmer formally introduces the corporate heritage identity and, arguably, this represents a meaningful advance apropos the corporate heritage canon. Moreover, it also introduces the multiple role identity notion in relation to corporate heritage identities and the relative invariance concept too. Significantly, too, it notes the importance of bilateral trust between organisations and stakeholders. The author argues that trust, authenticity, affinity and regulation all need to be considered in terms of the management and maintenance of corporate heritage identities. He also details a revised corporate heritage framework vis-à-vis the British Monarchy. As such, he extends the original elements as shown in Balmer *et al.* (2006). The new framework, therefore, includes eight dimensions: royal, religious, regal, ritual, relevant, respected, responsive and regulation dimensions. He argues that these dimensions can be adapted to corporate heritage entities. The appendix to this article is of note too, since it discusses the power of provenance and history in marketing; notes the dark side of history, heritage and provenance; explains the roles of history and the past in marketing; and provides a more detailed explanation of the revised corporate heritage identity framework vis-à-vis the British Monarchy.

The second article on monarchy, entitled "Scrutinising the British Monarchy: The corporate brand that was shaken, stirred and survived", also by John M. T. Balmer (2009), reprints an article which appeared in *Management Decision*. Again, this article provides not only insights on the British Monarchy but on heritage institutions per se. This time the focus is from a corporate heritage brand perspective rather than a corporate heritage identity perspective. The author identifies a few of the travails the British Monarchy has experienced over the centuries and explains how the institution has learnt from these and how these have shaped the institution's corporate heritage brand. The aforementioned resulted in one process for examining corporate heritage brand entitled: *Chronicling Corporate Heritage Brands*. In managing a corporate heritage brand – drawing on monarchical insights – it is conceptualised this requires a multidisciplinary approach based on *Continuity* (apropos the corporate brand and corporate identity), *Visibility* (apropos corporate communications), *Strategy* (apropos corporate strategy), *Sensitivity* (apropos leadership and crisis management), *Respectability* (apropos corporate image and corporate reputation), and *Empathy* (apropos stakeholder management/stakeholder orientation).

Section 2: Corporate heritage connoisseurship: Key concepts and theories

Three articles are included in this section.

The first article, by John Balmer (2013b), entitled "Corporate heritage, corporate heritage marketing, and total corporate heritage communications", reprints an article which appeared in *Corporate Communications: An International Journal.*

The article formally introduces the corporate heritage marketing, total corporate heritage communications and the corporate heritage sustainability notions and also provides frameworks pertaining to them. It details latent theoretical contributions vis-à-vis corporate heritage. It provides an overview of the literature as it existed in 2013 and details key dimensions of corporate heritage. The importance and salience of corporate heritage are noted along with the difficulties associated with the concept.

In the second article, by Mario Burghausen and John M. T. Balmer (2014), entitled "Repertoires of the corporate past: Explanation and framework. Introducing an integrated and dynamic perspective", reprints an article which appeared in *Corporate Communications: An International Journal*. The article meaningfully develops Balmer's (2011) earlier typology of the past. The authors do this by noting that a clear distinction should be made between instrumental and foundational concepts relating to the past, namely the corporate past, corporate memory, corporate history, corporate tradition, corporate heritage, corporate nostalgia and corporate provenance past-related corporate-level concepts, making a distinction between instrumental and foundational past-related corporate-level concepts. A framework is introduced and articulated detailing seven different modes of referencing the past of an organisation: corporate past, corporate memory, corporate history, corporate tradition, corporate heritage, corporate nostalgia and corporate provenance. The article introduces a framework which explicates seven routes by which a company's past can be referenced.

Finally, the article by Bradford T. Hudson and John M. T. Balmer (2013) entitled "Corporate heritage brands: Mead's theory of the past" reprints an article which appeared in *Corporate Communications: An International Journal*. The article has the aim of exploring the mechanisms of consumer behaviour apropos corporate heritage brands. The article draws on – and develops – George Herbert Mead's (1863–1931) theory of the past in this regard. Marshalling this theory, the authors explain why consumers engage with heritage and the past. The authors make a distinction between innate heritage, projective heritage, structural heritage, implied heritage, reconstructed heritage and mythical heritage. Thus, the article details why and how corporate heritage brands are appealing to consumers. A corporate heritage brand framework is introduced.

Section 3: Corporate heritage identity stewardship and corporate heritage tourism brand attractiveness

Two articles have been included in this section. Both are empirical studies and both relate to celebrated corporate heritage institutions having a patrimony dating back to the late seventeenth century. The first empirical research focusses on a British company and the second – unusually – on a Chinese institution.

The first article is a major theory-building case study of *Shepherd Neame*: it is Great Britain's oldest brewery and is one of the oldest heritage organisations in the world. It was established in 1698. Authored by Mario Burghausen and John

M. T. Balmer (2015) and entitled "Corporate heritage stewardship: A corporate marketing perspective", the research was published in the *European Journal of Marketing*. The study explores senior managers' collective understanding of Shepherd Neame's corporate heritage. In introducing and explicating a theory of corporate heritage stewardship, the authors outline how this strategic perspective is grounded in a distinctive management mind-set. The research found the aforementioned was underpinned by six stewardship temperaments, namely a sense of continuance, belongingness, self, heritage, responsibility and potency. The theoretical contribution of this study also is germane apropos the management/stewardship of corporate heritage institutions since the study revealed how a corporate heritage stewardship management mind-set can guide and apprise top executives of what, and what not, to do vis-à-vis their stewardship of a corporate heritage institution. This study is of particular note owing to the richness of the qualitative data informing this in-depth, theory-building, single case study.

The second article is also noteworthy. Co-authored by John M. T. Balmer and Weifeng Chen (2016) and entitled "Corporate heritage tourism brand attractiveness and national identity", it constituted the lead article in the *Journal of Product and Brand Management*. It is the first empirical study to focus on a corporate heritage tourism brand and the earliest to focus on a Chinese corporate heritage brand per se. The study conjoins corporate brand notion with the nascent corporate heritage brand domain and the established area of heritage tourism. The research focusses on what is arguably China's most celebrated corporate heritage brand: *Tong Ren Tang* (同仁堂). Arguably the most celebrated heritage shop in both Beijing and, moreover, China, it is also, unquestionably, the most fêted traditional Chinese medicine shop in greater China and the wider Chinese diaspora. Enjoying an unequalled heritage spanning five centuries, the shop was established in 1669. (As such, it is a contemporaneous institution in heritage terms to Shepherd Neame, detailed above.) Drawing on Balmer's (2013b) corporate heritage tourism notion, the article considers the reasons why Tong Ren Tang (TRT) is a popular attraction for Chinese domestic tourists. Informed by the multiple role identity/augmented role identity notion apropos corporate heritage institutions (Balmer 2011), this empirical study showed that the attractiveness of TRT as a corporate heritage brand was due to its national, temporal, familial and – most interestingly – imperial role identities. (The latter is fascinating, since the research revealed the ongoing saliency of China's erstwhile imperial identity.) The authors explain that visits to the TRT shop may be seen as expressing and reaffirming a sense of Chinese national community and identity. Traditional Chinese medicine is underpinned by Confucian and, moreover, by Daoist religious/philosophical precepts, and this shop is the principal exponent and symbol of traditional Chinese medicine in the Middle Kingdom. Also, because the shop was the sole provider of medicine to successive emperors, TRT enjoys an unparalleled imperial provenance among Chinese corporate heritage institutions. In short, the study revealed TRT to be a living link with China's imperial past. Moreover, today, as in centuries past, TRT's products and services are deemed to be "fit for a king" or, more appropriately, "fit for an emperor".

The second segment of the book consists of original contributions from leading scholars working in the corporate heritage domain. The contributors were requested to pen chapters which spoke to scholars, practitioners and students following taught courses in business schools. Thus, they seek to have an unambiguous pedagogical utility. To this end, the articles include questions for study and reflection which, therefore, enable them to be used on degree and diploma pathways.

Section 4: Corporate heritage and family businesses

Two contributions constitute this section.

The opening chapter is written by Australian scholars Dale Miller, Bill Merrilees and Holly Cooper and has the title "Contrasting cases of corporate heritage-in-use: Vibrant versus latent approaches". Many corporate marketing scholars will be familiar with the research scholarship of Dr Miller and Professor Merrilees in the broad corporate marketing domain. This chapter has a distinctly and interestingly "Old Commonwealth" dimension owing to its Australian and Canadian foci. To this end, this chapter focusses on two corporate heritage institutions: one based in Canada (Canadian Tire) and the other in Australia (David Jones). Both companies have strong family roots. By means of context, this article shares certain parallels with the distinction made by Urde, Greyser and Balmer in their second landmark article on corporate heritage (Urde *et al.* 2007) where they made a distinction between *a corporate heritage brand* and *a corporate brand with a heritage*. The former characterises companies which highlight their firm's heritage as part of its corporate brand identity whilst the second perspective denotes firms who have decided not to formally utilise the organisation's heritage. In this chapter, the authors refer to vibrant and latent heritage and their respective approaches in utilising corporate heritage, and this complements and extends the scholarship of Urde *et al.* (2007). In their chapter, the authors explain why David Jones represents the latent approach in contrast to Canadian Tire, which characterises the vibrant approach. A model of sustainable corporate heritage is introduced and explicated. Moreover, the chapter usefully offers guidance for managers who are concerned to highlight their firm's corporate heritage credentials.

Entitled "Family heritage in corporate heritage branding: Opportunities and risks", the second chapter is written by the Swedish scholar Olof Brunninge, celebrated for his scholarship on corporate heritage. This chapter provides a good introduction to this territory by detailing the nature of family firms and the utilisation of corporate heritage by them. Making reference to numerous case examples from Italy, Germany and Sweden (Barre, Bertelsmann, Brio, Falck, Hipp, IKEA, Rickmers and Spendrups), Brunninge's reflections demonstrate how a company's family heritage can represent a unique resource for heritage organisations: a core heritage trait from which an entity (and of course the family) have the potential to derive a unique and valuable competitive advantage. As Brunninge relates:

> For family firms not yet including family heritage in their corporate communications, this means that there is probably potential to construct a compelling

story around the family-related provenance of the organisation, enhancing the uniqueness of the firm and its brand.

However, for the sake of balance, Dr Brunninge also relates how certain family businesses have negative/undesirable heritage traits and reflects on the problems and instrumental approaches to the aforementioned. Thus, corporate heritage for family business not only presents opportunities but risks in addition. Clearly, for good or for ill, the corporate heritage notion is especially germane for many family businesses, large or small.

Section 5: Corporate heritage image, management and inheritance

Three chapters constitute this section.

The first chapter, "Corporate image heritage: A customer view of corporate heritage", written by the Finnish marketing scholar Anne Rindell, develops a core research interest of hers, namely *heritage image*. Making reference to Sweden's IKEA corporate brand and the Finnish retailer brand Anttila, Dr. Rindell explains that corporate heritage relates to a consumer's past images. These serve as reference points when evaluating company-related experiences of the present but have inferences for the future. As such, *corporate image heritage* links both past and present conceptualisations and experiences with future expectations. These need to be understood by corporate marketing managers, since they are part of a customer's corporate images construction processes. Usefully, the author explores the notion of time apropos corporate brand images. However, she urges caution, since the concept of time can be comprehended in a variety of ways. An updated, three-dimensional mapping tool focussed on customers is outlined. The aforementioned provides an overview of archetypal corporate heritage analysis but is augmented by incorporating systematic efforts to identify customers' corporate image heritage. By these means organisations can uncover what customers deem to be meaningful, authentic and genuine apropos a company's heritage.

Penned by US academic Bradford T. Hudson, the second chapter is entitled "Approaches to corporate heritage brand management: The cases of Cunard and Ritz-Carlton". Focussing on two well-known corporate heritage institutions that are remarkably similar on a number of dimensions, Cunard and Ritz-Carlton, this chapter is distinctive in that it is informed by the historical method research tradition. Readers are likely to find the historical narrative relating to Cunard and Ritz-Carlton thought-provoking from a corporate heritage perspective. A comparison of the two cases lends support to Urde, Greyser and Balmer's (Urde *et al.* 2007) binary division apropos corporate heritage. This relates to: (1) a corporate heritage brand (where an organisation employs its heritage as part of its strategic corporate marketing activities) and (2) a corporate brand with a heritage (where an organisation does not marshal its corporate heritage). Dr Hudson's utilisation of the historical method mode of analysis identifies Cunard to be an exemplar of the first category whilst Ritz-Carlton is an exemplar of the second. Furthermore, the conclusions reached in this chapter are supportive of the corporate heritage notion, with the author seeing merit in the multidimensional corporate heritage brand framework introduced by Urde *et al.* (2007).

The final chapter, by French scholars Fabien Pecot and Virginie de Barnier, has the title "Corporate heritage or corporate inheritance: A French perspective". It examines the epistemological distinction between heritage (*héritage*) and patrimony (*patrimoine*) from a French perspective. The contribution is a response to Balmer's (2013b) call for scholars to explore the historiography of key concepts and words. Taking up this challenge, these French scholars show how both the French and Latin origins of the words – and also the impact of French cultural contexts – have moulded contemporary meanings of heritage and patrimony. Marshalling four epistemological distinctions (content and process/content only; private/public; imposed/appropriated; and from past to present/from past to present to future), the authors suggest a definition for the study of corporate inheritance (French: *héritage d'entreprise*). This is qualitatively different from the study of corporate heritage (French: *patrimoine d'entreprise*). Reference is made to the Ferrero France heritage institution in expounding the above. The chapter, whilst mindful of the differences between Anglophone and Francophone understandings of heritage outlined by Balmer (2013b), is distinct in that it provides a fuller Francophone overview of the territory. As such, this contribution provides a useful and timely French perspective on the broad corporate heritage domain.

Final reflection

The publication of this book is propitious since it falls on the tenth anniversary of the exposition and formal introduction of the corporate heritage/corporate heritage brand notion by Professor Stephen A. Greyser, Dr. Mats Urde and myself (Balmer *et al.* 2006). At the time, our pithy reflections on corporate heritage – made in the final paragraphs of our article on monarchies – seemed little more than a significant aside; ten years on, it is becoming transparent that the corporate heritage phenomenon is of far greater consequence than was initially assumed. As we say in England: "Mighty oaks from little acorns grow."

This groundbreaking book is testimony not only of the above but of the progress made over the last decade. Today, there is a small, vibrant and growing community of scholars engaged in research and scholarship apropos corporate heritage. Encouragingly, research students are pursuing doctorates in the area, and Dr Mario Burghausen seemingly has the distinction of holding the first PhD in the field. Moreover, managers and consultants have begun to appreciate the strategic importance of corporate heritage: it is a concept that now enjoys prominence in business parlance.

In bringing this introduction to a close, I wish to thank my friends and colleagues who have contributed to this anthology along with my research collaborators whose articles are included in the first part of the book. Thanks are due to everyone at

Routledge who supported and encouraged this publication initiative. I also wish to acknowledge and salute my friends Professor Stephen A. Greyser of Harvard Business School and Dr. Mats Urde of Lund University, Sweden. It was we three who formally introduced and developed the corporate heritage notion (Balmer *et al.* 2006; Urde *et al.* 2007). We all owe them a huge debt of gratitude.

Foundations of Corporate Heritage aims to be a valuable and pivotal introduction to the field for scholars, managers and consultants alike: a collection which aims to capture something of my fascination and excitement with the depth and richness of the broad corporate heritage domain. Finally, it is my hope that readers will see this book as a *vade mecum*: a book they will wish to have to hand and frequently refer to; a book that with the passage of time will fashion its own exceptional heritage as a veritable, essential and accessible compendium. *Read on and enjoy!*

References

Balmer, J. M. T. (2011), Corporate heritage identities, corporate heritage brands and the multiple heritage identities of the British Monarchy. *European Journal of Marketing*, 45(*9–10*): 1380–1398.

Balmer, J. M. T. (2013a), Papers from the First International Symposium on Corporate Heritage, History and Nostalgia. Special Edition: *Corporate Communications: An International Journal*, 18(*3*): 285–382.

Balmer, J. M. T. (2013b), Corporate heritage, corporate heritage marketing, and total corporate heritage communications. *Corporate Communications: An International Journal*, 18(*3*): 290–326.

Balmer, J. M. T. and Burghausen, M. (2015a), Corporate heritage, corporate heritage brands, and organisational heritage. Special Edition: *The Journal of Brand Management*, 22(*5*): 361–484.

Balmer, J. M. T. and Burghausen, M. (2015b), Explicating corporate heritage, corporate heritage brands and organisational heritage. *Journal of Brand Management*, 22(*5*): 354–384.

Balmer, J. M. T. and Burghausen, M. (2015c), Introducing organisational heritage: Linking corporate heritage, organisational identity, and organisational memory. *Journal of Brand Management*, 22(*5*): 385–411.

Balmer, J. M. T. and Chen, W. (2016), Corporate heritage brands in China: Consumer engagement with China's most celebrated corporate heritage brand – Tong Ren Tang: 同仁堂. *Journal of Brand Management*, 23(*3*): 194–210.

Balmer, J. M. T., Greyser, S. A. and Urde, M. (2006), The crown as a corporate brand: Insights from monarchies. *Journal of Brand Management*, 14(*1–2*): 137–161.

Burghausen, M. and Balmer, J. M. T. (2014), Repertoires of the corporate past: Explanation and framework: Introducing an integrated and dynamic process. *Corporate Communications: An International Journal*, 19(*4*): 384–402.

Burghausen, M. and Balmer, J. M. T. (2015), Corporate heritage identity stewardship: A corporate marketing perspective. *European Journal of Marketing*, 49(*1–2*): 22–61.

Urde, M., Greyser, S. A. and Balmer, J. M. T. (2007), Corporate brands with a heritage. *Journal of Brand Management*, 15(*1*): 4–19.

SECTION 1

Corporate heritage and corporate heritage identities

Insights from monarchies

1

CORPORATE HERITAGE IDENTITIES, CORPORATE HERITAGE BRANDS AND THE MULTIPLE HERITAGE IDENTITIES OF THE BRITISH MONARCHY

John M. T. Balmer

Introduction

On first reading, Lampedusa's proposition may be seen as little more than a riddle wrapped up in a paradox. However, to me, a second reading of Lampedusa's thesis unwittingly divulges something of both the power and the paradox of corporate heritage identities. To me, corporate heritage identities:

- link identity change, identity continuance and the identities of time; and
- are an identity category that is both variable and invariable in that, although identities and symbolism may outwardly appear to be the same, the meanings we give to them can change.

This is what I call Relative Invariance. (In addition, I expand the theoretical notion of an individual's role identities to explain how this can be of saliency to corporate heritage identities: I call this phenomenon Institutional Role Identities.)

Although this article has as its focus the British Monarchy, my insights may be of pertinence for other corporate heritage identities. To me, corporate heritage identities represent an identity category that is, in organisational contexts, seemingly ubiquitous. To me, corporate heritage identities encompass famous, as well as infamous, heritage institutions such as Ambassador Cars (India), the BBC, the Berlin Philharmonic Orchestra, Coca-Cola, the Cooperative Movement, Harrods, Harvard Business School, Heinz, HSBC Bank, the Jesuits, Manchester United Football Club, the People's Liberation Army of China, Rolls-Royce, Philips, the Red Cross, Rotary Club, Toyota and Yale University.

This article focuses on corporate heritage identities per se. To date, heritage has received little attention in institutional contexts. This being noted, heritage has been the focus of attention in marketing and management in the fields of heritage marketing (Misiura, 2006), heritage tourism (Park, 2010) and the nascent area of corporate heritage brands (Balmer *et al.*, 2006; Urde *et al.*, 2007). Otnes and Maclaren (2007), for instance, have concluded that the intersections between heritage and consumption have largely been ignored by marketing scholars. Marketing scholars, both explicitly and implicitly, note the importance of heritage to a brand's worth and strength (George, 2004) and brand personality (Keller and Richey, 2006).

At this juncture I wish to make a distinction between corporate heritage identities and corporate heritage brands. The latter encompasses those institutional promises and stakeholder expectations that are, to a lesser or greater degree, seemingly immutable, and which are associated with a corporate brand name and marque. In contrast, corporate heritage identities relate to those institutional attributes and qualities that also are, to a lesser or greater degree, ostensibly invariable, and which, in part, meaningfully define an organisation's corporate identity.

Traditional power, the British Monarchy, and why heritage identities in institutional contexts matter

Max Weber, in his scrutiny of power modes, proffered a cogent, tripartite classification of power types: the rational, the traditional, and the charismatic. For Weber, monarchies were the embodiment of traditional authority, and, to Weber, their legitimacy was derived from tradition and from a seemingly eternal past (Mommsen, 1992). However, while the British Monarchy superficially appears to be invariable in identity terms as evinced by the centuries-old acclamation "God save the King", both public and monarch alike are fully cognizant of the fact that today, to draw on marketing parlance, "The customer is King" (as a direct consequence of the Crown's morphing into a constitutional monarchy). Heritage identities remain meaningful not only because of their provenance but because of their salience. Broadening the work of Smith (1991), I conclude that heritage identities can enter common consciousness and are of inestimable value vis-à-vis a group's collective memory not only in terms of the institution, but also as an embodiment of cultures, places and time frames. Heritage identities not only have but also give identity.

The British Monarchy: Not an ephemeral or a trivial institution

To me, a scrutiny of monarchy from marketing perspectives is not ephemeral or trivial but is a highly important and desirable corporate marketing undertaking. For instance, the monarchy has an impressive breadth and depth in institutional and in branding terms: Queen Elizabeth is Queen of 100 million people in the 16 realms where she is separately and divisibly Sovereign (Queen of Australia, Queen of Canada, etc.) In addition, She is titular head of the Commonwealth of Nations: the latter embraces one billion people: between a quarter and a third of mankind (Cannon and Griffiths, 1998). Moreover, the Crown has divulged important theoretical insights in terms of the historicity of organisations including the powerful notion of "invented tradition" (Cannadine, 1983; Hobsbawm, 1983) along with the identification of corporate heritage brands (Balmer *et al.*, 2006; Urde *et al.*, 2007). There is global interest in the institution as evinced by the wedding of Prince William in April 2011 when two billion people watched the celebrations on television and an additional 400 million households followed the wedding online (Ahmed, 2011; Starkey, 2011). In general terms, the British Monarchy seemingly appears to follow something of the precepts of corporate marketing in terms of its philosophy and culture. To me, the Crown has an increasingly explicit customer, stakeholder, societal, ethical/CSR orientation and is mindful not only of the present but also of the future and of the past (Balmer, 2011b).

The principal corporate-level constructs which draw on the past

A review of the literature on the past uncovered the following taxonomy of constructs, which appear to be of salience in institutional contexts. The principal constructs are: tradition, custom, nostalgia, melancholia, iconic branding, retro branding, heritage marketing, heritage tourism, corporate heritage identities and corporate heritage brands. In terms of time frames, for me, the aforesaid constructs can be characterised as follows:

- *Traditions* are rooted in the past.
- *Customs* evolve from the past.
- *Nostalgia* is embedded in the past.
- *Melancholia* is embedded in the past.
- *Iconic branding* of the past, and present, and which has a heightened cultural significance for the present (the past may be imagined).
- *Retro branding* reinterprets the past for the present; it evokes the past but is substantially of the present (e.g. a watch having a retro design but a contemporary technology).
- *Heritage marketing* celebrates a particular past through the lens of the present.
- *Heritage tourism* commemorates the places of the past through the lens of the present.
- *Corporate heritage identities* have certain perennial institutional traits, which are of the past, present, and prospective future.
- *Corporate heritage brands* have a perennial brand promise which is of the past, present and prospective future.

By means of context, Table 1.1 provides succinct explanations of the principal corporate-level constructs which draw on the past and Table 1.2 provides short overviews of the principal corporate-level constructs which draw on the past. Appendix 1 details the central role of history in marketing and in management contexts.

TABLE 1.1 Succinct explanations of the principal corporate-level constructs which draw on the past or which are linked to the past

Corporate-level	Succinct explanation	Emphasis constructs linked to the past
Tradition	"Maintaining the ceremonies of the past"	Ritual
Custom	"Maintaining the activities of the past"	Identity
Nostalgia	"Seeking the happiness of the past"	Emotional
Melancholia	"Seeking the sadness of the past"	Emotional
Iconic branding	"Deriving meaning from culturally dominant brands from the past"	Cultural
Retro branding	"Linking with a particular period of the past"	Historical
Heritage marketing	"Marketing the past"	Epochal
Tourism marketing	"Marketing the places of the past"	Locality
Corporate heritage identities	"Going forwards with a corporate identity's meaningful past"	Identity continuance
Corporate heritage brands	"Going forwards with a brand's meaningful past"	Brand guarantee/ continuance

TABLE 1.2 Scrutinising the principal corporate-level constructs which draw on the past

Constructs	
Tradition	Tradition especially refers to the maintenance of fixed behaviours, and conventions, which are characterised by their invariance. The purpose of tradition is to bind and to exclude and can be an activity of selection, revision and invention (Sarup, 1996). Tradition can be invented and the notion of invented tradition has been shown to be important to organisations such as monarchies and universities (Hobsbawm, 1983). Invented tradition can be a powerful blend of art and artifice. Invented tradition refers to a set of practices which seek to inculcate certain values and norms of behaviour by reputation and which implies – and the importance of the word "implies" needs to be stressed here – continuity with the past (Hobsbawm, 1983). In corporate marketing terms, events and rituals can accord an institution a degree of distinctiveness, differentiation and attraction. Consider the distinctiveness accorded to the USA's second oldest university – the College of William and Mary – which, since the early twentieth century, has introduced and communicated its historical ties with the British Monarchy and has an annual ceremony where the university's Royal Charter is read out in full: an event that is unique in the USA and almost certainly is unique in global terms (Balmer, 2011)

Constructs	
Custom	Custom refers to the behaviours, which – unlike tradition – are flexible and subject to change: tradition in contrast is invariant (or in the case of invented tradition is perceived to be invariant). As such custom refers to the substantive nature of behaviour rather than how a particular behaviour is enacted. Hobsbawm (1983), elucidating the difference between the two, observes that custom refers to the function of the judiciary, whereas tradition relates to symbols and ritualised practices of judges, their wigs and robes for instance
Nostalgia	Nostalgia is concerned with the positive associations – the seeking of happiness – relating to the past. Such feeling of nostalgia can give an individual a sense of certainty and security. Hewinson (1987) noted that individuals could turn to the past for comfort during times of great social change (and presumably other forms of change which bring anxiety). Holbrook and Schindler (2003) note that in later life an individual might seek out and still derive comfort from those brands with which they had a strong affinity from the ages of 16–20, and they characterise this as nostalgic bonding. Olfactory experience is especially germane vis-à-vis nostalgic bonding. Thus, a British person working overseas might derive considerable benefit of nostalgia by consuming Marmite (yeast spread) whereas Australians might derive an analogous benefit through the consumption of Vegemite (Australian yeast spread brand)
Melancholia	Melancholia is concerned with the seeking of sadness associated with the past. Although this is not covered in detail in marketing, such a mood can be actively sought and people can be attracted to this emotion and this can be marshalled by brands to meet a particular customer need. For instance, the music of certain pop groups which are associated with a particular time frame and which represent the sadness of a former time period can be powerful. For instance, some classical music lovers actively seek the melancholia associated with the Penitential music of Lent and Holy week at other times of the year namely: the Tenebrae musical settings of Victoria. Tourists, for instance, are sometimes attracted to stay in Venice in the depths of winter since they find the city's historic melancholia at that time especially appealing
Iconic branding	Iconic brand refers to those brands which are culturally dominant and distinctive. Nike is one example of an iconic brand. The work of Holt (2004) has been especially significant in this regard, and Holt concludes that myth making can be a key transformative activity in terms of a brand's metamorphosis into an iconic brand
Retro branding	Retro brands are redolent of a specific era (Brown *et al.*, 2003). Retro brands celebrate an idealised and – sometimes imagined – past, which is seen to be meaningful. The introduction of Volkswagen's new Beetle car exemplifies the retro branding

(*Continued*)

TABLE 1.2 (Continued)

Constructs	
Heritage marketing	Heritage marketing is primarily concerned with the tourism/heritage industry (Prentice, 1993; Herbert, 1995; Henderson, 2002; Misiura, 2006). In essence, it is concerned with the "marketing" of history and with brands that evoke and represent a particular era such as Boston's Freedom Trail, Brighton's Royal Pavilion and the Bund in Shanghai
Heritage tourism	Heritage tourism refers to clearly identifiable places which – in historical contexts – help to denote a tourist destination. Often, heritage tourism relates to historical phenomena that related to the distant past (Weaver, 2010). The focus of heritage tourism – old castles, churches, temples, etc. – require, in the context of heritage tourism, both protection and presentation. Among those who write on heritage tourism are Palmer (2005) and Park (2010). Examples would include the Forbidden City in Peking
Corporate heritage identity	This article makes a contribution to the broad area by making reference to corporate heritage identity and, therefore, makes a distinction between this identity type and corporate heritage brands. Corporate heritage identities should be viewed as a distinct identity type. Corporate heritage identities refer to those institutional identity traits which have remained meaningful and invariant over the passage of time and, as such, a corporate heritage identity is viewed as being of the past, present and future. This said, the meanings attached to particular facets of an institution's identity can vary with the passage of time. Heritage identity traits can include corporate competencies, cultures, philosophies, activities, markets and groups, etc. and may find, in addition, expression in distinctive visual identities, architecture and service offerings
Corporate heritage brands	Corporate heritage brands refers to a distinct category of institutional brand where there is a degree of continuity in terms of the brand promise as expressed via the institution's identity, behaviour and symbolism. The temporal dimension is a key aspect of the previous with corporate heritage brands being seen to have a meaningful past, present and prospective future: they inhabit all the aforementioned time frames (Balmer et al., 2006). Moreover, corporate heritage brands – in order to remain salient – need to be relevant and respected and, in addition, should not be sclerotic but should be capable of adaptation; in short, to be responsive to change (Balmer et al., 2006). Of especial note is the article on corporate brands with a heritage by Urde et al. (2007), which concluded that longevity, core values, use of symbols, history and track record represented key dimensions of corporate heritage brands. Examples of corporate heritage brands include Rolls-Royce, Patek Philippe, Fortnum & Mason, Tiffany, Burberry, and London Transport

The nature of heritage

Heritage in context

The precise denotation of heritage is "to inherit", or "to pass on". Apparently, the construct is French in origin (Heathcote, 2011). Heritage, although closely linked to history, is singularly different from it. As such, while history is concerned with the past, heritage in corporate marketing and in corporate branding contexts (Balmer *et al.*, 2006) relates to the present as well as to the past and to the future. Heritage identities can be real, imagined or contrived or a fusion of all three. Heritage can pertain to an object, monument, inherited skill or symbolic representation, and is a key identity component of a social group (Bessiere, 1998). An especial characteristic of heritage is its ability to clarify the past and make the past relevant for contemporary contexts and purposes (Lowenthal, 1998). Heritage is meaningful since it provides existential anchors. These anchors are valuable in times of uncertainty and offer a sense of continuity (Rapport, 2002). Heritage can impart a sense of security. Heritage is seen to be salient since it offers certainty in a world of uncertainty. This is especially the case in our own time when change has been, and is, dramatic and where we live in a shifting world (Wright, 1985; Hewinson, 1987). The very notion of heritage is a paradox since a concern with heritage is modernist. Heritage, it has been argued, implies a consciousness of our place outside – or beyond – history. As such, heritage is super historic rather than a seamless part of it (Heathcote, 2011). In sociological terms, heritage has been defined in terms of a material testimony of identity; as a discourse and a set of practices concerned with the continuity, persistence and substantiality of collective identity (Macdonald, 2006). The postmodern perspective of heritage adds a further degree of complexity to our comprehension of heritage since this allows individuals to define heritage in any way that they see fit (Fowler, 1989; Walton, 2009; Weaver, 2010). Moreover, our comprehension of heritage is further complicated owing to the existence of multiple stakeholders who may perceive heritage in different ways. A diverse set of meanings, therefore, can be attributed to heritage as a result of the identification, presentation and interpretation of heritage to and from these groups (Apostolakis, 2003). What is clear is that the heritage is a very rich construct and is pregnant with possibilities in terms of insight. Thus, it has the potential to be highly meaningful in corporate marketing contexts.

Heritage and time

The following outlines my viewpoints vis-à-vis corporate heritage identities and their links with time. Heritage identities subsist in temporal strata (multiple time stratums). Heritage is not about something that aims simply to be of our time but is meaningful for all times. In contrast, nostalgia, melancholia, retro brands, heritage marketing and heritage tourism invariably belong to a single time stratum. In addition, my perspective differs from that of Lowenthal (1998) who avers that heritage speaks to the past and present whereas we have argued that it has a tripartite temporal dynamic in that it is meaningful to the past, present and prospective future (Balmer *et al.*, 2006; Urde *et al.*, 2007). My perspective of heritage is in part informed by the notion of time and our understanding of times from the present. Russell (1957, p. 374), for instance, concludes: "The present of things past is memory; the present of things present is sight; and the present of things future is expectation." Russell also makes reference to the exegesis on time offered by the fourth-century philosopher Saint Augustine (354–430) who identified three categories of time: a present of things past, a present of things present, and a present of things future.

The footprints of corporate heritage identities

To me, corporate heritage footprints may be found, at the macro level, in terms of corporate purposes, activities, competencies, cultures, philosophies, strategies and at the micro level, the heritage footprint can be found in design heritage, advertising and communication heritage, sensory heritage, architectural heritage, etc. In terms of the management of corporate heritage identities there is a requirement to marry brand archaeology, a concern with a brand's provenance and historic attractiveness, with brand strategy, marshalling the brand heritage in order to maintain its brand salience and competitive advantage for the future (Balmer, 2011a). Appendix 2 provides an overview of heritage identities in the context of the previous and in the context of this article.

Methodology

As an embedded single case study a single category of institution was examined (monarchy) but there was a reliance on two units of analysis: the British Monarchy and, to a lesser extent, the Swedish Crown. Both monarchies are exemplar monarchical forms and both have a particular significance in terms of benchmarking. This research took place over a ten-year period. The efficacy of relying on a single case study approach has been advanced by Znaciecki (1934), Normann (1970) and Yin (1994), among others. Around four years were spent collecting data on the Swedish Monarchy in Stockholm as part of a collaborative research endeavour with Professor Mats Urde (Lund University, Sweden) and Professor Stephen Greyser (Harvard Business School) where we were granted lengthy audiences with their Majesties the King and Queen of Sweden, with HRH Crown Princess along with other members of the Royal Family and senior courtiers of the Royal Court of Sweden.

In very broad terms, a pattern matching logic informed the analysis of data. As such, the literature-based insights relating to the monarchy (in effect propositions) were confirmed by the empirical study of the Swedish Crown. Investigator triangulation informed our examination of the Swedish Crown where there was consensus among the researchers re the findings. The study was, among other lines of inquiry, informed by literature reviews on monarchies generally and the British

Monarchy in particular, a scrutiny of critical events in the annals of the British Monarchy from 1837 to the present. Research was also undertaken vis-à-vis the historical evolution of the British Crown. This article builds on earlier published work relating to this study (Balmer, 2004, 2008, 2009b, 2011a; Balmer *et al.*, 2006; Urde *et al.*, 2007).

Findings

There are three main contributions from this study:

(1) Heritage identities and the identification of the Relative Invariance phenomenon.
(2) Heritage identities and identity accretion and the identification of the Institutional Role Identities phenomenon.
(3) A revised heritage identity framework.

Heritage identities and the identification of the Relative Invariance phenomenon

In explaining why heritage identities appear to remain the same and yet change, the case study of monarchy showed that while certain attributes (the Royal status, Regal activities, Religious dimensions and Monarchical Rituals) in part remain unchanged, the meanings ascribed to them can change over time. Thus there is both change and continuity. I call this phenomenon Relative Invariance.

Heritage identities and identity accretion and the identification of the Institutional Role Identities phenomenon

Taking an historical perspective, heritage identities acquire new identities over the passage of time and thus take on board new meanings and greater relevance. For instance, they can become associated with places, cultures and with time frames and, importantly, with new institutional role identities. For instance, the study of monarchy has revealed new roles and expectations (the requirement to be Respected, Relevant, to be Responsive and to be Regulated). Consider, the broader international role the Crown has vis-à-vis Queen Elizabeth's position as Queen in 16 Realms and her position as titular head of the Commonwealth. As such, the British Monarchy – in heritage identity terms – is a composite of identity types. In their totality they communicate an astonishingly broad reper-toire of meanings and time frames, which can be drawn on by the institution for a wide variety of contexts and audiences. These identity types enable the Crown to play out various roles at various times and in various places in constitutional, cultural, emotional, legal, philanthropic and religious contexts. Some identity types have an institutional focus and are of considerable antiquity such as the Royal, Religious dimensions whereas others are linked to values and behaviour of a social group (Regal) and to symbolic enactments of identity (Ritual). Some of the identity types require a territorial adaptation such as when the Queen undertakes duties in her capacity as Head of State for her other realms (namely: Queen of New Zealand, Queen of Australia) or in an international mode as Head of the Commonwealth.

A revised heritage identity framework

An updated framework to that reported in Balmer (2011a) is outlined here. Drawing on the work of Schumpeter (1949), it was noted that: the heart of scholarship is not only vision, but re-vision. As such, this version of the framework has two, additional identity facets which, as a result of further scrutiny of the primary and secondary data, were found to be highly salient. As such, the framework includes the Religious and Ritual dimensions.

Trust, authenticity and affinity

At the heart of the framework is the notion of bilateral trust, which it is conceptualised should characterise institutional and stakeholder relationships of heritage identities. It is conceptualised that trust is dependent on authenticity (from the organisation's side in terms of the perseverance of salient corporate heritage features) and affinity (from customer and stakeholder perspectives in terms of the heritage identity remaining meaningful to them). There should be a dynamic equilibrium between the aforementioned. This central aspect of the framework is shown in diagrammatic form in Figure 1.1.

The 8Rs of corporate heritage identities vis-à-vis the British Monarchy

The revised framework includes eight dimensions: royal, religious, regal, ritual, relevant, respected, responsive, and regulation. The key identity modes (the 8Rs) are shown in diagrammatic mode in Figure 1.2 and an explanation of them is given in Appendix 3. In corporate heritage branding terms the framework can have a utility in seeing the 8Rs as a series of brand promises (from the organisational side) and expectations (from customer and from stakeholder perspectives).

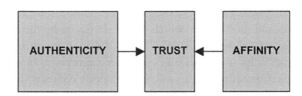

FIGURE 1.1 The importance of bilateral trust, authenticity and affinity vis-à-vis corporate heritage identities

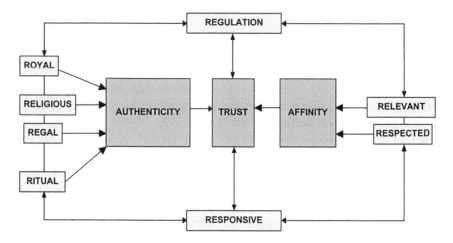

FIGURE 1.2 A revised heritage identity framework vis-à-vis the British Monarchy

Corporate heritage identities: Some reflections and directions for managers

The following reflections on corporate heritage identities aim to advance our comprehension of the territory and also aim to be of general utility to managers. As such I note:

- The importance of relative invariance, in terms of explaining why corporate heritage identities can change, and yet, seemingly, remain constant.
- Corporate heritage identities are shaped by the accretion of multiple institutional and other identity types over time and this may give them greater strength and saliency.
- Corporate heritage identities, in part, represent a nexus of time identities: this, again, may account for their strength.
- Corporate heritage identities have multiple role identities, which can be meaningful in different contexts (temporal, special, cultural, stakeholder, etc.).
- Corporate heritage identities need to be authentic but they may also be shaped, in addition, by contrived and imagined identities.
- The need to make a distinction between corporate heritage identities (activity and attribute based) and corporate heritage brands (based on promises and expectations).
- Corporate heritage identities can be powerful because they are a part of a group's collective memory vis-à-vis the institution per se and the institution's inextricable link with cultures, places and with time frames.
- Corporate heritage identities are especially meaningful in creating identity and in nurturing identification not only with the organisation, but with other meaningful identities.
- Heritage identities and heritage brands only remain meaningful if they embrace both change and continuity and remain salient.

Conclusion

> If we want things to stay the same, things will have to change.
>
> *(Lampedusa, 1958)*

The English translation of Lampedusa's book is *The Leopard*. Although it is some-times said that a leopard's spots do not change, the meanings we attach to those spots – and to leopards themselves – do change. Today, leopards tend to be cherished for what they are: formerly, they were widely hunted and were cherished for their fur. In an analogous fashion, we can note that heritage identities may have different meanings in different times and in different places even though on certain dimensions they remain the same (the phenomenon of relative invariance). To me, corporate heritage identities are special in that they are a fusion of continuity and of change; of differing identities, time frames and meanings. To build on the aforementioned, corporate heritage identities are multifaceted. For instance, they are invested with the omnipresence of time: they are of the past, present and future. Identities, which, through their accretion of various identities types over time, have an especial distinctiveness and roles (the phenomenon of institutional role identities). Importantly, heritage identities also have a role in giving identity. Arguably, they have a worth to the collective memory of a group. Heritage identities are attractive because they have changed and because they have remained the same. As such, they can be especially salient and powerful as an institutional identity type in corporate marketing contexts (Balmer, 1998, 2001b, 2009b; Balmer and Greyser, 2006). In bringing this commentary to a close we, perhaps, should note that there is more to Lampedusa's book than meets the eye. The same can surely be said in relation to corporate heritage identities and, of course, to the British Monarchy in particular.

References

Ahmed, M. (2011), "Ceremony clicks with internet age as 400 million watch on the web", *The Times*, 30 April, p. 25.

Apostolakis, A. (2003), "The convergence process in heritage tourism", *Annals of Tourism Research*, Vol. 30, pp. 795–812.

Askegaard, S. (2006), "Brands as a global ideoscape", in Schroeder, J.E. and Salzer-Morling, S. (Eds.), *Brand Culture*, Routledge, London, pp. 91–102.

Attenborough, Sir D. (2002), *Life on Air*, BBC Books, London.

Balmer, J.M.T. (1995), "Corporate branding and connoisseurship", *Journal of General Management*, Vol. 21 No. 1, pp. 24–46.

Balmer, J.M.T. (1998), "Corporate identity and the advent of corporate marketing", *Journal of Marketing Management*, Vol. 14 No. 8, pp. 963–96.

Balmer, J.M.T. (2001a), "The three virtues and seven deadly sins of corporate brand management", *Journal of General Management*, Vol. 27 No. 1, pp. 1–17.

Balmer, J.M.T. (2001b), "Corporate identity, corporate branding and corporate marketing: Seeing through the fog", *European Journal of Marketing*, Vol. 35 Nos. 3/4, pp. 248–91.

Balmer, J.M.T. (2004), *The British Monarchy as a Corporate Brand: Does the Crown as a Corporate Brand Fit?*, Working paper No. 04/16, Bradford School of Management, Bradford.

Balmer, J.M.T. (2011a), "Corporate heritage brands and the precepts of corporate heritage brand management: Insights from the British Monarchy on the eve of the wedding of Prince William (April 2011) and Queen Elizabeth II's Diamond Jubilee (1952–2012)", *Journal of Brand Management*, Vol. 18, April, pp. 517–44.

Balmer, J.M.T. (2011b), "Corporate marketing myopia and the inexorable rise of a corporate marketing logic: Perspectives from identity based views of the firm", *European Journal of Marketing*, Vol. 45 Nos. 9/10, pp. 1329–52.

Balmer, J.M.T. and Greyser, S.A. (2006), "Corporate marketing: Integrating corporate identity, corporate branding, corporate communications, corporate image and corporate reputation", *European Journal of Marketing*, Vol. 40 Nos. 7/8, pp. 730–41.

Balmer, J.M.T., Greyser, S.A. and Urde, M. (2006), "The crown as a corporate brand: Insights from monarchies", *Journal of Brand Management*, Vol. 14 Nos. 1/2, pp. 137–61.

Bessiere, J. (1998), "Local development and heritage: Traditional food and cuisine as tourist attractions in rural areas", *Sociologia Ruralis*, Vol. 38 No. 1, pp. 21–34.

Blomback, A. and Brunninge, O. (2009), "Corporate identity manifested through historical references", *Corporate Communications: An International Journal*, Vol. 14 No. 4, pp. 404–19.

Bogdanor, V. (1997), *The Monarchy and the Constitution*, Oxford University Press, Oxford.

Bond, J. (2002), *Reporting Royalty*, Headline, London.

Bronnenberg, B., Gentzkow, M. and Dube, J.-P. (2010), *The Evolution of Brand Preferences: Evidence from Migration*, NBER working paper no. 16267, Cambridge, MA, August.

Brown, S., Kozinets, R. and Sherry, J.F. (2003), "Teaching old brand new tricks: Retro branding and the revival of brand meaning", *Journal of Marketing*, Vol. 67, pp. 19–33.

Brunninge, O. (2009), "Using history in organizations: How managers make purposeful reference to history in strategic processes", *Journal of Organizational Change Management*, Vol. 22, pp. 8–26.

Cannadine, D. (1983), "The context, performance and meaning of ritual: The British Monarchy and the 'invention of tradition'", in Hobsbawm, E. and Ranger, T.E. (Eds.), *The Invention of Tradition*, Cambridge University Press, Cambridge.

Cannon, J. and Griffiths, R. (1998), *The Oxford Illustrated History of the British Monarchy*, Oxford University Press, Oxford.

Carroll, C. (2002), "Introduction: Special issue on the strategic use of the past and future in organisations", *Journal of Organizational Change Management*, Vol. 15 No. 6, pp. 556–62.

Fowler, P. (1989), "Heritage: A postmodernist perspective", in Uzzell, D. (Ed.), *Heritage Interpretation, 1: The Natural and Built Environment*, Belhaven, London, pp. 57–63.

Friedman, W.A. and Jones, G. (2008), "A special edition on Alfred D. Chandler Jr: Editors' note", *Business History Review*, Vol. 82 No. 2, pp. 203–6.

Galbraith, J.K. (1991), *A History of Economics: The Past as the Present*, Penguin, London.

Gellner, E. (1998), *Nationalism*, Phoenix, London.

George, M. (2004), "Heritage branding helps in global markets", *Marketing News*, Vol. 4 No. 13, p. 16.

Gioia, D.A., Corley, K.G. and Fabbri, T. (2002), "Revisiting the past (while thinking about the future-perfect tense)", *Journal of Organizational Change Management*, Vol. 15 No. 6, pp. 622–34.

Hatch, M.-J. and Rubin, J. (2006), "The hermeneutics of branding", *Journal of Brand Management*, Vol. 14 Nos. 1/2, pp. 40–59.

Heathcote, E. (2011), "How to build heritage", *Financial Times*, 8/9 January, p. 8.

Heilbrunn, B. (2005), "Brave new brands: Cultural branding between Utopia and A-topia", in Schroeder, J.E. and Salzer-Morling, S. (Eds.), *Brand Culture*, Routledge, London, pp. 103–17.

Henderson, J.C. (2002), "Conserving colonial heritage: Raffles Hotel in Singapore", *International Journal of Heritage Studies*, Vol. 7 No. 1, pp. 7–24.

Herbert, D.T. (1995), *Heritage, Tourism and Society*, Pinter, London.

Hewinson, R. (1987), *The Heritage Industry: Britain in a Climate of Decline*, Methuen, London.

Hobsbawm, E. (1983), "The invention of tradition", in Hobsbawm, E. and Ranger, T.E. (Eds.), *The Invention of Tradition*, Cambridge University Press, Cambridge.

Hobsbawm, E. (2002), *Interesting Times: A Twentieth-Century Life*, Allen Lane, London.

Hobsbawm, E. (2006), *The Age of Capital*, Abacus, London.

Hocart, A.M. (1927), *Kingship*, Oxford University Press, Oxford.

Holbrook, M. and Schindler, R. (2003), "Nostalgic bonding: Exploring the role of nostalgia in the consumption experience", *Journal of Consumer Behavior*, Vol. 3 No. 2, pp. 102–7.

Holt, D.B. (2004), *How Brands Become Icons*, Harvard Business School Publishing, Boston, MA.

Jeremy, D.J. (1998), *A Business History of Britain, 1900–1990s*, Oxford University Press, Oxford.

Kantrow, A. (1986), "Why history matters to managers: A roundtable discussion with Alfred D. Chandler Jr", *Harvard Business Review*, Vol. 64 No. 1, pp. 102–24.

Keller, K.L. and Richey, K. (2006), "The importance of corporate brand personality traits to a successful twenty-first century business", *Journal of Brand Management*, Vol. 14 Nos. 1/2, pp. 74–81.

Lampedusa, G.T. (1958), *Il Gattopardo*, Casa Editrice Feltrinelli, Milan.

Lowenthal, D. (1998), *The Heritage Crusade and the Spoils of History*, Cambridge University Press, Cambridge.

Macdonald, S. (2006), "Undesirable heritage: Fascist material culture and historical consciousness in Nuremberg", *International Journal of Heritage Studies*, Vol. 12 No. 1, pp. 9–28.

Misiura, S. (2006), *Heritage Marketing*, Butterworth-Heinemann, Oxford.

Moingeon, B. and Ramanantsoa, B. (1997), "Understanding corporate identity: The French school of thought", *European Journal of Marketing*, Vol. 31 Nos. 5/6, pp. 383–95.

Mommsen, W.J. (1992), *The Political and Social Theory of Max Weber: Collected Essays*, University of Chicago Press, Chicago, IL.

Normann, R. (1970), "A personal quest for methodology", *Scandinavian Institutes for Administrative Research*, Vol. 53, pp. 6–26.

Olsen, B. (1995), "Brand loyalty and consumption patterns: The lineage factor", in Sherry, J.F. Jr (Ed.), *Contemporary Marketing and Consumer Behavior: An Anthropological Sourcebook*, Sage Publications, Thousand Oaks, CA.

Otnes, C.C. and Maclaren, P. (2007), "The consumption of cultural heritage among a British Royal Family Brand Tribe", in Kozinets, R., Cova, B. and Shanker, A. (Eds.), *Consumer Tribes: Theory, Practice, and Prospects*, Elsevier/Butterworth-Heinemann, London.

Oui, C.-S. (2002), "Persuasive histories: Decentering, recentering and the emotional crafting of the past", *Journal of Organizational Change Management*, Vol. 15 No. 6, pp. 606–21.

Palmer, C.A. (2005), "An ethnography of Englishness: Experiencing identity through tourism", *Annals of Tourism Research*, Vol. 32 No. 1, pp. 7–27.

Park, H.-Y. (2010), "Heritage tourism: Emotional journeys into nationhood", *Annals of Tourism Research*, Vol. 37 No. 1, pp. 116–35.

Parker, J. (2002), "Contesting histories: Unity and division in a building society", *Journal of Organizational Change Management*, Vol. 15 No. 6, pp. 589–605.

Prentice, R. (1993), *Tourism and Heritage Attractions*, Routledge, London.

Rapport, N. (2002), *British Subjects: An Anthology of Britain*, Routledge, London.

Russell, B. (1957), *History of Western Philosophy*, George Allen & Unwin, London and New York, NY.

Sarup, M. (1996), *Culture and the Postmodern World*, Edinburgh University Press, Edinburgh.

Schumpeter, J. (1949), "Science and ideology", *Economic Review*, Vol. 29, March, pp. 358–9.

Smith, A.D. (1991), *National Identity*, Penguin, London.

Starkey, D. (2002), *Reinventing the Royals*, Channel 4 TV Programme, December.

Starkey, D. (2011), "Why this union symbolises a divided nation", *The Times*, 29 April, p. 35.

Urde, M., Greyser, S.A. and Balmer, J.M.T. (2007), "Corporate brands with a heritage", *Journal of Brand Management*, Vol. 15 No. 1, pp. 4–19.

VanRiel, C.B.M. and Balmer, J.M.T. (1997), "Corporate identity: The concept, its measurement and management", *European Journal of Marketing*, Vol. 31 Nos. 5/6, pp. 340–55.

Walton, J. (2009), "Prospects in tourism history: Evolution, state of play and future developments", *Tourism Management*, Vol. 30, pp. 783–93.

Weaver, D.B. (2010), "Contemporary tourism as heritage tourism: Evidence from Las Vegas and Gold Coast", *Annals of Tourism Research*, Vol. 38 No. 1, pp. 249–67.

Wilkins, M. (2008), "Chandler and global business history", *Business History Review*, Vol. 82 No. 2, pp. 251–6.

Wright, P. (1985), *On Living in an Old Country: The National Past in Contemporary Britain*, Verso, London.

Yin, R.K. (1994), *Case Study Research: Design and Methods*, Sage Publications, Thousand Oaks, CA.

Znaciecki, F. (1934), *The Method of Sociology*, Farrar and Rinehart, New York, NY.

Further reading

Balmer, J.M.T. (2008), "A resourced-based view of the British Monarchy as a corporate brand", *International Studies of Management and Organizations*, Vol. 37 No. 4, pp. 20–45.

Balmer, J.M.T. (2009a), "Corporate marketing: Apocalypse, advent and epiphany", *Management Decision*, Vol. 47 No. 4, pp. 544–72.

Balmer, J.M.T. (2009b), "Scrutinising the British Monarchy: The corporate brand that was shaken, stirred and survived", *Management Decision*, Vol. 47 No. 4, pp. 639–75.

Kunde, J. (2000), *Corporate Religion*, Financial Times/Prentice Hall, London.

Starkey, D. (2010), *Crown and Country: A History of England through the Monarchy*, Harper Press, London.

APPENDIX 1

The power of provenance: the central role of history in marketing and in management

Provenance is, perhaps, an under-utilised dimension within management and marketing scholarship. Not only organisations but management disciplines and constructs have a history and, with the passage of time, the origins and utility of the aforesaid are, sometimes, forgotten.

History can not only reveal how the identities of disciplines have shifted but can, moreover, help us to reveal key corporate identity traits of organisations.

For instance, the English university tradition is not only informed by the precepts of the Enlightenment but also from the traditions of the Catholic Church (the early universities were run by the Church). Vestigial elements of the latter can be found within all UK universities and are more pronounced at universities such as Oxford, Cambridge and Durham. As for the 2,000-year-old Catholic Church, it is also informed by earlier histories and identities. Tradition, for instance, is one pillar from which the Catholic Church claims its legitimacy and teaching. For instance, in terms of the Catholic Church's identity traits, it has been asserted that these are derived from its history, which was Jewish; from its theology, which was Greek; and from its government (canon law), which was Roman (Russell, 1957, p. 17).

Within the English legal system, along with statute law and case law, custom is also seen to have, in certain circumstances, the force of law namely: where certain activities and rights have existed since time immemorial.

Within management research, history remains a salient mode of inquiry: the *Journal of Business History* is significant in this regard. The importance of business history has been noted in various *Harvard Business Review* articles (Kantrow, 1986). In broader contexts, scholars have variously noted that important normative insights can be discerned when examining an organisation's – or an industry's – historiography (Jeremy, 1998; Carroll, 2002; Gioia *et al.*, 2002; Oui, 2002; Parker, 2002).

While it is indubitably the case that many management scholars have argued that history can be highly meaningful, for others, it is reasonable to surmise that history can be characterised as opaque, disadvantageous and, even, extraneous. It is more often the exception than the rule that business history is taught in business schools: Harvard Business School is a long-time exception in this regard.

Adopting a Chandlerian perspective (see: Wilkins, 2008), scholars have asserted that an organisation's history gives institutions identity and distinctiveness (e.g. Friedman and Jones, 2008; Wilkins, 2008). Galbraith (1991) concludes that the past actively shapes not merely the present but also, importantly, the future. He also observes that in economic terms history is highly functional. History can also be used as a control mechanism for managers (Brunninge, 2009).

Drawing on broader perspectives, studies of national identity and culture, for instance, have shown that marshalling the past (tradition for instance) has a utility in maintaining identity against the threat of heterogeneity, discontinuity and contradiction. As such, the impulse to preserve the past is to preserve the self (Sarup, 1996). Gellner (1998) notes that our identity as individuals is derived from:

- society;
- religion;
- intellect; and
- national roots.

The recollection of a distinctive past, whether authentic or merely claimed, can create a powerful sense of self-identity (national roots are important in this regard).

To me, the observations of Sarup are worthy of scrutiny, in institutional and corporate branding contexts, while the work of Gellner might also be meaningfully augmented, by taking account of the role of corporate identities and corporate brands in the creation of identity formation. Moreover, marketing and management scholars might usefully give greater accord to the work on national and cultural identity in explicating the nature of corporate identities and institutional brands.

The dark sides of history, heritage and provenance

While the various literatures tend to put a positive gloss in terms of the benefits of the past, of history and heritage to organisations, there are contrary and critical perspectives as well. For example, the rise of heritage marketing (and probably heritage tourism as well) has been lambasted by Sarup (1996). Sarup is of the view that such concerns are entropic and are symptoms of a deep-seated societal disorder. In addition, there is always the danger of being an uncritical celebrant of a particular perspective, and the same is true of corporate heritage identities and brands.

Certainly, there are disadvantages in having an undue focus on the past. For instance, where heritage is closely linked to a particular technology this may, sometimes, lead to corporate brand obsolescence (Polaroid vis-à-vis instant photography and Olivetti vis-à-vis typewriters). Moreover, reference to the past can also serve as a control mechanism, as noted by Hobsbawm – what he called the tyranny of tradition in terms of resistance to change (Hobsbawm, 2006). It was the Oxford classicist

Cornforth who, in 1903, espoused the principle of "unripe time"; the notion that now (de facto never) was not quite the time for change (Hobsbawm, 2002).

The role of history and of the past in marketing

History, hermeneutics, and corporate branding

Within marketing, the fascination with heritage, iconic brands and nostalgia have, in recent times, surfaced as prominent research strands within the branding canon (Brown et al., 2003; Holt, 2004; Balmer et al., 2006: Urde et al., 2007; Bronnenberg et al., 2010).

Increasingly, brands are seen to be central historical and institutional phenomena. Heilbrunn (2005) concluded that brands progressively occupy the space once occupied by politics and religion. Moreover, they are – and therefore will be seen to be – of seminal importance for contemporary organisations for a variety of reasons, not least of which is the pivotal role vis-à-vis globalisation (Askegaard, 2006). Taking a branding and sociological perspective, Olsen (1995), for instance, noted that brands, which are associated with a cultural past, could have considerable meaning to immigrant communities in terms of maintaining identity.

In broader terms, the view that corporate brands are derived from an organisation's historical attributes has also been asserted (Balmer, 1995, 2001a).

Recently, the hermeneutic tradition – which has its origins in the scrutiny of scriptural and legal texts – has been found to have a utility vis-à-vis the branding literature. In this regard, it has been observed that our current comprehension of brand meaning may result from collective interpretations by different stakeholders over time. This being said, with the passage of time a brand may remain true to its origins. Often, it is possible to detect key features of a brand's identity traits (Hatch and Rubin, 2006). As such, the hermeneutic perspective has a clear utility to the nascent domain of corporate heritage identities.

Corporate marketing, corporate identity, and history

The corporate marketing philosophy accords importance to the past in terms of former stakeholder groups and company founders (Balmer, 2001a). Within the identity canon, a number of marketing scholars have underscored the importance of history in corporate identity formation in its various forms (Moingeon and Ramanantsoa, 1997; VanRiel and Balmer, 1997; Blomback and Brunninge, 2009). In general terms, the importance of history and the past within the corporate marketing/marketing canons are demonstrated in a number of ways. The following provides an indicative list relating to the previous, namely:

- History is a key dimension of corporate identity and organisational identity.
- History and heritage can be key means of creating brand value.
- Nostalgia can be a key dimension of consumer buying behaviour vis-à-vis brands.

- The consumption, collection and display of brand and identity artefacts which have an historic dimension is a key means of creating identity.
- History is a key dimension in corporate communication in expressing both continuity and change.
- History can be a key dimension in terms of internal group identity and identification.
- The rediscovery of heritage identity and its utilisation as a competitive advantage.
- Historical rituals and myths can be a key means to engender identification via recourse to historical rituals and symbols.

APPENDIX 2

Reflections on corporate heritage identities

- Corporate heritage identities are concerned with history – sometimes real, sometimes idealised and sometimes imagined – and history in the making: a concern with the future.
- Corporate heritage identities are not stuck in the past or unduly hidebound by history but are informed by the precept of "pressing forwards with the past".
- At the macro level, the corporate heritage footprint may be found in terms of corporate purposes, activities, competencies, cultures, philosophies, strategies.
- At the micro level, the heritage footprint can be found in design heritage, advertising and communication heritage, sensory heritage, architectural heritage, etc.
- Corporate heritage identities can have a symbiotic relationship with other heritage brands (place, communities, professions, etc.) and can have a meaningful/defining bilateral relationship with other corporate heritage brands, e.g. in the USA, the close association between the college of William and Mary and the British Monarchy.
- In terms of corporate heritage identity management there is a requirement to marry brand archaeology (a concern with a brand's provenance and historic attractiveness) with brand strategy (marshalling the brand heritage in order to maintain its brand saliency and competitive advantage for the future).
- Corporate heritage identities are not merely about history, but of history in the making: a history informed by continuity and by change.

APPENDIX 3

The 8Rs of corporate heritage identities vis-à-vis the British Monarchy

Royal

A critical, and distinctive, dimension of monarchies as corporate heritage identities is their royal identity. This heritage identity dimension gives the monarch an especial eminence and, in broader contexts, accords a royal status to the country (the UK), its people (British subjects), government (Her Majesty's government and opposition) and so on.

> The whole point of having Royalty is that the Sovereign is not the same as other people. Wars were fought about that issue in the eighteenth century, and the nations still like to believe to some degree in the divine right of kings.
>
> *(Sir David Attenborough, 2002, p. 313)*

Religious

The religious dynamic imbues the British Monarchy with spiritual, sacred and ethereal identity attributes. The religious dimensions – three were identified – of the Crown imbue the heritage brand with transcendental attributes. The study revealed there to be tripartite manifestations of this religious dimension in terms of orthodox/theocratic religion, civil religion and brand religion:

> The earliest known religion is the belief in Kings.
>
> *(Hocart, 1927, p. 7)*

Regal

The regal status requires that the actions and behaviours of the British Monarchy as an institutional brand should be regal. This is both in accordance with the age-old traditions of monarchy and with the more modern requirements of a constitutional monarchy. It defines what is, as well as what is not, acceptable:

> We are sometimes criticised that we are too common in a sense. Young people, for example, often want us to be like them – but at the same time there are expectations that we should be role models and "behave like a royal". I feel that dealing with this paradox is sometimes very hard.
>
> *(Audience with Her Royal Highness Crown Princess Victoria*
> *of Sweden, Balmer et al., 2006, p. 152)*

Ritual

Monarchical rituals and symbolism are not ethereal. They have a legitimising effect; inculcate beliefs and values; create a sense of identification. Rituals and symbolism have defined the Crown since time immemorial and, in terms of heritage, link the past with the present:

> The impact of monarchy itself on subjects has always depended greatly on visual magnificence – the awe inspired by coronations, the sense of participation engendered by jubilees, the solemnity of great funeral ceremonies.
>
> *(Cannon and Griffiths, 1998, p. ix)*

Relevant

Change, and the need for the Crown to remain meaningful to all facets of British society, emerged as a prominent theme of this study. The relevance of the Crown in heritage identity terms can be seen in terms of its pivotal role in providing identity: in corporate marketing terms this is a key USP. This is important in an increasingly homogenised world. For instance the Crown remains relevant for our times through its philanthropic and charitable credentials. It does this by marshalling its privileged position in order to shed light on the plight of the disadvantaged in society. Most royal visits relate to these welfare concerns.

> My role is to represent Sweden for my country; some people would use the modern word "trademark".
>
> *(Audience with His Majesty King Carl XVI Gustaf of*
> *Sweden, Balmer et al., 2006, pp. 140–141)*

> [Vis-à-vis the title of Queen of Sweden] The title serves the nation.
>
> *(Audience with Her Majesty King Queen Silvia of Sweden,*
> *Balmer et al., 2006, p. 152)*

Respected

Britain's monarchy endures because there is widespread respect for the institution. Without public consent the Crown would not only lose its allure but, also, its right to exist. An imperative for the British Monarchy, in terms of winning public respect, is its ability to interpret the nation to itself (Bogdanor, 1997). The Crown needs to deal honourably with men at all times and keep faith with them, and public respect cannot be taken for granted.

> In the age of democracy the Crown has to be like any other brand: it has to win the respect of the people.
>
> *(Dr David Starkey, 2002)*

Responsive

With the passage of time the brand has metamorphosed from having a theocratic and aristocratic focus to the position today whereby it has a democratic and societal role: the Crown has an obligation to all walks of society. As such, the Crown as a brand is in the service of the people and *not* vice versa as was formerly the case. Those monarchies that have not been responsive face the ultima ratio of obsolescence. The hard-headed pragmatics and shrewdness of the Crown in the wake of changes in the political, economic, social, ethical and technological environment have, to date, ensured that it has endured and flourished: a sclerotic monarchy is a waning dying monarchy.

> Responsive implies flexibility, in terms of doing what the people want their head of state to do. It is not about being an opportunist, but it means having priorities. But one's responsiveness must be authentic.
>
> *(Interview with Elisabeth Tarras-Wahlberg: Senior Swedish Courtier, Balmer et al., 2006, p. 146)*

Regulation

Regulation and reinforcement of the brand emerged as prerequisites to ensure the maintenance of the brand. Ongoing stewardship of the heritage identities of the Crown is not only the responsibility of the Monarch and Royal Family but also includes the Queen's private secretary and members of the Royal Household along with the Prime Minister and Government.

> The monarchy is more of a business today than it ever was in previous reigns. In a typical company you have a chairman, a chief executive who reports to the chairman, and four or five departmental heads, who report to the chief executive. All these posts exist in the royal household, by one name or another, but in the final analysis the Queen makes the decisions.
>
> *(Bond, 2002, p. 32)*

2

SCRUTINISING THE BRITISH MONARCHY

The corporate brand that was shaken, stirred and survived

John M. T. Balmer

Introduction

The perspective advanced in this article is that the survival of many contemporary organisations is dependent on them being understood and managed as corporate brands. This is especially so for an arcane institution such as the British Crown. Therefore, a key task of management is to ensure that the corporate brand remains meaningful; this means that executives, as brand custodians, should both respond to as well as effect change. In this article a general methodology for informing the previous is outlined, which I term, "Chronicling the Corporate Brand", and is based on the premise that there is much to be gained through examining a brand's history; this is especially so for corporate heritage brands and, most notably, the British Monarchy.

The Crown is no stranger to change; some of it has been quite radical. Whereas today, the Monarchy as a brand is seen to be associated with Britain's democratic traditions, it has, in the past, also been associated with theocratic and aristocratic systems of rule. Initially, British Kings were viewed as being servants of God, then the people were seen as subjects of the King, and finally, today, Kings are seen to be in the service of the people.

Our current understanding of corporate brands is predicated on the notion that emotional ownership of brands resides with its brand community. For the British Monarchy as a brand, it follows that those charged with managing the Monarchy as a corporate brand should, therefore, be sensitive to the fact that emotional ownership of the Crown is vested in the public at large. For this reason, monarchs need to be mindful of their obligation to serve the public in a variety of meaningful ways. Contemporary notions of Constitutional Monarchy in Great Britain require a recognition that the real power and the significance of monarchy are in terms of its iconic, branding role, as a symbol of both people and of nation, rather than in the Crown's constitutional role (important though this still is) with regards to the polity of the UK.

In broader contexts, the notion that the Crown is analogous to the modern firm and, moreover, that it is akin to a corporate brand is occasionally to be found from those who write about monarchy and even from those from within the institution. For example, within the Royal Family and Royal Household the British Monarchy is often described in colloquial terms as "The Firm" (Micklethwait and Wooldridge, 2005, p. xv).

Tellingly, the prominent British historian David Starkey (2002) unambiguously acknowledged the importance of branding to Britain's Monarchy when he declared:

> In the age of democracy the crown has to be like any other brand. It has to win the respect of the people.

If it is an irrefutable fact that the British Crown is a corporate brand then it is indubitably the case that it needs to be managed as such. Just as in examining our past we can find our future, a failure to take account of history can mean that history is repeated: this is especially true of venerable institutions such as the British Monarchy. As they say in Russia: "Dwell on the past and you'll lose an eye. Forget the past and you'll lose both eyes" (Cohen and Major, 2004, p. xx).

Appendix 1 provides a short, broad overview of the British Monarchy, with the roles, responsibilities and scope of the Crown in both British and Commonwealth contexts.

For the main, this article focuses on critical events that have shaped the Crown during the twentieth century along with one example from the eleventh century. However, there have been some recent, and not so recent, events that, in addition, have also been highly significant in the annals and development of the British Monarchy, and I go on to briefly detail a few of these in the next section.

The British Monarchy: Travails and prevails

Sunday, August 31, 1997

Stunned, the British public woke up to the news that Princess Diana had been fatally injured in a car crash in Paris. Public grief metamorphosed into disbelief as the Royal Family stayed away from London and this boiled over into anger in the funeral panegyric delivered by Earl Spencer, Princess Diana's brother (Pimlott, 2002, pp. 606, 627). It was as if the dogged, stoic and phlegmatic character of the British had been put to one side for something more emotional and immediate.

At the time, the Crown was subject to a good deal of public and media censure, and some political analysts surmised that the world, in all probability, was witnessing the death throes of a once great, but now enfeebled, institution. Sir Robert Worcester (1997a), a leading UK image-research consultant, reflecting on these traumatic events noted that the monarchy: "stood on the brink of the abyss, staring down in the chasm of the dismay of a growing number of British subjects".

Of course, the institution had suffered similar travails before (Bogdanor, 1997; Cannon and Griffiths, 1998; Gardiner and Wenborn, 1995). Consider the issuance of the Magna Carta by the much-reviled King John in 1215 and the execution of King Charles I in 1649. Forty years on, the Glorious Revolution of 1688–1689 ended the medieval notion that Kings ruled by Divine Right. In the eighteenth century, the Crown's prestige was severely impaired by the American Revolution of 1776 which ended monarchical rule in much of British North America (but not in what became known as Canada). A more recent predicament for the Crown was the highly public, acrimonious and debilitating divorce of the Prince and Princess of Wales (Princess Diana) in 1996.

In synthesising why the British Crown has endured, I attribute this to three characteristics: Provenance, Pertinence and Popularity. These characterisations are related to, but are distinct from, the insights detailed later on in terms of the management of monarchy. Exhibit 1 outlines these three characteristics vis-à-vis the British Crown.

What is clear is that in numerous instances (both in recent as well as in past history) by design, as well as by good fortune, the monarchy has been shaken, stirred and has survived (see Exhibit 1).

The literature

Three literatures were found to be pertinent to this study: the literature on corporate brands; the literature on the British Monarchy; and the literatures on corporate organisational and social identity.

Some of the principal insights from these reviews are as follows:

The literature on corporate brands

The literature on corporate brands was used to verify the corporate branding credentials of the Crown and also served to highlight the importance of adopting a multidisciplinary perspective in terms of its management.

The nascent literature on corporate brands revealed the strategic and multidisciplinary character of corporate brand management, and this suggested that a similar perspective was likely to characterise insights vis-à-vis the British Crown (Aaker, 2004; Aaker and Joachimsthaler, 2000; Argenti and Druckenmiller, 2004; Balmer, 1995, 2001b; Balmer and Gray, 2003; Balmer et al., 2009; Hatch and Schultz, 2001, 2003; Holt et al., 2004; Kapferer, 2002; King, 1991; Knox and Bickerton, 2003; Mukherjee and Balmer, 2008; Schultz and Hatch, 2003; Urde, 2001).

EXHIBIT 1. PROVENANCE, PERTINENCE AND POPULARITY: THE DETERMINANTS OF THE BRITISH CROWN AS A HERITAGE CORPORATE BRAND

Provenance

The British Monarchy is the last of the truly great imperial and sacerdotal monarchies. The institution dates back to the ninth century. It is the world's most famous monarchy and is one of the oldest. Until comparatively recently somewhere between a quarter to a third of the world's population were subjects of the British Monarch. The British sovereign is surrounded by sumptuous ceremonies, many of which are of considerable antiquity. For instance, the sovereign is sanctified by the Church during the Coronation Service at Westminster Abbey. The genesis of the British Coronation can be traced back to the Coronation of the Emperor Charlemagne in 800 when Pope Leo III crowned him (Cannadine and Price, 1992; Sullivan, 1959). For many, the attributes and rituals of the British Monarchy have, in global contexts, entered into common consciousness (the idea of a monarch wearing a crown for instance: most monarchs today no longer wear the crown). For these (and other) reasons it is viewed by many as the archetypal monarchy. Britain's democratic traditions have materially altered the role of the monarchy over successive centuries. For instance, constitutional experts as far back as Montesquieu (1748) saw it as the prototypical constitutional monarchy. The doctrine underpinning the notion of a constitutional monarchy is encapsulated in the dictum that: "the sovereign reigns but does not rule" (Bogdanor, 1997).

Pertinence

The status of the monarchy as an iconic British heritage brand is widely accepted both in the UK and overseas. One former US Ambassador to the UK compared the British Crown to an intricate tapestry since it provided a constant background to everyday events (Seitz, 1999). An anthropological study of the Monarchy by a US scholar concluded that the institution chimed with fundamental British values: a love of both hierarchy and democracy (Hayden, 1987).

Popularity

Although the Crown is sometimes portrayed as little more than an enjoyable and irrelevant spume on the British and world stage, this appears to be at odds with the facts. In relation to the UK, the Monarchy remains a surprisingly meaningful corporate brand. Research undertaken among British teenagers showed that, for them, it was a key icon of their British sense of identity

(Smithers, 2006), and surveys undertaken by MORI revealed that support for the Crown has remained over 70 per cent for many years (Granada/MORI, 2002; Kennedy, 2004). Research undertaken by the Mass Observation Day Surveys in the early part of the twentieth century also revealed a high degree of public support for the monarchy (Jennings and Madge, 1937).

In a global context, and as a consequence of the UK's imperial past, the footprint of Britain's monarchy is to be found in all parts of the globe. Even today, the Queen is Head of State in 16 countries and is titular Head of the British Commonwealth of Nations. It is a brand loyalty that many contemporary national and global corporate brands are likely to covet.

Moreover, the literature provided criteria against which the corporate branding credentials of the British Monarchy as a corporate brand could be determined (Balmer, 2008b): this is detailed as follows (see Exhibit 2).

The literatures on the British Monarchy

Remarkably, the British monarchy (including its English and Scottish antecedents) has endured for over a millennium, and the history of the institution along with the genealogy and its incumbents are awesome in their telling. Consider, for instance, the claimed royal provenance of Queen Elizabeth II. The Queen is descended from no less than Charlemagne, the Emperor Barbarossa and Rodrigo the Cid (Sampson, 1962). Of course, British monarchs have come in all shapes, sizes, nationalities and personalities. There have been saints (St Edward the Confessor), sinners (King Henry II) and scholars (Queen Elizabeth I). Some were famous (King Henry VIII), infamous (King John), mad (King George III), sad (King Edward VIII) and indolent (King George V).

It is frequently forgotten that in addition to her roles as British Head of State Queen Elizabeth is separately and divisibly Queen of 100,000,000 people in her 16 realms including Canada, Australia and New Zealand (Bogdanor, 1997). She is also titular Head of the British Commonwealth of Nations, which has a constituency in excess of 1,000,000,000 people; between a quarter and a third of all mankind (Cannon and Griffiths, 1998, p. 632).

EXHIBIT 2. THE CORPORATE BRANDING CRITERIA OF THE BRITISH MONARCHY

Brands have distinctive visual and verbal identifiers
(The Monarchy has the visual symbol of Crown along with the powerful verbal identifier of Royal.)

Brands are associated with key values
(The Monarchy is seen to represent traditional British values: a love of tradition, hierarchy, ceremony, etc.)

Brands may rent their prestige through endorsement
(The Monarchy de facto endorses other brands via the granting of Royal Warrants to organisations such as Fortnum and Masons and by conferring the use of the Royal prefix such as the Royal Albert Hall. It also, in effect, endorses nation states where the Queen is Head of State such as in Canada, New Zealand and Papua New Guinea for example.)

Brands are supported by brand communities
(The Monarchy has a legal brand community of many millions in the UK and hundreds of millions around the world by virtue of the Queen's position as Monarch in over 15 countries and her role as Head of the Commonwealth. Significantly, the Crown has brand communities of those who are interested in the brand in nations that have no formal ties with the institution as in France, Italy and the USA. The two and a half billion people worldwide who watched the funeral of Princess Diana on television is symptomatic of the global interest in the institution in good times and bad.)

Brands can be iconic and can be heritage brands in addition
(The Monarchy represents a familiar and meaningful reference point to many in an ever-changing world.)

Source: Balmer, 2008b

Although there is a good deal of popularist material on the monarchy, this can obfuscate the not inconsiderable scholarly literature on the British Crown.

The Crown has been studied from a variety of perspectives including anthropology (Hayden, 1987; Hocart, 1927; Murray, 1954), art history (Molesworth, 1969), British cultural studies (Couldry, 2001), commonwealth studies (Butler and Low, 1991), constitutional history (Chrimes, 1967), constitutional law (Brazier, 2003), heraldic science (Innes, 1978), history (Hobsbawn and Ranger,1983; Pimlott, 2002), philosophy (Montesquieu, 1748), political science (Bogdanor, 1997; Mayer and Sigelman, 1998; Thompson, 1971), sociology (Shils and Young, 1953), applied psychoanalysis (Jones, 1951); social psychology (Billig, 1998; Black, 1953), social policy (Prochaska, 1995) and theology (Bradley, 2002). Also of note is the medieval doctrine of the King's two bodies (the sovereign as an individual and the monarchy as a mystical institution), which still has some utility in terms of discussions relating to monarchy (Kantorowicz, 1953).

As an ancient, prominent and unique organisational brand, it seems irrefutable that there is merit in scrutinising this institution from both marketing and management perspectives, and yet the review of these literatures confirmed that the Crown, until comparatively recently, had rarely been the subject of substantive scrutiny from marketing and management scholars. An exception is the work of and Greyser *et al.*, 2006 along with the author's individual and collaborative work on the territory (Balmer, 2008b; Balmer *et al.*, 2004, 2006) relating to the British and Swedish monarchies. In addition, the work of Otnes and Maclaren (2007) is notable; their work examined the creation of individual identities via the collection and display of artefacts associated with the British Crown.

In terms of advice for monarchs and would-be monarchs there appears to be a surprising dearth of material. Of note, however, are the venerable tomes of Dante (in Church, 1879): *De Monarchia*; Defoe (c.1690): "Of Royall Educacion: A Fragmentary Treatise"; Erasmus (1516): "The Education of a Christian Prince"; Machiavelli (in Marriott, 1949): *The Prince*; and Viscount Bolingbroke (1738): *The Idea of a Patriot King*. All of the previous tomes offer advice for the education and political formation of monarchs and heirs apparent; some of the advice relates to the former, political role of monarchs as absolute rulers, but Bolingbroke does advocate the role of King in terms of being the "Father of the nation" which, arguably, chimes with the current role of constitutional monarchy with regard to the polity of the UK.

More recently, Bagehot's (1867) observations on the roles and functions of the Crown are noteworthy. The most notable of these is Bagehot's celebrated tripartite dictum relating to the Monarch's role vis-à-vis the British Prime Minister and Ministers of the Crown. It was, he said, the constitutional duty of the Sovereign to encourage, advise and to warn the government of the day.

Although frequently examined at a visceral level, the British Crown is an important and legitimate area of scrutiny at a cerebral level.

In Great Britain an environment of deference often militates against the Crown being the subject of debate, as none other than HM Queen Elizabeth II has noted (Hames and Leonard, 1998).

The identity literature

Finally, the literatures on corporate, organisational and social identity were scrutinised in order to see whether meaningful insights could be applied to corporate brand identities.

An examination of these literatures was found to be salient in comprehending the Crown as a Corporate Brand (Balmer, 1995, 2002, 2008a; Cornelissen *et al.*, 2007; He and Balmer, 2007). This is because the Crown not only has meaning as a legal and constitutional entity (Head of State) but also in terms of its symbolic and cultural role (Head of Nation).

The notion that organisations have dual as well as multiple identities is a *leit motif* within the management literature (Albert and Whetten, 1985; Balmer and Greyser, 2002). Additionally, it has been argued that there needs to be meaningful alignment between various identity types (Balmer and Greyser, 2002).

These insights from the identity literatures in management were important, in that the literature on the Crown tends to focus on its constitutional role (Bogdanor, 1997) and its symbolic importance (Hayden, 1987), but its importance to both States as well as to people is not always accorded prominence.

Methodological approach

In addition to a review of the previous literatures, the findings are also informed by case study research and historical research. By drawing on both methodological perspectives the objective is to provide normative insights vis-à-vis the management and maintenance of the British Crown as a corporate brand.

In methodological terms, case studies are viewed as efficacious where the research is explanatory in nature and where the researchers are, in effect, faced with a *tabula rasa* as was the case here (Easterby-Smith *et al.*, 2002; Easton, 2003; Gummesson, 2001, 2003, 2005; Normann, 1970; Yin, 1994; Znaniecki, 1934).

Historical research represents a distinct branch of inquiry within management. The literature reveals that normative insights may be discerned when scrutinising an organisation's, or an industry's, historiography (Carroll, 2002; Gioia *et al.*, 2002; Jeremy, 1998; Ooi, 2002; Parker, 2002; Phillips and Greyser, 2001). Such a perspective does of course underpin leading academic journals such as the *Journal of Business History* and has been acknowledged in the *Harvard Business Review* (Kantrow, 1986; Smith and Steadman, 1981).

Within the literature on business history, there is a tradition where normative insights are derived by exploring key historical events and their implications for contemporary corporations. These include Nelson's victory over Napoleon and the events, and management decisions, which resulted in the sinking of the Vasa Warship in Sweden: see, also, Coleman (1969), Dellheim (1987), Ferrier (1982), Kessler *et al.* (2001), Kroll *et al.* (2000) and Pringle and Kroll (1997). As cogently observed by Lowenthal (1988), drawing on and clarifying the past can be relevant for contemporary contexts: this approach has informed this study and is especially apposite for the Crown as a corporate brand.

This article draws from, as well as builds on, both of the previously mentioned traditions. This is based on the premise that the Crown has the capacity to learn from critical events in its past such is its extraordinarily long, rich and eventful history. However, since the monarchy stretches back to the mists of time, certain parameters were set in terms of the sovereigns to be studied.

For this study, it was decided to examine the last six British Monarchs (from Queen Elizabeth II back to Queen Victoria) along with a much earlier and celebrated monarch: King William ("William the Conqueror"), who gained the English throne by conquest in 1066. Such an approach was undertaken to find whether important insights could be gleaned from each reign. In all instances, the answer was affirmative.

In terms of the scrutiny of the last six monarchs it was possible to find critical events for each reign that shed light on key aspects of managing the British Crown as a brand.

Six insights: managing the British Monarchy as a corporate brand

The six insights are as follows:

(1) Continuity (maintaining heritage and symbolism).
(2) Visibility (having a meaningful and prominent public profile).
(3) Strategy (anticipating and enacting change).
(4) Sensitivity (rapid response to crises).
(5) Respectability (retaining public favour).
(6) Empathy (acknowledging that brand ownership resides with the public).

Each insight comprises three elements: a brief description of a critical event in the institution's history, followed by the implications in terms of the management and maintenance of the Crown as a corporate brand (normative insights), along with a brief comment relating to one of the nascent theories of corporate branding.

Insight 1. The reign of King William I (1066–1087): "Maintaining brand symbolism and heritage"

Critical event: The Coronation of King William I in 1066, shortly after winning the throne of England at the Battle of Hastings, confirmed, sanctified and legitimatised William of Normandy's status as King of England.

Christmas Day 1066 was a defining moment in the annals of English history. On this day French hegemony over the English was confirmed. There was the imposition of a new Sovereign, Royal Family, and Dynasty and, moreover, a new ruling class, a new culture and a new language (Cannon and Griffiths, 1998; Gardiner and Wenborn, 1995, p. 554). Earlier that year, under the command of William, Duke of Normandy (pretender to the throne of England), the English army was crushed. England's King, the last of the Anglo-Saxon line, King Harold II, was slain at the Battle of Hastings.

Questions of legitimacy, and authenticity, were very much on the mind of England's new ruler: William, Duke of Normandy (Barker, 1979). It came with a realisation that the throne of England could only be authentically and completely his if he underwent the traditional Catholic Coronation ceremony, where he was anointed, consecrated, crowned and acclaimed as King. Of course, the English Coronation service closely replicated that used by the celebrated Coronation of the Emperor Charlemagne (who was crowned) and, earlier on, the custom of anointing Kings; the inauguration of Pippin in 751 is a case in point (Enright, 1985; Nelson, 1992, p. 142). Today, in Great Britain, the Coronation is very much seen to be part of the country's heritage and of its collective memory. The Coronation was seen then, and still is seen now, by the public at large as the defining ritual that accords legitimacy to a Monarch (even though, today, the status of the monarch as Head of State is no longer dependent on such rites: the situation was materially different in eleventh-century Europe).

From an ecclesiastical perspective, Coronations invest a Sovereign with sacerdotal eminence; this is especially the case relating to the anointing of monarch, which is by seen both by monarchs and prelates as the most central of all the liturgical rites: in effect, a quasi-sacrament. In addition to the previous, the rituals and tokens of monarchy as used in the Coronation (such as the crown, orb and sceptre) connote, as well as project, considerable symbolic power (Barker, 1979; Cannadine and Price, 1992; Hayden, 1987). The Coronation, and the symbols of Monarchy, were critical to William since it gave his reign both legal legitimacy and ecclesiastic approbation. Of particular importance was for King William to reinforce the view that he was Sovereign by Divine Right. The cross at the apex of the Crown is not there only for aesthetic and decorative purposes. Then, as today, the Crown is unquestionably the brand marque *par excellence* with, perhaps, the exception of the crucifix vis-à-vis the Roman Catholic Church. Surprisingly, perhaps, an opinion poll undertaken in the 1960s showed that 30 per cent of the British public thought that the Queen had been especially chosen by God to be the British Sovereign (Prochaska, 2001, p. 204).

The symbolic meaning of the crown is such that it is not simply a mark of Kingship but also one of authority and sovereignty (Barker, 1979; Tresidder, 2004). This perhaps explains why King William was eager to be invested with the Crown as soon as possible after his defeat of King Harold at the infamous Battle of Hastings. After 1066:

> He wore his crown three times each year, as often as he was in England. At Easter he wore it in Winchester, at Pentecost at Westminster, at mid-winter in Gloucester; and there were then with him all the powerful men over all England.
>
> (Anglo Saxon Chronicle, *1086/1087*)

The viewpoint of King William still resonates with the Crown and Royal Household today. One confidant of Queen Elizabeth II related how there had, de facto, never been an abdication vis-à-vis the British Monarchy and confirmed the centrality of the Coronation in according legitimacy and authority:

> You see, Edward (King Edward VIII, 1936) ran away before he was crowned. He was never anointed, so he never really became King. So he never abdicated.
>
> (Paxman, 2007, p. 125)

The rite of anointing the monarch with Holy Chrism is one that, significantly, because of its sacramental nature, was hidden from the gaze of the congregation and television viewers during the Coronation of Queen Elizabeth: a coronation that closely follows the pattern of King William's coronation and which, of course, takes place in exactly the same Abbey Church.

Normative advice regarding the management of the Crown as a corporate brand

(1) Symbolism and rituals can be critically important dimensions in managing and maintaining the corporate brand.
(2) It is important to understand and maintain brand heritage and to keep the saliency of the brand's authentic nature.

Theoretical insight

This critical incident appears to support something of the nascent theory of corporate heritage brands which notes that for a heritage brand to claim to be authentic it has to meet two criteria:

(1) Its ability to clarify the past.
(2) To make the past relevant for contemporary contexts (Urde *et al.*, 2007).

The criterion appears to apply to the Coronation of King William I.

Insight 2. The reign of Queen Victoria (1837–1901): "Visibility" (having a meaningful and prominent public profile)

Critical event: The crisis caused by Queen Victoria's lack of public visibility in the aftermath of the death of her husband, Prince Albert (the Prince Consort).

In 1861 Prince Albert, the consort of Queen Victoria, died. Overcome with grief the Queen withdrew from public gaze and strictly limited her activities to the administrative affairs of State (the approval of legislation, reading papers of state and meeting the Prime Minister, etc.). The Queen eschewed events that brought her into the presence and gaze of the general public; what is sometimes called affairs of Nation (Hardman, 2007).

Victoria's absence for almost a decade led to growing disquiet among much of British society and led to the rise of republicanism and the formation of republican clubs throughout Great Britain (Thomson, 1967, p. 171). In a celebrated action by a member of the public, a handbill was fixed to the walls of Buckingham Palace; it captured something of the *Zeitgeist* and read as follows:

> These extensive premises to be let or sold, the late occupant having retired from business.
>
> *(Prochaska, 2001, p. 101)*

Fortuitously, if not paradoxically, it was the recovery from a life-threatening illness of the Prince of Wales (the future King Edward VII) in 1871 that brought the Queen out of mourning. The public rejoicing that followed the news of his recovery struck a chord with the Monarch who, once again, took up affairs of the nation. By embracing the more ceremonial aspects of the Crown, Queen Victoria successfully rekindled the bond between the monarchy and public. In subsequent years the monarch, and monarchy, grew in esteem as a corporate brand as evinced by the populist jubilee celebrations of 1887 and 1897 (Ormrod, 2001, p. 245).

The previous provides a salient lesson for constitutional monarchies in that they need to be *seen*. The importance of public visibility to the survival of the Crown was emphasised by Bolingbroke in 1738 in his treatise "The Idea of a Patriot King" (Prochaska, 2001), who noted that popularity was the sole foundation of Royal authority and asserted that the Crown's charisma was dependent on Royal appearances.

In broader contexts, public service is a cornerstone of constitutional monarchy. The very earliest notions of Kingship had little to do with dynastic inheritance but a great deal to do with an individual's suitability to become the Sovereign. Then, as now, monarchs might usefully heed the ancient monarchical precept of *ad vitam aut culpam*: "for life until removed for fault". It was this dictum that informed the appointment and removal of the first Christian monarchs (Manchester, 1993, p. 18).

In surveying the reasons for failed monarchies the Oxford constitutional expert Vernon Bogdanor (1997) concludes that most failed because they had been discredited and, thereby, fatally wounded. It might also be added that a lack of visibility has the potential to undermine the institution: a lesson from the Reign of Queen Victoria that the Royal Household of today failed to take account of in the aftermath of the death of Princess Diana with destructive effect.

Normative advice regarding the management of the Crown as a corporate brand

(1) Being visible and adopting appropriate behaviour (public service) is, arguably, the most powerful form of corporate brand communication.
(2) The Brand Promise is akin to an emotional contract. If broken, an institution can be undermined and even fatally damaged.

Theoretical insight

This critical incident also supports the general theory vis-à-vis corporate communications that behaviour is the most powerful form of communication, what Balmer and Gray (1999a, b) term primary communications as part of what they call their total corporate communications mix.

Insight 3. The reign of King Edward VII (1901–1910): "Strategy" (anticipating and enacting change)

Critical event: Redefining the Crown's brand identity by emphasising its symbolic role and philanthropic credentials.

The short reign of King Edward VII marked a vital transition in the corporate brand identity of Britain's monarchy. With Edward's reign came the realisation that in a more open, technologically advanced and increasingly less deferential age, the survival of monarchy was not so much dependent on its vestigial constitutional powers and obligations but on its ceremonial, public and philanthropic roles (Hobsbawn and Ranger, 1983; Prochaska, 1995; Taylor, 1977, p. 206).

As such, the King and his advisers repositioned the crown as a corporate brand along the above lines.

Cannadine and Price (1992, p. 7) mused that although Monarchs no longer rule by Divine Right, the divine rites of Monarchs, in our contemporary times, continue to beguile and enhance our society and civilisation. King Edward and his advisers understood this and realised that there was merit in the monarchy being seen to be magnificent. As one courtier has noted, the pomp and circumstance of monarchy make the strong meek and the meek tremble (Shea, 2003, pp. 146–7).

Aided by his advisers, the King invigorated the pomp and ceremonial aspects of the British Monarchy. The panache and precision we now take for granted vis-à-vis the British Monarchy owes much to King Edward VII; in earlier reigns it had been horrendously slipshod. The Coronation of Queen Victoria was a case in point: the clergy lost their place in the order of service; the Archbishop of Canterbury placed the ring on the wrong finger, which occasioned the Queen to wince with pain; another Bishop managed to fall over; the singing by the choir was wretched; a Lord tripped on his robes and tumbled down the stairs and two of the trainbearers talked throughout the entire coronation ceremony. There was more. On leaving Westminster Abbey Queen Victoria was scandalised to see that in a side chapter an altar was covered with half-eaten sandwiches along with empty bottles of wine (Cannadine, 1983, p. 119; Paxman, 2007, p. 128). Clearly, Queen Victoria was not amused.

As part of the King's strategy for effecting a renaissance of royal ritual, ancient ceremonies were revived, revisited and reinvigorated – especially the annual State Opening of Parliament. The environs of Buckingham Palace were radically refashioned in order to allow for grand ceremonial displays and to more comfortably accommodate the large crowds in an area that is now colloquially and appropriately known as "Ceremonial London".

The approach taken by Edward and his advisers might seem to be counterintuitive since, both then and now, making the modern monarchy relevant invariably leads to calls for the institution to "innovate" via strategies of "modernisation" and "simplification".

To Edward, "innovation" entailed the revisiting and rediscovery of brand heritage; especially in terms of symbolism. Thus, whereas most other monarchies were pensioning off their carriages, simplifying their coronation rituals and eschewing the wearing of crowns, King Edward, paradoxically, brought the carriages back into use and commissioned a new state landau; he elaborated the coronation rites and reinstituted the tradition of wearing the crown and coronation robes at the annual state opening of Parliament.

In addition, realising that all ceremonial is preposterous unless perfectly meticulously executed, King Edward VII took care to ensure that crown ceremonies were very carefully planned and choreographed. In a profound sense of the phrase, King Edward invented the tradition of the ceremonial monarchy. It worked and it was liked.

It still is, of course, as evidenced by the large crowds who witness the Changing of the Guard, the State Opening of Parliament and Trooping the Colour (the ancient military ceremonial that takes place on the monarch's official birthday.)

The importance of ceremony to the polity of democratic societies was averred by Keynes (1936). He concluded that one explanation why so many democracies were unsuccessful was their failure to recognise the importance of ceremony. By the same token, I note how ceremonies were of central importance to the Nazi regime in Germany in the last century and to North Korea today. What is certain is that rituals and ceremonies are unquestionably of considerable importance and can bolster democratic as well as despotic regimes.

As Sovereign, Edward did much to lay the foundations of Britain's monarchy as we know it today whereby the monarch is not merely Head of State but, moreover, the Head and focus of Civil Society. This was the second, critical, strand of the new strategy for the Crown.

As a public monarch, Edward performed his public obligations as constitutional monarch with skill and reached out to the public by travelling indefatigably through the length and breadth of the Realm (Cannon and Griffiths, 1998, p. 583).

As a philanthropic sovereign, Edward VII realised that if the institution was to survive and flourish it had to be of relevance to the British public at large and that the monarchy by doing good would be seen to be doing well: the doctrine of noblisse oblige. As such, particular attention was accorded to activities associated with public welfare and benevolence and highlighting the plight of the poor, weak and disadvantaged; this established what has been termed "The Welfare Monarchy" (Prochaska, 1995, p. 282). This is not unlike the CSR activities that are now undertaken by many contemporary corporate brands (Brammer and Pavelin, 2004; The Economist, 2008a, b). It was as if King Edward VII had written "the triple bottom line" into the articles of association of the Crown. Before Edward's reign monarchs appeared to follow the *bon mot*: "Remember who you are," but, from Edward's reign onwards, to me this doctrine appears to have been modified to "Not only remember who you are but be guided by what you can do."

Today, the philanthropic activities of the Crown are realised to be of particular saliency, and this was confirmed by a Mass Observation Survey undertaken in the 1960s (Prochaska, 2001, p. 224). More recently, as a senior member of staff of Prince Charles observed:

> The Monarchy is moving from being an institution principally famous for ceremonial occasions to being an institution principally of value for what it can add to the country through public service.
>
> *(Prochaska, 2001, p. 225)*

Normative advice regarding the management of the Crown as a corporate brand

(1) Anticipating and accommodating change are necessary to maintain brand saliency.
(2) Adopting a more explicit philanthropic/CSR stance has been necessary for the Crown's survival by monarchs, both past and present.
(3) Sensitivity (rapid response to crises).

Theoretical insight

In theoretical terms the repositioning of the corporate brand at this time supports the general theory of identity that: "Differences of identity highlight distinctiveness in identity" (Balmer, 2008a, p. 889). Normally, this theory has an intra-organisational context but in this instance, clearly applies to instances where there has been a meaningful repositioning of a corporate brand identity. Theoretical insights from organisational identity also appear to resonate here in terms of corporate brand identity. For instance, Czarniawska and Wolff (1998) found that organisational identities are created via the adoption of symbolic behaviour and language. Glynn (2000) and Pratt and Rafaeli (1997) noted the importance of rites and rituals, artefacts and organisational dress, etc. in identity creation. Mead (1934), of course, advanced the theory that identities are symbolically enacted.

Insight 4. The reign of King George V (1911–1936): "Sensitivity" (rapid response to crises)

Critical event: The affirmation of the Crown's British credentials via the adoption of a new, dynastic, corporate brand name during World War I. The British Monarchy then had a German Dynastic name (Saxe-Coburg Gotha). This was unacceptable to the public and opinion formers when Great Britain was at war with Germany.

One of the most remarkable, and successful, examples of re-branding anywhere over the last 100 years must surely be the one that took place during the reign of King George V. His reign marked the end of one dynasty and the birth of another. Why did this happen?

During the Great War of 1914–1918 when Britain was at war with Germany there was widespread loathing towards all things German. At that time, the dynastic name of Britain's Royal Family was Saxe-Coburg and Gotha: and (for many) at a time when Britain was at war the notion that the dynastic name (i.e. brand) was foreign, and seemingly of the enemy, was abhorrent. The Crown's Teutonic links were conspicuous in several other regards in that there were close blood ties with the German Crown and Aristocracy and the British Royal Family still held German aristocratic titles. In addition, both the King and Queen spoke English with a discernible German accent (Cannon and Griffiths, 1998, p. 591). As such, King George V was seen as Britain's "German" King and there were calls for his abdication (Hayden, 1987, p. 45).

A drastic re-branding exercise was called for and in what was unquestionably a masterstroke, the King's Private Secretary suggested that the dynastic name should be changed to that of Windsor (Hayden, 1987, p. 46). This dynastic name seemed so safe, solid, timeless and traditional because it connoted a Royal House that was (or appeared to be) quintessentially English and insinuated a dynasty that had an enviable English and British provenance. Nevertheless, it was, in effect, the adoption of a faux corporate brand heritage, something that is not uncommon today.

As part of this exercise the Royal Family gave up their claim to German titles and, importantly, abolished the bar on members of the Royal Family marrying non-royals. The response was a timely one since, as noted by Nicolson (1952), by the end of the Great War the world had seen the disappearance of five Emperors, eight Kings and 18 dynasties and there was no certainty that Britain's Monarchy would have endured. As has been judiciously explained by Bogdanor (1997) in his analysis of monarchy, most monarchies disappear as either a consequence of war/conquest or because they self-destruct: both phenomena threatened the Crown during the 1914–1918 war.

Lord Stamfordian, the King's private secretary (and, de facto, corporate brand manager to the British Crown) and whom King George V credited with teaching him how to be a king, in 1918 penned the following guidance:

> I am not concerned at the possible sacrifice of old traditional ideas and customs regarding Royalty. Some of these have already been sacrificed. Sovereigns must keep pace with the times.
>
> *(Prochaska, 2001, pp. 157, 169)*

Interestingly, HM King Carl XVI Gustaf of Sweden has the motto: "For Sweden – with the times". The King explained to us the significance of his motto:

> "For Sweden – with the times". To me it means being a monarch in a modern society – that is, to adapt the role by meeting the demands of a changing world. Not being ahead of the times, not being behind the times. But rather being in our time. It's about sensing feelings and what is right at the time – what the Swedish people wish and expect from a modern monarch.
>
> *(Audience with His Majesty King Carl XVI Gustaf, 17 February 2004)*

See the collaborative study on the Swedish Crown undertaken by Balmer *et al.* (2004, 2006).

Normative advice regarding the management of the Crown as a corporate brand

(1) Respond swiftly, skilfully and resolutely in response to sudden changes in the environment.
(2) Ensure that senior courtiers/managers are of a sufficiently high calibre and realise the importance of corporate brand management and maintenance.

Theoretical insight

The theory of corporate brand building is made up of a number of building blocks (Mukherjee and Balmer, 2008), and among these are values and priorities (Aaker, 2004) and image (Hatch and Schultz, 2001). However, during the Great War, the Monarchy's associations, communications, image and values were felt (rightly or wrongly) to be highly inappropriate by the British Public (its brand community). The major re-branding exercise (including significant changes to the Crown's identity traits) did much to assuage public unease.

Insight 5. The reigns of King Edward VIII (1936) and King George VI (1936–1952): "Respectability" (retaining public favour)

Critical events: The abdication of King Edward VIII did great damage to the Crown. However, it was the bombing of Buckingham Palace during the World War II in the reign of George VI which re-established public respect for the Crown and as such for King George VI and Queen Elizabeth (the mother of Queen Elizabeth II).

On the morning of January 21, 1936, the centre of London shuddered as the artillery of the British Army boomed out a royal salute. Following time-honoured tradition, and with great pomp and ceremony, a Royal Proclamation announcing the accession of the new King Emperor was declaimed by Kings of Arms in the capital cities of London and Edinburgh. Britain had a new king: the second of three kings who were to reign as monarchs in 1936 but the only one not to be crowned.

The monarch was King Edward VIII, but his position as sovereign came to an abrupt end on 11 December, at precisely 1:52 p.m., when in a cataclysmic act in the annals of the British Monarchy, King Edward VIII gave his Royal Assent to a Bill of Abdication and relinquished his status as King-Emperor in favour of his brother: the Duke of York. That evening, in what has become the most extraordinary of all royal broadcasts, Prince Edward (as he had become) uttered the following, fateful words to the peoples of the British Empire: "A few hours ago I discharged my last duty as King and Emperor." He continued: "I have found it impossible to carry the heavy burden of responsibility and discharge my duties as King as I would wish to do without the help and support of the woman I love" (Broad, 1936, p. 224). The woman was Mrs Wallis Warfield Simpson, a US divorcee and a close companion of the King of several years standing.

The affair had scandalised many (but by no means all) in Britain. The King's relationship with Mrs Simpson was considered to be both *outré* and unbecoming of a British Monarch. The Prime Minister and Bishops were not quiescent on the matter and moved to oust the King.

The dethronement of Edward VIII was a powerful reminder that British monarchs reigned on sufferance, and that the pomp and sycophancy that accompanied the monarch counted for nothing if the "rules" were disobeyed (Bogdanor, 1997,

p. 269; Pimlott, 2002, p. 37). Respect was not an unalienable right of monarchy or monarchs: it had to be earned and it had to be maintained.

Edward VIII was removed to save the monarchy (Powell in Hennessy, 1996, p. 20): it was (and is) the survival of the institutional brand and not the continuance of the individual (celebrity) brand that is in the end critical. This explains why the Royal Household, Government and Church focused on monarchy rather than monarch or, indeed, dynasty.

The primary task for the new King, George VI (the younger brother of Edward VIII), was to assuage the acute damage caused by his brother's omission and the loss of respect for the Crown.

With the outbreak of World War II in 1939, King George's resolve in this matter was all too soon put to the test. It was the bombing of Buckingham Palace in 1940 that cemented, once again, the nation's respect for the monarchy (Ormrod, 2001). Surveying the rubble of Buckingham Palace, Queen Elizabeth (the King's consort) made the following celebrated comment:

> I'm glad we've been bombed. It makes me feel as if I can look the East End in the face.
>
> *(Prochaska, 2001, p. 194)*

The people of London's East End had taken a good deal of the brunt of the bombing of London and had suffered greatly.

Curiously, just as the Crown's German associations during World War I nearly undermined the Monarchy, it was, paradoxically and by a twist of fate, a German bomb which had, unwittingly, restored public respect in the Monarchy during the World War II.

Normative advice regarding the management of the Crown as a corporate brand

(1) The loss of corporate brand reputation can be fatal to a corporate brand, but the seemingly catastrophic loss of it can, with careful management, be regained.
(2) Corporate brand managers should be mindful of the fact that corporate brand reputations take time in their creation but can be destroyed very quickly. It is the institutional brand rather than the individual (celebrity) brand "the King" that in extremis must take priority and should endure.

Theoretical insight

In general terms, the previously mentioned incident also supports the general theory of corporate brand building (Mukherjee and Balmer, 2008) where importance is accorded to the importance of primitives or building blocks; a key one of which is the maintenance of (a favourable) image.

Insight 6. The reign of Queen Elizabeth II (1952–): "Empathy" (recognising that emotional ownership of the corporate brand resides with the public)

Critical event: The Crown's dramatic climb-down to public and media demands that the 1953 Coronation should be televised by the British Broadcasting Corporation (BBC).

It is sometimes forgotten that the Coronation of Queen Elizabeth II in 1953 was marred by considerable controversy – a quarrel that resulted in a clash of wills among the Crown, British public, and media.

In the run-up to the Coronation, the Palace, Prime Minister, and the senior Prelate of the Anglican Church were all obdurate in their opposition in having the Coronation televised. A resolute public, spirited lobbying from the BBC, and a concerted campaign by the British press led to a *volte-face* on the part of the establishment and the cameras were, finally, allowed into the Abbey (Cannadine, 1983; Cockerell, 1988; Hennessy, 2007; Pimlott, 2002).

Among the ineffectual objections raised against having the ceremony televised by the great and the good were those voiced by the British Prime Minister, Sir Winston Churchill, and the Queen's Private Secretary, who were worried that considerable strain would be placed on the Queen caused by the TV cameras and studio lights. The Palace was also concerned that any imperfections in the ceremony, or in behaviour, could be a national embarrassment.

For his part, the Archbishop of Canterbury was exercised at the thought that the general populace might not show due decorum while viewing the ceremony: he was especially horrified at the thought that some might watch the ceremony while imbibing beer in a public house.

As noted by Macmillan, the will of the people prevailed and the establishment had to affect a gracious climb-down (Catterall, 2003; Hennessy, 2007, pp. 243–4).

In a powerful way, the televising of the Coronation had "democratised" the Crown to a degree hitherto unknown. It came with a realisation that the real power behind the throne was the British public who watched the Coronation at home on their TV screens, rather than those on the choir side of the rood screen within Westminster Abbey. The effect of the broadcast was momentous with two eminent US sociologists who in analysing public response to the Coronation Rites concluded that it was nothing less than a religious experience on a national scale (Shils and Young, 1953).

On Coronation Day (2 June 1953) an extraordinary 20 million people (40 per cent of the population) watched the service on television in a country which still had only 2.5 million television sets. Arguably, Queen Elizabeth II was the first British Sovereign to be truly crowned "in the sight of the people", as the coronation service has long ordained (Cannadine, 1983, p. 158). The broadcast revealed that in a more egalitarian and technology-orientated age the Rites of Monarchy can no longer be the preserve of the few but should be accessible to the Crown's brand community of millions both at home and overseas. Indeed, such was the global interest in the ceremony that the US-based *Time Magazine* made a bold and atypical claim that "The whole world is royalist now" (Shawcross, 2002, p. 54).

In retrospect, what was surprising about the controversy was the myopic mindset of Court, Cabinet and Clergy who failed to grasp that the *meaning* of the Coronation had and should change: ceremonies, rites and symbols can, over time, acquire different meanings.

The imbroglio was a powerful reminder that theocratic and aristocratic power of monarchy had progressively been supplemented by democratic power: the monarchy was there for the people and not vice versa. As Lampedusa (1958) cogently observed in his classic novel, *Il Gattopardo* (*The Leopard*): "If we want things to stay the same, things will have to change." The televising of the Coronation underpinned the *actualité*: the Monarchy, at its quintessence, through the course of a millennium had become a plebeian and democratic symbol and very much less a symbol of the aristocracy let alone a theocracy. British monarchs need to be mindful not only of the *vox dei* (the voice of God) but importantly the *vox populi* (the voice of the people). In terms of corporate brand heritage, *both were critical* to the Carolingian Coronation rituals of the ninth century (Nelson, 1992). Of course, elites have always buttressed their rule with ritual, ceremony and symbolism: King William and King Edward VII knew this all too well, however, increasingly, the ceremonies of monarchy reflect not so much that sovereignty resides with the monarchy but with the populace. The televising of the Coronation of Queen Elizabeth was a potent reproach to those who had failed to acknowledge the brand-like nature of the Crown where it was no longer the case of the monarch having a people but of the people having a monarch. Constitutional monarchies and corporate brands in addition ignore the de facto public ownership of brands at their peril.

As one senior courtier recently remarked:

> The Monarchy cannot just exist. It depends on popular support to survive, and that means adapting.
>
> *(Hardman, 2007, p. 13)*

Thus, although to all outward appearances the Coronation of Queen Elizabeth II is similar to that of William the Conqueror some 900 years earlier, the meaning of the Coronation had morphed over the passage of time.

The Coronation was not so much about the British Monarch but, in reality, was more about the British along with her Commonwealth subjects.

Interestingly, research undertaken by Black (1953, p. 28) sought to explain why, in the Queen's Canadian Realm, there was such extraordinary public exuberance spirited during the Queen's visit to her Dominion. His explanation was that Canadians coveted bilateral adulation; from them to their sovereign and, significantly, from the Canadian Queen to them. Black provides a cogent psychological explanation of what is, in effect, a revised notion of the point of monarchy by giving the following account:

> The (Canadian) public is on display because it desires to be loved. It wants the smile of Monarchy, the Royal sign of gratitude. It craves to display its ability,

its planning, its intelligence, its kind-heartedness and courage. The public in effect says: "Look on us, O Monarch. We are your people; we are good!"

It is a telling reminder that contemporary notions of monarchies as corporate brands are such that it is more appropriate to speak of nations having kings rather than kings having subjects; the monarchs of today are in the service of their subjects and not vice versa.

Black's research can be drawn on, and augmented, to explain the negative reaction to the Crown after the death of Diana, Princess of Wales, when the Queen and Royal Family went into private mourning.

This is because monarchs have two familial obligations: to their immediate family and, importantly, to the family that is the British public. It could well be that the Crown, for some, fills a vacuum that was once filled by the extended family and the support offered by the mainstream churches and religions.

Unlike the past, to me, contemporary notions of monarchy would appear to demand that the Sovereign's public role has been augmented to include public commiserations as well as celebrations.

Thus, in the aftermath of the death of the Princess of Wales, many wished the public to engage in bilateral expressions of grief and mourning in the same way as the Canadian public sought bilateral expressions of adulation. As such, in describing the scene outside Buckingham Palace when Queen Elizabeth (and also Princes William and Harry and others) were consoled, and when they, in turn, consoled the public, I *offer* the following explanation (adapting that of Black):

> The British public was on display because it desired to be consoled as well as to console. It wants to witness the tears of Monarchy, the Royal sign of grief and mourning. It too, also offers tears of grief; tears which display their humanity and empathy. The public in effect says: "Look on us, O Monarch. We are your people and we too are sad."

Recently, the British Crown appears to have recognised the imperative of seeing the institution through the eyes of the public. The statement made by Queen Elizabeth II in 1997 on the occasion of her 50th wedding anniversary is, perhaps, one of the most remarkable of her reign:

> Despite the huge constitutional difference between a hereditary monarchy and an elected government, in reality the gulf is not so wide. They are complementary institutions, each with its own role to play. Each, in its different way, exists only with the support and consent of the people. That consent, or the lack of it, is expressed for you, Prime Minister, through the ballot box. It is a tough, even brutal, system but at least the message is clear for all to read. For us, a Royal Family, however, the message is often harder to read, obscured as it can be by deference, rhetoric or the conflicting attitudes of public opinion. But read it we must.
> *(cited in Hames and Leonard, 1998)*

Normative advice regarding the management of the Crown as a corporate brand

(1) A distinction needs to be made between the legal ownership of the monarchy as a corporate brand (by the dynasty and by the apparatus of the nation state) and its emotional ownership by the general public. The Crown's corporate brand power is dependent on the latter and there are important obligations that flow from this.

(2) Customs and traditions need to be considered so that they remain meaningful to the crown's brand community. This may mean that some traditions are ended, altered, reinstated or although retained are reinterpreted by key stakeholders.

Theoretical insight

This critical incident supports the theoretical contributions of Lawer and Knox who state that, in part, an effective corporate brand requires customer involvement (the public in this case) and fostering knowledge-creating customer partnerships. Balmer (2008b) in his corporate branding mix includes relevance and responsiveness as key corporate brand management determinants; both were very apparent in the previous critical incident. The "Latin school of thought" in marketing (Badot and Cova, 1995) is also salient in terms of our comprehension of the Crown as a brand since it argues that marketing management should, in part, be focused on the creation of social ties between individuals via an individual's membership of a corporate brand community. The British Monarchy very much appears to fulfil this role.

Managing the British Monarchy as a corporate brand: Normative insights

A principal aim of this article was to provide some normative insights in terms of managing the monarchy as a corporate brand. The six critical incidents examined in the case history revealed the significance of continuity (maintaining heritage and symbolism); visibility (having a high public profile); strategy (anticipating and enacting change); sensitivity (rapid response to crises); respectability (retaining public favour); and empathy (acknowledging that brand ownership resides with the public).

With explicit reference to the insights from this case history it is possible to align each insight to an area of a specific zone of management or management activity. For instance:

Insight 1. Continuity is analogous to corporate identity and corporate brand heritage (Balmer, 2008b; Urde *et al.*, 2007).

Insight 2. Visibility is analogous to corporate communications (Christensen *et al.*, 2008; Greyser *et al.*, 2006; VanRiel, 2003).

Insight 3. Strategy is analogous to corporate strategy (Andrews, 1980) but also is analogous to ideal identity (Balmer and Greyser, 2002).

Insight 4. Sensitivity is analogous to crisis management/leadership (Nelson and Kanso, 2008).

Insight 5. Respectability is analogous to corporate image and reputation (Fombrun and Shanley, 1990; Gray and Balmer, 1998; Worcester, 1997b).

Insight 6. Empathy is analogous to marketing (Kotler, 2003), corporate marketing (Balmer and Greyser, 2006) and also is analogous to stakeholder management (Mitchell *et al.*, 1997).

Beyond Bagehot. A new tripartite monarchical dictum: "To be dutiful, devoted and dedicated"

To date, the responsibilities of the British Sovereign have emphasised the constitutional imperatives of the position as captured in Bagehot's insightful dictum that the obligations of the Monarch are to encourage, advise and to warn the Government of the day. However, when perceiving the Crown through a corporate branding lens it is apparent that this represents a narrow conceptualisation of the Monarchy's corporate brand promise.

In response, I suggest that the tripartite precepts of constitutional monarchy are in terms of being *dutiful, devoted and dedicated*: this encapsulates the Crown's constitutional, societal and symbolic roles.

As such, it is expected that the Monarch, and those supporting to the institution of monarchy, will be mindful of their obligations to be:

- dutiful to the tenets of a constitutional monarchy;
- devoted to the peoples of the realm; and
- dedicated to maintaining royal symbolism.

The previous list can be explained in a little more detail as follows:

> *Dutiful:* Bagehot's tripartite dictum may usefully inform the Monarch's responsibilities to the constitution.
>
> *Devoted:* In terms of the Crown's obligations to the peoples of the Realm, I suggest that this should be informed by the following concerns: to celebrate their achievements; to commiserate with them in times of adversity and to illuminate the plight of the ill, dispossessed, vulnerable and/or forgotten.
>
> *Dedicated:* Upholding the dignity, symbolism and traditions of Kingship so that they remain meaningful to both nation and to society at large.

"Chronicling the corporate brand": A modus operandi for the management of corporate heritage brands

There is a wealth of management insight, which can be extracted from the history of heritage brands; the discovery and comprehension of corporate brand values are cases in point (Balmer *et al.*, 2006; Urde *et al.*, 2007). Heritage brands, it should be remembered, imbue institutions with long-held values that in contemporary contexts mean that such brand values are relevant and distinctive. As such, decision makers should be *au courant* with a brand's history and the critical events that have marked as well as shaped its corporate brand identity. Organisations in examining their past often find their future, and a brand's history has the potential to guide management decision making for those having custodianship of a heritage brand. In short, a brand's history can be regarded as a key resource. This retrospective of the British Monarchy has revealed the efficacy of adopting such a perspective. Such an approach is likely to be efficacious for a variety of heritage brands, from a gargantuan brand such as the Catholic Church, to celebrated consumer brands such as Raffles Hotel as well as to small-scale brands such as Morgan (car makers) and Balmer (Swiss watch maker).

However, institutions, both ancient and modern, sometimes forget, misunderstand, or ignore their history. As such, critical insights in terms of managing an institution as a meaningful corporate brand may no longer inform contemporary decision-making processes. Critical insights from an organisation's past should be viewed as a critical institutional resource and part of an organisation's collective memory. As such I advocate a basic, five-stage *modus operandi*, relating to the previous – i.e. chronicling/assembling/documenting and communicating/marshalling/revisiting – as follows:

(1) *Chronicling* the brand's history in order to uncover key dimensions of a brand's values as well as to reveal critical events which have shaped the brand and which also have the potential to inform current decision-making activities.

(2) *Assembling* a cross-section of senior managers from key directorates to set down the corporate brand narrative and the lessons that flow from scrutinising key events of a brand's history. In addition, outside specialists such as management academics and consultants could be appointed in order to provide greater insight and objectivity; also, the cerebral prowess of more junior staff who are potential "high fliers" should not be ignored. Where possible the group should include a range of ages and representatives of both sexes. Non-management staff should also be a key part of the process since frontline staffs invariably have a wealth of experience as well as insight.

(3) *Documenting and communicating* the insights from the previous retrospective so that they might be used as a key resource in terms of the organisation's corporate branding and marketing activities along with strategy formulation, corporate communications, staff training and induction programmes as well as providing a key template in terms of providing insight vis-à-vis a brand's values.

(4) *Marshalling* historical insights may be used by senior managers as an element of scenario training vis-à-vis crisis management and might usefully be referred to when confronted with an actual crisis.

(5) *Revisiting* the brand's history needs to be undertaken since new insights may be gleaned by different individuals with different perspectives and when an organisation is, potentially, facing what appears to be uncharted territory.

The process of chronicling a brand's history also has the benefit of confirming/augmenting key aspects of a brand's heritage. For some brands, such an activity may lead to the discovery of a brand heritage: this occurred in the years leading up to the bi-centenary celebrations of the University of Strathclyde in 1996, with which I was intimately involved. More specifically, it led to the formal adoption of a full coat of arms along with the motto "Useful Learning", which was explicitly derived from the University's founder, John Anderson, who founded an institution which was charged with engaging in research and teaching that had a practical utility. The motto comes from his own words that his University should be: "A seminary of useful learning".

Of course, we should be mindful of the canard that history never repeats itself in precisely the same way and contexts are invariably different. However, a powerful riposte to the previously mentioned is to note the pedagogical value of examining critical events in an organisation's history and development.

In broader contexts, I note that the examination of past campaigns (successful or otherwise) is an important part of the training of cadets at British military and naval colleges. A similar doctrine informs postgraduates reading for MBA degrees at leading business schools and which include courses on business history. Clearly, chiefs of staff along with many in the business school professoriate are mindful of the celebrated adage that those who forget history are forced to repeat it.

The findings vis-à-vis theories relating to corporate branding, corporate identity and corporate marketing

The insights from this retrospective of the British Monarchy reveal that many facets need to be considered in terms of the management of the Crown as a corporate brand. This supports a key theory relating to corporate brand management in that a broad, multidisciplinary approach is required; this is somewhat different from the management of product and services brands (Balmer, 1995; Balmer and Gray, 2003; King, 1991; Knox and Bickerton, 2003; Schultz et al., 2005).

With regard to broader identity theory, the examination of the British Monarchy supports the theory that organisations are inhabited by multiple identities; for instance, many institutions have both a corporate identity in addition to a corporate brand identity (Balmer and Greyser, 2002). The study also suggests that in addition to Albert and Whetten's (1985) notion that entities have a utilitarian (for the Crown: its constitutional role) as well as a normative identity (for the Crown: its emblematic role as an iconic symbol of state), they also have a cultural identity (for the Crown: its societal covenant and obligations). More generally, in terms of medieval theories of monarchy which cogitated over the King's two bodies (Kantorowicz, 1953) relating to the parameters of the person of the monarch and the monarchy as an institution, from this study it is clear that theories of Kingship in the twenty-first century need to accommodate additional perspectives of monarchy.

In a related vein, the analyses of the Crown reveal both explicitly and implicitly that key corporate-level activities are interrelated and that there are multilateral relationships between them. For these reasons, corporate brand management, although undoubtedly of considerable importance, may in certain contexts be viewed as a key element of a much broader gestalt: that of corporate marketing (Balmer, 1998). The nascent theory of corporate marketing is that it should be viewed as an organisational-wide philosophy and one that marshals corporate-level activities relating to corporate branding, communications, identity and corporate image/reputation, etc. Its position as an explicit function should be secondary to its status as an organisational-wide philosophy. Moreover, the theoretical notion regarding the efficacy of aligning key zones of corporate marketing is one that has been a key concern for the Crown and would suggest the efficacy of such an approach (Balmer and Greyser, 2002).

The importance of stakeholder management is also significant since a careful scrutiny of the key events detailed in this retrospective reveals that the relative importance of stakeholder groups has shifted, quite markedly, with the passage of time. Agle and Wood's (1997) theory of stakeholder identification is predicated on the existence of meaningful institutional-group relationships; as such one, or more, of the following attributes should characterise such an association, namely, power, legitimacy and/or urgency. This analysis of the monarchy would suggest that this theory could be augmented in order to accommodate temporal analyses of stakeholder relationships in terms of power, legitimacy and/or urgency. This could provide meaningful insight for the future dynamic of the brand/stakeholder dynamic; this is equally important for the Monarchy as a brand along with other heritage brands.

A key question of corporate marketing is the following: "Can we, as an institution, have meaningful, positive and profitable bilateral on-going relationships with customers, and other stakeholder groups and communities?" (Balmer and Greyser, 2006).

For the British Monarchy, for which the concepts of corporate marketing and corporate branding are likely to be displeasing, the previously mentioned can, as a first attempt, be amended as follows: "Can we, the British Monarchy* have meaningful, positive and beneficial bilateral on-going relationships with British* people, society, institutions and culture mindful of the promises made at the Coronation and in accordance with the precepts of the UK's constitutional monarchy?" (*can be adapted for the Queen's other Realms/the Commonwealth).

The management of corporate marketing accords particular importance to corporate brands, among other concepts, and requires that particular attention is accorded to the meaningful and dynamic alignment of each of the six components of Balmer's corporate marketing mix (the 6Cs); collectively, and individually, they require the attention of those having ongoing responsibility for the institution (Balmer, 2006). The mix elements as applied/adapted to the British Monarchy are detailed as follows:

(1) *Character* (the defining institutional traits of the Monarchy).
(2) *Culture* (the collective feeling of British people and society towards the Crown).

Balmer's Corporate Marketing Mix
CHARACTER
*"What we indubitably
are"*

CULTURE
"What we feel we are"

COMMUNICATION
"What we say we are"

CONCEPTUALISATIONS
"What we are seen to be"

CONSTITUENCIES
"Whom we seek to serve"

COVENANT
"What is promised and expected"

FIGURE 2.1 Balmer's corporate marketing mix

Source: Balmer (2006)

(3) *Communication* (coordinating outward-bound formal communications which mirror the Monarchy's identity [character] and corporate brand [covenant]).

(4) *Conceptualisation* (the regular monitoring of the Monarchy's image and reputation among British society and among key stakeholder groups).

(5) *Constituencies* (recognising the importance of serving different stakeholder groups and adopting a stakeholder approach in terms of the day-to-day management of the institutions).

(6) *Covenant* (being mindful of the Monarch's/institution's corporate brand promise but also realising that the evolutionary nature of corporate brand promises).

Balmer's corporate marketing mix is shown in diagrammatic form (see Figure 2.1).

Conclusion

The British Monarchy provides some penetrating insights with regard to the management and maintenance of corporate brands. Such insights confirm previously made observations in relation to the efficacy of adopting a multidisciplinary approach to the management of corporate brands within the literature (Balmer, 1995,

2001a, b; Hatch and Schultz, 2001; Knox and Bickerton, 2003) and the efficacy of embracing the principles of corporate marketing (Balmer, 1998; Balmer and Greyser, 2006).

This study has as its particular focus the management of the British Monarchy as a corporate brand. However, the normative insights from this research clearly have a utility for other constitutional monarchies (Belgium, Denmark, Japan, Luxembourg, the Netherlands, Malaysia, Norway, Sweden, Spain, and Thailand). Moreover, the normative findings might also be found generalisable to those having responsibility for heritage (corporate) brands along with corporate brands per se.

There are other, important, parallels between monarchy and the world of business (Jenkins and Wiesmann, 2005). This is because our current comprehension of constitutional monarchy, as it exists in Britain, means that the monarch is the servant of the institution in a way that corporate brands, their management and personnel are in the service of their brand community.

Today, just as there is no place in an advanced democratic and economic society such as Britain for the autocratic, self-serving monarchs of old, the same should also be true to sovereigns of the boardroom.

This article confirms the view that ultimate responsibility for the corporate brand resides with the senior manager and especially the CEO (Balmer, 1995; King, 1991): in the case of the British Crown the ultimate custodians are senior courtiers, the government and, of course, the person of the monarch. As with many contemporary organisations, the survival of the British Crown is to a considerable degree dependent on it recognising that not only is it a corporate brand but that, critically, it needs to be managed as such.

Finally, the modern Monarchy, as with any corporate brand, is dependent for its continued existence on its saliency to its corporate brand community.

There is a centuries-old Royal motto which goes to the heart of corporate brand management: "Ich Dien" ("I serve"). It is the motto of the Prince of Wales. A motto that, perhaps, can be meaningfully customised for all staff so that it resonates with what is a central tenet of corporate branding as well as corporate marketing: "We serve."

Acknowledgement

The examination of monarchies as corporate brands has been a prominent theme at recent ICIG Symposia and includes, for instance, the collaborative work undertaken by the author with Professor Stephen A. Greyser (Harvard Business School) and Professor Mats Urde (Lund University) on the Swedish Monarchy.

The author is indebted to his good friend and colleague Professor Greyser of Harvard Business School for his generosity of spirit in kindly reading this manuscript and in making a number of suggestions. He is also grateful to his faculty colleagues at Brunel University, London, for their continued support and encouragement. This paper has its origins in a major collaborative study undertaken by scholars from Great Britain, North America and Sweden which explored the notion that monarchies are brand-like in character: see Balmer *et al.* (2004, 2006). Moreover, it draws on the author's extensive review of the literature on monarchy which took place from 2001 to the present time. The author is grateful for the reactions from faculty colleagues at Brunel University and Bradford School of Management to earlier presentations of some of the ideas contained in this article.

References

Aaker, D.A. (2004), "Leveraging the corporate brand", *California Management Review*, Vol. 46 No. 3, pp. 6–26.

Aaker, D.A. and Joachimsthaler, E.A. (1999), "The lure of global branding", *Harvard Business Review*, November–December, pp. 137–44.

Aaker, D.A. and Joachimsthaler, E.A. (2000), "The brand relationship spectrum: The key to the brand architecture challenge", *California Management Review*, Vol. 42 No. 4, pp. 8–23.

Agle, B.R. and Wood, D.J. (1997), "Towards a theory of stakeholder identification and salience: Defining the principle of who and what really counts", *Academy of Management Review*, Vol. 22 No. 4, pp. 853–86.

Albert, S. and Whetten, D.A. (1985), "Organizational identity", in Cummings, L.L. and Staw, B.M. (Eds.), *Research in Organizational Behavior*, JAI Press, Greenwich, CT, Vol. 7, pp. 263–95.

Andrews, K.R. (1980), *The Concept of Corporate Strategy*, Irwin, Homewood, IL.

Anglo-Saxon Chronicle (1086/1087) (2004), "Peterborough manuscript (1996 translation)", in *History in Quotations* (trans. Cohen, M.J. and Major, J.), Cassell, London, p. 217.

Argenti, P.A. and Druckenmiller, B. (2004), "Reputation and the corporate brand", *Corporate Reputation Review*, Vol. 6 No. 4, pp. 368–74.

Badot, O. and Cova, B. (1995), "Communaute´ et consommation: Prospective pour un marketing tribal", *Revue Franc aise du Marketing*, Vol. 1 No. 151, pp. 5–17.

Bagehot, W. (1867), *The English Constitution*, Chapman & Hall, London.

Balmer, J.M.T. (1995), "Corporate branding and connoisseurship", *Journal of General Management*, Vol. 21 No. 1, pp. 24–46.

Balmer, J.M.T. (1998), "Corporate identity and the advent of corporate marketing", *Journal of Marketing Management*, Vol. 14 No. 8, pp. 963–96.

Balmer, J.M.T. (2001a), "Corporate identity, corporate branding and corporate marketing: Seeing through the fog", *European Journal of Marketing*, Vol. 35 Nos. 3/4, pp. 248–91.

Balmer, J.M.T. (2001b), "The three virtues and seven deadly sins of corporate brand management", *Journal of General Management*, Vol. 35 Nos. 3/4, pp. 248–91.

Balmer, J.M.T. (2002), "Of identities lost and identities found", *International Studies of Management and Organizations*, Vol. 32 No. 3, pp. 10–27.

Balmer, J.M.T. (2005), "Corporate brand cultures and communities", in Schroeder, J.E. and Salzer-Morling, M. (Eds.), *Brand Culture*, Routledge, London, pp. 34–48.

Balmer, J.M.T. (2008a), "Identity based views of the corporation: Insights from corporate identity, organisational identity, social identity, visual identity and corporate image", *European Journal of Marketing*, Vol. 42 Nos. 9/10, pp. 879–906.

Balmer, J.M.T. (2008b), "A resource-based view of the British Monarchy as a corporate brand", *International Studies of Management and Organizations*, Vol. 37 No. 4, pp. 20–45.

Balmer, J.M.T. and Gray, E.R. (1999a), "Corporate identity and corporate communications: Creating a competitive advantage", *Corporate Communications: An International Journal*, Vol. 4 No. 4, pp. 171–6.

Balmer, J.M.T. and Gray, E.R. (1999b), "Corporate identity and corporate communications: Creating a competitive advantage", in Balmer, J.M.T. and Greyser, S.A. (Eds.), *Revealing the Corporation: Perspectives on Identity, Image, Reputation, Corporate Branding and Corporate Level Marketing*, Routledge, London, pp. 126–35.

Balmer, J.M.T. and Gray, E.R. (2003), "Corporate brands: What are they? What of them?", *European Journal of Marketing*, Vol. 37 Nos. 7/8, pp. 972–97.

Balmer, J.M.T. and Greyser, S.A. (2002), "Managing the multiple identities of the corporation", *California Management Review*, Vol. 44 No. 3, pp. 72–86.

Balmer, J.M.T. and Greyser, S.A. (2006), "Corporate marketing: Integrating corporate identity, corporate branding, corporate communications, corporate image and corporate reputation", *European Journal of Marketing*, Vol. 40 Nos. 7/8, pp. 730–41.

Balmer, J.M.T., Greyser, S.A. and Urde, M. (2004), "Monarchies as corporate brands", working paper, Division of Research, Harvard Business School, Boston, MA.

Balmer, J.M.T., Greyser, S.A. and Urde, M. (2006), "The crown as a corporate brand: Insights from monarchies", *Journal of Brand Management*, Vol. 14 Nos. 1/2, pp. 137–61.

Balmer, J.M.T., Stewart, H. and Greyser, S.A. (2009), "Aligning identity and strategy: Corporate branding at British", *California Management Review*, Vol. 51 No. 3, pp. 6–23.

Barker, B. (1979), *The Symbols of Sovereignty*, David and Charles, North Pomfret, VT, p. 35.

Bartlett, C.A. and Nanda, A. (1990), *Ingvar Kamprad and IKEA*, Case No: 390–132, Harvard Business School, Boston, MA.

Berner, R. and Kiley, D. (2005), "Global brands", *Business Week*, Vol. 5 No. 12, September, pp. 56–63.

Billig, M. (1998), *Talking of the Royal Family*, Routledge, London.

Black, P. (1953), *The Mystique of Modern Monarchy: With Special Reference to the British Commonwealth*, Watts, London.

Bogdanor, V. (1997), *The Monarchy and the Constitution*, Oxford University Press, Oxford.

Bradley, I. (2002), *God Save the Queen: The Spiritual Dimension of Monarchy*, Darton Longman & Todd, London.

Brammer, S. and Pavelin, S. (2004), "Building a good reputation", *European Journal of Management*, Vol. 22 No. 6, pp. 704–13.

Brazier, R. (2003), "The Monarchy", in Bogdanor, V. (Ed.), *The British Constitution in the Twentieth Century*, The British Academy/Oxford University Press, Oxford, pp. 69–96.

Broad, L. (1936), *Crowning the King*, Hutchinson & Co., London.

Butler, S.L. and Low, D.A. (1991), *Sovereigns and Surrogates: Constitutional Heads of State in the Commonwealth*, Macmillan, London.

Cannadine, D. (1983), "The context, performance and meaning of ritual: The British Monarchy and the invention of tradition *circa* 1820–1977", in Hobsbawn, E. and Ranger, T. (Eds.), *The Invention of Tradition*, Cambridge University, Cambridge, pp. 101–64.

Cannadine, D. and Price, S. (1992), *Rituals of Royalty*, Cambridge University Press, Cambridge.

Cannon, J. and Griffiths, R. (1998), *Oxford Illustrated History of the British Monarchy*, Oxford University Press, Oxford.

Capon, N., Berthon, P., Hulbert, J.M. and Pitt, L.F. (2001), "Brand custodianship: A new primer for senior managers", *European Management Journal*, Vol. 19 No. 3, pp. 215–27.

Carroll, C. (2002), "Introduction: Special edition on the strategic use of the past and future in organizations", *Journal of Organizational Change Management*, Vol. 15 No. 6, pp. 556–62.

Catterall, P. (2003), *The Macmillan Diaries: The Cabinet Years, 1950–1957*, Macmillan, London.

Chrimes, S.B. (1967), *English Constitutional History*, Oxford University Press, Oxford.

Christensen, L.T., Firat, A.F. and Torp, S. (2008), "The organisation of integrated communications: Towards flexible integration", *European Journal of Marketing*, Vol. 42 Nos. 3/4, pp. 423–52.

Church, F.J. (1879), *Dante Alighieri. De monarchia*, Macmillan, London.

Cockerell, M. (1988), *Live from Number 10: The Inside Story of Prime Ministers and Television*, Faber, London.

Cohen, M.J. and Major, J. (2004), *History in Quotations*, Cassell, London.

Coleman, D.C. (1969), *Courthaulds: An Economic and Social History*, Vol. 1, Clarendon Press, Oxford.

Cornelissen, J.P., Haslam, S.A. and Balmer, J.M. (2007), "Social identity, organizational identity and corporate identity: Towards an integrated understanding of processes, patternings and products", *British Journal of Management*, Vol. 18, pp. S1–S16.

Couldry, N. (2001), "Everyday royal celebrity", in Morley, D. and Robins, K. (Eds.), *British Cultural Studies: Geography, Nationality and Identity*, Oxford University Press, Oxford.

Czarniawska, B. and Wolff, R. (1998), "Constructing new identities in established organization fields", *International Studies of Management and Organization*, Vol. 28, pp. 32–56.

Defoe, D. (c.1690), "Of Royall Educacion: A Fragmentary Treatise", in Bulbring, K.D. (Ed.), David Nutt, London, (1895).

Dellheim, C. (1987), "The creation of a company culture: Cadbury, 1861–1931", *American Historical Review*, Vol. 92.

Easterby-Smith, M., Thorpe, R. and Lowe, A. (2002), *Management Research*, Sage, London.

Easton, G. (2003), "One case study is enough", paper presented at Academy of Marketing Annual Conference, Aston University, Birmingham.

(The) Economist (2005a), "Brand new: Samsung's success shows the value of brands even in a world of new digital gadgets", *The Economist*, January 15, pp. 10–11.

(The) Economist (2005b), "A special report: Toyota", *The Economist*, January 29, pp. 61–3.

(The) Economist (2005c), "The benefits of woodworm", *The Economist*, September 10, p. 65.

(The) Economist (2006), *The Economist*, April 1, p. 13.

(The) Economist (2008a), "A special report on corporate social responsibility", *The Economist*, January 17, pp. 1–22.

(The) Economist (2008b), "How good should your business be?", *The Economist*, January 19, pp. 12–13.

Enright, M.J. (1985), *Iona, Tara and Soissons: The Origins of the Royal Anointing Ritual*, Walter de Gruyter, Berlin.

Erasmus, D. (1516), *The Education of a Christian Prince* (trans. Cheshire, N.M. and Heath, M.J.), edited by Jardine, L., Cambridge University Press, Cambridge.

Fang, N. (2004), "Starbucks brewing plans for Singapore region", *The Straits Times (Singapore)*, June 23, p. A19.

Ferrier, R.W. (1982), *The History of the British Petroleum Company, Vol. 1: The Developing Years 1901–1932*, Cambridge University Press, Cambridge.

Fombrun, C. and Shanley, M. (1990), "What's in a name? Reputation building and corporate strategy", *Academy of Management Journal*, Vol. 33 No. 2, pp. 233–58.

Frears, S. (2006), *The Queen (Film)*, Pathé Pictures, London.

Gardiner, J. and Wenborn, N. (1995), *The History Today Companion to British History*, Collins & Brown, London.

Gioia, D.A., Corley, K.G. and Fabbri, T. (2002), "Revisiting the past (while thinking about the future perfect tense)", *Journal of Organizational Change Management*, Vol. 15 No. 6, pp. 622–34.

Glynn, M.A. (2000), "When cymbals become symbols: Conflict over organizational identity within a symphony orchestra", *Organization Science*, Vol. 11, pp. 285–98.

Granada/MORI (2002), *Britain's Latest Views on the Monarchy*, Granada/MORI, London.

Gray, E.R. and Balmer, J.M.T. (1998), "Managing corporate image and corporate reputation", *Long Range Planning*, Vol. 31 No. 5, pp. 695–702.

Greyser, S.A., Balmer, J.M.T. and Urde, M. (2006), "The monarchy as a corporate brand: Some corporate communications dimensions", *European Journal of Marketing*, Vol. 40 Nos. 7/8, pp. 902–8.

Gummesson, E. (2001), *Qualitative Methods in Marketing Research*, Sage, London.

Gummesson, E. (2003), "All research is interpretive!", *Journal of Business & Industrial Marketing*, Vol. 18 No. 6, pp. 482–92.

Gummesson, E. (2005), "Qualitative research in marketing: Roadmap for a wilderness of complexity and unpredictability", *European Journal of Marketing*, Vol. 39 Nos. 3/4, pp. 309–27.

Hall, W. (1997), "Striking a balance between familiarity and efficiency", *Financial Times*, October 17, p. 12.

Hames, T. and Leonard, M. (1998), *Modernising the Monarchy*, Demos, London.

Hardman, R. (2007), *Monarchy*, Ebury Press, London.

Hatch, M.J. and Schultz, M. (2001), "Are the strategic stars aligned for your corporate brand?", *Harvard Business Review*, February, pp. 128–34.

Hatch, M.J. and Schultz, M. (2003), "Bringing the corporation into corporate branding", *European Journal of Marketing*, Vol. 37 Nos. 7/8, pp. 1041–64.

Hayden, I. (1987), *Symbol and Privilege: The Ritual Context of British Royalty*, University of Arizona Press, Tucson, AZ.

He, H.-W. and Balmer, J.M.T. (2007), "Identity studies: Multiple perspectives and implications for corporate-level marketing", *European Journal of Marketing*, Vol. 41 Nos. 7/8, pp. 22–34.

Hennessy, P. (1996), *Muddling through: Power, Politics and the Quality of Government in Postwar Britain*, Indigo, London.

Hennessy, P. (2007), *Having It So Good: Britain in the Fifties*, Penguin Books, London.

Hobsbawn, E. and Ranger, T. (1983), *The Invention of Tradition*, Cambridge University Press, Cambridge.

Hocart, A.M. (1927), *Kingship*, Oxford University Press, London.

Holt, D.B., Quelch, J.A. and Taylor, E.L. (2004), "How global brands compete", *Harvard Business Review*, September, Reprint R0409D.

Innes, Sir T. (1978), *Scots Heraldry*, rev ed., Johnston & Bacon, London.

Jenkins, P. and Wiesmann, G. (2005), "The powerful patriarch", *Financial Times*, October 8–9, p. 13.

Jennings, H. and Madge, C. (1937), "May the twelfth", in *Mass-Observation Day Surveys 1937*, Faber & Faber, London.

Jeremy, D.J. (1998), *A Business History of Britain 1900–1990s*, Oxford University Press, Oxford.

Jones, E. (1951), "The psychology of constitutional monarchy", in *Essays in Applied Psychoanalysis*, Vol. 1, Hogarth Press, London.

Kantorowicz, E.H. (1953), *The King's Two Bodies: A Study in Medieval Political Theology*, Princeton University Press, Princeton, NJ.

Kantrow, A. (1986), "Why history matters to managers: A roundtable discussion with Alfred D. Chandler Jr", *Harvard Business Review*, Vol. 64 No. 1, pp. 102–24.

Kapferer, J.-N. (2002), "Corporate brands and organizational identity", in Moingeon, B. and Soenen, G. (Eds.), *Corporate and Organizational Identities*, Routledge, London.

Kennedy, C. (2004), "Ahead in the polls", in *The Director*, Institute of Directors, London, p. 66.

Kessler, E.H., Bierley, P.E. III and Gopalakrishnan, S. (2001), "Vasa syndrome: Insights from a seventeenth century new-product disaster", *The Academy of Management Executive*, Vol. 15 No. 3, pp. 80–91.

Keynes, J.M. (1936), "Art and the state", *The Listener*, 26 August.

King, S. (1991), "Brand building in the 1990s", *Journal of Marketing Management*, Vol. 7 No. 11, pp. 3–13.

Kling, K. and Goteman, I. (2003), "IKEA CEO Anders Dahlvig on international growth and IKEA's unique corporate culture and brand identity", *The Academy of Management Executive*, Vol. 1 No. 1, pp. 31–7.

Knox, S. and Bickerton, D. (2003), "The six conventions of corporate branding", *European Journal of Marketing*, Vol. 37 Nos. 7/8, pp. 998–1016.

Kotler, P. (2003), *Marketing Management*, 11th ed. (International version), Prentice-Hall, Englewood Cliffs, NJ.

Kroll, M.J., Tooms, L.A. and Wright, P. (2000), "Napoleon's tragic march home from Moscow", *The Academy of Management Executive*, Vol. 14 No. 1, pp. 117–28.

Lampedusa, G.T. (1958), *Il Gattopardo*, Casa Editrice Feltrinelli, Italy.

Larsson, R., Brousseau, K.R., Driver, M.J., Holmqvist, M. and Tarnovskaya, V. (2003), "International growth through cooperation: Brand driven strategies leadership, and career development in Sweden", *Academy of Management Executive*, Vol. 17 No. 1, pp. 7–24.

Laundry, P. (1973), *Canada's Parliament*, The Canadian House of Commons, Ottawa.

Lowenthal, D. (1988), *The Heritage Crusade and the Spoils of History*, Cambridge University Press, Cambridge.

Machiavelli, N. (1949), *The Prince* (trans. Marriott), Dent, London.

Manchester, W. (1993), *A World Lit Only by Fire: The Medieval Mind and Renaissance*, Little Brown, Boston, MA.

Martin, G., Beaumont, P., Doig, R. and Pate, J. (2005), "Branding: A new performance discourse for HR", *European Management Journal*, Vol. 23 No. 1, pp. 76–88.

Masters, B. (1988), *Dreams about HM the Queen*, Grafton Books, London.

Mayer, J.D. and Sigelman, L. (1998), "Zog for Albania, Edward for Estonia, and Monarchs for all the rest? The royal road to prosperity, democracy, and world peace", *Political Science and Politics*, December, pp. 773–95.

Mead, G.H. (1934), *Mind, Self and Society*, University of Chicago Press, Chicago, IL.

Micklethwait, J. and Wooldridge, A. (2005), *The Company: A Short History of a Revolutionary Idea*, Modern Library, New York, NY.

Mitchell, R.K., Agle, B.R. and Wood, D.J. (1997), "Towards a theory of stakeholder identification and salience: Defining the principle of who and what really counts", *Academy of Management Review*, Vol. 22 No. 4, pp. 853–86.

Molesworth, H.D. (1969), *The Princes*, Weidenfeld & Nicolson, London.

Montesquieu, C.-L. de Secondat, Baron de (1748), *De l'esprit des lois ou du rapport que les lois doivent avoir avec la constitution de chaque government*, Barrillon, Geneva.

Mukherjee, A. and Balmer, J.M.T. (2008), "New frontiers and perspectives in corporate brand management", *International Studies of Management and Organization*, Vol. 37 No. 4, pp. 3–19.

Murray, M.-A. (1954), *The Divine Kings in England: A Study in Anthropology*, Faber & Faber, London.

Nairn, T. (1988), *The Enchanted Glass: Britain and Its Monarchy*, Century Hutchinson, London.

Nelson, J.L. (1992), "Carolingian royal ritual", in Cannadine, D. and Price, S. (Eds.), *Rituals of Royalty: Power and Ceremonial in Traditional Societies*, Cambridge University Press, Cambridge.

Nelson, R.A. and Kanso, A.M. (2008), "Employing effective leadership in a crisis", in Melewar, T.C. (Ed.), *Facets of Corporate Identity, Communication and Reputation*, Routledge, London, pp. 141–60.

Nicolson, Sir H. (1952), *King George the Fifth*, Constable, London.

Normann, R. (1970), "A personal quest for methodology", *Scandinavian Institutes for Administrative Research*, Vol. 53, pp. 6–26.

Olins, W. (2000), "How brands are taking over the corporation", in Schultz, M., Hatch, M.J. and Larsen, M.H. (Eds.), *The Expressive Organization*, Oxford University Press, Oxford, pp. 51–65.

Ooi, C.-S. (2002), "Persuasive histories: Decentering, recentering and the emotional crafting of the past", *Journal of Organizational Change Management*, Vol. 15 No. 6, pp. 606–21.

Ormrod, W.M. (2001), *The Kings and Queens of England*, Tempus, Stroud.

Otnes, C.C. and Maclaren, P. (2007), "The consumption of cultural heritage among a British Royal Family Brand Tribe", in Kozinets, R., Cova, B. and Shanker, A. (Eds.), *Consumer Tribes, Theory, Practice and Prospects*, Elsevier/Butterworth-Heinemann, London.

Parker, J. (2002), "Contesting histories: Unity and division in a building society", *Journal of Organizational Change Management*, Vol. 15 No. 6, pp. 589–605.

Paxman, J. (2007), *On Royalty*, Penguin, London.

Phillips, P.M. and Greyser, S.A. (2001), "Bank one: The uncommon partnership", in Balmer, J.M.T. and Greyser, S.A. (Eds.), *Revealing the Corporation*, Routledge, London and New York, NY.

Pimlott, B. (2002), *The Queen: Elizabeth II and the Monarchy*, HarperCollins, London.

Pratt, M.G. and Rafaeli, A. (1997), "Organizational dress as a symbol of multilayered social identities", *Academy of Management Review*, Vol. 25, pp. 862–98.

Pringle, C.D. and Kroll, M.J. (1997), "Why Trafalgar was won before it was fought: Lessons from resource-based theory", *The Academy of Management Executive*, Vol. 11 No. 4, pp. 73–89.

Prochaska, F. (1995), *Royal Bounty: The Making of a Welfare Monarchy*, Yale University Press, New Haven, CT.

Prochaska, F. (2001), *The Republic of Britain 1760–2000*, Penguin, London.

Sampson, A. (1962), *Anatomy of Britain*, Hodder & Stoughton, London.

Schultz, M., Antorini, Y.M. and Csaba, F.F. (2005), *Corporate Branding: Purpose/People/Process*, Copenhagen Business School Press, Copenhagen.

Schultz, M. and Hatch, M.J. (2003), "The cycles of corporate branding", *California Management Review*, Vol. 46 No. 1.

Seitz, R. (1999), *Over Here*, Phoenix, London, p. 82.

Shawcross, W. (2002), *Queen and Country*, BBC Worldwide Limited, London.

Shea, M. (2003), *A View from the Sidelines*, Sutton Publishing, Stroud.

Shils, E.A. and Young, M. (1953), "The meaning of the coronation", *Sociological Review*, Vol. 1, pp. 68–81.

Smith, A. (1998), "Moving out of the shadows", *Financial Times*, June 5, p. 32.

Smith, G.D. and Steadman, L.E. (1981), "Present value of corporate history", *Harvard Business Review*, Vol. 59 No. 6, November–December, pp. 164–73.

Smithers, R. (2006), "Young Britons value nation's history and values", *The Guardian*, November 6, p. 9.

Starkey, D. (2002), *Reinventing the Royals*, Channel 4 TV Programme, London.

St John, H. Viscount Bolingbroke (1738), *The Idea of a Patriot King*, Carey & Hart, Philadelphia, PA, p. 380.

Sullivan, R.E. (1959), *The Coronation of Charlemagne*, D.C. Heath, Boston, MA.

Taylor, A.J.P. (1977), *The Use of Monarchy in Essays in English History*, Book Club Associates, London.

Thompson, J.A. (1971), "Labour and the modern British Monarchy", *South Atlantic Quarterly*, Vol. 20 No. 3, Summer.

Thomson, D. (1967), *The Pelican History of England: 8. England in the Nineteenth Century*, Penguin, London.

Tresidder, J. (2004), *The Complete Dictionary of Symbols*, Duncan Baird Publishers, London, p. 132.

Urde, M. (2001), "Core, value-based corporate brand building", *European Journal of Marketing*, Vol. 37 Nos. 7/8, pp. 1017–40.

Urde, M., Greyser, S.A. and Balmer, J.M.T. (2007), "Brands with a heritage", *Journal of Brand Management*, Vol. 15 No. 1, pp. 4–19.

VanRiel, C.B. (1995), *Principles of Corporate Communication*, Prentice-Hall, London.

VanRiel, C.B. (2003), "The management of corporate communications", in Balmer, J.M.T. and Greyser, S.A. (Eds.), *Revealing the Corporation: Perspectives on Identity, Image, Reputation, Corporate Branding and Corporate-Level Marketing*, Routledge, London and New York, NY, pp. 161–70.

Willman, J. (1997), "Shimmering symbols of the modern age", *Financial Times*, October 17, p. 12.

Worcester, Sir R. (1997a), "The power of public opinion: Princess Diana, 1961–1997", *Journal of the Market Research Society*, Vol. 39 No. 4.

Worcester, Sir R. (1997b), "Managing the image of your bank: The glue that binds", *International Journal of Bank Marketing*, Vol. 15 No. 5, special issue on Corporate Identity, pp. 146–52.

Yin, R.K. (1994), *Case Study Research: Design and Methods*, Sage Publications, Thousand Oaks, CA.

Znaniecki, F. (1934), *The Method of Sociology*, Farrar & Rinehart, New York, NY.

Further reading

Balmer, J.M.T. and Greyser, S.A. (2003), *Revealing the Corporation: Perspectives on Identity, Image, Reputation, Corporate Branding and Corporate Level Marketing*, Routledge, London and New York, NY.

(The) Economist (2005), "The fall of a corporate queen", *The Economist*, February 5, pp. 61–2.

Hocart, A.M. (1970), "In the grip of tradition", in *The Life Giving Myth and Other Essays*, Methuen & Company, London.

Keller, K.L. (1999), "Brand mantras: Rationale, criteria and examples", *Journal of Marketing Management*, Vol. 15, pp. 43–51.

Lacey, R. (1977), *Majesty: Elizabeth II and the House of Windsor*, Harcourt, Brace, Jovanovich, New York, NY.

Oliver, T. (1986), *The Real Coke, the Real Story*, Penguin Books, New York, NY.

Rose, C. and Thomsen, S. (2004), "The impact of corporate reputation on performance: Some Danish evidence", *European Management Journal*, Vol. 22 No. 3, pp. 201–10.

Schultz, M. and Hatch, M.J. (2000), *The Expressive Organization*, Oxford University Press, Oxford.

APPENDIX 1

The British Monarchy in context

Monarchy has been the ordinary mode of government for by far the greater history of mankind.

In Great Britain, with the exception of the seventeenth-century Commonwealth Period which followed the English Revolution, it has been the preferred form of constitutional governance and has metamorphosed from being a theocratic, to an autocratic and finally a constitutional monarchy: a shift from having political power to symbolic power. Unlike many other corporate brands, the monarchy has entered the subconsciousness of thousands of people in the UK and overseas: many have dreamt about meeting the Queen, for instance (Masters, 1988).

In the context of the previously mentioned it is, perhaps, not surprising that the world's first national anthem was Britain's "God Save the King!" and that it has an explicit religious dimension, since anthems are a musical form that is very common within the English cathedral tradition.

For many constitutional authorities, in global contexts, the British Monarchy is regarded as the prototypical constitutional monarchy. A constitutional monarchy is where the King reigns but does not rule and reflects the notion that a nation can be both democratic and self-governing and yet have as its titular head a hereditary crowned head of state. As noted by the American Political Association, monarchies although exerting little discernible effect on democracy did bolster the conditions that promoted democracy (Mayer and Sigelman, 1998).

To date, a good deal of the literature on the British Monarchy focuses on the utilitarian aspects of the Crown rather than on its normative credentials. The importance of the utilitarian role of the Crown has been highlighted by no less than the distinguished English historian A.J.P. Taylor. He concluded that the continuance of Britain's Constitutional Monarchy was not so much dependent on its executive power but on upholding its emotional and symbolic links with the British public (Taylor, 1977, p. 206).

The Crown, de facto, no longer wields real political power, although its reserve constitutional powers are considerable: the appointment and dismissal of prime ministers and governments are still within its purview. Nonetheless, it still exercises significant brand power via the Monarch's role as the symbolic Head of the British Nation. In addition, albeit to a lesser degree, there are 15 or so other sovereign monarchies where she is Queen; Canada is one prominent case in point.

Moreover, the potential reach of the Crown's global brand community in terms of those individuals who are avid followers of the monarchy and derive great pleasure thereon includes many in ostensibly republican nations such as France, Italy and the USA. Also included are those in the Queen's non-British realms (New Zealand, Jamaica, etc.).

Of especial significance to the reach of the Crown's global brand community is the Queen's status as titular Head of the Commonwealth; this association encompasses well in excess of 50 nation states, and includes around a third of mankind, binding those nations who have, or had, constitutional links with the British Crown. Included are India, Kenya, Malaysia, Singapore, South Africa, etc. Many are, of course, republics. Recently Mozambique successfully petitioned to join the Commonwealth even though it has never had the British Monarch as its Head of State but had been under the colonial rule of the Portuguese.

For all of the previously mentioned reasons, the British Crown is one that is analogous to a multinational entity and the British Monarchy is unquestionably a highly significant global corporate brand. The famous "Solemn Act of Dedication" made by Princess Elizabeth (the future Queen Elizabeth II) to the British Commonwealth in 1947 is revelatory with regard to global scope of the corporate brand promise:

> I declare before you that my whole life, whether it be long or short, shall be devoted to your service and the service of our great Imperial Commonwealth to which we all belong.
>
> *(Shawcross, 2002, pp. 41–2)*

Significantly, on the 25th anniversary of becoming Queen she reaffirmed her vow to Britain and the Commonwealth, even though most Commonwealth nations were now republics:

> When I was 21, I pledged my life to the service of our people, and I ask for God's help to make good that vow. Although that vow was made in my salad days when I was green in judgement, I do not regret or retract one word of it.
>
> *(Shawcross, 2002, p. 19)*

Of course, the Queen, Prince Philip, the Prince of Wales and Prince William are, indubitably, celebrity brands in their own right. An examination of global media coverage of the British Crown reveals that the activities of monarch and royal family engender considerable fascination. Although periodically tarnished by impropriety from within, the British Monarchy as an institution still retains a charisma, distinctiveness, and worth to its brand community within the Commonwealth and beyond. Consider the phenomenal success of the award-winning film *The Queen* (Frears, 2006) and the insatiable public appetite for books on the British Crown such as *On Royalty* (Paxman, 2007) and *Monarchy* (Hardman, 2007).

The British Monarchy does have its detractors who see the institution as an outdated and expensive irrelevance (Nairn, 1988). Such a stance has recently been adopted by The Economist (2006), which argued that the institution was arcane and had lacked utility and concluded, in short, that its "time has passed".

In certain Commonwealth countries such as Australia, where the Queen is Head of State, the monarch is, by some, seen as a vestigial element of British administration and the institution would not appear to have been internalised and accepted as a quintessential Australian institution. The Sovereign is a non-resident head of state, and this can understandably be viewed as an outdated notion. Moreover, in recent years the national sense of self of Australians, Canadians and New Zealanders has meant that many of them no longer see themselves as having a meaningful affinity with Britain in the way that, say, their grandparents might have done.

The current constitutional position of Australia is that it is a sovereign constitutional monarchy; one that is separate and divisible from the UK along with Queen Elizabeth's other realms and where Queen Elizabeth's status is that of Queen of Australia as she is Queen of Canada, Queen of New Zealand and so on. Thus, if the UK or one of the other realms were to become a republic this would not alter the constitutional position of the Queen in the other monarchies where she is Head of State.

However, having a monarch as a Head of State can be one of the most conspicuous symbols in terms of national identity. Consider the UK vis-à-vis France and Canada vis-à-vis the USA. In Canada, the visible differences with the USA are not very apparent but the monarchy provides the country with one defining characteristic. Unlike Australia, the Crown is viewed as a key Canadian institution which was: "Chosen by the Fathers of the Confederation, who made it plain that they felt perfectly free to do so otherwise" (Laundry, 1973, p. 99).

Of course since time immemorial there has been opposition to the tenets of hereditary monarchy on strong philosophical, political, moral and religious grounds and also on economic grounds.

There are equally strong arguments in favour of the institution, many of which stress the legitimacy and efficacy of the Crown in practical, emotional and historical terms. What is indisputably the case is that the British Monarchy is, and has been, resilient as well as protean in character.

Sometimes, republican and monarchical forms of government are discussed as if they were irreconcilable forms of rule. Yet kingship is not inconsistent with republican government since, in the strict meaning of the word, a republic does not denote any particular form of government (Prochaska, 2001, pp. xv–xvi).

The classical definition of a republic is government undertaken in the public interest and is derived from the Latin phrase *res publica*, "the public thing". Following the previous definition, it is undeniably the case that the monarchies of the UK, Canada, Denmark, Sweden, are republics. All of them have democratic systems of polity and have sophisticated systems of social support and healthcare. As such, Britain is sometimes described as being a "Crowned Republic". Interestingly, the US President John Adams liked the phrase "monarchical government". He did, of course, detest despotic kingship (Prochaska, 2001, p. 1), as have the English and British generally. The English Revolution predates the French and American revolutions.

In Britain, having a president as Head of State remains an unpopular option; especially since it would almost certainly mean having a politician as both Head of State and of Nation. As noted by Paxman (2007, p. 269), the notion that presidents would be less self-important, or cheaper, than the British Monarchy is a matter of opinion. Paxman observes that we might take heed of the conduct of the President of the People's Republic of China. He famously refused an invitation to stay with Queen Elizabeth because in his estimation Buckingham Palace was: "not quite five-star enough".

APPENDIX 2

Corporate brands: An overview

Since 1995 a distinct literature has emerged in relation to corporate brands, and this reflects the growing importance accorded to corporate brand as a discrete branding category: a category that is distinct from product and service brands. See: Aaker (2004); Aaker and Joachimsthaler (2000); Argenti and Druckenmiller (2004); Balmer (1995, 2001a, b, 2005); Balmer and Gray (2003); Balmer *et al.* (2009); Hatch and Schultz (2001, 2003); Holt *et al.* (2004); Kapferer (2002); King (1991); Knox and Bickerton (2003); Schultz and Hatch (2003); and Urde (2001).

A corporate brand identity represents a set of expectations relating to a brand name in terms of corporate service, performance and philosophy and so on. As such, the corporate brand can be compared to a covenant: based on promise/promises associated with the brand. In effect it is akin to an informal contract between an organisation and its diverse stakeholders. In contrast, a corporate identity relates to the distinguishing attributes of the organisation. Organisations need to ensure, therefore, that there is a meaningful alignment between the corporate identity and the corporate brand identity. Many good examples of this phenomenon are to be found among franchisees that align their identity so that it is tightly coupled with the brand identity; as such, most customers are unaware of the individual shop's distinct identity: the Body Shop brand and the Hilton brand are among many organisations that have franchise arrangements with other institutional entities.

For many companies their core competency appears to rest not so much on what they make but on what they brand as an organisation (Olins, 2000). This is just as apposite to a corporate behemoth such as Tesco as to niche players such as Wood-worm, a corporate brand of cricket bat fame (The Economist, 2005c).

Executives of major corporations such as Nestlé and Procter & Gamble regard their corporate brands as key strategic assets (Hall, 1997) and have realised that raising the corporate umbrella in certain markets can create value (Smith, 1998). Balmer and Gray (2003) have argued that corporate brands are strategic resources of critical importance and have marshalled the theory of the resourced-based view of the firm to support their hypothesis.

Corporate brands can be a key component of an organisation's strategy: the successes of Samsung and Toyota have, to a large part, been attributed to their corporate brands (The Economist, 2005a, b). They also facilitate ease of entry into overseas markets as the examples of IKEA and Starbucks illustrate. See Aaker and Joachimsthaler (1999), Bartlett and Nanda (1990), Capon et al. (2001), Fang (2004), Kling and Goteman (2003), Larsson et al. (2003). In addition, corporate brands, as pointed out by Willman (1997), can accord a competitive advantage in business-to-business contexts and can be of importance to an organisation's Human Resources policies (Martin et al., 2005).

Recently, it has been argued by Balmer (2005) that the value of corporate brands can be seen in terms of their crucial role as currencies, languages and navigational tools.

As currencies they have a worth in one or more markets (local, national, regional and global). Consider McDonald's, American Express, BP and Sony. Of course, corporate brands can also operate at a more local level. For instance, small shops may have a particular worth in very local markets such as butchers, bakers and even fish and chip shops!

As languages, corporate brands (as a form of communication) can transcend linguistic and cultural boundaries. Prominent (global) corporate brands in this regard include Heinz, Microsoft and the BBC.

As navigational tools, corporate brand identities are of importance to numerous stakeholder groups including customers, employees, business partners and shareholders. In their totality such groups comprise a corporate brand community. However, the brand is "consumed" by different groups in different ways including purchase, employment and association.

In short, it would appear that not only has the business landscape become a brandscape, but has moreover become a corporate brandscape. Indicative of this is Interbrand's valuation of the world's top 100 brands, which are largely made up of corporate brands (Berner and Kiley, 2005).

A failure to keep the corporate brand covenant (the promise that is associated with a particular brand by customers and other stakeholders) is one of the most serious failings that can beset any organisational brand. This is because corporate brands need to be credible and trustworthy to customers and other groups. It has, for instance, been argued that the latter are, in an important regard, owners of the corporate brand. More specifically, whereas legal ownership of the corporate brand resides with an organisation, emotional ownership of the brand resides with customers and other stakeholder groups. The real value of a brand, therefore, is derived from the emotional ownership of the brand (Balmer, 2005).

From the previous it can be inferred that a corporate brand covenant should be projected not only through corporate communications (VanRiel, 1995) but, moreover, through total corporate communications (Balmer and Gray, 1999): the latter is based on the notion that the activities, behaviours and communications associated with a corporate brand have a communications effect. Based on the premise, the corporate brand promise should be manifest unceasingly, and over time, through service quality, product performance, price, salary, conditions of work, corporate and boardroom behaviour, as well as through corporate symbolism and architecture.

Consider the brand promise associated with well-known corporate brands such as Disney (wholesome family entertainment), the city of Paris (romance), and BBC (authoritative news and quality radio and TV output). Strap lines often attempt to capture the essence of the brand promise. Consider IBM's "business solutions", Philips' "sense and simplicity", and HSBC's "local knowledge".

The management of corporate brands is typically more difficult than the management of product brands. In part this is because a corporate brand community consists of many stakeholder groups whereas a product brand's primary focus is its customers and the distribution channels that reach them. It is the task of senior executives to know the breadth and depth of their corporate brand community and to communicate with them, marshalling the plethora of corporate communications channels that are available.

One way of conceptualising the previous is to consider the relevance of a particular corporate brand to:

- its customers; and
- its stakeholder groups.

Of course, there are many forms of brand association, and for some individuals there will be multiple forms of association owing to their membership of several stakeholder groups. The relevance of corporate brands can be seen in terms of consumption (e.g. customer loyalty to the BMW brand), employment (a preference to work for Waitrose vis-à-vis other supermarkets), endorsement (industrial endorsement evidenced by loyalty to Boeing rather than Airbus), association (the prestige accorded to parents whose daughter has won a place at Yale University), acquisition (the Tata Group's procurement of celebrated car marques such as Jaguar and Range Rover) and aspiration (the purchase of a Brooks Brothers tie rather than the coveted Brooks Brothers suit).

SECTION 2

Corporate heritage connoisseurship

Key concepts and theories

3

CORPORATE HERITAGE, CORPORATE HERITAGE MARKETING, AND TOTAL CORPORATE HERITAGE COMMUNICATIONS

What are they? What of them?

John M. T. Balmer

Introduction

The explicit aims of this article are to augment the nascent corporate heritage canon; to more fully particularise the foundational precepts of corporate heritage and introduce and explicate the notions of corporate heritage marketing and corporate heritage communications. Attention is also given to instrumental insights and implications. Where appropriate I make reference to *prima facie* corporate heritage identities and corporate heritage brands. As befits an opening article of the first special edition devoted to corporate heritage, this article is conceptual and instrumental in character. In many regards it reflects my personal perspective on the domain and, for the sake of expediency, I make significant reference to my own/ collaborative work on the domain. The article marshals the extant literature from the broad heritage along with the more specific corporate heritage canons. Corporate heritage can be understood at the visceral as well as at the cerebral level, and this article attempts to accommodate both perspectives.

The reflections in this article come at a time when slowly, but assuredly, the broad corporate heritage phenomenon has generated interest, and is gaining legitimacy, within the corporate marketing and corporate communications fields. To date, the notion of heritage as it applies to extant institutions (rather than to museums, the historic built environment, sites and tourism attractions) has largely – and perplexingly – been eschewed within the heritage canon and, until comparatively recently, has not been taken up in any meaningful way within the corporate marketing, corporate communications and management fields as well.

Recently, however, there has been a sea change. For instance, in the corporate marketing domain, this has come with a realisation that corporate heritage institutions can, because of their especial provenance, be a peerless corporate asset: an asset that can be highly meaningful to customers and other stakeholders across the generations. Internally, within organisations, it is also viewed to be of consequence – in ancestral terms – to company owners and managers alike as a quick scrutiny of the websites of many organisations will show. What is starting to transpire is that institutions with a corporate heritage not only have a unique asset but one that is perennial and profitable to organisations too.

Organisations which are endowed with a corporate heritage have an ambient asset. It is an institutional trait (traits) which may appreciably contribute to any entity's survival and ongoing success and is of saliency to successive generations of stakeholders. For this reason, perceiving an organisation via a corporate heritage prism can be of inestimable value in uncovering, identifying, maintaining and communicating an institution's heritage and provides an additional means by which a companies and stakeholders alike can profit from the inherent latent value of corporate heritage identities. Dating back to 1844, the enduring corporate heritage traits of the British Co-operative Movement, and more especially, the continual ethical corporate heritage traits of the Co-operate Bank (with roots back to 1872) are cases in point (Wilkinson and Balmer, 1996; Balmer, 2009).

To expand the above point: to me, corporate heritage is not about something that only aims to be of our own time but is meaningful for all times. Corporate heritage subsists in temporal strata, that is, in multiple time stratums (Balmer, 2011a). As such, it is a powerful realisation of the juridical notion that organisations have the potential to exist in perpetuity: most organisations have this dimension written into their legal articles of association.

The profit of corporate heritage identity

Corporate heritage institutions can be of inestimable value to organisations and to their owners and are profitable along many dimensions. Marshalling the economic theory of the resource-based view of the firm in corporate branding contexts (Balmer and Gray, 2001), it is arguably the case that heritage institutions imbued with a meaningful and unique heritage may be invested with valuable resource: and one can impart long-lasting strategic value. Consider *Hōshi* (a traditional Japanese Ryokan/Inn). Dating back to 717, remarkably, 46 generations of the same family have owned and managed this establishment (www.ho-shi.co.jp).

For commercial entities, and in financial terms, this may find expression via "financial goodwill", that is, the enhanced monetary worth, over and above capital assets, which is accorded to an organisation.

Significantly, too, can be the stand-alone fiscal value that is accrued to a corporate brand's latent worth and which is attractive to managers, shareholders, investors and commentators in terms of corporate brand equity. McDonald's is a case in point. As a major corporate heritage brand – with roots going back to 1940 – in 2012 the London-based brand consultancy Interbrand reported that the stand-alone value of this global foodservice retailer was $40,062 (US) million (www.interbrand.com).

For not-for-profit institutions this may find expression in meeting their organisation's societal and/or charitable objectives over successive generations: examples include the Thomas Coram Foundation for Children established by Royal Charter in 1739 (and still going strong) and the London-based Anti-Slavery International. Founded in 1839, and sadly still very active, it is the world's oldest international human rights organisation.

For public sector corporate heritage concerns this is expressed in meeting the goals as set out by the state via its government: a prominent example of this is the Royal Canadian Mounted Police (RCMP). Formed in 1920, but having much earlier roots, it is the national police force of the Canadian Realm and has responsibility for enforcing federal laws throughout the Dominion of Canada. It is indubitably the case that the RCMP, one of Canada's most prominent icons, is a reminder of the important symbolic role of many corporate heritage entities to peoples, cultures and places.

The long-standing importance accorded to the past in uncovering corporate identity traits and in revealing the corporation has been recognised and asserted by marketing and communication scholars for some time now (Balmer, 1995; Blombäck and Brunninge, 2009). Also, the importance of the past was noted by the little-known work of French scholars Larcon and Reitter (1979) and Moingeon and Reitter (1997). The latter argued that a corporate identity imbues organisations with specificity, stability and coherence: stability being of importance here. Their work presaged the more widely cited work of Albert and Whetten (1985), who refer to an organisation's claims re central character, distinctiveness and continuity.

Of course, over recent times, scholars of corporate marketing and corporate communications increasingly have noted the utility of history and, importantly, of corporate heritage too. For example, the increased interest in, and the saliency of, constructs focussing on the past within the corporate marketing domain has led to the introduction of new concepts/zones of marketing scholarship.

An overview of these concepts – including their natures and importance – has been provided by Balmer (2011c). See Table 3.1. To reiterate, a company's history – and especially its heritage – can meaningfully impart value to customers and other stakeholders across the generations.

Corporate heritage: Catholic in scope

To me, what is irrefutable is that there are a considerable number of organisations – large, medium and small – which inhabit the private, public, not-for-profit and other sectors, which belong to a unique institutional identity category of their own in that they have a corporate heritage identity.

Such organisations are invested with an inimitable mix of corporate heritage traits that are perennial in terms of intent, time and title: traits which habitually beguile stakeholders of the present-time; have enthralled successive generations in past-times and, conceivably, will captivate consumers and other stakeholders in future-times too.

TABLE 3.1 Scrutinising the principal corporate-level constructs which draw on the past

Tradition

Tradition especially refers to the maintenance of fixed behaviours, and conventions which are characterised by their invariance. The purpose of tradition is to bind and to exclude and can be an activity of selection, revision and invention (Sarup, 1996, p. 182). Tradition can be invented and the notion of invented tradition has been shown to be important to organisations such as monarchies and universities (Hobsbawm, 1983). Invented tradition can be a powerful blend of art and artifice of tradition. Invented tradition refers to a set of practices which seeks to inculcate certain values and norms of behaviour by reputation and which implies – and the importance of the word *implies* needs to be stressed here – continuity with the past (Hobsbawm, 1983). In corporate marketing terms, events and rituals can accord an institution a degree of distinctiveness, differentiation and attraction. Consider the distinctiveness accorded to the USA's second oldest university, the College of William and Mary, which, since the early twentieth century, has introduced and communicated its historical ties with the British Monarchy and has an annual ceremony where the University's Royal Charter is read out in full: an event that is unique in the USA and – almost certainly – is unique in global terms (Balmer, 2011a, b, c)

Custom

Custom refers to the behaviours which – unlike tradition – are flexible and subject to change: tradition in contrast is invariant (or in the case of invented tradition is perceived to be invariant). As such custom refers to the substantive nature of behaviour rather than how a particular behaviour is enacted. Hobswabm (1983a, b), elucidating the difference between the two, observes that custom refers to the function of the judiciary whereas tradition relates to symbols and ritualised practices of judges, their wigs and robes for instance

Nostalgia

Nostalgia is concerned with the positive associations – the seeking of happiness – relating to the past. Such feeling of nostalgia can give an individual a sense of certainty and security. Hewison (1987) noted that individuals can turn to the past for comfort during times of great social change (and presumably other forms of change which bring anxiety). Holbrook and Schindler (2003) note that in later life individuals might seek out and still derive comfort from those brands which they had a strong affinity with from the ages of 16–20, and they characterise this as nostalgic bonding. Olfactory experience is especially germane vis-à-vis nostalgic bonding. Thus, a British person working overseas might derive considerable benefit of nostalgia by consuming Marmite (yeast spread) whereas Australians might derive an analogous benefit through the consumption of Vegemite (Australian yeast spread brand). The scholarship of Loveland et al. (2010), for instance, focusses on customer preferences for nostalgic products

Melancholia

Melancholia is concerned with the seeking of sadness associated with the past. Although this is not covered in detail in marketing, such a mood can be actively sought and people can be attracted to this emotion and this can be marshalled by brands to meet a particular customer need. For instance, the music of certain pop groups which are associated with a particular time frame and which represent the sadness of a former time period can be powerful. For instance, some classical music lovers actively seek the melancholia associated with the Penitential music of Lent and Holy week at other times of the year, namely the Tenebrae musical settings of Victoria, or are attracted to a weekend visit to Venice in the depths of winter

Iconic branding

Iconic brand refers to those brands which are culturally dominant and distinctive. Nike is one example of an iconic brand. The work of Holt (2004) has been especially significant in this regard, and Holt concludes that mythmaking can be a key transformative activity in terms of a brand's metamorphosis into an iconic brand

Retro branding

Retro brands are redolent of a specific era (Brown et al., 2003). Retro brands celebrate an idealised – and sometimes imagined – past which is seen to be meaningful. The introduction of Volkswagen's New Beetle car exemplifies the retro branding

Heritage marketing

Heritage marketing is primarily concerned with the tourism/heritage industry (O'Guinn, 1989; Prentice, 1993; Herbert, 1995; Henderson, 2002; Misiura, 2006). In essence, heritage marketing it is concerned with the "marketing" of history and with brands that evoke and represent a particular era, such as Brighton's Royal Pavilion Palace, the Bund in Shanghai and the Colonial architecture of Georgetown in Penang (Malaysia)

Heritage tourism

Heritage tourism refers to clearly identifiable places which – in historical contexts – help to denote a tourist destination. Often, heritage tourism relates to historical phenomena relating to the distant past (Weaver, 2010). The focus of heritage tourism – old castles, churches, temples, etc. – requires, in the contexts of heritage tourism, both protection and presentation. Among those who write on heritage tourism are Palmer (2005) and Park (2010). Examples would include the Forbidden City in Peking, the Eiffel Tower in Paris and the Coliseum in Rome

Source: Derived from Balmer (2011a, b, c)

This being said, there appears, to me, to be a considerable absence of nuance in comprehending the heritage domain: this is because heritage is often narrowly conceived by some social scientists in terms of heritage sites and the heritage built environment. As a consequence, the notion that heritage (including heritage sites and the heritage built environment) can also meaningfully pertain to extant – to "living-entities" – is either not understood or, perhaps, is not explored. Perhaps there is another reason: a reluctance to focus on organisations or to engage with commerce, marketing and communications. Possibly some social scientists narrowly conceive marketing and management studies in terms of capitalism (and with "trade") and with wealth-generation. As such, for them, applying the heritage notion to organisations may, perhaps, be viewed by some as vulgar and below the pale. The fault, of course, may also substantially reside with marketing and management scholars who, historically, have failed to progress the heritage domain within their own fields.

From my perspective, corporate heritage may be covert and tacit (heritage manifestations are not, perhaps, easily identifiable and are not communicated externally). For example, an organisation may have a heritage which is manifested via internal cultural traits which may only be known to organisational members. It can also be overt and communicated (heritage manifestations are identifiable and are communicated to customers and other stakeholders). For example, an organisation may have an espoused and codified institutional doctrine grounded in its heritage and this, for instance, may inform an organisation's corporate communications activities.

Corporate heritage institutions are valuable because they are repositories of meaningful multiple heritage identities and because of their apparent capacity to bestow multiple identities to individuals, families, groups, cultures, territories across the generations. The importance of the latter – of inheritance and the multigenerational character of corporate heritage – cannot be over-stressed.

Moreover, corporate heritage is about multiple continuities, and permanencies too in terms of time, identity, heredity, stakeholder loyalty and saliency, institutional profitability and corporate adaptability.

The above being said, the extant literature has shown that the corporate heritage notion and its saliency is, arguably, due to its richness in terms of its meanings (Balmer, 2011a). Clearly, corporate heritage brands (Balmer et al., 2006; Urde et al., 2007) and corporate heritage identities characterise many institutions and institutional brands.

From these foundational steps it is entirely logical to apply the corporate marketing domain and philosophy (what in the context of this article I call corporate heritage marketing) and the corporate communications domain (what in this article I call corporate heritage communications/total corporate heritage communications) to the field. Such a move represents a meaningful step change in terms of advancing the field, and the introduction and articulation of the aforementioned is one of the objectives of this article.

Corporate heritage brands

A singular characteristic of the corporate heritage marketing domain relates to the notion of corporate heritage brands. The reason for this is because of the simple reason (and one that surprisingly many corporate marketing and corporate communications scholars have not always adequately grasped) that a corporate heritage brand can be shared by one, several or many organisations (Balmer and Gray, 2003). Since the mid-2000s (Balmer et al., 2006), of course, there has been a realisation that some corporate brands are also invested with a heritage and, to advance the point made here, some of these corporate heritage brands pertain to several entities. Consider the very large and British-owned Rolls-Royce aero engine firm and the small German-owned (BMW) Rolls-Royce automotive company. Both institutions meaningfully inform the enviable corporate brand heritage of Rolls-Royce and – as I have long argued – are a salient reminder that corporate brands (and corporate heritage brands too) quite often relate to several, and sometimes to very many, companies.

In context: Problems and possibilities vis-à-vis corporate heritage

By means of context, this article proceeds by providing an overview of the embry-onic, and foundational, corporate heritage canon. It begins by discussing the growth of interest in corporate heritage whilst noting that corporate heritage (the heri-tage construct as applied to extant institutions and corporate brands) has, for the main, been studiously ignored. This is followed by a discussion of the problems and possibilities afforded by the corporate heritage construct. Following on from this, developments vis-à-vis corporate heritage within the corporate marketing domain are enumerated.

The heritage phenomenon and why corporate heritage matters but, largely, has been ignored

Developing an earlier observation, as a rule, social scientists with an interest in heritage have eschewed meaningful reference to organisations – corporate heri-tage institutions – and most certainly in relation to corporate heritage brands per se. For this reason, a somewhat skewed understanding of the heritage milieu has prevailed. What is clear is that a privileged status has been accorded to the heri-tage construct as it relates to historical sites and, more especially, to the historic built environment, and in broad business contexts the importance of industrial heritage can be noted. Moreover, the particular regard given to heritage build-ings and heritage sites all too often scrutinises heritage via a restricted spectrum in terms of time and locus. A good many heritage sites and buildings are unduly associated with royal, aristocratic and sacerdotal groups and, as such, accord especial attention to the privileged and the rich. In contrast, corporate heritage – with its broad utility – is meaningful to all groups, classes and time frames. This more inclusive prism coupled with the omni-temporal characteristic are especial characteristics pertaining to corporate heritage. Arguably, it may also be viewed as a corrective to a good deal of the extant heritage literature where there can be a mono-temporal (respective) focus.

Yet, the heritage canvas is far greater and deeper than buildings and historic landscapes. Perhaps a slight thaw among many rank-and-file social scientists will, slowly if not grudgingly, take place in light of developments in corporate marketing and corporate communications.

Two indicators of this can be found in relation to heritage tourism and to marketing heritage, which have emerged as significant domains. The inter-est in heritage tourism may be seen to have mirrored the broader attention given to heritage in other disciplines (Fowler, 1989; Urry,1995; Bessiere, 1998; Lowenthal, 1998; Macdonald, 2002, 2006) and, in turn, the interest in heritage tourism appears to have informed the literature on heritage marketing (Misiura, 2006).

This being said, the above two areas are only tangentially aligned to corporate heritage. To reiterate, this is because both areas accord primary attention to the temporal dimension of the past. In contrast, corporate heritage identity and corporate heritage brands are linked with the time frames of the past, present and future. The total temporal characteristic is also a defining characteristic of a corporate marketing logic.

Thus, to me, unlike traditional notions of heritage (buildings and sites) which, in temporal and functional terms have a largely static identity and one which is different from its original purpose (erstwhile palaces being characterised as museums), corporate heritage institutions and brands have living, durable but also – importantly – adaptable corporate identity traits.

Corporate heritage: Utility, pregnant possibilities and complexity

Scrutinising the formal corporate communications of organisations reveals the degree to which entities, over recent times, have increasingly made reference to their institution's heritage. Of course, many corporations make the claim that they are heritage institutions or have a corporate heritage brand. For example, the utility of the corporate heritage appellation is apparent in the People's Republic of China, where the government accords the designation "time honoured companies" to long-established (largely small-scale) companies. In the Anglo sphere these entities would, in general terms, be known as corporate heritage institutions.

The utility of these organisations can be seen in terms of what I call appropriated corporate heritage. This is where an institution appropriates a heritage in one or another form. For instance, Brunel University, London, has sequestered the heritage associations of the British engineer Brunel in the institution's name. More typically is the requisition of corporate heritage in the form of company takeovers. Recently, corporations with the rapidly emerging economies of India and China have acquired celebrated corporate heritage automotive brands including Jaguar/Land Rover, Volvo, MG, and London Taxis International. Of course, US companies have long sought out celebrated British corporate heritage brands such as Cadburys and Cunard.

Corporate heritage identities both reveal but also conceal. This, in part, can be due to the degree to which heritage organisations communicate their heritage but also because some stakeholders may not recognise, appreciate or even seek out certain corporate heritage institutions. Clearly, some heritage institutions are meaningful in territorial (associations with a city, region or country), cultural (the values of a nation, region or city or of a class, profession, etc.) and ancestral (the familial dimension in terms of multigenerational ownership of a firm and multigenerational loyalty to a company as customers, suppliers, investors, etc.) and, absolutely critically, in institutional terms (what a company makes, stands for, etc.).

However, for certain territories, cultures, groups and peoples a particular corporate heritage may be meaningless and may engender an antipathetic reaction.

Consider the antipathy that exists on the part of supporters of Manchester United vis-à-vis Manchester City football clubs and vice versa.

Elaborating this point and drawing on the work of Pecheux (1982) in relation to the corporate heritage notion, it can be deduced that corporate heritage identities can encapsulate a variety of individual, group and institutional associations, and non-associations, to the institution as per the original and developed aspects of social identity theory (see Tajfel and Turner, 1985). Moreover, not only will there be group and individual and corporate heritage identification, but also counter-identification and dis-identification with a particular heritage identity.

It is conceivable that these identifications may vary along different corporate heritage traits. This can, for instance, be seen in relation to the British Monarchy (the Crown) as a corporate heritage institution, namely: an individual having strong affinity to the Crown's symbolic role as head of state whilst, for instance, being indifferent to the Crown's positions as titular head of the Church of England and/ or of the Commonwealth. The multiple role identities of the Crown were detailed earlier in my earlier work on the corporate heritage territory.

Developments in corporate marketing

Archetypal marketing scholarship (which primarily focusses on products, services and their brands rather than on corporate identities and corporate brands) has both explicitly and implicitly noted the significance of heritage in terms of brand-worth (George, 2004), brand-strength (Ritson, 2003) and brand-personality (Keller and Richey, 2006). Some highly significant work has been undertaken in this regard, for instance in terms of operationalising brand heritage (Hakala et al., 2011). Also of note is a stream of work relating to the consumption of cultural heritage (Otnes and Maclaren, 2007). However, a good deal of the traditional product and services-focussed marketing literature has not adequately engaged with or developed the heritage notion as it applies to the corporate level per se.

In addition is the more general marketing literature which focusses on heritage (Goulding, 2000, 2001), and the nascent domain of heritage marketing (Misiura, 2006). Both of the aforementioned areas owe something to the more substantive literature on heritage tourism (Waitt, 2000; Halewood and Hannam, 2001; Henderson, 2002; Chhabra et al., 2003; Palmer, 2005; Gu and Ryan, 2008; Park, 2010; Hudson, 2011).

However, it is the corporate heritage notion which, increasingly and distinctly, has informed the heritage notion within the corporate marketing domain. To date, the primary focus has focussed on corporate heritage brands, but the explanations and engagement with the construct, it has to be noted, is highly variable (Balmer et al., 2006; Urde et al., 2007; Hudson, 2011; Wiedmann et al., 2001a, b, c). More recently, the importance of corporate heritage identities has been acknowledged (Balmer, 2011a).

Reflections on foundational articles within the nascent corporate heritage canon

From the outset, the extant literature on corporate heritage has its genesis in two cornerstone articles penned by a triumvirate of scholars from Great Britain, the USA and Sweden namely Balmer, Greyser and Urde. In this section the key contributions of the above are detailed and I very much draw on my own, more recent, published output on the domain.

Introducing the corporate heritage brand notion

The first article (Balmer *et al.*, 2006) was informed by earlier work on the field (Balmer, 2004, 2008). The article formally introduced the notion of corporate heritage brands and noted four key aspects of corporate brands in that they were:

(1) of the past, present and future;
(2) stable reference points in a changing world;
(3) invariably linked to place; and
(4) valuable in that they harness positive public emotions.

An instrumental model pertaining to monarchy (but that in retrospect may be seen to have a wider utility for corporate heritage brands and corporate heritage identities) was articulated. Here, I have slightly amended the labels of the categories so that they are more easily applicable to corporate entities; the original terms are shown in parenthesis.

In essence five imperatives may be seen to have informed the aforementioned in terms of five requirements vis-à-vis corporate brand custodianship: to have a requisite corporate heritage identity (royal) relevant, respected, responsive and reliable (regal). See Table 3.2 for more information.

Buttressing the corporate heritage brand notion

Building on the above insights (Balmer *et al.*, 2006), the corporate heritage brand notion was further explicated and its nature more clearly articulated by the same triumvirate of scholars (Urde *et al.*, 2007). To me, this article made an advance in further explicating the nature and value of corporate heritage brands, and these insights may be seen to augment earlier insights. In this article, the view was advanced that the determinants of a corporate heritage brand were its track record, longevity, core values, use of symbols and an institution's belief that its history is important.

Whereas the earlier article (Balmer *et al.*, 2006) was derived from empirical findings and conceptual insights from constitutional monarchies, this article marshalled case study reflections and conceptualisations from a wide variety of corporate heritage brands. See Table 3.2.

TABLE 3.2 Insights (empirical and conceptual) from foundational articles on corporate heritage brands

---

Balmer *et al.* (2006)

The introduction and initial characterisation of the corporate heritage brand construct

The first article (Balmer et al., 2006), based on empirical case study insights on monarchies, introduced and identified the corporate heritage brands notion. The article is informed by Balmer's earlier work on the British monarchy including a detailed scrutiny of the literature on and historiography of monarchy (Balmer, 2004, 2008). In this seminal article on corporate heritage brands, explicit instrumental insights relating to monarchies as corporate heritage brands (and implicit insights vis-à-vis corporate heritage brands) were detailed along with empirical and conceptual contributions in relation to the nature of corporate heritage brands. In terms of instrumental insights, five criteria for the effective management and maintenance of monarchies/corporate heritage brands were articulated in a quinquepartite model which marshalled earlier work on the territory (Balmer, 2004)

The core of the model is the dimension relating to the institution's identity (what in the original model was called the royal identity) – those institutional attributes which accord a royal heritage (corporate heritage) both differentiation and distinctiveness. Managing the royal (corporate heritage dimension), whilst important, was also insignificant since four other dimensions demanded management attention to a further quartet of concerns. The five requirements of this instrumental approach have, for the sake of expediency, been adapted here so that they speak to institutions per se and not merely to constitutional monarchies:

(i) The requirement to have a requisite corporate heritage identity (corporate identity being the basis of a corporate heritage brand. In the original monarchical model this was called royal)
(ii) The requirement to have a relevant corporate heritage brand
(iii) The requirement to have a respected corporate heritage brand
(iv) The requirement to have a responsive corporate heritage brand
(v) The requirement to have a reliable corporate heritage brand

(In the original monarchical model this was called regal. This can be explained as follows: the need for the institution's behaviours, rituals and symbols which are appropriate to the institution)

The articulation of the 5Rs of monarchies as corporate heritage brands – the royal, regal, relevant, responsive and respected dimensions (see Balmer, 2004, 2008; Balmer *et al.*, 2006) – may, perhaps, be seen as a precursor to latter frameworks on the territory (Urde *et al.*, 2007). The inference, the study of the Swedish monarchy, also suggested that corporate heritage brands are often inextricably linked to a nation (place) and to a national culture (place)

The custodianship of corporate heritage brands (informed by monarchical management) requires senior managers to focus on identity (what was called the royal dimension) and on behaviour and symbolism (what was called the regal dimension) by ensuring that the heritage corporate brand remains relevant, respected and responsive to the needs of stakeholders

---

(Continued)

TABLE 3.2 (Continued)

Urde *et al.* (2007)

A broader disquisition vis-à-vis the corporate heritage construct

Nature

1 Corporate brand heritage is a dimension of a corporate brand's identity found in its track record, longevity, core values, use of symbols and an institution's belief that its history is important

2 A corporate heritage brand is qualitatively different from a corporate brand with a heritage. The key distinctions are in terms of orientation, strategy and management. The former relates to those institutions that have chosen to emphasise their provenance as history as part of their brand identity and positions and strategic direction. Some organisations have decided not to do this, and these are corporate brands with a heritage. (To me, this can be through ignorance but also through default/design)

3 There is no contradiction between using and expressing a corporate heritage brand and having the company be (and be seen as) up to date, cutting edge, high tech and modern

4 Corporate heritage brand characterises for example multigenerational owned value

5 Corporate heritage brands can be harnessed and employed as a strategic resource and can create value as part of an institution's corporate marketing proposition to customers and to stakeholders

6 Corporate heritage brands do not, inherently, have value, only the opportunity to do so

Balmer (2009)

The management of corporate heritage brands

In detailing the obligations of management in terms of their custodianship of corporate heritage brands stated that attention should be focused on: 1: Continuity (maintaining heritage and symbolism); 2: Visibility (having a meaningful and prominent public profile); 3: strategy (anticipating and enacting change); 4: Sensitivity (rapid response to crises); 5: Respectability (retaining public favour), and 6: Empathy (acknowledging that brand ownership resides with the public). Also showed how the management of a corporate heritage brand is informed by corporate marketing and by other disciplinary perspectives. This explained by making reference to the: Continuity (corporate identity and corporate brand management) Visibility (corporate communications) Strategy (corporate strategy) Sensitivity (leadership and crisis management) Respectability (corporate image and corporate reputation) and Empathy (stakeholder management and the customer and stakeholder orientation which is of fundamental importance in corporate marketing). In addition, introduced a process for uncovering corporate heritage brands: "Chronicling corporate heritage brands"

Balmer (2011a)

Introduced the corporate heritage identity construct, and theoretical notions of multiple corporate heritage role identities, relative invariance and the importance of bilateral organisational-stakeholder trust, along with authenticity, affinity and regulation vis-à-vis the management of corporate heritage identities

This article formally introduced the notion of corporate heritage identities and this refers to an entity's identity traits that have remained perennial. Also advanced the perspective that corporate heritage identities are meaningful in that they have multiple role identities. That is they can be imbued with identities of people, places and the identities of time, etc. These additional identity modes often burnish the organisation's corporate identity. As such, corporate heritage identities not only confer identification to the organisation but also to territories, times, communities and cultures, etc. The notion of relative invariance was also advanced in that whilst identities may appear to be invariant they may in fact be variant (for instance symbols may endure their meanings may change). Importantly, the article noted the importance of bilateral trust vis-à-vis organisations and stakeholders, and noted, too, the importance of authenticity and affinity to corporate heritage brands. The article introduces a revised framework for the management of corporate heritage identities (see Balmer, 2004; Balmer et al., 2006). Reflected in terms of a model the original five dimensions are included (royal-requisite, regal, relevant, respected, responsive and regulation, plus the additional dimension of regulation (the requisite for corporate heritage to be managed): Trust is at the core of the model and this is bolstered by issues of authenticity and affinity. The insights from this article were informed by on-going work on the British Monarchy as a corporate heritage institution

Corporate heritage brand management and its multidisciplinary perspective

The obligations of corporate brand custodianship inform this article (Balmer, 2009). These are underpinned by six management precepts – each of which is underpinned by a distinct area of management. As such managers should focus on:

(1) continuity (corporate heritage identity and corporate heritage brand management);
(2) visibility (corporate communications);
(3) strategy (corporate strategy);
(4) sensitivity (leadership and crisis management);
(5) respectability (corporate image and corporate reputation); and
(6) empathy (stakeholder management and the need for both a customer and moreover a stakeholder orientation which is a fundamental tenet of corporate marketing).

This article introduced a process which may uncover a corporate heritage brand and shed light on salient dimensions and is called: "Chronicling corporate heritage brands". See Table 3.2.

Introducing the corporate heritage identity construct, and theoretical notions of multiple corporate heritage role identities, relative invariance and the importance of bilateral organisational-stakeholder trust, along with authenticity and affinity (Balmer, 2011a). In this article, the centrality of bilateral trust between corporate heritage institutions and stakeholders was emphatically articulated. Trust is dependent on authenticity and affinity. Thus, on the organisational side, trust this was dependent on the organisation ensuring that corporate brand authenticity was maintained. In terms of customers and stakeholder they had to have a strong sense of affinity toward the corporate brand. Marshalling the above in the context of the earlier model of corporate heritage (Balmer, 2004; Balmer *et al.*, 2006) a new framework vis-à-vis the management/custodianship of corporate heritage identities was introduced consisting of trust, authenticity, affinity, requisite (royal), relevant, respected, responsive and reliable (regal) and regulation (the need for the on-going management of corporate heritage by senior managers). See Table 3.2 for more information. A good deal of this article marshals ongoing insights relating to corporate heritage scholarship focussing on the British Monarchy.

A brief overview of heritage

The article continues by positing a number of foundational questions focussing on heritage-rather than corporate heritage-as a means of context. As such, an explication is given of the fundamental nature of heritage (What is it?) and the degree to which it is important (What of it?).

Heritage: What is it?

The widespread interest in heritage very much mirrors the contemporary *Zeitgeist*. As I noted in an earlier article (Balmer, 2011), heritage, as a word, has its origins in France and the precise meaning of heritage, means to "inherit": to pass on (see Heathcote, 2011). As observed by Macdonald (2006) heritage is inextricably linked with issues of continuity, persistence and substantiality of identity.

This being said, scholars need to be circumspect in considering the historiography and definitions of heritage since the concept is accorded different meanings in the broad canon. On the one hand heritage is aligned to patrimony and in another sense legacy as I would conclusively argue in terms of corporate heritage.

For example, in France and more generally in the Francophone sphere heritage (*patrimone*), typically, relates to peoples and societies. In contrast in Great Britain and more usually in Anglophone nations, heritage characteristically, focusses on buildings and on landscapes (Cohen, 2002).

For me, the heritage concept is catholic in scope. This is because the heritage notion is germane to tangibles (buildings, landscapes, entities), intangibles (skills, competencies), the metaphysical (cultural, corporate, and spiritual values and precepts) and the institutional too (corporate identities and brands).

Heritage is meaningful at a number of levels: individual, communitarian, regional and national (Rapport, 2002, p. 87) and, as re-articulated earlier with the corporate marketing canon, is of significance at the organisational level vis-à-vis corporate brands and corporate identities (Balmer et al., 2006, 2011a): the corporate heritage notion, in other words.

As I have previously noted (Balmer, 2011a), and drawing on the above, it will be apparent that, in considering corporate heritage, notions of bequest, inheritance and custodianship/stewardship are all highly germane. Where a bequest is passed on from generation to generation the nature of ownership of the bequest takes on an especial form. This is because ownership is seen to be transient and the ownership role is perhaps therefore more appropriately characterised as a custodianship role.

The very notion of heritage is of itself a paradox since a concern with heritage is modernist.

To elaborate, although heritage is seen, albeit in varying degrees, as an historically rooted construct, the broad inquisitiveness in heritage is very much a contemporary concern. As such, the concern with heritage – and by inference with the past/historical – is very much a characteristic of our own time. For this reason, heritage, whilst associated with the past, can equally, and powerfully, be characterised as being a decidedly contemporary/modernist phenomenon. Of course, in one sense, there is a certain irony vis-à-vis the exponential growth of scholarly, societal and institutional interest in heritage – and especially so in relation to corporate heritage – since heritage, increasingly, is both of the present as well as of the past and, moreover, is increasingly viewed to be part of the future. As my initial scrutiny of the heritage construct in institutional contexts showed, heritage is subject to change, transformation and reinterpretation (Balmer, 2011a).

Heritage: What of it?

From the scrutiny of the literature it is apparent that heritage is seen to be of especial value. At the individual level, it has been argued that heritage implies a consciousness of an individual's place outside – or beyond – history. As such, heritage is super-historic rather than a seamless part of it (Heathcote, 2011). This, among other reasons, explains why heritage is a highly salient perspective and affords one explanation why some scholars actually prefer the heritage notion to history. The above also, perhaps, reveals why heritage, over recent times, has been especially attractive for some corporate marketing and corporate communications scholars in focussing on extant institutions with seemingly strong corporate heritage credentials.

Heritage and a shared collective memory

Within the heritage canon, it has been argued that our mental state is in part shaped by a *musie imaginaire*. This is based on the idea that our minds are moulded by both knowledge and experience gained over time and from a variety of sources (Jenks, 1984). At the group level, the notion of collective memory is of importance since corporate heritage identities can be attractive of themselves and also in helping to define a group via a shared collective memory (Smith, 1991, p. 25). Indeed, Smith (1991, p. 11) concludes that homogeneous national identities are underpinned by common historical memories, myths, symbols and traditions.

To me, the notion of the shared collective memory – and positive collective memory at that – is one important dimension of why corporate heritage identities are attractive. Corporate heritage identities, clearly, may create identities at the level of the group.

Identity perspectives: National, sociological, stakeholder, postmodern and corporate marketing/corporate communications perspectives

A number of scholars have contemplated the value of heritage from a variety of disciplinary and philosophical perspectives vis-à-vis national (Sarup, 1996), sociological (Macdonald, 2002, 2006), stakeholder (Apostolakis, 2003), postmodern (Fowler, 1989; Walton, 2009; Weaver, 2010) – and, of course, corporate marketing and corporate communications contexts too. This being noted, these five perspectives sometimes differ. Table 3.3 delineates, albeit in abridged form, the significance of heritage: sociological, national/national cultural, institutional and corporate marketing, stakeholder and postmodern perspectives.

TABLE 3.3 Delineating the significance of heritage: sociological, national/national cultural, institutional and corporate marketing, stakeholder and postmodern perspectives

a. The sociological significance of heritage	
Clarifies the past and makes the past relevant for contemporary contexts and purposes	Lowenthal (1998)
Offers continuity, and this is especially valuable in terms of uncertainty	Rapport (2002)
Is valuable in contemporary times and in a shifting world – a world where change is often dramatic	Hewison (1985); Wright (1985)
Older generations, for instance, have a propensity to seek out – and derive comfort from – those heritage institutions with which they were associated in their youth	Holbrook and Schindler (2003)
Heritage symbols are like cosmetics which when applied make the world more attractive and desirable	Hayden (1987)
The impulse to preserve the past is to preserve the self and, to me, the notion of holding on and going forward with the past is a key characteristic of the heritage doctrine	Sarup (1996)
b. The national/cultural significance of heritage	
Heritage is important in communicating and embodying national identity	Gellner (1983); Smith (1986, 1991, 1994); Nairn (1997); Kumar (2003)
Reminds citizens of the symbolic roots from which a sense of national belonging is grounded	Rapport (2002); Park (2010)
Makes up for the (national) deficit, loss, or, indeed, trauma caused by the past	
Of heightened importance and meaning during periods of (national) change and uncertainty	Hewison (1987)

*c. The institutional and corporate marketing significance
     of heritage*

Corporate heritage brands are stable reference points in a changing world which can harness positive public emotions and are linked to the past, present and prospective future too	Balmer et al. (2006)
Imbue corporate brands with a distinctiveness and attractiveness which may be rare and, in many cases, unique, and the above can be attractive and meaningful for consumers	Urde et al. (2007); Balmer (2011a, b, c)
Customers value heritage	Wiedmann et al. (2011a, b)
d. Stakeholder significance of heritage	
Different stakeholder groups' sense of identification with heritage and their interpretation of a particular heritage are variable. In part, these views are shaped by the ways in which heritage is presented to stakeholders	Apostolakis (2003)
e. Postmodern significance of heritage	
The postmodern perspective allows heritage to be understood and defined in a multifarious number of ways. As such, it allows an individual to define heritage in any way the individual deems to be fit	Fowler (1989); Walton (2009); Weaver (2013)

Sociological significance

In sociological terms, heritage has been defined in terms of a material testimony of identity; as a discourse and a set of practices concerned with the continuity, persistence and substantiality of a group's collective identity (Macdonald, 2006).

National significance

The heritage literature vis-à-vis national identity is also significant. It communicates and embodies national identity; reminds citizens of the symbolic roots from which a sense of national belonging is grounded; makes up for the (national) deficit, loss, or, indeed, trauma caused by the past; is of heightened importance and meaning during periods of (national) change and uncertainty. Often, within this literature, the importance of image, symbol, habit, ritual and mythology are seen to be of significance to heritage (Gellner, 1983; Hewison, 1987; Smith, 1991; Edensor, 2002; Rapport, 2002, 2003; Kumar, 2003; Park, 2010).

Institutional and corporate marketing significance

Institutional and corporate marketing perspectives on heritage stress the importance of continuity in that heritage, invariably, is of value in that corporate heritage identities and brands are stable reference points for stakeholders and others (Balmer *et al.*, 2006; Balmer, 2011a, b, c).

Stakeholder significance

The stakeholder viewpoint vis-à-vis heritage is mindful of different stakeholder groups whose sense of identification with and interpretation of heritage varies. The aforementioned is shaped by the ways in which heritage is presented to them and interpreted by them as a group. As such, heritage is complex owing to the viewpoints of various stakeholders and owing to issues of identification, presentation and interpretation of heritage to and from these groups (Apostolakis, 2003). For me, this perspective is highly salient for corporate marketing generally and for corporate communications specially.

Postmodern significance

For its part, the postmodern perspective affords a huge degree of licence in terms of how heritage in characterised. As such, heritage can be understood and defined in a multifarious number of ways. For instance, it allows an individual to define heritage in any way the individual deems to be fit (Fowler, 1989; Walton, 2009; Weaver, 2013).

Corporate heritage. Foundational precepts: Six criteria

In this section, some of the foundational precepts of corporate heritage are elucidated. As such, six criteria can be said to pertain so that an institution can be regarded as having a *bona fide* corporate heritage. They are not necessarily placed in any specific order:

(1) omni-temporality;
(2) institution trait constancy;
(3) external/internal tri-generational heredity;
(4) augmented role identities;
(5) ceaseless multigenerational stakeholder utility; and
(6) unremitting management tenacity.

1st corporate heritage criterion: Omni-temporality

Corporate heritage identities subsist in temporal strata (multiple time stratums). This is because a corporate heritage interacts with all three time frames: past, present as well as prospective future (Balmer, 2011a, b, c). Of course, this reflects the common juridical notion that organisations have the potential to exist in perpetuity: the legal aspects of identity – and of company law – are, alas, very rarely known or understood even though it is of material importance in comprehending institutions of all types.

From the outset, it can be deduced that corporate heritage institutions are perennial entities in terms of time (the focus of this section) but also in terms of their
traits and, more often than not, their title too.

The omni-temporal corporate heritage trait of heritage is one of the most
important, valuable, attractive – and arguably difficult – characteristics of the corporate heritage notion. Typically corporate heritage institutions have endured and
have remained meaningful.

Whilst many institutions will have a corporate heritage over time it is possible
that an entity's heritage traits may disappear, the geneses and significance of the traits
might elapse, be forgotten, loose their saliency or be eschewed.

Heritage and time

Heritage is not about something that aims simply to be of our time but, I conclude,
is meaningful for all times. Lowenthal (1998) argues that heritage speaks to the past
and present whereas, in the context of corporate heritage, it has been argued that
it has a tripartite temporal dynamic in that it is meaningful to the past, present and
prospective future (Balmer *et al.*, 2006). In short, it subsists in temporal strata or
multiple time stratums (Balmer, 2011a).

The notion – and conundrum – that heritage is of the past whilst being resolutely part of the present (Balmer *et al.*, 2006), although a comparatively new notion
in the corporate marketing domain, is not unfamiliar to other fields of scholarship.
For instance, when the philosophy canon is examined we can see that the notion of
time has been an enduring concern among philosophers and from different schools
of thought since time immemorial. For instance, Russell (1957, p. 374), in explaining the nature of time, provided the following definition:

> The present of things past is memory; the present of things present is sight;
> and the present of things future is expectation.

Informed by this perspective, we can posit that corporate heritage, from this particular philosophical perspective (there are others), can be seen to be an amalgam
of memory, sight and expectation. The above may perhaps bring to mind for some
readers the exegesis on time offered by the fourth-century bishop and philosopher
Saint Augustine, who in his *Confessions* averred there to be three categories of time:
a present of things past, a present of things present, and a present of things future.
Interestingly, and controversially, perhaps, Augustine sees the tripartite identities of
time as being firmly fixed in the present.

The heritage canon articulates the importance of heritage along a number of
dimensions. For instance, heritage can imply a sense of our consciousness of our
place – and in the context of corporate heritage, an institution's place – outside,
or beyond, history. To reiterate an earlier point, and drawing on the broad heritage canon (Heathcote, 2011), for me corporate heritage is super-historic and its
omni-temporal traits mean that it is of value since it provides existential anchors.

Recently, Balmer (2011a) introduced the notion of Relative Invariance (and the identities of time) in relation to corporate heritage. This is based on the notion that whilst individuals and groups may perceive things to be the same there, often, they are not. For instance, the symbols of age-old heritage institutions such as the Catholic Church, the British Monarchy along with the universities of Oxford, Durham and Harvard, whilst they have endured the meanings attached to some of them, have been transformed. To me (Balmer, 2011a), the renowned Sicilian author Lampedusa (1958), in his famous book, *The Leopard*, penned an adage of penetrating luminosity which, arguably, goes to the core of my notion of Relative Invariance. Lampedusa mused that if we want things to stay the same, things will have to change.

2nd corporate heritage criterion: Institution trait constancy

One key criterion of corporate heritage is for there to be meaningful trait consistency on one or, ideally, two or more dimensions of the 11 identified here. Reflecting on corporate heritage entities, 11 traits have been uncovered, namely:

(1) ownership;
(2) organisational-type;
(3) organisational rationales/cultures and ethos;
(4) product and service focus;
(5) manufacturing processes and the delivery of services;
(6) quality levels;
(7) location;
(8) group and class associations;
(9) design and style;
(10) sensory utilisation; and
(11) corporate communications.

Figure 3.1 shows the 11 key institutional trait constancy types I have identified.

A requirement of institution trait constancy is that the aforementioned of what, sometimes, are called corporate identity anchors, should be invariant. As we pointed out earlier (Urde *et al.*, 2007), whilst all organisations have a history, not all institutions have a heritage. In this article, the latter refers to a firm's key corporate identity anchors which have remained constant. Sometimes, of course, managers are unaware of their heritage or chose to ignore it. As such, determining whether an organisation has a corporate heritage can be of material importance.

A key question relating to the above is: What is an abiding corporate identity trait? In truth, there are many. As such, some organisations will have a plethora of heritage traits, some will have only one or two, and their significance will vary and may fluctuate in different times, places and among stakeholder groups of course. Heritage identity traits can in part be substantiated, but, also, may be imagined, or contrived. Sometimes they are a fusion of all three. Such perspectives – as with images – can vary from individual to individual and from group to group and, for

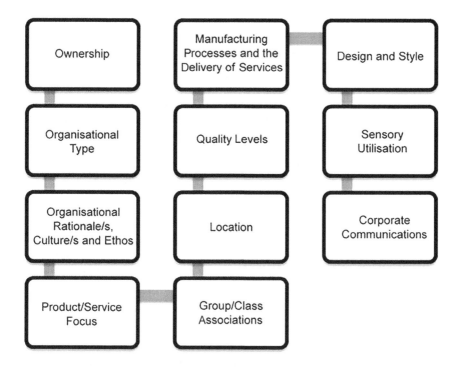

FIGURE 3.1 Key institutional trait constancy types

this reason, heritage can have a variety of connotations and, therefore, represents trajectories of meanings, values and times. Table 3.4 provides an explanation of the 11 institutional trait constancy modes and also provides explanations and examples of them.

3rd corporate heritage criterion: External/internal tri-generational heredity

In my earlier articulation of this dimension of corporate heritage (Balmer, 2011a), the idea of corporate heritage bequest was introduced. Elaborating this perspective, the notions of legacy and/or bequest and inheritance are important since they give the corporate heritage dimension tractive force vis-à-vis the future. To me, one practical way of conceptualising corporate heritage is to be mindful of the precept "forward with the past". The ancestral, legacy and hereditary aspects of corporate heritage can sometimes be overlooked (especially when some of the broad heritage literature is retrospective in character) but, to me, are apropos to our comprehension of the domain.

However, this raises the following, key question, namely: at what point in time can it reasonably be deduced – all things being equal – that an institution, in temporal terms, can be found to meet the above criteria?

TABLE 3.4 Institutional trait constancy modes: explanations and examples

Trait (and indicative corporate heritage appellation/s)	Explanation	Examples
Ownership Corporate heritage ownership	Ownership type, for instance, as a family business, etc., can accord an entity with a heritage distinctiveness if it has prevailed over time	Enjoying a high-profile presence on the UK High Street, Clarks shoes is unusual among similar entities in that it continues to be a family-owned and managed entity, and this (being a family-owned entity), therefore, represents an especial corporate heritage characteristic
Organisational type Corporate heritage type	Mutuals, partnerships, co-operatives, and unlimited companies, etc. can accord an entity with a heritage distinctiveness if it has prevailed over time	The John Lewis Partnership is owned by personnel. This affords a distinctive corporate heritage trait to this well-known British High Street retailer (John Lewis and Waitrose)
Organisational rationales, cultures and ethos Corporate heritage rationale Corporate heritage culture Corporate heritage ethos	An entity's *raison d'être* can accord an entity with a heritage distinctiveness if it has prevailed over time. Some organisation have a distinct corporate heritage rationale/culture and/or ethos	The UK's National Health Service (NHS) is a corporate heritage that is rare. Since its inception after the Second World War, a key rationale of the NHS is that there should be a comprehensive healthcare service for all, which is free at the point of need. This is a key and perennial precept of the NHS. Abiding corporate heritage cultures underpin religious orders such as the Benedictines, Carthusians, and, in the commercial realm, the family-owned private bankers Hoare and Co.
Product and service focus Corporate heritage competency/ies	What an organisation makes, or provides as a service – a core manufacturing/service creation competency – can accord an entity with a heritage distinctiveness if it has prevailed over time	Oxford University for almost 1,000 years has focussed on advanced-level research, scholarship and teaching which, on many fronts but not all, is without obvious parallel among other corporate heritage identities in the higher education sector

Trait (and indicative corporate heritage appellation/s)	Explanation	Examples
Manufacturing processes and the delivery of services Corporate heritage processes	The processes underpinning the manufacture of products and the provision of services can accord an entity with a heritage distinctiveness if it has prevailed over time	The Morgan car company uses methods of construction which have largely remained unchanged. Cars are entirely hand-built and the cars all have a wooden chassis. This is, increasingly, very rare among analogous automotive corporate heritage identities
Quality levels Corporate heritage quality	Organisations can be known for the pursuit of certain quality levels, which can accord an entity with a heritage distinctiveness if it has prevailed over time	The P&O (Peninsular and Oriental) ocean/cruise liner, as a corporate heritage identity, has long been known for offering good-value, middle of the range ocean journeys and cruises. It initiated the concept of cruise holidays
Location (country and territory of origin) Corporate heritage territorial identities	An entity's strong association with a location can accord an entity with a heritage distinctiveness if it has prevailed over time	Newcastle United Football Club is a powerful symbol/icon of the northeastern English town and, arguably, has a unique corporate heritage status vis-à-vis the city of Newcastle
Group and class associations Corporate heritage communities	Firms can accord an entity with a heritage distinctiveness if it has prevailed over time	The Co-operative Societies (running shops, a bank, funeral directors, etc., and also having a political wing in sponsoring members of the British Parliament) is in corporate heritage terms distinct owing to its strong association with blue-collar workers/the working class
Design and style corporate heritage design Corporate heritage architecture Corporate heritage house style Corporate heritage visual identity	The pursuance and continuance of certain design features vis-à-vis products, graphic design, architecture, livery, etc. can accord an entity with heritage distinctiveness if it has prevailed over time. Also relates to having a coherent visual system in place (corporate design/house style/visual identity)	Consider the distinctive chequered pattern of Burberry, the inimitable design of Louis Vuitton and the graphic design heritage of London Transport. In their different ways the above entities burnish their corporate heritage via their pursuance of a distinctive corporate design and style

(Continued)

TABLE 3.4 (Continued)

Trait (and indicative corporate heritage appellation/s)	Explanation	Examples
Sensory utilisation Corporate heritage sensory identity Corporate heritage auditory identity Corporate heritage taste identity Corporate heritage olfactory identity Corporate heritage visual identity Corporate heritage touch identity	Sound, scent, touch, vision, and taste – individually, as a combination or in their entirety – can accord an entity with a heritage distinctiveness if it has prevailed over time	The auditory heritage identity of the instrumentalists of Vienna Philharmonic Orchestra (in terms of their sound and distinctive style of playing their core repertoire) is distinctive, as is the distinctive vocal heritage timbre produced by the men and boy choristers of Westminster Metropolitan Cathedral Choir (London) which blends a centuries-old southern European head-voice projection with the English-precision of English Cathedral Choral practise. In the commercial ambit the taste of "Classic Coke" is, arguably, a key corporate heritage sensory trait of the Coca-Cola corporation
Corporate communications Corporate heritage communications Corporate heritage total communications Corporate heritage integrated communications Corporate heritage advertising	The pursuance of certain corporate communications activities (advertising, corporate PR) along with integrated corporate communications activities (and the broader notion of total corporate communications) all, to varying degrees, can accord an entity with a heritage distinctiveness if it has prevailed over time	Consider – at a micro level – the celebrated Christmas corporate heritage advertising campaign of Coca-Cola, which is without obvious parallel as part of an organisation's corporate heritage. At the macro level, the corporate heritage total communications of London's celebrated Dorchester Hotel is noteworthy (primary communications: activities; secondary communications: formal communications; tertiary communications: word of mouth and general commentary)

The tri-generational/50-year corporate heritage requisite

To me, there is logic in saying that if key identity traits have endured for a minimum of three generations – say 50 years – then this criterion of corporate heritage may apply. Of course, context is a vital factor here since countries, societies and organisations differ. For instance, some associations with entities may well occur later on in an individual's life cycle.

It is worth bearing in mind that there are multiple modes of inheritance. For instance, whilst it is not, strictly speaking, an absolute prerequisite for corporate heritage to be passed on in stringent familial terms over three generations, this is likely to be the case, but of course corporate heritage bequest and inheritance does not necessarily have to have the family as its *locus*.

Corporate heritage identities – because they are passed on from generation to generation – are invested with and can invest to others a *charism* (a gift). Why? This is because corporate heritage identities and corporate heritage brands not only have and are invested with enduring and meaningful identity traits but also transmit these highly meaningful identities to successive generations.

Corporate heritage can be adopted (adopted corporate heritage): consider Anglophiles and Francophiles who may, respectively, develop a penchant for British corporate heritage identities such as the British Monarchy, the BBC, the Royal Shakespeare Company and Burberry and for French corporate heritage identities such as Pol Roger champagne, Lacoste, the Hôtel Ritz Paris and Le Figaro. Corporate heritage can be received (received corporate image) not only from parents but from teachers, friends who can introduce and instil an appreciation and loyalty to a corporate heritage and, of course, it can simply be made known via communication (communicated corporate heritage).

From this, corporate heritage institutions – because of their multigenerational characteristics – tend to be very much part of the collective memory of a social group.

Internal and external legacies

Moreover, tri-generational and above, corporate heritage legacy may manifest itself internally (internal tri-generational heredity +) in terms of ownership (family businesses for instance), employment and education, etc. as well as externally (external tri-generational heredity +) vis-à-vis customers, suppliers and other shareholders. It is logical to suppose that the corporate heritage legacy dimension will be more robust where the hereditary dimension is manifest both internally and externally, but it may of course be manifest on only one of these dimensions. The aforementioned is reflected in diagrammatic form in Figure 3.2.

FIGURE 3.2 External/internal tri-generational heredity criterion

4th corporate heritage criterion: Augmented role identities

Corporate heritage identities are infused with multiple role identities, namely the temporal. Territorial, cultural, social and ancestral identity: these burnish an entity's institutional identity. Since corporate heritage institutions are invested with multiple identities they can, in omni-temporal terms, be emblematic of groups, and societies and places, etc. (Balmer, 2011a). Moreover, and importantly, they confer these identities to groups, societies and places in multigenerational terms (Balmer, 2011a).

The importance of the latter is, arguably, of immense and of immeasurable significance: long-established universities are a case in point and often confer cultural, national, or territorial identities across the generations, namely: Aberdeen University (Scotland: est. 1495); University of Bologna (Italy: est. 1088); Cambridge University (England: est. 1209); Dartmouth College, Hanover (USA: est. 1769); and Trinity College, Dublin (Ireland: est. 1592).

Sui generis

One of the reasons why corporate heritage institutions are *sui generis* – one of a kind – is because they are imbued with significant non-corporate identities. These identity modes include the temporal (identities of time), territorial (identities of place), cultural (identities of culture), social (identities of peoples including classes, professions, etc.) and familial (identities linked to ancestry). Corporate heritage institutions are likely to be associated with one or several of the aforementioned. It is clear that many corporate heritage entities are significant symbols of places, peoples and cultures: consider the importance of the National Railway of India and Coca-Cola in terms of their national importance and cultural significance vis-à-vis India and the USA.

Multiple role identities

In explaining the above corporate heritage characteristic, Balmer (2011a) asserted that heritage institutions are imbued with multiple role identities and, as such, have a number of referents. Over time, nascent corporate heritage institutions are imbued with these additional identity traits. Again, and to recapitulate, this provides one reason for the success of corporate heritage institutions, since they are invariably invested with multiple identity modes which are linked to, and evoke, significant cultural, territorial identities, etc. which burnish an entity's institutional and temporal properties.

Arguably, each additional role identity should meet the tri-generational criterion before it can be regarded as a meaningful corporate heritage role identity. A prominent institution which is imbued with multiple role identity is the British Broadcasting Corporation (BBC): not only does it have a distinct corporate identity but, over time, became associated with the territorial role identity of Great Britain

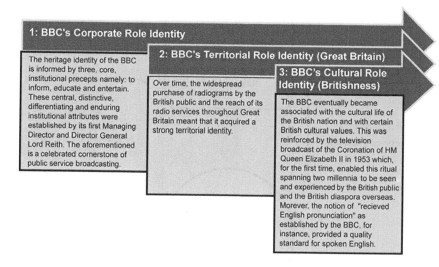

1: BBC's Corporate Role Identity

The heritage identity of the BBC is informed by three, core, institutional precepts namely: to inform, educate and entertain. These central, distinctive, differentiating and enduring institutional attributes were established by its first Managing Director and Director General Lord Reith. The aforementioned is a celebrated cornerstone of public service broadcasting.

2: BBC's Territorial Role Identity (Great Britain)

Over time, the widespread purchase of radiograms by the British public and the reach of its radio services throughout Great Britain meant that it acquired a strong territorial identity.

3: BBC's Cultural Role Identity (Britishness)

The BBC eventually became associated with the cultural life of the British nation and with certain British cultural values. This was reinforced by the television broadcast of the Coronation of HM Queen Elizabeth II in 1953 which, for the first time, enabled this ritual spanning two millennia to be seen and experienced by the British public and the British diaspora overseas. Morever, the notion of "recieved English pronunciation" as established by the BBC, for instance, provided a quality standard for spoken English.

FIGURE 3.3 Augmented role identities – indicative example of the BBC

and, later on, became closely allied to British culture. Typically, organisations make reference to their entity's time line (key dates in an organisation's history). In the corporate heritage sphere it is more apposite to refer to a heritage: the identification of the process of accrual and sequence via which an institution is imbued with multiple role identities. An example of this is shown in Figure 3.3 in terms of three prominent role identities of the BBC.

5th corporate heritage criterion: Ceaseless multigenerational stakeholder utility

This criterion, informed by but extending the nascent corporate marketing logic (meeting stakeholders wants and needs so that there is mutual benefit for customers and the corporation too), is an obvious one but one that, all the same, needs to be said. In short, once an institution no longer has a utility to one generation of customers and other stakeholders – even if it has been valuable to former generations – then it will, most likely, wane and ultimately expire. Of course institutional termination is inevitable but is, for the main, not preordained and may be accelerated by a failure for corporate heritage institutions to focus on multigenerational utility.

In ensuring that corporate heritage identities are demonstrably salient for consecutive generations of stakeholders, to me, building on my earlier model by adding the ability dimension (Balmer, 2011a), corporate heritage institutions should:

- have the continuous ability to meet the wants and needs of successive generations of customers and other stakeholders;
- be mindful of, and also nurture, multiple generational affinities with the entity; and
- ensure the authenticity of the corporate heritage.

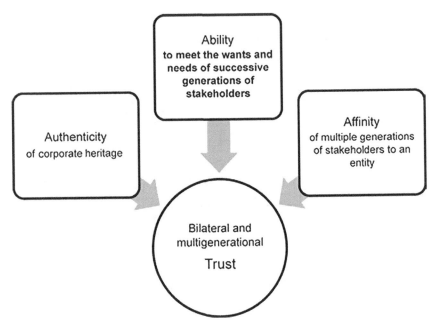

FIGURE 3.4 Multigenerational stakeholder dimensions vis-à-vis corporate heritage institution trust

The above tripartite dimensions can help to foster ongoing and, importantly, bilateral and multigenerational trust between institutions and stakeholders. Figure 3.4 reproduces the updated exhibit. Balmer (2011a) conceptualised that corporate heritage brands were dependent on bilateral trust between customers/stakeholders and the corporate brand.

6th corporate heritage criterion: Unremitting management tenacity

The assiduous management of corporate heritage identities is critical in ensuring the survival and saliency of a given corporate heritage. This view was advanced in an earlier scrutiny of corporate heritage identities – based on work on the British Monarchy – where the significance of regulation (management) vis-à-vis corporate heritage was underlined (Balmer, 2011a, b, c).

Of course, institutional success and corporate survival are core tenets of management. Whilst serendipity can account, in part and perhaps even in whole, for the survival and success of a given corporate heritage, we should not discount the role of corporate heritage custodianship and the requisite of unremitting management tenacity in this regard. As such issues pertaining to strategy rather than serendipity are fundamental to the success and maintenance of corporate heritage, it is a *sine non qua*, therefore, that senior and other managers are apprised of their institution's corporate heritage in terms of its character and value, whilst being cognisant that it can be a precious, valuable but also a vulnerable corporate resource.

Moreover, corporate heritage institutions require a reappraisal and a good deal of nuance on the part of strategic planners and other managers and consultants – including those focussing on corporate marketing and corporate communications – in more fully accommodating the requisites of corporate heritage management.

In part, the extant literature has begun to take cognisance of the aforementioned. As such, it is more appropriate to see heritage ownership (from consumer and institutional proprietorship perspectives) in terms of a custodianship (Balmer, 2011a) or a stewardship rather than management (Urde *et al.*, 2007).

Corporate heritage sustainability theory

In theoretical terms, even at this nascent stage of the area's development, and drawing on the insights detailed in this article, it is possible to articulate a preliminary articulation of what, to me, is an expansive theory of sustainable corporate heritage. This postulated theory will need to be tested and verified. This theory is mindful and in part is informed by two critical management theories: the core competencies of the corporation theory of Prahalad and Hamel (1990), and the resourced-based view of the firm theory of Grant (1991). However, these theories are blended and are, importantly, expanded so that they are meaningful as what, to me, is something approaching a grand theory of corporate heritage. They form a part, but not the major part, of this pregnant theory. Corporate heritage sustainability theory may, provisionally, be articulated as follows:

> Corporate heritage sustainability theory requires omni-temporal company longevity and is underpinned by institutional trait constancy and durable company capabilities and mandates organisational continuity and, usually, company prosperity. It is dependent on multigenerational stakeholder inheritance in terms of trust and loyalty to the organisation. This is based on a company's constant capacity to confer, as well as bequeath, manifold benefits to customers and other stakeholders. These benefits can be multiple and wide-ranging and can relate to what a firm makes, does and represents, especially in relation to broad identity terms vis-à-vis the organisation's social, cultural, territorial and temporal associations among others.

The final substantive section of this article introduces two corporate heritage notions: corporate heritage marketing and corporate heritage communications. With the increased recognition of the importance of corporate heritage, the aforementioned are likely to be of increased importance.

Corporate heritage marketing and total corporate heritage communications

With the growing realisation of the importance of corporate heritage identities and corporate heritage brands there is a *prima facie* case need to accommodate such developments within the corporate communications and corporate marketing fields: thus, the need for the corporate marketing and corporate communications fields to be adapted. With this in mind, in this section I introduce and briefly explicate what I call corporate heritage management and total corporate heritage communications.

A preliminary explication of corporate heritage marketing

Modifying my earlier definition of corporate marketing (Balmer, 2011c, p. 1345), I present the following definition of corporate heritage marketing:

> Corporate heritage marketing is an organisational-wide philosophy which is underpinned by a multigenerational-focussed customer, stakeholder, societal and CSR/ethical-focussed ethos.
>
> It is enacted and created over successive generations and should broadly meet a tri-generational criterion.

In corporate heritage institutions, importance is accorded to the institutions' corporate identity and omni-temporal, cultural, social and ancestral heritage traits. Importantly, the aforementioned will meaningfully inform an organisation's corporate heritage brand promise/covenant.

In maintaining a corporate heritage marketing doctrine, equilibrium has to be achieved in relation to the requisite of corporate heritage continuity and the expediency of corporate heritage change.

A corporate heritage institution's multiple role identities provide distinctive and perennial multigenerational platforms from which multilateral, organisational and stakeholder/societal relationships are fostered to all-round advantage.

Corporate heritage institutions, once established, can perennially confer corporate, temporal, territorial, and cultural and other meaningful identities.

Corporate heritage marketing, as with corporate marketing per se, is also concerned with meeting the wants and needs of successive generations of customers and other stakeholders to mutual advantage and profit. Also, corporate heritage marketing – as with corporate marketing – is also sensitive to an institution's provenance and inheritance and to its prospective future too.

A corporate heritage marketing logic, as an institutional-wide philosophy, is also mindful of its ongoing societal, ethical and CSR roles and responsibilities.

Successive generations of senior managers bequeath responsibility for a corporate heritage marketing orientation to newer generations, as can organisational members generally.

In family-owned businesses, both corporate heritage inheritance and corporate heritage marketing responsibility are linked and, significantly, are limited – and sometimes constrained – by ancestry.

In most organisations, both collectively and across the generations, CEOs share ultimate responsibility for the corporate heritage identity/brand and, ideally, in nurturing and maintaining a corporate heritage marketing orientation.

The espoused and enduring benefits of a corporate heritage marketing logic include the establishment of multigenerational and bilateral positive organisational/customer-stakeholder relationships that are of mutual financial and or social profit. The establishment of multigenerational stakeholder trust/positive corporate heritage reputations is another benefit. In addition, the maintenance of multigenerational institutional saliency in its markets and among its stakeholders (corporate survival and profitability) can be invaluable vis-à-vis the organisation's license to operate.

For many corporate heritage organisations, the creation of long-term shareholder and/or stakeholder value is achieved via the establishment of strong, salient and enduring appealing corporate heritage brands will be desirable and for some institutions (universities, for example) a long-term strategic imperative.

Figure 3.5 shows the dimensions of corporate heritage marketing whilst Table 3.5 provides an overview of the dimensions and explanations of the corporate heritage marketing mix.

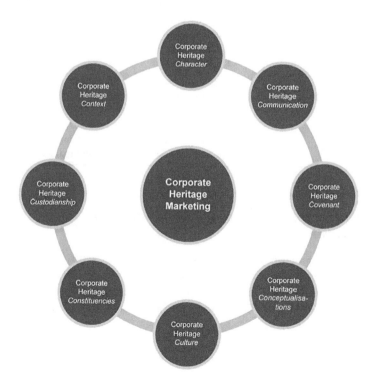

FIGURE 3.5 The corporate heritage marketing mix

TABLE 3.5 Dimensions and explanations of the corporate heritage marketing mix

Corporate heritage marketing mix dimensions	Explanation
Corporate heritage CHARACTER	The organisation's perennial corporate identity traits
Corporate heritage COMMUNICATION	The organisation's perennial communication of its core corporate identity traits
Corporate heritage COVENANT	The perennial promise/covenant underpinning the organisation's corporate heritage brand
Corporate heritage CONCEPTUALISATIONS	The perennial images/reputations held of the organisation by successive generations of customers and other stakeholders
Corporate heritage CULTURE	The perennial sense of who we are on the part of successive generations of organisational members and, where applicable, owners (family-owned businesses for example)
Corporate heritage CONSTITUENCIES	The perennial organisational concern in meeting the wants and needs of successive generations of customers and other key stakeholders
Corporate heritage CONTEXT	The perennial organisational concern in taking cognisance of the political, economic, ethical, social and technological environment and ensuring the corporate heritage remains relevant and requires perennial adaptation vis-à-vis the above
Corporate heritage CUSTODIANSHIP	The perennial senior management stewardship of the organisation and, importantly, the shared perennial custodianship of the corporate heritage by all organisational members. A corporate heritage institution is the ongoing and multigenerational responsibility of everyone with an organisation

A preliminary explication of corporate heritage total communication

The total corporate heritage communications notion is substantively based on the long-standing notion that everything an organisation says, makes and does communicates (Balmer, 1995). The total corporate communications has, variously, informed my earlier work vis-à-vis corporate communications (Balmer, 1995, 1998; Balmer and Gray, 1999).

With corporate heritage identities and corporate heritage brands in its sights, a key difference of total corporate heritage communications is that it accords importance to the omni-temporal and multigenerational dimensions of corporate heritage.

Total corporate heritage communication represents:

(1) the nexus which exists between a corporate heritage identity and/or the corporate heritage brand;

(2) the focus in providing experiences and knowledge about a corporate heritage, and also provides a perennial platform by which corporate heritage images and reputations of the corporate heritage identity/corporate heritage brand are meaningfully shaped and

(3) finally, the effect in terms of multigenerational customer and other stakeholder relationships and engagement with a corporate heritage identity/brand.

Although it is difficult to coordinate total communications – especially in multi-generational and in temporal terms – this is important, all the same, for corporate heritage entities.

Figures 3.6 and 3.7 respectively show the focus, nexus and effect of total corporate heritage communications and its quadripartite character.

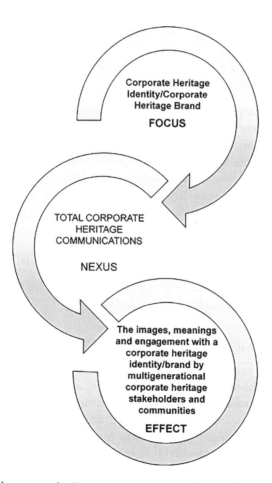

FIGURE 3.6 Total corporate heritage corporate communications: focus, nexus and effect

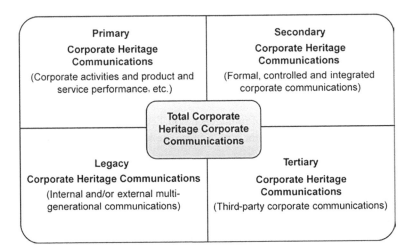

FIGURE 3.7 Quadripartite dimensions of total corporate heritage corporate communications

Primary, secondary, tertiary and legacy corporate heritage communications

To reiterate, total corporate heritage communications is mindful of the communications effects not only of formal and integrated corporate communications channels across the time but, importantly, across the generations. Therefore, whereas the classic total corporate communications approach is tripartite in nature, the total corporate heritage communications doctrine is quadripartite in character. Thus in addition to the primary, secondary and tertiary dimensions, a fourth dimension is added: that of legacy corporate communications is important and accommodates the multigenerational perspective of the above.

Primary corporate heritage communications (primary CHC)

Relates to the omni-temporal corporate communications effects of product, services, management and employee actions and similar.

Secondary corporate heritage communications (secondary CHC)

Relates to the omni-temporal corporate communications effects of more orthodox and formally controlled corporate communications vehicles including corporate advertising, corporate communication using new technology, corporate public relations, corporate sponsorship and similar. Much of the aforementioned will be integrated and should be informed by common starting points vis-à-vis corporate heritage identity/the corporate heritage brand.

Tertiary corporate heritage communications (tertiary CHC)

Relates to the omni-temporal corporate communications generated by third parties including stakeholders, competitors, media commentary and a variety of interest groups.

Various vehicles are utilised for the above, including the spoken word, print, broadcast media and, more importantly today, on new media such as the Web, etc.

Legacy corporate heritage communications (legacy CHC)

Relates to multigenerational and omni-temporal communications. These are transmitted across three or more generations: this notion takes cognisance of the fact that corporate heritage communications may also be bequeathed and inherited and for good or bad. Individuals and groups may see themselves as custodians of messages relating to an organisation.

Internal legacy corporate heritage communications accommodate the above as it relates to multigenerational groups of managers and other organisational managers and also, in family-owned businesses, as it relates to ancestry (internal familial legacy CHC).

External legacy corporate heritage communications is broadly the same as above except that it relates to multigenerational groups of customers, and other stakeholders. Importantly, legacy corporate heritage communications among customers and stakeholders can also have a familial characteristic where a corporate heritage is passed down from grandparents via their children to their grandchildren, who may receive the double legacy corporate heritage communications effect from both grandparents and parents (external familial legacy CHC).

The downsides of corporate heritage

Just as the heritage domain has its celebrants and detractors, the same will be true for corporate heritage. For intellectual reasons, some may reason that an undue focus on corporate heritage is entropic and is indicative of a deep-seated disorder. Such perspectives are prevalent in relation to the heritage tourism field (Sarup, 1996).

A focus on corporate heritage can, in certain cases, achieve a degree of corporate utopia but can also lead to dystopia too. Here, I provide a short list of some of the downsides of corporate heritage:

• Contested corporate heritage and organisational provenances represent severe shortcomings. Since corporate heritage narratives can change across space, time and context, promulgated corporate heritage narratives may be contested by different groups. Corporate heritage is context specific and can evoke contradictory and opposite reactions. Whilst many British, Canadians and New

Zealanders are proud of their monarchical heritage, in Ireland there typically is an aversion to their monarchical provenance (Balmer, 2009, 2011b, c).

- Organisations may advance positive corporate heritage characteristics and downplay the negative – consider Cadbury's, the US-owned, British choco-latier corporate brand which seemingly has a corporate identity heritage linked slavery (Balmer, 2009).
- Undue focus on an organisation's heritage – and an unwillingness to adapt or change – can result in corporate myopia.
- Organisations that are invested with neutral corporate heritage traits may determine that it is not expedient to be informed by corporate heritage or to usefully communicate it.
- The complexity of corporate heritage may be viewed as an encumbrance owing to its multifaceted nature and the need to simultaneously accommodate identity continuity and change, composite time frames and the need to dis-criminate between corporate heritage identities and corporate heritage brands.

Further research and impending theoretical advances

Clearly, with an area that is in its infancy there is merit in garnering insights from philosophical, sociological, anthropological, psychological domains along with the literatures pertaining to nationality and nationalism. More specifically, to me, there are a number of latent theories relating to corporate heritage which are likely to be elaborated on in the future. In the meantime a distinct domain of corporate heritage tourism (focussing on institutions which have dual identities derived from corpo-rate, economic, social identities and which are of interest to domestic and overseas tourists) is one area which is pregnant with possibilities.

Latent theoretical contributions vis-à-vis corporate heritage

- *Corporate Heritage Core Competencies Theory.* Developing traditional core com-petencies theory (Prahalad and Hamel, 1990).
- *Corporate Heritage Resourced-Based View Theory.* Developing traditional resource-based view theory (Grant, 1991).
- *Corporate Heritage Brand Orientation Theory.* Developing traditional product/ service brand orientation theory of Urde (1994).
- *Corporate Heritage Relationships Theory.* Developing traditional relationship mar-keting approach of Grönroos (1997).
- *Corporate Heritage Social Identity Theory.* Developing social identity theory (Tajfel and Turner, 1979).
- *Corporate Heritage Commitment-Trust Theory.* Developing traditional commitment-trust theory (Morgan and Hunt, 1994).
- *Corporate Heritage Stakeholder Theory.* Developing stakeholder theory (Freeman, 1984).

- *Corporate Heritage Customer-Company Theory.* Developing customer-company theory (Bhattacharya and Sen, 2003).
- *Corporate Heritage Organisational Type Theory.* Developing the theory of organisational types (Parsons, 1960; Blau and Scott, 1963).
- *Corporate Heritage Institutional Theory.* Developing institutional theory (Powell and DiMaggio, 1991).

Corporate heritage tourism

Corporate heritage tourism usefully links the nascent corporate heritage domain and that of heritage tourism. As such, there is a subcategory of corporate heritage institution/brands which, because of their provenance and multiple meanings, attracts not only customers but also tourists: some may be classified as (corporate heritage) customer/tourists. London Transport, Selfridges, The Vienna Boys' Choir, Maxim's (Paris) and Darjeeling Himalayan Railway (India) are *prima facie* cases in point.

Reflection

By means of reprise, and adopting a broad vista, it is clear that over recent, successive decades the new and novel has been embraced and past and the traditional has been disregarded and, in extremis, eliminated. Arguably, this has led to a feeling of rootlessness and a sense of heritage loss. Sometimes this is sudden and dramatic, as in the case in the People's Republic of China.

The above helps to explain why, for a small but steadily growing body of corporate marketing and communications scholars, the broad heritage notion – with its focus on the past, present, and future – has come to the fore. Corporate heritage identities and corporate heritage brands, because they have stood to the test of time and therefore are seemingly stable entities, can be of especial value because of their capacity to confer a sense of stability, continuity and identity to successive generations of customers and other stakeholders.

This article has sought to advance corporate heritage scholarship and practice by further reflecting on the nature of corporate heritage institutions and, in particular, through the introduction and explication of the new notions of corporate heritage marketing and total corporate heritage communications. Whilst fully appreciating that the field is still very much in its infancy, and also recognising that a good deal more work is required in the territory, we should not discount the importance of naissance and, in terms of the broad heritage domain, the significance of "new beginnings" in relation to the corporate heritage field and of course in the wider heritage domain.

Arguably, the introduction of corporate heritage marketing and corporate heritage communications will result in new and distinct fields of management consultancy which, in instrumental terms, have the potential to be highly significant. Moreover, the broadening of the corporate heritage domain, as advanced in this article, can lead to a broadening and wider recognition of the strategic importance of corporate heritage.

To me, scholars of corporate marketing and corporate communications are in pole positions to advance our comprehension of the territory and, as such, have the potential – in the very near future – to make meaningful advances to both areas. Moreover, these contributions have the capacity to be of inestimable value to both corporate heritage theory and practice. Of course, making groundbreaking advances of this kind, arguably, is very much part of the embryonic heritage of both corporate communications and corporate marketing.

References

Albert, S. and Whetten, D.A. (1985), "Organizational identity", in Cummings, L.L. and Staw, B.M. (Eds.), *Research in Organizational Behavior*, Vol. 7, JAI Press, Greenwich, CT, pp. 263–295.

Apostolakis, A. (2003), "The convergence process in heritage tourism", *Annals of Tourism Research*, Vol. 26 No. 3, pp. 795–812.

Balmer, J.M.T. (1995), "Corporate branding and connoisseurship", *Journal of General Management*, Vol. 21 No. 1, pp. 24–47.

Balmer, J.M.T. (1998), "Corporate identity and the advent of corporate marketing", *Journal of Marketing Management*, Vol. 14 No. 8, pp. 963–996.

Balmer, J.M.T. (2004), "The British Monarchy: Does the British Crown as a corporate brand fit?", Working Paper No. 04/16, School of Management, Bradford University, Bradford, April.

Balmer, J.M.T. (2008), "Corporate brands, the British Monarchy and the resource-based view of the firm", *International Studies of Management and Organizations*, Vol. 37 No. 4, pp. 20–45.

Balmer, J.M.T. (2009), "Scrutinising the British Monarchy: The corporate brand that was shaken, stirred and survived", *Management Decision*, Vol. 47 No. 4, pp. 639–675.

Balmer, J.M.T. (2011a), "Corporate heritage identities, corporate heritage brands and the multiple heritage identities of the British Monarchy", *European Journal of Marketing*, Vol. 45 Nos. 9/10, pp. 1380–1398.

Balmer, J.M.T. (2011b), "Corporate heritage brands and the precepts of corporate heritage brand management: Reflections on the British Monarchy on the eve of the wedding of Prince William (April 2011) and the Diamond Jubilee celebrations of Queen Elizabeth II (1952–2012)", *Journal of Brand Management*, Vol. 18 No. 8, pp. 517–544.

Balmer, J.M.T. (2011c), "Corporate marketing myopia and the inexorable rise of a corporate marketing logic: Perspectives from identity-based views of the firm", *European Journal of Marketing*, Vol. 45 Nos. 9/10, pp. 1329–1352.

Balmer, J.M.T. and Gray, E.R. (1999), "Corporate identity and corporate communications: Creating a competitive advantage", *Corporate Communications: An International Journal*, Vol. 4 No. 4, pp. 171–176.

Balmer, J.M.T. and Gray, E.R. (2003), "Corporate brands: What are they? What of them?", *European Journal of Marketing*, Vol. 37 Nos. 7/8, pp. 972–997.

Balmer, J.M.T., Greyser, S.A. and Urde, M. (2006), "The crown as a corporate brand: Insights from monarchies", *Journal of Brand Management*, Vol. 14 Nos. 1/2, pp. 137–161.

Bessiere, J. (1998), "Local development and heritage: Traditional food and cuisine as tourist attractions in rural areas", *Sociologia Ruralis*, Vol. 38 No. 1, pp. 21–34.

Bhattacharya, C.B. and Sen, S. (2003), "Consumer-customer identification: A framework for understanding consumer's relationship with companies", *Journal of Marketing*, Vol. 67, pp. 76–88.

Blau, P.M. and Scott, W.R. (1963), *Formal Organizations: A Comparative Approach*, Routledge and Kegan Paul, London.

Blombäck, A. and Brunninge, O. (2009), "Corporate identity manifested through historical references", *Corporate Communications: An International Journal*, Vol. 14 No. 4, pp. 404–419.

Brown, S., Kozinets, R. and Sherry, J.F. (2003), "Teaching old brand new tricks: Retro branding and the revival of brand meaning", *Journal of Marketing*, Vol. 67 No. 3, pp. 19–33.

Chhabra, D., Healy, R. and Ills, E. (2003), "Staged authenticity and heritage tourism", *Annals of Tourism Research*, Vol. 30 No. 3, pp. 702–719.

Cohen, A.P. (2002), "The best of British – with more to come", in Rapport, N. (Ed.), *British Subjects: An Anthropology of Britain*, Routledge, London.

Fowler, P. (1989), "Heritage: A post-modernist perspective", in Uzzell, D. (Ed.), *Heritage Interpretation, Vol. 1: The Natural and Built Environment*, Belhaven, London, pp. 57–63.

Freeman, R.E. (1984), *Strategic Management: A Stakeholder Approach*, Pitman, Boston, MA.

Gellner, E. (1983), *Nations and Nationalism*, Blackwell, Oxford.

George, M. (2004), "Heritage branding helps in global markets", *Marketing News*, Vol. 4 No. 13, p. 16.

Goulding, C. (2000), "The commodification of the past, postmodern pastiche, and the search for authentic experiences at contemporary heritage attractions", *European Journal of Marketing*, Vol. 34 No. 7, pp. 835–853.

Goulding, C. (2001), "Romancing the past: Heritage visiting and the nostalgic consumer", *Psychology and Marketing*, Vol. 18 No. 6, pp. 565–592.

Grant, R.M. (1991), "The resourced-based view of competitive advantage: Implications for strategy formulation", *California Management Review*, Vol. 33 No. 3, pp. 114–135.

Grönroos, C. (1997), "From marketing mix to relationship marketing-towards a paradigm shift in marketing", *Management Decision*, Vol. 35 No. 4, pp. 322–339.

Gu, H. and Ryan, C. (2008), "Place attachment, identity and community impacts of tourism: The case of a Beijing hutong", *Tourism Management*, Vol. 29 No. 4, pp. 637–647.

Hakala, U., Lätti, S. and Sandberg, B. (2011), "Operationalising brand heritage and cultural heritage", *Journal of Product & Brand Management*, Vol. 20 No. 6, pp. 447–456.

Halewood, C. and Hannam, K. (2001), "Viking heritage tourism: Authenticity and commodification", *Annals of Tourism Research*, Vol. 28 No. 3, pp. 565–580.

Hayden, I. (1987), *Symbol and Privilege*, University of Arizona Press, Tucson, AZ.

Heathcote, E. (2011), "How to build heritage", *The Financial Times*, Vol. 8–9, January, p. 8.

Henderson, J.C. (2002), "Conserving colonial heritage: Raffles Hotel in Singapore", *International Journal of Heritage Studies*, Vol. 7 No. 1, pp. 7–24.

Herbert, D.T. (Ed.) (1995), *Heritage, Tourism and Society*, Pinter, London.

Hobsbawm, E. (1983a), "Introduction: Inventing traditions", in Hobsbawn, E. and Ranger, T.E (Eds.), *The Invention of Tradition*, Cambridge University Press, Cambridge, pp. 1–14.

Hobsbawm, E. (1983b), "Mass-producing traditions: Europe, 1870–1914", in *The Invention of Tradition*, Cambridge University Press, Cambridge.

Holbrook, M. and Schindler, R. (2003), "Nostalgic bonding: Exploring the role of nostalgia in the consumption experience", *Journal of Consumer Behavior*, Vol. 3 No. 2, pp. 102–107.

Hudson, B.T. (2011), "Brand heritage and the renaissance of Cunard", *European Journal of Marketing*, Vol. 45 Nos. 9/10, pp. 1538–1556.

Kumar, K. (2003), *The Making of English National Identity*, Cambridge University Press, Cambridge.

Larcon, J.P. and Reitter, R. (1979), *Structures de Pouvoir et Identite´ de L'Enterprise*, Nathan, Paris.

Loveland, K.E., Smeesters, D. and Mandel, N. (2010), "Still preoccupied with 1995: The need to belong and preference for nostalgic products", *Journal of Consumer Research*, Vol. 37 No. 3, pp. 393–408.

Lowenthal, D. (1998), *The Heritage Crusade and the Spoils of History*, Cambridge University Press, Cambridge.

Macdonald, S. (2002), "On old things: The fetishization of past everyday life", in Rapport, N. (Ed.), *British Subjects: An Anthropology of Britain*, Routledge, London, pp. 31–48.

Macdonald, S. (2006), "Undesirable heritage: Fascist material culture and historical consciousness in Nuremberg", *International Journal of Heritage Studies*, Vol. 12 No. 1, pp. 9–28.

Misiura, S. (2006), *Heritage Marketing*, Butterworth-Heinemann, Oxford.

Morgan, R.M. and Hunt, S.D. (1994), "The commitment-trust theory of relationship marketing", *Journal of Marketing*, Vol. 58, July, pp. 20–38.

Nairn, T. (1997), *Faces of Nationalism: Janus Revisited*, Verso, London.

Otnes, C.C. and Maclaren, P. (2007), "The consumption of cultural heritage among a British Royal family brand tribe", in Kozinets, R., Cova, B. and Shanker, A. (Eds.), *Consumer Tribes: Theory, Practice, and Prospects*, Elsevier/Butterworth-Heinemann, London.

Palmer, C.A. (2005), "An ethnography of Englishness: Experiencing identity through tourism", *Annals of Tourism Research*, Vol. 32 No. 1, pp. 7–27.

Park, H.-Y. (2010), "Heritage tourism: Emotional journeys into nationhood", *Annals of Tourism Research*, Vol. 37 No. 1, pp. 116–135.

Parsons, T. (1960), *Structure and Process in Modern Society*, The Free Press, Glencoe, IL.

Powell, W. and DiMaggio, P. (1991), *The New Institutionalism in Organizational Analysis*, University of Chicago Press, Chicago, IL.

Prahalad, C.K. and Hamel, G. (1990), "The core competence of the corporation", *Harvard Business Review*, May/June, pp. 79–91.

Prentice, R. (1993), *Tourism and Heritage Attractions*, Routledge, London.

Rapport, N. (Ed.) (2002), *British Subjects: An Anthology of Britain*, Routledge, London.

Russell, B. (1957), *History of Western Philosophy*, George Allen and Unwin, London.

Sarup, M. (1996), *Identity, Culture and the Postmodern World*, Edinburgh University Press, Edinburgh.

Smith, A.D. (1986), *The Ethnic Origins of Nations*, Blackwell, Oxford.

Smith, A.D. (1991), *National Identity*, Penguin, London.

Smith, A.D. (1994), "The problem of national identity: Ancient, medieval and modern?", *Ethnic and Racial Studies*, Vol. 17 No. 3, pp. 375–399.

Tajfel, H. and Turner, J.C. (1985), "The social identity theory of intergroup behavior", in Worchel, S. and Austin, W.G. (Eds.), *Psychology of Intergroup Relations*, Vol. 2, Nelson-Hall, Chicago, IL, pp. 7–24.

Urde, M. (1994), "Brand orientation: A strategy for survival", *Journal of Consumer Marketing*, Vol. 11 No. 3, pp. 18–32.

Urde, M., Greyser, S.A. and Balmer, J.M.T. (2007), "Corporate brands with a heritage", *Journal of Brand Management*, Vol. 15 No. 1, pp. 4–19.

Urry, J. (1995), *Consuming Places*, Routledge, London.

Walton, J. (2009), "Prospects in tourism history: Evolution, state of play and future developments", *Tourism Management*, Vol. 30 No. 6, pp. 783–793.

Wiedmann, K.-P., Hennigs, N., Schmidt, S. and Wuestefeld, T. (2011a), "The importance of brand heritage as a key performance driver in marketing management", *Journal of Brand Management*, Vol. 19 No. 3, pp. 182–194.

Wiedmann, K.-P., Hennigs, N., Schmidt, S. and Wuestefeld, T. (2011b), "Drivers and outcomes of brand heritage: Consumers' perception of heritage brands in the automotive industry", *The Journal of Marketing Theory and Practice*, Vol. 9 No. 2, pp. 205–220.

Wilkinson, A. and Balmer, J.M.T. (1996), "Corporate and generic identities: Lessons from the Co-operative Bank", *International Journal of Bank Marketing*, Vol. 14 No. 4, pp. 23–35.

Wright, P. (1985), *On Living in an Old Country: The National Past in Contemporary Britain*, Verso, London.

Further reading

Balmer, J.M.T. and Greyser, S.A. (2006), "Corporate marketing: Integrating corporate identity, corporate branding, corporate communications, corporate image and corporate reputation", *European Journal of Marketing*, Vol. 40 Nos. 7/8, pp. 730–741.

Banerjee, S. (2008), "Strategic brand-culture fit: A conceptual framework for brand management", *Journal of Brand Management*, Vol. 15 No. 5, pp. 312–321.

Foster, W.M., Suddaby, R., Minkus, A. and Wiebe, E. (2011), "History as social memory assets: The example of Tim Hortons", *Management and Organizational History*, Vol. 6 No. 1, pp. 101–120.

Gellner, E. (1998), *Nationalism*, Phoenix, London.

Illia, L. and Balmer, J.M.T. (2012), "Corporate communication and corporate marketing: Their nature, history and similarity", *Corporate Communication: An International Journal*, Vol. 17 No. 4, pp. 415–433.

Moingeon, B. and Ramanantsoa, B. (1997), "Understanding corporate identity: The French school of thought", *European Journal of Marketing*, Vol. 31 Nos. 5/6, pp. 383–395.

O'Guinn, T.C. and Belk, R.W. (1989), "Heaven on earth: Consumption at Heritage Village, USA", *Journal of Consumer Research*, Vol. 16, September, pp. 227–238.

4

REPERTOIRES OF THE CORPORATE PAST

Explanation and framework: introducing an integrated and dynamic perspective

Mario Burghausen and John M. T. Balmer

Introduction

The purpose of this paper is to consolidate and expand our extant comprehension of the past within the corporate marketing and corporate communication domains so that the general discernment of the corporate past and its multifarious actualisations in the present can be of utility to scholars and practitioners alike.

This conceptual paper is informed by the extant literatures on the past not only within corporate marketing and communication but also the salient literature within the social sciences. Our aim, to reiterate and to expand, is to provide a more comprehensive and, arguably, nuanced, mapping of the aforementioned terrains. The contributions of our paper are as follows: first, consolidating previously discussed conceptualisations vis-à-vis corporate heritage by differentiating them into two main categories of concepts referring to an organisation's past; and second, expanding on the extant literature in this nascent field by introducing a sevenfold conceptual framework: the repertories of the corporate past.

First, we found the past to be increasingly debated as a substantive, symbolic, and communicative resource for corporate marketing and communication, especially within the nascent area of corporate heritage scholarship (Balmer *et al.*, 2006; Urde *et al.*, 2007; Balmer, 2011b, c, 2013). Drawing on previously published output – taking into account the four stages of conceptual development recently suggested by Balmer (2013) – we articulate a fifth stage of conceptual development in this paper. Our paper advances the extant literature by making a distinction between instrumental and foundational past-related corporate-level concepts.

Second, we expand on the aforementioned, partially drawing on earlier work by Balmer (2011c, 2013), by detailing seven foundational past-related corporate-level concepts of referring to an organisation's past in terms of core concepts of the past. All these different concepts have the potential to inform instrumental corporate marketing and communication concepts and policy, such as corporate heritage brands and corporate heritage identities (Balmer *et al.*, 2006; Urde *et al.*, 2007; Balmer, 2011b, c, 2013). A conceptual framework detailing and delineating the seven foundational corporate-level concepts relating to the past is introduced. We call the framework and the integrative and dynamic perspective it represents "Repertoires of the Corporate Past".

In relation to the above, we argue that such a differentiated and dynamic view of the past in corporate-level contexts carries scholarly and pragmatic relevance. As such, the suggested conceptual framework is a development and expansion of earlier work. It is also broadly scoped and tentative, as befits such a nascent area. This allows for future amendments in the light of new empirical insights and conceptual reflections.

Approach

We reviewed the extant literature addressing temporal issues specifically within the domain of corporate marketing (for a discussion of corporate marketing see, for instance, Balmer, 1998, 2011a; Balmer and Greyser, 2006), while taking the dedicated corporate communication perspective initially introduced by Balmer (1995) and later expanded by Balmer and colleagues (Balmer and Gray, 1999; Balmer, 2001; Balmer and Greyser, 2003; Illia and Balmer, 2012). In addition, we broadened our disciplinary vista and selectively marshalled contributions within the social sciences and humanities in general, which is an approach that is consistent with recent conceptual work in the area (e.g. Balmer, 2013; Hudson and Balmer, 2013).

This review of the literature is multidisciplinary in scope and, importantly, is informed by moderate constructionist convictions. In reflecting on the corporate marketing and communication literatures and those outside these areas, we detected sufficient conceptual overlap. This conceptual overlap between different concepts across disciplinary boundaries warrants the (at least metaphorical) importation of the most salient concepts into the domain of corporate marketing. Hence, in combining extant conceptualisations within corporate marketing – while explicitly drawing on the tentative conceptual discussions of Balmer (2011c, 2013) in particular – with the borrowed concepts from the wider discourses in the social sciences and humanities, we articulated and derived at the seven different but dynamically interrelated foundational concepts of referring to the past in corporate-level marketing and communication contexts.

Structure

Our paper is structured in the following way. First, we provide a short reflection of the territory vis-à-vis the corporate marketing and corporate communications perspectives; scrutinise the extant literature within the nascent area of corporate marketing from a total corporate communication perspective; note the conceptual and semantic ambiguity in the canon; and identify the lack of empirical work (vis-à-vis temporal modes) between the past, present, and future in corporate-level marketing contexts. Significantly, seven salient modes of the past are presented within a conceptual framework: detailing each regarded as foundational constructs. Finally, the theoretical and pragmatic implications of our differentiated view of the past and avenues for future scholarly work are outlined.

Initial reflections on the corporate marketing and communication perspective

Recently, corporate marketing (Balmer, 2009, 2011a) and corporate communications scholars (Illia and Balmer, 2012) and practitioners have begun to stress and explore the temporal dimension of organisations and its relevance for corporate marketing and communication. Illia and Balmer (2012) found that a degree of "temporal sensitivity" now – at least partially – characterises both domains (i.e. a growing number of scholars accord importance to research specifically concerned with the temporality and temporal relations of corporate-level phenomena and concepts). Balmer (2013) introduced the notion of total and corporate heritage communications, which he defined in terms of primary, secondary, tertiary, and legacy communications. Our review shows the past to be increasingly debated as a substantive, symbolic, and communicative resource for corporate marketing and communication.

For example, corporate marketing scholars identified a distinct category of corporate brand (corporate heritage brands) and articulated some key dimensions of the aforementioned (Balmer *et al.*, 2006), and the subsequent literature further explored the nature and significance of corporate heritage brands (Urde *et al.*, 2007; Balmer, 2011b; Hudson, 2011; Hudson and Balmer, 2013) and, more recently, corporate heritage identities (Balmer, 2011c, 2013; Burghausen and Balmer, 2014). Within the corporate communication canon, practitioners have variously stressed the differentiating potential of "heritage communication" (Bühler and Dürig, 2008), noted the importance of history and tradition for corporate brand communication (Herbrand and Röhrig, 2006), and identified "history marketing" as an integral part of corporate communication and corporate marketing strategy per se (Schug, 2003). Moreover, the efficacy of historical references for corporate-level marketing and corporate communication as expounded by marketing and communications scholars have been noted (Blombäck and Brunninge, 2009) in both general and in specific institutional contexts, with family businesses being notable (Blombäck and Brunninge, 2013) and corporate heritage in CSR communication contexts (Blombäck and Scandelius, 2013). All of the aforementioned developments indicate a heightened scholarly interest among corporate communications and corporate marketing scholars.

In addition, the academic attention accorded to nostalgia (Holbrook and Schindler, 2003; Muehling and Sprott, 2004; Loveland *et al.*, 2010), retro-branding (Brown, 2001; Brown *et al.*, 2003), or brand heritage (Wiedmann *et al.*, 2011a, b; Hakala *et al.*, 2011) is significant in consumer marketing and brand communication contexts. Also, hermeneutics and interpretative approaches (Hatch and Rubin, 2006) exemplify heightened cultural and linguistic sensitivities in consumer marketing (Moisander and Valtonen, 2006). Beyond corporate marketing and corporate communication there is growing recognition of the past's strategic and managerial pertinence and there have been frequent calls for a "historical turn" within business and management studies in general (Clark and Rowlinson, 2004; Booth and Rowlinson, 2006).

Mindful of the considerable advances made within the canon to date – including significant work which has laid some important foundations to the domain – the field is embryonic in character. To date comparatively few scholars have written in the territory from a dedicated corporate marketing communication perspective. Consequently, the efficacy in providing even greater depth, clarity, and consistency in regard to the ways in which organisations link with a past can be understood and utilised.

Distinguishing instrumental vs. foundational past-related corporate-level concepts

A growing number of scholarly as well as more popular business writers (Carson and Carson, 2003; Schug, 2003; Herbrand and Röhrig, 2006; Bühler and Dürig, 2008; Balmer, 2009, 2011b, c; Blombäck and Brunninge, 2009; Delahaye *et al.*, 2009) accord importance to the past's instrumental value and practical utility for corporate-level marketing and communication purposes. This development is exemplified, for instance, by the growing number of communication and brand consultancies now offering specialised services in regard to corporate history (Carson and Carson, 2003; Delahaye *et al.*, 2009). It is also indicated by the increasing number of corporate museums (Nissley and Casey, 2002; Hollenbeck *et al.*, 2008) or the widespread use of history-related sections on corporate websites (Delahaye *et al.*, 2009), to mention just a few. Thus, the corporate past is increasingly seen as an important strategic resource and an asset to be leveraged for the differentiation, authentication, and legitimation of corporate identities and corporate brands vis-à-vis internal and external stakeholders (Balmer, 2009; Blombäck and Brunninge, 2009) contributing to their identification with a corporate identity or a corporate brand (Feldenkirchen, 2006; Bühler and Dürig, 2008). Further, the notion of corporate heritage brands and identities has generated increased scholarly interest recently (Balmer *et al.*, 2006; Urde *et al.*, 2007; Balmer, 2011b, c; Hudson, 2011; Wiedmann *et al.*, 2011a, b; Hudson and Balmer, 2013).

However, these contributions – as one would expect with an embryonic area – largely focus on instrumental corporate marketing concepts such as corporate brands or activities such as corporate communication that draw on the past in different ways rather than the foundational concepts (e.g. history, heritage) that underpin them. Hence, there is already a well-established academic discourse concerning the instrumental impact and utility of the corporate past in general or corporate history and corporate heritage in particular. In this context, we also note the recent contributions differentiating various past-related instrumental marketing concepts such as (corporate) heritage brands and identities, retro brands, iconic brands, heritage marketing, history marketing, or heritage tourism (Urde *et al.*, 2007; Balmer, 2011c; Wiedmann *et al.*, 2011a, b).

In contrast, there is still an understandable muteness, owing to the nascent character of the field, in regard to the underlying foundational concepts' specificities and likely differences between them, which is partially attributable to a general dearth of academic work in regard to the temporal and historical dimension of corporate marketing and communication phenomena in general (Blombäck and Brunninge, 2009; Leitch and Davenport, 2011). Moreover, there appears to be a lack of appreciation for the differences between instrumental concepts and foundational basic concepts the former draw on. Hence, whilst broad categorisations of the past have been detailed recently (Balmer, 2011c, 2013), they remain underspecified in terms of their distinct roles as foundational concepts.

In view of the above, the past of an organisation is frequently being treated in the literature as an "unproblematic" aspect – whether as a contingency factor or as a constitutive element – receiving little further conceptual elaboration. Thus, there appears to be little evidence within the corporate marketing and communication literature yet (apart from the literatures specifically concerned with business history and the history of marketing, communication, etc.) that would indicate a heightened awareness for the ontological and epistemological limitations and ambiguities of the very notion of "the past" itself. Therefore, there is not yet a discourse amongst the majority of corporate marketing and communication scholars similar to the theoretical and conceptual discussions that have increased the historical and temporal sensitivities in other fields of the social sciences and humanities (Booth and Rowlinson, 2006). This state of the field is not surprising though, as the extant corporate marketing/corporate communications literature relating to the above is in its infancy and, to date, only a small number of scholars have written on the area. Moreover, corporate marketing/corporate communication scholarship is sensitive to the practical and instrumental concerns of an area/business phenomenon and then develops a body of theoretical work around a domain. In contrast, the applied and instrumental aspects of other management areas are quite often given little and sometimes no significance.

The above being noted, we found little conceptual clarity in terms of the differences between constructs such as history or heritage as dynamically interrelated but independent concepts, "independent" in the sense that they warrant further empirical and conceptual scrutiny. Similar observations have been made in regard to management research and the use of the past in organisations in general (Clark and Rowlinson, 2004; Booth and Rowlinson, 2006; Brunninge, 2009).

Nonetheless, it is noteworthy that Balmer (2011c, 2013) more recently has elaborated some past-related concepts in an attempt to define corporate heritage more clearly. These and other more recent contributions (e.g. Hudson and Balmer, 2013) indicate a growing awareness of the subtle differences between various manifestations of an organisation's temporality and historicity (i.e. temporal sensitivity).

More importantly for the purpose of this paper, these authors have looked beyond marketing, communication, and management for inspiration.

Further, Balmer (2013) recently identified four distinct stages in the conceptual development within this nascent field of corporate-level scholarship. Building on this we focus on the categorical distinctions between various concepts. To this end, our paper consolidates the extant literature by differentiating extant conceptualisations into instrumental and foundational past-related corporate-level concepts with a focus on the latter. We argue that our paper heralds a necessary fifth stage of conceptual development: consolidation and expansion. Table 4.1 details the different

TABLE 4.1 Towards repertories of the corporate past, development stages in the literature

Developmental stage of concepts	Key conceptual contribution	Key article
Stage 1: recognition	Reflection on the strategic relevance of the past and identification of institutional heritage as an organisational/corporate phenomenon based on case-study work on monarchies as corporate brands	Balmer et al. (2006)
Stage 2: introduction	Development of corporate heritage brands and brands with a heritage as distinct branding types; development of instrumental framework for their identification and management; differentiation between heritage and history	Urde et al. (2007)
Stage 3: synthesis	Identification of different aspects of the past as a corporate marketing and communication phenomenon; introducing the umbrella concept of historical references and developing propositions	Blombäck and Brunninge (2009)
Stage 4: differentiation	Elaboration of corporate heritage and its delineation from other past-related corporate-level constructs; introduction of corporate heritage identities as distinct identity type	Balmer (2011c)
Stage 5: consolidation and expansion	Identification of different perspectives and developmental stages re the relevance of the past within corporate marketing and communication; differentiation between instrumental and foundational past-related corporate-level concepts; integration of latter within a comprehensive dynamic framework	This paper

stages as suggested by Balmer (2013) by summarising the conceptual contributions of key works exemplifying each stage and how this paper contributes to its further development (the fifth stage).

Repertoires of the corporate past perspective: Seven modes of referring to the past

As with the above mentioned more recent articles (Balmer, 2013; Hudson and Balmer, 2013), we marshal insights from the wider social sciences and humanities literatures.

Such an approach has the potential to expand on our knowledge and understanding of these constructs. Moreover, it reinforces extant work and thus provides an even stronger foundation on which to further advance conceptual and theoretical developments. In addition, it can aid future conceptual development, critical scholarly discourse, and empirical enquiry. With this general caveat in mind, our approach partially utilises as a point of departure the initial categorisations and explanations of past-related corporate-level constructs advanced by Balmer (2011c) (see Table 4.2).

From our reading of the extant literature we identified seven salient modes of referring to the past and we transposed them into seven corporate-level concepts:

TABLE 4.2 Balmer's (2011c, p. 1383) tentative categorisation of past-related corporate-level concepts

Corporate-level concepts	Succinct explanation	Emphasis
Tradition	"Maintaining the ceremonies of the past"	Ritual
Custom	"Maintaining the activities of the past"	Identity
Nostalgia	"Seeking the happiness of the past"	Emotional
Melancholia	"Seeking the sadness of the past"	Emotional
Iconic branding	"Deriving meaning from culturally dominant brands from the past"	Cultural
Retro branding	"Linking with a particular period of the past"	Historical
Heritage marketing	"Marketing the past"	Epochal
Tourism marketing	"Marketing the places of the past"	Locality
Corporate heritage identities	"Going forwards with a corporate identity's meaningful past"	Identity continuance
Corporate heritage brands	"Going forwards with a brand's meaningful past"	Brand guarantee/ continuance

corporate past, corporate memory, corporate history, corporate tradition, corporate nostalgia, corporate provenance, and corporate heritage. All concepts are conceived as dynamically linked social categories that are constantly constructed and recon-structed in the light of contemporary purposes and concerns in the present.

Within the framework the corporate past represents the most basic category that underpins all the other concepts. Corporate memory constitutes a kind of conceptual "bridge" between the corporate past as such and three interrelated pri-mary modes (in instrumental terms) of referring to the past, which are corporate history, corporate tradition, and corporate heritage. The latter concept (corporate heritage) is distinct from all the other concepts in terms of its temporal orientation by being transtemporal (concurrently retrospective and prospective) while the other modes are all retrospective in orientation. Finally, corporate nostalgia and corporate provenance represent secondary modes that are more or less relevant for the oth-ers. Table 4.3 summarises the different concepts. The table provides a succinct (i.e. adage-like), conceptual (i.e. indicating the main type of reference to the past) and pragmatic (i.e. action word describing the primary activity involved) explanation for each foundational concept. In addition, the table indicates the aforementioned main temporal orientation of the concepts (column: "temporal focus" in the table) and categorises their role within the repertoires framework (column: "conceptual

TABLE 4.3 The repertoires of the corporate past, foundational past-related corporate-level concepts

Foundational concept	Succinct explanation	Conceptual explanation	Pragmatic explanation	Temporal focus	Conceptual category
Corporate past	"All that ever happened"	Discovered, rediscovered and invented past	Resourcing	Retrospective	Base
Corporate memory	"All that is known (accessible)"	Remembered and forgotten past	Knowing	Retrospective	Bridge
Corporate history	"All that is told"	Narrated and storied past	Telling	Retrospective	Primary
Corporate tradition	"All that is done"	Enacted and embodied past	Doing	Retrospective	Primary
Corporate nostalgia	"All that is felt"	Emotive past	Feeling	Retrospective	Secondary
Corporate provenance	"All that is rooted"	Situated past	Belonging	Retrospective	Secondary
Corporate heritage	"All that is (still) relevant"	Appropriated and valorised past	"Relevancing" (making relevant)	Retrospective and prospective	Primary

category" in the table). The framework itself is introduced after our discussion of each foundational concept.

Corporate past

The corporate past in our framework refers to "all that ever happened" during the existence of a company, following heritage scholars Graham *et al.* (2000) with this rather broad definition of "the past". As such, it refers to all past events (including social actors and contextual circumstances involved) that had a direct bearing on the company or vice versa.

Yet, due to the past's absence in the present (i.e. we cannot directly relive or witness past events), its ontological status is uncertain (see Koselleck, 2002; Ricoeur, 2006; White, 2010) and its epistemological accessibility is limited to residual traces and sources (Megill, 2007) in material and non-material form (with traces referring to all past remains and sources indicating already pre-interpreted records or documents about a company's past) such as corporate buildings, documents, objects, traditions, orally transmitted anecdotes, and so on (Megill, 2007). However, past remains do not constitute the past per se (i.e. in ontological terms) nor do they inherently ascertain any epistemological veracity in terms of a unitary version of the past, yet they provide the only available basis for our comprehension and interpretation of an organisation's past in the present, albeit a contestable and often multiple one (Megill, 2007) depending on how and by whom those traces and sources are appropriated in the present (the company, customer groups, local communities, NGOs, etc.).

This limitation that poses a potential problem in academic historical research, we argue, provides pragmatic flexibility in the corporate domain. In particular, we argue that the different modes of representing the corporate past presented here may potentially draw on a wider historical context; a context where no or only scant direct residual traces of a company's involvement can be found. It provides the opportunity – within not yet specified limits – to temporally "reposition" the company or to "adopt" a past as corporate past that is more fiction than fact but has symbolic relevance for corporate-level marketing and communication in the present nonetheless. Therefore, the corporate past might be discovered or rediscovered as much as it may be an adopted past or an invention (see Hobsbawm and Ranger, 1983).

As a cautious reminder, this epistemological limitation and flexibility also entails potential for contestation, cynicism, and conflict in a multi-stakeholder environment in regard to the veracity, authenticity, or ownership of a particular version of the corporate past. For example, German companies were publicly forced to acknowledge and come to terms with their complicity in the Nazi crimes, an episode of their past most of them had preferred previously to conveniently "forget", with serious repercussions for corporate reputation, culture, and identity (see Booth *et al.*, 2007). It has been argued that this development has partially contributed to the heightened awareness of the past's corporate marketing and communication relevance amongst practitioners in Germany (Schug, 2003).

The preceding discussion leads to the next concept that provides a conceptual bridge between the corporate past per se and the other mode of referring to the past, that of corporate memory.

Corporate memory

Given the preceding discussion and drawing on the interdisciplinary field of cultural and collective memory studies (see Misztal, 2003; Erll, 2010; Olick *et al.*, 2011), corporate memory is defined as the remembered and forgotten past of a company representing all forms of present knowledge (understanding and meaning)[1] about an organisation's past that is constructed and reconstructed by processes and practices of remembering and forgetting at the individual, collective, and institutional level (it carries the notion of memory as "all that is known" in the present about a company's past).

As such, corporate memory is predicated on the discovered, rediscovered, invented, or adopted residual traces and sources that constitute the accessible corporate past (see previous section), which are meaningfully interpreted and reinterpreted in the present by successive generations of stakeholders inside and outside the organisation. However, these interpretations only become corporate memory in so far as they are manifested in cognitive, social, or cultural form. Consequently, corporate memories are socially constituted forms of an individually embodied corporate past (e.g. of an employee or the CEO) as well as refer to collectively shared, communicated, and enacted corporate pasts (e.g. oral stories and anecdotes, cognitive and habitual dispositions shared by organisational members or certain groups inside and outside the organisation such as consumer communities). Further, corporate memories manifest also as disembodied cultural forms of memory such as corporate documents, buildings, ceremonies, or other cultural artifacts and practices that act as mnemonic devices for the former (Coser in Halbwachs, 1992; Assmann, 2010). Yet, not all residual traces and sources of the past are deliberately chosen (i.e. "remembered") and some might willingly or inadvertently be discarded (i.e. "forgotten") in the light of changing demands, conditions, or interests in the present (see Connerton, 1989, 2009). For example, Nissley and Casey (2002) have shown that corporate museums represent mnemonic sites for active remembering as well as forgetting that are strategically deployed in order to remember a particular version of the past that supports and facilitates the current identity of an organisation.

In light of the above, corporate memory represents a broad and multifarious category, which other forms of referring to an organisation's past, such as corporate history, corporate tradition, corporate nostalgia, corporate provenance, and corporate heritage, draw on. Concurrently, these different modes of reference to the past can be understood as particular forms of corporate memory as well. Thus, corporate memory represents not only the aforementioned conceptual bridge but also a kind of perceptual "filter" and discursive "scaffolding" guiding the conceptual transition between the corporate past per se (as "all that ever happened") and the different modes of referencing that past to be discussed next.

Corporate history

Corporate history is defined as the narrated and storied past or "all that is told" about an organisation's past. Thus, a corporate history provides an interpreted account of the historical trajectory and development of an organisation, representing an attempt in the present to explain, celebrate, justify, or otherwise make sense of changes over time (see Ricoeur, 2006; White, 2010).

Following the argument recently advanced by Delahaye *et al.* (2009), corporate history is understood as a particular genre or discourse that tells the past in a specific way predicated on present corporate concerns and purposes that is not confined to textual representations exhibiting its own set of formal (e.g. type of media used, the combination of textual and audio-visual materials, authorship) and thematic (e.g. type and content of narrative, characters and plotline used) features and instrumental purposes (Delahaye *et al.*, 2009). Corporate history understood as a particular narrative genre is, as such, always open to revision and reinterpretation in the light of changing circumstances, purposes, and interests in the present and varies in regard to its epistemological status. For instance, corporate histories may be written based on academic research by a business historian but might also represent mere corporate eulogies drafted by a PR agency. Either way, as organisations are increasingly understood as "storytelling organisations" (Boje, 1995; Christensen and Cheney, 2000) in regard to identity construction and stakeholder identification, corporate histories understood as the narrated and storied past can be seen as an important element of identity and identification in corporate-level marketing and communication contexts.

This understanding of corporate history is consistent with extant discussions of the past's relevance while concurrently expanding it beyond the earlier mentioned limits of a mere instrumental conceptual understanding. However, corporate history represents only one particular form of referring to the past. Hence, another important concept that captures a different dimension is discussed next: corporate tradition.

Corporate tradition

Corporate tradition refers to the enacted and embodied past or "all that is done" in reference to an organisation's past (e.g. corporate celebrations, rituals, annual commemorations). Hence, corporate traditions represent all cultural practices that are predicated on a symbolic and/or substantial link to a company's past (actual or invented) and carries the notion of intergenerational exchange (Shils, 1981) between past, present, and future that is also central to the conceptualisation of corporate heritage as will be shown shortly.

Within the canon, as so often happens, there are some differences. For example, it is possible to categorise customs in terms of being flexible and changing and traditions as fixed and invariable (cf. Balmer, 2011c), but this is dependent on how they are defined, and thus different perspectives can emerge and different definitions be advanced (Giddens, 1999; see Misztal, 2003). The view is advanced here that corporate traditions are primarily legitimated by their substantive and/ or symbolic link with an actual or invented past while customs are largely perpetuated on pragmatic grounds (Hobsbawm, 1983). However, corporate traditions can be more or less customary in terms of their pragmatic relevance as well (Giddens, 1999; see Misztal, 2003). Thus, for the sake of expediency (and contrary to the well-known differentiation advanced by Hobsbawm, 1983), the concept of custom is incorporated within the category of corporate tradition but we are mindful and highly sensitive of the fact that others may wish to accord custom an important and distinct status.

Further, corporate traditions are not necessarily confined to the internal realm of a company but may also be enacted by external stakeholders (e.g. company-specific rituals at annual general meetings, company-sponsored festivals or activities, activities of brand communities). What they have in common is their reference to the company and its past as a source of legitimacy and identity for the company itself or the collective and individual identities of different stakeholders derived from it. In a similar vein, Balmer (2011b) recently argued that in the context of corporate-level marketing corporate traditions "can accord an institution a degree of distinctiveness, differentiation, and attraction" (Balmer, 2011b, p. 1384).

Corporate nostalgia

Corporate nostalgia is defined as "all that is felt" in reference to a company's past relative to the present representing a particular collectively shared, usually positively charged, emotional mentality (manifested in emotional and affective individual moods) amongst internal (e.g. organisational nostalgia) or external stakeholders (e.g. customer nostalgia) towards an organisation's past predicated on socio-cultural or autobiographical conditions in the present; a kind of affective retrospection in the present – an emotive past so to speak – that can provide a sense of belonging and emotional attachment with an organisation based on its past rather than its contemporary status.

Again, for the sake of expediency, we have not included melancholia – as identified by Balmer (2011c) – as a distinct construct in the repertoires of the corporate past perspective. For Balmer (2011c), nostalgia is of pertinence vis-à-vis "the happiness of the past" whereas melancholia is redolent of the "sadness of the past". However, the perspective advanced in this paper suggests that nostalgia – while characterising the emotive relevance of the past per se – does not qualify the directional motivation or emotional significance of that "longing" for the past as such, which can be more or less melancholic in nature but still be preferred over the present.

Further, corporate nostalgia can overlap with different modes of referring to the past as well that are often, especially in corporate marketing and communication contexts, positively charged. However, corporate nostalgia is not a necessary condition for a positively narrated corporate history or time-honoured corporate traditions as such. Thus, it is to some degree a secondary contingent mode in the context of the other forms of referencing the corporate past introduced here. Within the marketing and management canons, there are many significant articles on the domain (e.g. Gabriel, 1993; Goulding, 2001; Brown and Humphreys, 2002; Holbrook and Schindler, 2003). The broader social sciences literature is also significant (e.g. Davis, 1977; Strangleman, 1999; Pickering and Keightley, 2006). Our understanding advanced here draws on both literatures.

Corporate provenance

Corporate provenance refers to the historical origins of an organisation that represent a kind of spatio-temporally and culturally situated past. It is "all that is rooted" in a particular version of the past that is relevant for contemporary purposes and concerns. Corporate provenance conflates temporal beginnings with cultural belonging, thus representing a recurrent theme in regard to identity and identification in corporate-level marketing contexts exemplified by the importance accorded to the corporate founder or the founding stages of an organisation (Blombäck and Brunninge, 2009).

Generally, the concept is predicated on the significance accorded to origins and primordial roots (Lowenthal, 1985, 1998) within society in general that reflects the "special mnemonic status of beginnings" (Zerubavel, 2004, p. 101) and the importance of "origin myths" and "founding ancestors" for the constitution and legitimation of collective identities (Zerubavel, 2004). Our understanding of corporate provenance is partially informed by and relates to the corporate marketing and marketing literature on the importance of (corporate) brand origin (e.g. Thakor and Kohli, 1996; Wilson, 2005; Simms and Trott, 2006; Balmer, 2011c).

It is another secondary mode of referencing the past (similar to corporate nostalgia) that may inform (or is informed by) corporate history, corporate tradition, and collective memories as much as corporate heritage derived from a company's origins "in a time and in a place".

Corporate heritage

Arguably, drawing on the interdisciplinary field of heritage studies (see Lowenthal, 1998; Graham et al., 2000; Howard, 2003; Smith, 2006; Bendix, 2009), corporate heritage as introduced and explicated within the canon (Balmer et al., 2006; Balmer, 2009, 2011b, c, 2013) is defined as all the traits and aspects of an organisation that link its past, present, and future in a meaningful and relevant way. Thus, it refers to some aspect of an organisation's past that is still deemed by current internal and/or external stakeholders to be relevant and meaningful for contemporary concerns and purposes but concurrently perceived as worth to be maintained and nurtured for future generations; it is the selectively appropriated and valorised past of a company or "all that is (still) relevant" in the light of contemporary concerns and purposes.

What distinguishes corporate heritage from the other modes of referencing the past is that the latter are all retrospective in nature, despite the important notion of being similarly constituted in the light of present concerns. Corporate heritage instead is appropriated and valorised not only because of its retrospective link between past and present (as an inherited legacy) but concurrently also because it is perceived as relevant for future generations whoever they may be (as a bequeathed legacy). Although, corporate traditions, for instance, are as well predicated on the notion of intergenerational exchange, their symbolic relevance and legitimacy in the present is solely based on their reference to the past. Corporate heritage, however, derives its legitimacy and relevance for the present retrospectively from its link with the past but at the same time from its prospective link to the future.

Hence, corporate heritage is transtemporal (Balmer *et al.*, 2006; Urde *et al.*, 2007; Balmer, 2011c, 2013) in that it refers to the three organisational time frames of past, present, and future at once and as such constitutes a different conceptual category altogether. Corporate heritage may draw on the other forms of referencing the past (e.g. corporate history or traditions being "ennobled" as heritage, see Bendix, 2009), but it expands their temporal reach and relevance by valuing the past not only for its contribution to the present but also for its role in the present as well as its potential role for the future of an organisation. Consequently, corporate heritage is constantly imbued with new value (i.e. valorised). Further, due to its transtemporal qualities, the notion of corporate heritage is closely associated with questions of corporate identity and identification for which actual or perceived temporal continuity are a fundamental conceptual building block in general (Albert and Whetten, 1985; see Balmer and Greyser, 2003).

Having discussed the different basic concepts of referencing the corporate past, Figure 4.1 schematically depicts and synthesises the dynamic interrelationships between them (this is represented by the double arrows between the concepts in

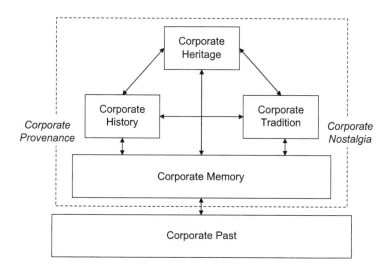

FIGURE 4.1 The repertoires of the corporate past, schematic framework

Figure 4.1). Thus, the corporate past represents the broadest and most basic concept that provides the traces and sources that are (and need to be) appropriated in one way or another in order to be of relevance for corporate marketing and communication (depicted at the bottom of Figure 4.1 as the "base" for the other concepts). Corporate memory instead functions as a kind of "filter" and as a conceptual "bridge" in between the corporate past per se and the three interlinked primary ways in which the corporate past can be articulated for corporate marketing and communication purposes: as corporate history, as corporate tradition, and as corporate heritage.

While all three modes draw on corporate memories – which make the corporate past as such accessible – corporate history, corporate tradition, and corporate heritage are also mutually linked in a dynamic way in that they potentially reinforce or contradict each other. Corporate heritage has the additional advantage, in instrumental terms, of being at once not only retrospective (i.e. past–present link) but also prospective, linking past, present, and future in a meaningful way.

The remaining two concepts of corporate nostalgia and corporate provenance are secondary or contingent modes that more or less underpin the others (indicated by the dotted frame in Figure 4.1). As such, corporate memories and their translations into corporate history, corporate tradition, or corporate heritage can have varying degrees of emotive import (i.e. corporate nostalgia) and can vary in regard to their temporal situatedness in cultural and spatial terms (i.e. corporate provenance).

The transition between the different concepts is characterised by interpretative processes (again indicated by the double arrows in Figure 4.1) at the individual and collective level. These multiple interpretations provide companies with a strategic opportunity to reinterpret aspects of their past in the light of contemporary concerns and purposes but potentially also impose strategic constraints in regard to the various interpretations amongst internal and external stakeholders that may lead to conflicting accounts of the corporate past. This is irrespective of whether the corporate past is constituted as corporate memory at large or in more specific terms as corporate history, as corporate tradition, or indeed as corporate heritage. Thus, we argue that a better understanding of these phenomena – individually and in conjunction – is conceptually and instrumentally warranted.

Theoretical contribution

This paper makes several theoretical contributions to the nascent area of corporate-level marketing from a dedicated total corporate communication perspective, particularly in regard to its transtemporal orientation:

(1) Advances extant work which detailed the repertoire of concepts and noted their instrumental significance by further highlighting their foundational significance.
(2) Extends our comprehension of the multiple ways in which an organisation's past can be understood and scrutinised.

(3) Provides greater conceptual clarity, consistency, and depth vis-à-vis the temporal dimensions of organisations in corporate marketing/communications contexts purposes.

(4) Introduces enhanced conceptual lenses that highlight different aspects in which the past can be relevant in corporate marketing/communications purposes.

(5) Details, confirms, and advances the nature of corporate heritage as a foundational concept by virtue of its transtemporal orientation as indicated by Balmer *et al.* (2006), Urde *et al.* (2007), and Balmer (2011c, 2013) by clearly delineating it from the other solely retrospectively orientated foundational corporate-level constructs referring to an organisation's past.

Practical implications

The repertories of the corporate past framework introduced here have potential practical relevance for practitioners in the following ways:

(1) details how a company's past can be relevant to stakeholders;

(2) explains the different ways in which the past can be communicated to them;

(3) explicates how the past is not a mere factual given but can be malleable for strategic and communication purposes;

(4) reveals the past represents a resource that can variously be discovered and rediscovered but also invented and appropriated;

(5) shows how the past can be differentiated in terms of how it is known, told, performed, felt, and made relevant for and by stakeholders;

(6) presents numerous instrumental opportunities, since an organisation's past manifests in different forms;

(7) sensitises managers in terms of the emotive power of historical references such as nostalgia while corporate provenance indicates the important role of belonging;

(8) reveals the need for managers to go beyond narrated histories and written documents when trying to uncover and appropriate the corporate past and that they should marshal oral stories and anecdotes as much as rituals, customs, etc.; and

(9) provides a concise and succinct framework that can guide corporate marketing/communication practice and consultancy work.

Future research

In terms of future research, the repertories of the corporate past perspective, which substantially expands and elaborates extant conceptual insights (e.g. Balmer, 2011c, 2013), can be further developed. The nascent character of the corporate heritage domain means that the potential for theoretical, conceptual, and instrumental advances on the territory is vast. Based on our framework of foundational concepts, different aspects and dimensions of an organisation's temporality and historicity can be more fully highlighted and scrutinised within the corporate marketing and corporate communications domains.

Note

1   Please note that this notion of "knowledge" does not make any statement about its epistemological status, hence incorporates a notion of belief as well. This is consistent with the broad conception of history as the narrated past that also includes the notion of myths, legends, or sagas.

References

Albert, S. and Whetten, D.A. (1985), "Organizational identity", *Research in Organizational Behavior*, Vol. 7, pp. 263–295.

Assmann, J. (2010), "Communicative and cultural memory", in Erll, A. and Nünning, A. (Eds.), *A Companion to Cultural Memory Studies: An International and Interdisciplinary Handbook*, de Gruyter, Berlin, pp. 109–118.

Balmer, J.M.T. (1995), "Corporate branding and connoisseurship", *Journal of General Management*, Vol. 21 No. 1, pp. 24–46.

Balmer, J.M.T. (1998), "Corporate identity and the advent of corporate marketing", *Journal of Marketing Management*, Vol. 14 No. 8, pp. 963–996.

Balmer, J.M.T. (2001), "Corporate identity, corporate branding and corporate marketing: Seeing through the fog", *European Journal of Marketing*, Vol. 35 Nos. 3/4, pp. 248–291.

Balmer, J.M.T. (2009), "Corporate marketing: Apocalypse, advent and epiphany", *Management Decision*, Vol. 47 No. 4, pp. 544–572.

Balmer, J.M.T. (2011a), "Corporate marketing myopia and the inexorable rise of a corporate marketing logic: Perspectives from identity-based views of the firm", *European Journal of Marketing*, Vol. 45 Nos. 9/10, pp. 1329–1352.

Balmer, J.M.T. (2011b), "Corporate heritage brands and the precepts of corporate heritage brand management: Insights from the British Monarchy on the eve of the royal wedding of Prince William (April 2011) and Queen Elizabeth II's Diamond Jubilee (1952–2012)", *Journal of Brand Management*, Vol. 18 No. 8, pp. 517–544.

Balmer, J.M.T. (2011c), "Corporate heritage identities, corporate heritage brands and the multiple heritage identities of the British Monarchy", *European Journal of Marketing*, Vol. 45 Nos. 9/10, pp. 1380–1398.

Balmer, J.M.T. (2013), "Corporate heritage, corporate heritage marketing, and total corporate heritage communications: What are they? What of them?", *Corporate Communications: An International Journal*, Vol. 18 No. 3, pp. 290–326.

Balmer, J.M.T. and Gray, E.R. (1999), "Corporate identity and corporate communications: Creating a competitive advantage", *Corporate Communications: An International Journal*, Vol. 4 No. 4, pp. 171–176.

Balmer, J.M.T. and Greyser, S.A. (Eds.) (2003), *Revealing the Corporation: Perspectives on Identity, Image, Reputation, Corporate Branding, and Corporate-Level Marketing: An Anthology*, Routledge, London.

Balmer, J.M.T. and Greyser, S.A. (2006), "Corporate marketing: Integrating corporate identity, corporate branding, corporate communications, corporate image and corporate reputation", *European Journal of Marketing*, Vol. 40 Nos. 7/8, pp. 730–741.

Balmer, J.M.T., Greyser, S.A. and Urde, M. (2006), "The crown as a corporate brand: Insights from monarchies", *Journal of Brand Management*, Vol. 14 Nos. 1/2, pp. 137–161.

Bendix, R. (2009), "Heritage between economy and politics: An assessment from the perspective of cultural anthropology", in Smith, L. and Akagawa, N. (Eds.), *Intangible Heritage*, Routledge, London, pp. 253–269.

Blombäck, A. and Brunninge, O. (2009), "Corporate identity manifested through historical references", *Corporate Communications: An International Journal*, Vol. 14 No. 4, pp. 404–419.

Blombäck, A. and Brunninge, O. (2013), "The dual opening to brand heritage in family businesses", *Corporate Communications: An International Journal*, Vol. 18 No. 3, pp. 327–346.

Blombäck, A. and Scandelius, C. (2013), "Corporate heritage in CSR communication: A means to responsible brand image?", *Corporate Communications: An International Journal*, Vol. 18 No. 3, pp. 362–382.

Boje, D.M. (1995), "Stories of the storytelling organization: A postmodern analysis of Disney as 'Tamara-Land'", *Academy of Management Journal*, Vol. 38 No. 4, pp. 997–1035.

Booth, C., Clark, P., Delahaye, A., Procter, S. and Rowlinson, M. (2007), "Accounting for the dark side of corporate history: Organizational culture perspectives and the Bertelsmann case", *Critical Perspectives on Accounting*, Vol. 18 No. 6, pp. 625–644.

Booth, C. and Rowlinson, M. (2006), "Management and organizational history: Prospects", *Management & Organizational History*, Vol. 1 No. 1, pp. 5–30.

Brown, A.D. and Humphreys, M. (2002), "Nostalgia and the narrativization of identity: A Turkish case study", *British Journal of Management*, Vol. 13 No. 2, pp. 141–159.

Brown, S. (2001), "The retromarketing revolution. l'imagination au pouvoir", *International Journal of Management Reviews*, Vol. 3 No. 4, pp. 303–320.

Brown, S., Kozinets, R.V. and Sherry, J.F. (2003), "Teaching old brands new tricks: Retro branding and the revival of brand meaning", *Journal of Marketing*, Vol. 67 No. 3, pp. 19–33.

Brunninge, O. (2009), "Using history in organisations: How managers make purposeful reference to history in strategy processes", *Journal of Organizational Change Management*, Vol. 22 No. 1, pp. 8–26.

Bühler, H. and Dürig, U.-M. (Eds.) (2008), *Tradition kommunizieren: Das Handbuch der Heritage Communication*, Frankfurter Allgemeine Buch, Frankfurt am Main.

Burghausen, M. and Balmer, J.M. (2014), "Corporate heritage identity management and the multi-modal implementation of a corporate heritage identity", *Journal of Business Research*, Vol. 67 No. 11, pp. 2311–2323.

Carson, P.P. and Carson, K.D. (2003), "An exploration of the importance of history to managers: The meaningful, manipulative, and memorable uses of milestones", *Organizational Dynamics*, Vol. 32 No. 3, pp. 286–308.

Christensen, L.T. and Cheney, G. (2000), "Self-absorption and self-seduction in the corporate identity game", in Schultz, M., Hatch, M.J. and Larsen, M.H. (Eds.), *The Expressive Organization: Linking Identity, Reputation, and the Corporate Brand*, Oxford University Press, Oxford, pp. 246–270.

Clark, P. and Rowlinson, M. (2004), "The treatment of history in organisation studies: Towards an 'historic turn'?", *Business History*, Vol. 46 No. 3, pp. 331–352.

Connerton, P. (1989), *How Societies Remember*, Cambridge University Press, Cambridge.

Connerton, P. (2009), *How Modernity Forgets*, Cambridge University Press, Cambridge.

Davis, F. (1977), "Nostalgia, identity and the current nostalgia wave", *Journal of Popular Culture*, Vol. 11 No. 2, pp. 414–424.

Delahaye, A., Booth, C., Clark, P., Procter, S. and Rowlinson, M. (2009), "The genre of corporate history", *Journal of Organizational Change Management*, Vol. 22 No. 1, pp. 27–48.

Erll, A. (2010), "Cultural memory studies: An introduction", in Erll, A. and Nünning, A. (Eds.), *A Companion to Cultural Memory Studies: An International and Interdisciplinary Handbook*, de Gruyter, Berlin, pp. 1–15.

Feldenkirchen, W. (2006), "Kontinuität und Wandel. Geschichte als Element der Marken- und Unternehmensidentität der Siemens AG", in Herbrand, N.O. and Röhrig, S. (Eds.), *Die Bedeutung der Tradition für die Markenkommunikation*, Edition Neues Fachwissen, Stuttgart, pp. 265–285.

Gabriel, Y. (1993), "Organizational nostalgia: Reflections on 'the golden age'", in Fineman, S. (Ed.), *Emotion in Organizations*, SAGE, London, pp. 118–141.

Giddens, A. (1999), "Reith lectures 1999: Runaway world, Lecture 3 Tradition", *Reith Lectures*, Vol. 3, available at: www.bbc.co.uk/radio4/reith1999/lecture3.shtml (accessed 20 March 2013).

Goulding, C. (2001), "Romancing the past: Heritage visiting and the nostalgic consumer", *Psychology and Marketing*, Vol. 18 No. 6, pp. 565–592.

Graham, B.J., Ashworth, G.J. and Tunbridge, J.E. (2000), *A Geography of Heritage: Power, Culture, and Economy*, Arnold, London.

Hakala, U., Lätti, S. and Sandberg, B. (2011), "Operationalising brand heritage and cultural heritage", *Journal of Product & Brand Management*, Vol. 20 No. 6, pp. 447–456.

Halbwachs, M. (1992), "On collective memory", in *The Heritage of Sociology*, (Trans and Edited by Lewis A. Coser), University of Chicago Press, Chicago.

Hatch, M.J. and Rubin, J. (2006), "The hermeneutics of branding", *Journal of Brand Management*, Vol. 14 Nos. 1/2, pp. 40–59.

Herbrand, N.O. and Röhrig, S. (Eds.) (2006), *Die Bedeutung der Tradition für die Markenkommunikation*, Edition Neues Fachwissen, Stuttgart.

Hobsbawm, E.J. (1983), "Introduction: Inventing tradition", in Hobsbawm, E.J. and Ranger, T.O. (Eds.), *The Invention of Tradition*, Canto ed., Cambridge University Press, Cambridge, pp. 1–14.

Hobsbawm, E.J. and Ranger, T.O. (Eds.) (1983), *The Invention of Tradition*, Canto ed., Cambridge University Press, Cambridge.

Holbrook, M.B. and Schindler, R.M. (2003), "Nostalgic bonding: Exploring the role of nostalgia in the consumption experience", *Journal of Consumer Behaviour*, Vol. 3 No. 2, pp. 107–127.

Hollenbeck, C.R., Peters, C. and Zinkhan, G.M. (2008), "Retail spectacles and brand meaning: Insights from a brand museum case study", *Journal of Retailing*, Vol. 84 No. 3, pp. 334–353.

Howard, P. (2003), *Heritage: Management, Interpretation, Identity*, Continuum, London.

Hudson, B.T. (2011), "Brand heritage and the renaissance of Cunard", *European Journal of Marketing*, Vol. 45 Nos. 9/10, pp. 1538–1556.

Hudson, B.T. and Balmer, J.M.T. (2013), "Corporate heritage brands: Mead's theory of the past", *Corporate Communications: An International Journal*, Vol. 18 No. 3, pp. 347–361.

Illia, L. and Balmer, J.M.T. (2012), "Corporate communication and corporate marketing: Their nature, histories, differences and similarities", *Corporate Communications: An International Journal*, Vol. 17 No. 4, pp. 415–433.

Koselleck, R. (2002), *The Practice of Conceptual History: Timing History, Spacing Concepts*, (Trans by Todd Samuel Presner, with others), Stanford University Press, Stanford, CA.

Leitch, S. and Davenport, S. (2011), "Corporate identity as an enabler and constraint on the pursuit of corporate objectives", *European Journal of Marketing*, Vol. 45 Nos. 9/10, pp. 1501–1520.

Loveland, K.E., Smeesters, D. and Mandel, N. (2010), "Still preoccupied with 1995: The need to belong and preference for nostalgic products", *Journal of Consumer Research*, Vol. 37 No. 3, pp. 393–408.

Lowenthal, D. (1985), *The Past Is a Foreign Country*, Cambridge University Press, Cambridge.

Lowenthal, D. (1998), *The Heritage Crusade and the Spoils of History*, Cambridge University Press, Cambridge.

Megill, A. (2007), *Historical Knowledge, Historical Error: A Contemporary Guide to Practice*, (Contributions by Steven Shepard and Phillip Honenberger), University of Chicago Press, Chicago, IL.

Misztal, B.A. (2003), *Theories of Social Remembering*, Open University Press, Maidenhead.

Moisander, J. and Valtonen, A. (2006), *Qualitative Marketing Research: A Cultural Approach*, SAGE, London.

Muehling, D.D. and Sprott, D.E. (2004), "The power of reflection: An empirical examination of nostalgia advertising effects", *Journal of Advertising*, Vol. 33 No. 3, pp. 25–35.

Nissley, N. and Casey, A. (2002), "The politics of the exhibition: Viewing corporate museums through the paradigmatic lens of organizational memory", *British Journal of Management*, Vol. 13 No. S2, pp. S35–S45.

Olick, J.K., Vinitzky-Seroussi, V. and Levy, D. (2011), "Introduction", in Olick, J.K., Vinitzky-Seroussi, V. and Levy, D. (Eds.), *The Collective Memory Reader*, Oxford University Press, Oxford, pp. 3–62.

Pickering, M. and Keightley, E. (2006), "The modalities of nostalgia", *Current Sociology*, Vol. 54 No. 6, pp. 919–941.

Ricoeur, P. (2006), *Memory, History, Forgetting*, (Trans by Kathleen Blamey and David Pellauer), University of Chicago Press, Chicago, IL.

Schug, A. (2003), *History Marketing: Ein Leitfaden zum Umgang mit Geschichte in Unternehmen*, Transcript, Bielefeld.

Shils, E. (1981), *Tradition*, Faber and Faber, London.

Simms, C.D. and Trott, P. (2006), "The perceptions of the BMW Mini brand: The importance of historical associations and the development of a model", *Journal of Product & Brand Management*, Vol. 15 Nos. 4/5, pp. 228–238.

Smith, L. (2006), *Uses of Heritage*, Routledge, New York, NY.

Strangleman, T. (1999), "The nostalgia of organisations and the organisation of nostalgia: Past and present in the contemporary railway industry", *Sociology*, Vol. 33 No. 4, pp. 725–746.

Thakor, M.V. and Kohli, C.S. (1996), "Brand origin: Conceptualization and review", *Journal of Consumer Marketing*, Vol. 13 No. 3, pp. 27–42.

Urde, M., Greyser, S.A. and Balmer, J.M.T. (2007), "Corporate brands with a heritage", *Journal of Brand Management*, Vol. 15 No. 1, pp. 4–19.

White, H.V. (2010), "The discourse of history", in Robert, D. (Ed.), *The Fiction of Narrative: Essays on History, Literature, and Theory, 1957–2007*, Johns Hopkins University Press, Baltimore, pp. 187–202.

Wiedmann, K.-P., Hennigs, N., Schmidt, S. and Wuestefeld, T. (2011a), "Drivers and outcomes of brand heritage: Consumers' perception of heritage brands in the automotive industry", *The Journal of Marketing Theory and Practice*, Vol. 19 No. 2, pp. 205–220.

Wiedmann, K.-P., Hennigs, N., Schmidt, S. and Wuestefeld, T. (2011b), "The importance of brand heritage as a key performance driver in marketing management", *Journal of Brand Management*, Vol. 19 No. 3, pp. 182–194.

Wilson, I. (2005), "The Bentley brand", *Marketing Review*, Vol. 5 No. 3, pp. 277–293.

Zerubavel, E. (2004), *Time Maps: Collective Memory and the Social Shape of the Past*, University of Chicago Press, Chicago, IL.

Further reading

Balmer, J.M.T. (2008), "Identity based views of the corporation insights from corporate identity, organisational identity, social identity, visual identity, corporate brand identity and corporate image", *European Journal of Marketing*, Vol. 42 Nos. 9/10, pp. 879–906.

He, H.-W. and Balmer, J.M.T. (2007), "Identity studies: Multiple perspectives and implications for corporate-level marketing", *European Journal of Marketing*, Vol. 41 Nos. 7/8, pp. 765–785.

Micelotta, E.R. and Raynard, M. (2011), "Concealing or revealing the family? Corporate brand identity strategies in family firms", *Family Business Review*, Vol. 24 No. 3, pp. 197–216.

Suddaby, R., Foster, W.M. and Quinn-Trank, C. (2010), "Rhetorical history as a source of competitive advantage", in Baum, J.A.C. and Lampel, J. (Eds.), *The Globalization of Strategy Research: Advances in Strategic Management*, Vol. 27, Emerald, Bingley, pp. 147–173.

Walsh, I.J. and Glynn, M.A. (2008), "The way we were: Legacy organizational identity and the role of leadership", *Corporate Reputation Review*, Vol. 11 No. 3, pp. 262–276.

5

CORPORATE HERITAGE BRANDS

Mead's theory of the past

Bradford T. Hudson and John M. T. Balmer

Introduction

Brand heritage has been a leitmotif within the marketing canon for at least three decades (Smith and Steadman, 1981), while the notion of corporate brands has evolved over the past twenty years (Balmer, 1995, 1998). However, it is only recently that the more specific idea of corporate heritage brands has entered the corporate marketing management lexicon.

Interest in the concept of corporate heritage brands dates back to the work of a triumvirate of scholars, who first identified the notion and articulated some of the key characteristics of the corporate heritage brand construct via their scrutiny of monarchies as corporate brands (Balmer *et al.*, 2006). A year later, a second paper provided a more substantive scrutiny of the corporate brand heritage phenomenon (Urde *et al.*, 2007). Since then, scholarly interest in the territory has begun to burgeon (Blombäck and Brunninge, 2009; Hudson, 2011; Wiedmann *et al.*, 2011).

While we recognise that extant scholarship has greatly advanced our understanding of customer preference and management action in this area, nonetheless many tangential questions remain unanswered. Perhaps most importantly, the fundamental mechanisms of consumer behaviour relating to heritage brands remain elusive.

We hope to contribute to this topic by adapting a relatively obscure theory about the role of the past in human behaviour, which was first developed by the pioneering sociologist George Herbert Mead (1929, 1932). Drawing on his ideas, we conceptualise why and how corporate heritage brands, and more especially their historical dimensions, appeal to consumers. We also offer a framework, based on a four-part taxonomy of heritage effects, which can assist practitioners in developing more effective corporate communications for older companies.

Although the primary focus of this article is corporate heritage brands per se, there are many corporate-level constructs relating to the past (Balmer, 2011a). We believe that Mead's theory is also of considerable utility in understanding other historically related concepts, such as authenticity and nostalgia.

In communications terms, researchers have observed that the corporate communications and corporate design strategies of long-established companies habitually – through one or more of their outward-directed formal corporate communications channels – make reference to organisational provenance or history. In certain instances, the aforementioned are emblematic of a category of institution whose brands can be characterised as corporate heritage brands. These are brands which have bona fide heritage characteristics and whose strategic positioning is informed by corporate brand heritage or corporate identity heritage (Balmer, 2009, 2011a, b; Balmer *et al.*, 2006; Hudson, 2011; Urde *et al.*, 2007).

Mead's theory of the past

George Herbert Mead (1863–1931) was a pioneer of the sociology discipline. Although his scholarship is almost a century old, much of it remains valid and useful for contemporary scholars (Stryker, 2008). A search of recent academic literature yielded more than 1,000 articles that cite Mead, including more than 800 in sociology and more than 175 in business journals.

Mead is best known for his contributions to the theory of symbolic interactionism. This suggests that an individual develops a sense of self through reflection about and comparison to external people, entities or objects (Mead, 1934). In the marketing and consumer behaviour literature, Mead has been cited repeatedly on the subject of symbolic interactionism (Goulding, 1999; Leigh and Gabel, 1992; Reed, 2002; Schouten, 1991; Solomon, 1983) and related topics such as identity (Belk, 1989; Christensen and Askegaard, 2001; Mittal, 2006).

While Mead is less well known for his theory of the past, it has been suggested that his thoughts about the historical process inform his other work (Adam, 1990; Flaherty and Fine, 2001). For Mead, time was a fundamental component in his larger effort to understand identity. He argued that events and people in the past, including prior versions of oneself, serve as points of comparison in the process of symbolic interaction. As subsequent scholars have observed, "Mead shows us that the self is above all a temporal process" (Flaherty and Fine, 2001). This has influenced some to conclude that we should "reconceptualise human agency as a temporally embedded process of social engagement, informed by the past" (Emirbayer and Mische, 1998).

The Mead theory of the past has received some attention in the discipline of sociology (Adam, 1990; Bergmann, 1992; Emirbayer and Mische, 1998; Flaherty, 1987; Flaherty and Fine, 2001; Luckmann, 1983; Urry, 1996). Of particular interest is an article by sociologists Maines *et al.* (1983) that proposes a four-part model to amplify the Mead theory of the past, as it applies broadly to human behaviour. Their model serves as the foundation for our own typology, which is applicable more specifically to the field of consumer behaviour and the concept of heritage brands.

To date, Mead's theory of the past has received little attention in marketing and consumer behaviour literature. Notable exceptions include a discussion of the role of possessions in personal identity (Belk, 1990) and a literature review related to temporality in financial services (Gibbs, 1998). As such, we believe that the framework below offers an important new perspective on the dynamics of heritage brands.

Applying Mead to corporate heritage brands

In this section, the sociological perspectives of the past articulated by Maines *et al.* (1983) and Mead (1929, 1932) are applied to the corporate heritage brand construct. Using this prior scholarship as a theoretical foundation, we have developed a conceptual model with four dimensions of corporate heritage brands. These will be discussed in turn by means of proffering an explanation, verification and illustration for each.

Structural heritage

Explanation

This dimension refers to the historical process as commonly understood, namely the progress of time in sequential fashion. The nature of the present depends on the outcome of events that occurred in the past, which cannot be altered. Structural heritage involves a succession of causation from past to present. If considered in a legal or institutional sense, this is consistent with a legacy that legitimises ownership or a precedent that provides authorisation for action.

Verification

Claims of differentiation or superiority on behalf of heritage brands are validated by the existence of a pedigree connecting the current company to the moment of origination and the people instrumental in establishing the company. It may also be evidenced through references to pioneer status within an industry or product category.

Illustration

Practical examples of structural heritage abound within many industries and sectors. For instance, some companies refer to founding dates in corporate marketing communications or in packaging design, such as the phrase *"Fondé en 1743"* (Founded in 1743) on labels of Moët et Chandon champagne bottles or the phrase "Established 1820" on bottles of Johnnie Walker Whisky. Companies also frequently employ representations of their founders. Examples include the appearance of Colonel Sanders in the logo for KFC restaurants, or the image of

Samuel Cunard that is prominently featured in historical displays aboard *Queen Mary 2* (Hudson, 2011). Corporate websites often refer to founders in sections devoted to their history. A film from the German coffee producer Melitta shows the company's original location and also accords prominence to the founder, Melitta Bentz (Blombäck and Brunninge, 2009). Universities also do much of the same. Consider the College of William and Mary in Virginia, which has recently introduced a ceremony in which the institution's Royal Charter is declaimed (Balmer, 2011a).

Implied heritage

Explanation

This dimension describes the characteristics of the past that may be inferred or understood from present conditions. As in the structural dimension, the objective past involves a progression of causation from past to present, but in this case the circumstances of the present provide verification of the past. In an institutional sense, if an organisation is vibrant and respected in the present, then it must have existed and developed during the past in a manner that explains its current status. The present characteristics of the brand logically require that these attributes emerged during the past, and support the construction of realities that explain causation in the development of the related company. Heritage is expressed by displaying current attributes that imply historical antecedents, by demonstrating congruence between current attributes and historical attributes, or by describing patterns of accomplishment across time. This dimension may also be indicated by references to the age of a brand. As Desai *et al.* (2008) noted, longevity alone may act as a signal or substitute for more substantial measures of performance. In certain situations, corporate brand survival for an extended period of time may generate veneration, even where a firm's accomplishment or the saliency of a corporate brand during the interim is somewhat vague.

Verification

Claims of differentiation or superiority by the firm are validated through statements of longevity, or demonstrations of continuity between past and present.

Illustration

Practical examples of implied heritage include recent centennial events orchestrated by corporate brands such as Disney, Ford, Fortnum and Mason, or Whirlpool. Implied heritage may also be signalled by referencing an historic artefact linked to brand identity. For example, the original silver trophy presented to Samuel Cunard upon completion of his first transatlantic voyage in 1840 is displayed aboard the new Cunard ship *Queen Mary 2* (Hudson, 2011). Corporate visitor centres are often created to showcase such items, as exemplified by museums for Harley-Davidson in Milwaukee, Bentley in Crewe, and Mercedes-Benz in Stuttgart. Implied heritage is also exemplified by anniversary celebrations for other types of organisations, such as Cambridge University. The British Monarchy has been adept at reintroducing and reinvigorating rituals and ceremonies that seek to bolster the Crown's historical associations (Balmer, 2009).

Reconstructed heritage

Explanation

This dimension suggests that our relationship to the past is interpretive and our understanding of prior events is enhanced through contemplation. The process is interactive and may involve not only re-classification of the past resulting from comparison to the present, but also re-conceptualisation of the present through comparison to a reconstructed past. This idea is similar to aspects of heritage discussed by Lowenthal (1998). The process may also involve a conclusion that the past was somehow superior to the present, which may be accompanied by an affective reaction in the form of sentimental or nostalgic feelings (Maines *et al.*, 1983). Reconstructed heritage usually involves an invitation to compare past and present, which may be explicitly communicated or may be implied through the asynchronicity of images and other references. The brand or its subsidiary products become associated with idealised qualities that are superior to those in modern products or in the current experience of consumers. This can be discussed in the context of the work of Belk *et al.* (1989) and Holt (2004), who have averred that brands can have significant symbolic roles in our contemporary society where change is ongoing and rapid. It has been noted within the identity literature that heritage brands are attractive because they appear to be invariable in an increasingly variable world (Balmer, 2011b).

Verification

Claims of differentiation or superiority by the firm are validated by the familiar or reminiscent character of the brand or its associated products.

Illustration

A commonly cited example of reconstructed heritage is the new Volkswagen Beetle, which was introduced in 1998 with design elements reminiscent of the original Beetle that became a cultural icon during the 1960s (Brown *et al.*, 2003). The success of the new Beetle inspired similar efforts by other automobile manufacturers, including the new Mini by BMW (Simms and Trott, 2006). Reconstructed heritage may also be found in packaging design and the design of consumer environments. The former is illustrated by the plastic version of the classic Coca-Cola hourglass bottle, while the latter is exemplified by the interior decor of newly built Cunard ships that is reminiscent of classic vessels from the past (Hudson, 2011).

Mythical heritage

Explanation

This dimension refers to fictitious inventions that offer an "aura of reality" through their contextual relevance, and constitute "part of the consensual basis of truth" in "shared consciousness" (Maines *et al.*, 1983). These often harken back to a "Golden Age" in which human relations and natural conditions are idealised or romanticised (Lowenthal, 1985; McCracken, 1988). Mythical heritage refers to pasts that are partly or wholly fictitious, and which facilitate the projection or escape of consumers into imaginary worlds that relate to the brand. Mythical heritage is often expressed through fantasy or illusion, especially within communications narratives or the design of environments and products. This is where faux heritage is most evident and appropriate.

Verification

Claims of differentiation or superiority by the firm are validated by the archetypal, universal or quintessential nature of brand attributes.

Illustration

Mythical heritage is often expressed through vintage design elements within products and consumer environments. Examples of the former include vehicles from Chrysler such as the PT Cruiser, which are reminiscent of Hot Wheels toys (Brown, 1999). A prominent example of the latter is provided by the Main Street arcade at the Disney Magic Kingdom, which is reminiscent of a small American town of yesteryear. Mythical heritage may also be invoked through marketing communications. This is exemplified by recent print advertisements for the Cunard Line, which promised that "each Cunard voyage will take you back to the Golden Age of Ocean Travel, when timeless elegance and refined British traditions ruled the day" (Hudson, 2011). Of course, the British Monarchy has made considerable recourse to mythical heritage in terms of its own positioning. Consider the introduction of seemingly ancient ceremonies by the Crown, which were in fact new, and which led Hobsbawm (1983) to propose the notion of "invented tradition." The British Crown's adoption of the brand (dynastic) name of Windsor is a prime example of communicating a mythical heritage. Although the British Monarchy had strong Teutonic family ties and was closely linked to the House of Hanover, the introduction of the Windsor brand communicated a faux English heritage. This was important during the first war with Germany, when many in Britain viewed the monarchy with considerable suspicion due to its dynastic names Saxe-Coburg and Gotha (Balmer, 2009).

Corporate heritage brands: A unifying framework

The four dimensions detailed above – structural heritage, implied heritage, reconstructed heritage and mythical heritage – constitute a unifying conceptual framework for corporate heritage brands. This is shown in Figure 5.1, which includes a summary of descriptive attributes and provides a mnemonic sequence to assist recollection.

The grouping of different types of heritage into an integrated typology suggests the need to explore the similarities and differences between these types. In this regard, several points deserve clarification.

Heritage conveys permanence and can infer strength and stability

Structural heritage and implied heritage both convey permanence and perpetuation, and generate associations with stability and strength. Consumers may select such brands because these attributes suggest that associated products can be trusted

INNATE HERITAGE		PROJECTED HERITAGE	
Historical elements of the brand serve as signals regarding the attributes or benefits of the brand itself		Brand becomes an instrument of existential definition upon which consumers project their own historical associations	
• Prospective • Brand identity • History of the brand • Indexical authenticity		• Retrospective • Brand identity and consumer identity • History through the brand • Iconic authenticity	
STRUCTURAL HERITAGE	IMPLIED HERITAGE	RECONSTRUCTED HERITAGE	MYTHICAL HERITAGE
Origination	Survival	Reunion	Adventure
Genuine	Continuous	Familiar	Quintessential
CONSUMER VALUE PROPOSITION			
Leadership Authenticity	Expertise Reliability	Personal Nostalgia	Historical or Utopian Nostalgia
Legacy	Longevity	Longing	Legend

FIGURE 5.1 A framework for brand heritage

for their utility and quality. In such cases, the age or history of the brand serves as an indicator of its other characteristics, in manner consistent with an extrinsic cue (Desai *et al.*, 2008).

Founding dates have different meanings in different dimensions

Although structural heritage and implied heritage may both refer to the founding dates of companies, two different dynamics are in play. In structural heritage, founding dates serve as signals of origin and precedence. In implied heritage, founding dates serve as starting boundaries for determining the duration of existence, and the operative factors are longevity and development during the interim.

Heritage often involves idealised and romanticised versions of history

Reconstructed heritage and mythical heritage both involve idealised and romanticised versions of history that are explicitly understood to be diversions from or interpretations of the objective past. Consumers may select such brands because their attributes facilitate the alleviation of present concerns, the escape from present constraints, or the indulgence of a desire for adventure or amusement.

Some types of heritage can be differentiated on the basis of personal experience

Although reconstructed heritage and mythical heritage may both involve retrospection, they can be differentiated on the basis of personal experience. Some of the mythical examples mentioned earlier have been inspired by real events or places, but the originals have not been personally experienced or observed by the consumers in question. It is not the absence of reality in these products that designates them as mythical, but rather the absence of reality in the experience of related consumers.

Mythical heritage does not require historical comparison

In reconstructed heritage, the mixture of historical and contemporary references encourages comparison between past and present. In mythical heritage, such asynchronicity may be present, but it is irrelevant. Genuine historical references are embedded in the mythical past merely to provide contextual recognition. The juxtaposition and comparison of different time periods is not a necessary functional component of the mythical past.

Mythical heritage may involve design elements that are not genuine

Vintage design may be employed in support of any of the four heritage dimensions. However, design in mythical heritage is disconnected from particular brand antecedents. Such products are not direct updates of older models, but rather fanciful creations based on nonspecific stylistic elements that evoke a bygone era.

Only some types of heritage effects are "retro"

All four types of heritage involve consideration of the past. However, structural heritage and implied heritage both involve a viewpoint or action sequence from past to present. Conversely, reconstructed heritage and mythical heritage both involve a viewpoint or action sequence from present to past. In other words, the former two are prospective, while the latter two are retrospective. Thus, while all older products reflect heritage dynamics, not all older products can be properly deemed "retro." Only reconstructed heritage and mythical heritage are examples of the retro phenomenon.

The four dimensions of heritage can be divided into two metacategories – innate heritage and projected heritage – which are differentiated by the object of heritage effects

Structural heritage and implied heritage refer solely to the identity of the brand and its inherent characteristics, while reconstructed heritage and mythical heritage also involve the identity of the consumer who is external to the brand. The former may be termed innate heritage, while the latter may be termed projected heritage. In projected heritage, individuals seek to understand themselves through their engagement with the past. As consumers, they project their own identity onto the brand and employ the brand as an instrument of existential definition. Brands therefore serve as "symbolic resources for the construction of identity" (Elliott and Wattanasuwan, 1998). Similar phenomena have been observed in relation to possessions (Belk, 1988, 1990; Csikszentmihalyi and Rochberg-Halton, 1981; McCracken, 1988; Solomon, 1983) and the behaviour of collectors (Belk *et al.*, 1989; Slater, 2001). This also relates to scholarship regarding identity myths (Holt, 2004; Thompson, 2004; Thompson and Tian, 2008).

All four dimensions of heritage may be evident in a single brand

The dimensions in our framework represent ideal types that are frequently interwoven with ambiguous boundaries that may not be easily differentiated in practice. This is illustrated by the case of Cunard (Hudson, 2011). The silver trophy displayed aboard the ocean liner *Queen Mary 2* serves not only as evidence of the legacy of

Samuel Cunard (structural heritage), but also as a symbol of continuity across time. If the new Cunard possesses the artefact, then it must be the same company that emerged more than a century ago (implied heritage). Similarly, the elements of vintage design aboard *Queen Mary 2* appeal not only to older passengers who may have personal experience with the original *Queen Mary* (reconstructed heritage), but also to younger consumers who have romantic fantasies about classic ocean travel (mythical heritage).

Broadening the discussion: Authenticity and nostalgia

The brand heritage phenomenon may usefully be considered relative to other historically informed concepts in marketing and consumer behaviour, namely authenticity and nostalgia. These constructs have their own attendant literatures, but it can be argued that the Mead theory of the past offers a unifying structure that can also encompass these ideas.

Authenticity

The authenticity construct focuses on the dichotomy that may exist between the true and false nature of people or objects. A key premise of authenticity is that originality is not only legitimate and preferential but also, by inference, ethical. The subject of authenticity represents a prominent line of scholarship in the marketing and consumer behaviour canons (Alexander, 2009; Ballantyne *et al.*, 2006; Belk, 1990; Belk *et al.*, 1989; Beverland, 2005, 2006; Gilmore and Pine, 2007; Goulding, 2000; Grayson and Martinec, 2004; Holt, 2002, 2004; Leigh *et al.*, 2006; Peñaloza, 2000).

The reconstructed heritage and mythical heritage dimensions elaborated upon earlier raise an important question about the nature of authenticity in heritage brand scenarios. If authenticity is a measure or expression of original status, and if originality is generally preferred, then why would consumers accept historical pastiche or reproductions in relation to brands or products?

The solution may be found in the idea that authenticity has two dimensions, namely indexical authenticity and iconic authenticity. It has been suggested that "indexical authenticity" refers to the distinction between genuine and counterfeit status (Grayson and Martinec, 2004). This aligns with the structural heritage and implied heritage dimensions, because the genuine status of brands can be determined by objective evidence, such as patent documents or photographs.

In contrast, "iconic authenticity" refers to the degree of "verisimilitude" with an ideal type (Grayson and Martinec, 2004). As such, the notion of iconic authenticity may explain the consumer acceptability of historical reproductions, the appropriation of selected heritage elements in new brands and products, and the creation of products and brands in the spirit of an homage. This relates to literature that considers the possibility of "constructed" or "staged" authenticity (Alexander, 2009; Chhabra *et al.*, 2003; Leigh *et al.*, 2006). Iconic authenticity aligns with the reconstructed heritage and mythical heritage dimensions, because genuine status is determined by consumers, who must subjectively perceive quintessential properties in the brand.

Nostalgia

Equally significant is the idea of nostalgia. This is a powerful construct, as it encapsulates an individual or group yearning for the past. It represents a sentimental cognitive recollection of yesteryear, or a penchant for objects or experiences that are associated with a prior era. Nostalgia has been a recurrent topic within marketing and consumer literature (Belk, 1990; Brown *et al.*, 2003; Goulding, 2001; Havlena and Holak, 1991; Holbrook and Schindler, 2003; Sierra and McQuitty, 2007; Stern, 1992).

Nostalgia has been variously characterised as a romantic preference for antiquity, a psychological disorder related to displacement and alienation, or an emotional coping mechanism in reaction to dissatisfaction with the modern era. In a manner consistent with Mead, it has also been suggested that nostalgia is operative in "constructing, maintaining, and reconstructing our identities" and that "the essence of nostalgic experience [is] to cultivate appreciative stances of former selves" (Davis, 1979, pp. 31–36).

Several variations of nostalgia are evident in brand heritage. The idea of personal nostalgia refers to the recollection of events personally experienced earlier in life (Stern, 1992). This is illustrated by the pilgrimage of adults to their first elementary school. It may also refer to memories about events in which the consumer was not directly involved, but which were experienced second-hand at the time they occurred, for example through media reports or cocktail party discussions. This is exemplified by the reactions of older Americans to the death of Marilyn Monroe or older British citizens to the funeral of Sir Winston Churchill.

In terms of our heritage construct, personal nostalgia is aligned with reconstructed heritage, because it represents an affective response to real events that have personal meaning for the consumer, and which are remembered either directly through lived experience or indirectly through participation in the contemporaneous cultural milieu. Brands, products or design attributes that existed during prior eras may serve as cues for such recollections.

The idea of historical nostalgia refers to knowledge of the past as opposed to lived experience. Real events are recalled in memory, but knowledge of such occurrences is derived from historical writings, works of popular culture, or collective memory (Halbwachs, 1992; Stern, 1992). Examples include the romantic portrayal of the Woodstock Festival by children of the baby boom generation who were not alive at the time of the event, or the attraction toward undergraduate life at Oxford or Cambridge (as characterised in films and television series) by those who never attended these universities.

In terms of our heritage construct, historical nostalgia aligns with mythical heritage, because it represents affective responses to events that are not part of the personal experience of the consumer. This relates to literature regarding "vicarious nostalgia" (Goulding, 2001). Brands, products or design attributes that existed during prior eras (or which can be associated with these eras) may serve as cues for such effects.

The idea of utopian nostalgia is entirely fictional in character. It refers to events that never occurred or places that never existed, but which could have or should have occurred or existed during a mythical Golden Age (Boym, 1995). This may be illustrated by a romantic longing to experience life at Camelot, as described in Arthurian legend and as dramatised in theatre and film productions.

In terms of our heritage construct, utopian nostalgia aligns with mythical heritage, because it represents affective responses to fictional events or mythical narratives that are envisioned solely through the imagination. This relates to literature regarding "synthetic" nostalgia (DaSilva and Faught, 1982). Brands, products or design attributes that are connected to such narratives (or which create their own) may serve as catalysts for such feelings.

Discussion

Our framework, along with the characterisation of corporate heritage brands detailed in this article, aims to clarify the internal logic of the brand heritage concept, and aims to build on the extant literature to provide a solid foundation for further scholarly research regarding the dynamics of corporate heritage brands. The framework also represents a tool that executives and consultants may use to recognise and classify different types of heritage phenomena.

Our recent interactions with practitioners indicate that this model offers new insight into the management of brands with a heritage, and is particularly useful in formulating decisions about different communications approaches. Our typology clarifies the complex conceptual and vernacular landscape upon which discussions about older brands occur. Executives may use it to make explicit connections between the selection of specific signals that are intended to trigger associations on the one hand, and the cognitive and behavioural effects that they are hoping to induce on the other.

For example, the model suggests that references to company founders will produce consumer associations with the firm and its products, and should be used to support utility claims such as reliability or trustworthiness. Similarly, the model suggests that references to contextual cues from historic eras are more likely to produce reactions that are affective or introspective, and should be used to engage consumers in more intuitive appeals. Differentiating these two approaches can have a meaningful influence on decisions about images or narratives that may be employed in corporate advertising and corporate communications generally.

Conclusion

This article has demonstrated that the theory of the past articulated by George Herbert Mead (1929, 1932) and amplified by Maines *et al.* (1983) can be adapted to provide a unifying framework for the brand heritage concept. Our proposed typology is comprised of four dimensions denoted as structural heritage, implied heritage, reconstructed heritage and mythical heritage.

Structural heritage refers to occurrences in the past that condition the future and provide precedent for claims by brands. Implied heritage refers to the past that is implied by the current status of brands. Reconstructed heritage refers to the remembrance of brands that were encountered earlier in the lifetimes of consumers. Mythical heritage refers to historical brand elements that are fictitious, and which facilitate the escape of consumers into imaginary scenarios. These four dimensions represent ideal types that are frequently interwoven.

According to Mead, the interaction of the present and the past is integral to the process of identity formation. In our adaptation for brand heritage, the dimensions of structural heritage and implied heritage together form the innate heritage category, which concerns the identity of the brand itself. The historical characteristics of the brand serve as cues to influence buyer preference. In contrast, the dimensions of reconstructed heritage and mythical heritage together form the projected heritage category, which concerns both the identity of the brand and the identity of the consumer. This involves the projection of personal identity onto the brand or its associated products, and appropriation of the brand as an instrument of existential definition.

Based on the findings of our article, the following alternative definition of corporate brand heritage effects is hereby proposed:

> Corporate brand heritage is an approach to corporate marketing that involves reference to the past. It encourages the engagement of consumers with the history of the brand, or the engagement of consumers with history through the brand. The former is operative in defining the identity of the brand alone, while the latter is also operative in defining the identity of the consumer. The corporate brand heritage concept encompasses a wide variety of historical references in contemporary corporate marketing, including interpretations and *faux* applications, provided that they relate to the brand and support the process of identity definition. A heritage brand is a specific variant of this phenomenon, differentiated by an organisational commitment to heritage and a strategic position that emphasises the past.

This characterisation and the related framework clarify the internal logic of the corporate brand heritage concept, and provide additional foundation for further scholarly research regarding the dynamics of corporate heritage brands. The framework also represents a tool that executives and consultants may use to recognise and classify different types of heritage phenomena. As such, it contributes to both theoretical and practical endeavours related to the management of corporate heritage brands.

References

Adam, B. (1990), *Time and Social Theory*, Temple University, Philadelphia, PA.
Alexander, N. (2009), "Brand authentication: Creating and maintaining brand auras", *European Journal of Marketing*, Vol. 43 Nos. 3/4, pp. 551–562.

Ballantyne, R., Warren, A. and Nobbs, K. (2006), "The evolution of brand choice", *Journal of Brand Management*, Vol. 13 Nos. 4/5, pp. 339–352.

Balmer, J.M.T. (1995), "Corporate branding and connoisseurship", *Journal of General Management*, Vol. 21 No. 1, pp. 24–46.

Balmer, J.M.T. (1998), "Corporate identity and the advent of corporate marketing", *Journal of Marketing Management*, Vol. 14 No. 8, pp. 963–996.

Balmer, J.M.T. (2009), "Scrutinising the British Monarchy: The corporate brand that was shaken, stirred and survived", *Management Decision*, Vol. 47 No. 4, pp. 639–676.

Balmer, J.M.T. (2011a), "Corporate heritage brands and the precepts of corporate heritage brand management: Insights from the British Monarchy on the eve of the royal wedding of Prince William (April 2011) and Queen Elizabeth II's Diamond Jubilee (1952–2012)", *Journal of Brand Management*, Vol. 18 No. 8, pp. 517–544.

Balmer, J.M.T. (2011b), "Corporate heritage identities, corporate heritage brands and the multiple heritage identities of the British Monarchy", *European Journal of Marketing*, Vol. 45 Nos. 9/10, pp. 1380–1398.

Balmer, J.M.T., Greyser, S.A. and Urde, M. (2006), "The crown as a corporate brand: Insights from monarchies", *Journal of Brand Management*, Vol. 14 Nos. 1/2, pp. 137–161.

Belk, R.W. (1988), "Possessions and the extended self", *Journal of Consumer Research*, Vol. 15 No. 2, pp. 139–168.

Belk, R.W. (1989), "Extended self and extending paradigmatic perspective", *Journal of Consumer Research*, Vol. 16 No. 1, pp. 129–132.

Belk, R.W. (1990), "The role of possessions in constructing and maintaining a sense of past", *Advances in Consumer Research*, Vol. 17, pp. 669–676.

Belk, R.W., Wallendorf, M. and Sherry, J.F. (1989), "The sacred and the profane in consumer behavior: Theodicy on the odyssey", *Journal of Consumer Research*, Vol. 16 No. 1, pp. 1–38.

Bergmann, W. (1992), "The problem of time in sociology", *Time and Society*, Vol. 1 No. 1, pp. 81–134.

Beverland, M.B. (2005), "Brand management and the challenge of authenticity", *Journal of Product & Brand Management*, Vol. 14 No. 7, pp. 460–461.

Beverland, M.B. (2006), "The real thing: Branding in the luxury wine trade", *Journal of Business Research*, Vol. 59 No. 2, pp. 251–258.

Blombäck, A. and Brunninge, O. (2009), "Corporate identity manifested through historical references", *Corporate Communications: An International Journal*, Vol. 14 No. 4, pp. 404–419.

Boym, S. (1995), "From the Russian soul to post-communist nostalgia", *Representations*, Vol. 49, pp. 133–166.

Brown, S. (1999), "Retro-marketing: Yesterday's tomorrows, today", *Marketing Intelligence and Planning*, Vol. 17 No. 7, pp. 363–376.

Brown, S., Kozinets, R.V. and Sherry, J.F. (2003), "Teaching old brands new tricks: Retro branding and the revival of brand meaning", *Journal of Marketing*, Vol. 67 No. 3, pp. 19–33.

Chhabra, D., Healy, R. and Sills, E. (2003), "Staged authenticity and heritage tourism", *Annals of Tourism Research*, Vol. 30 No. 3, pp. 702–719.

Christensen, L.T. and Askegaard, S. (2001), "Corporate identity and corporate image revisited: A semiotic perspective", *European Journal of Marketing*, Vol. 35 Nos. 3/4, pp. 292–315.

Csikszentmihalyi, M. and Rochberg-Halton, E. (1981), *The Meaning of Things: Domestic Symbols and the Self*, Cambridge University, Cambridge.

DaSilva, F.B. and Faught, J. (1982), "Nostalgia: A sphere and process of contemporary ideology", *Qualitative Sociology*, Vol. 5 No. 1, pp. 47–61.

Davis, F. (1979), *Yearning for Yesterday: A Sociology of Nostalgia*, Free Press, New York, NY.

Desai, P.S., Kalra, A. and Murthi, B.P.S. (2008), "When old is gold: The role of business longevity in risky situations", *Journal of Marketing*, Vol. 72 No. 1, pp. 95–107.

Elliott, R. and Wattanasuwan, K. (1998), "Brands as symbolic resources for the construction of identity", *International Journal of Advertising*, Vol. 17 No. 2, pp. 131–144.

Emirbayer, M. and Mische, A. (1998), "What is agency?", *American Journal of Sociology*, Vol. 103 No. 4, pp. 962–1023.

Flaherty, M.G. (1987), "The neglected dimension of temporality in social psychology", in Denzin, N.K. (Ed.), *Studies in Symbolic Interaction*, Vol. 8, JAI, Greenwich, CT, pp. 143–155.

Flaherty, M.G. and Fine, G.A. (2001), "Present, past, and future: Conjugating George Herbert Mead's perspective on time", *Time and Society*, Vol. 10 Nos. 2/3, pp. 147–161.

Gibbs, P.T. (1998), "Time, temporality and consumer behaviour", *European Journal of Marketing*, Vol. 32 Nos. 11/12, pp. 993–1007.

Gilmore, J.H. and Pine, B.J. (2007), *Authenticity: What Consumers Really Want*, Harvard Business School, Boston, MA.

Goulding, C. (1999), "Consumer research, interpretive paradigms and methodological ambiguities", *European Journal of Marketing*, Vol. 33 Nos. 9/10, pp. 859–873.

Goulding, C. (2000), "The commodification of the past, postmodern pastiche, and the search for authentic experiences at contemporary heritage attractions", *European Journal of Marketing*, Vol. 34 No. 7, pp. 835–853.

Goulding, C. (2001), "Romancing the past: Heritage visiting and the nostalgic consumer", *Psychology and Marketing*, Vol. 18 No. 6, pp. 565–592.

Grayson, K. and Martinec, R. (2004), "Consumer perceptions of iconicity and indexicality and their influence on assessments of authentic market offerings", *Journal of Consumer Research*, Vol. 31 No. 2, pp. 296–312.

Halbwachs, M. (1992), *On Collective Memory*, University of Chicago, Chicago, IL.

Havlena, W.J. and Holak, S.L. (1991), "The good old days: Observations on nostalgia and its role in consumer behaviour", *Advances in Consumer Research*, Vol. 18, pp. 323–329.

Hobsbawm, E. (1983), "Inventing traditions", in Hobsbawm, E. and Ranger, T. (Eds.), *The Invention of Tradition*, Cambridge University, Cambridge, pp. 1–14.

Holbrook, M.B. and Schindler, R.M. (2003), "Nostalgic bonding: Exploring the role of nostalgia in the consumption experience", *Journal of Consumer Behaviour*, Vol. 3 No. 2, pp. 107–127.

Holt, D.B. (2002), "Why do brands cause trouble? A dialectical theory of consumer culture and branding", *Journal of Consumer Research*, Vol. 29 No. 1, pp. 70–90.

Holt, D.B. (2004), *How Brands Become Icons: The Principles of Cultural Branding*, Harvard Business School, Boston, MA.

Hudson, B.T. (2011), "Brand heritage and the renaissance of Cunard", *European Journal of Marketing*, Vol. 45 Nos. 9/10, pp. 1538–1556.

Leigh, J.H. and Gabel, T.G. (1992), "Symbolic interactionism: Its effects on consumer behavior and implications for marketing strategy", *Journal of Services Marketing*, Vol. 6 No. 3, pp. 5–16.

Leigh, T.W., Peters, C. and Shelton, J. (2006), "The consumer quest for authenticity: The multiplicity of meanings within the MG subculture of consumption", *Journal of the Academy of Marketing Science*, Vol. 34 No. 4, pp. 481–493.

Lowenthal, D. (1985), *The Past Is a Foreign Country*, Cambridge University, Cambridge.

Lowenthal, D. (1998), *The Heritage Crusade and the Spoils of History*, Cambridge University, Cambridge.

Luckmann, T. (1983), "Remarks on personal identity: Inner, social and historical time", in Jacobson-Widding, A. (Ed.), *Identity: Personal and Socio-Cultural*, Academiae Upsaliensis, Uppsala, pp. 67–91.

Maines, D.R., Sugrue, N.M. and Katovich, M.A. (1983), "The sociological import of G.H", *Mead's Theory of the Past, American Sociological Review*, Vol. 48 No. 2, pp. 161–173.

McCracken, G. (1988), *Culture and Consumption: New Approaches to the Symbolic Character of Consumer Goods and Activities*, Indiana University, Bloomington, IN.

Mead, G.H. (1929), "The nature of the past", in Coss, J. (Ed.), *Essays in Honor of John Dewey: On the Occasion of His Seventieth Birthday*, Henry Holt, New York, NY, pp. 235–242.

Mead, G.H. (1932), *The Philosophy of the Present*, Open Court, Chicago, IL.

Mead, G.H. (1934), *Mind, Self and Society: From the Standpoint of a Social Behaviorist*, University of Chicago, Chicago, IL.

Mittal, B. (2006), "I, me, and mine: How products become consumers extended selves", *Journal of Consumer Behaviour*, Vol. 5 No. 6, pp. 550–562.

Peñaloza, L. (2000), "The commodification of the American west: Marketers production of cultural meanings at the trade show", *Journal of Marketing*, Vol. 64 No. 4, pp. 82–109.

Reed, A. (2002), "Social identity as a useful perspective for self-concept-based consumer research", *Psychology and Marketing*, Vol. 19 No. 3, pp. 235–266.

Schouten, J.W. (1991), "Selves in transition: Symbolic consumption in personal rites of passage and identity reconstruction", *Journal of Consumer Research*, Vol. 17 No. 4, pp. 412–425.

Sierra, J.J. and McQuitty, S. (2007), "Attitudes and emotions as determinants of nostalgia purchases: An application of social identity theory", *Journal of Marketing Theory and Practice*, Vol. 15 No. 2, pp. 99–112.

Simms, C.D. and Trott, P. (2006), "The perceptions of the BMW Mini brand: The importance of historical associations and the development of a model", *Journal of Product & Brand Management*, Vol. 15 No. 4, pp. 228–238.

Slater, J.S. (2001), "Collecting brand loyalty: A comparative analysis of how Coca-Cola and Hallmark use collecting behavior to enhance brand loyalty", *Advances in Consumer Research*, Vol. 28, pp. 362–369.

Smith, G.D. and Steadman, L.E. (1981), "Present value of corporate history", *Harvard Business Review*, Vol. 59 No. 6, pp. 164–173.

Solomon, M.R. (1983), "The role of products as social stimuli: A symbolic interactionism perspective", *Journal of Consumer Research*, Vol. 10 No. 3, pp. 319–329.

Stern, B.B. (1992), "Historical and personal nostalgia in advertising text: The *fin de sie'cle* effect", *Journal of Advertising*, Vol. 21 No. 4, pp. 11–22.

Stryker, S. (2008), "From Mead to a structural symbolic interactionism and beyond", *Annual Review of Sociology*, Vol. 34, pp. 15–31.

Thompson, C. (2004), "Marketplace mythology and discourses of power", *Journal of Consumer Research*, Vol. 31 No. 1, pp. 162–180.

Thompson, C. and Tian, K. (2008), "Reconstructing the south: How commercial myths compete for identity value through the ideological shaping of popular memories and countermemories", *Journal of Consumer Research*, Vol. 34 No. 5, pp. 595–613.

Urde, M., Greyser, S.A. and Balmer, J.M.T. (2007), "Corporate brands with a heritage", *Journal of Brand Management*, Vol. 15 No. 1, pp. 4–19.

Urry, J. (1996), "How societies remember the past", in Macdonald, S. and Fyfe, G. (Eds.), *Theorizing Museums: Representing Identity and Diversity in a Changing World*, Blackwell, Oxford, pp. 45–65.

Wiedmann, K.P., Hennigs, N., Schmidt, S. and Wuestefeld, T. (2011), "Drivers and outcomes of brand heritage: Consumers' perception of heritage brands in the automotive industry", *Journal of Marketing Theory and Practice*, Vol. 19 No. 2, pp. 205–220.

Corporate heritage identity stewardship and corporate heritage tourism brand attractiveness

6

CORPORATE HERITAGE IDENTITY STEWARDSHIP

A corporate marketing perspective

Mario Burghausen and John M. T. Balmer

Introduction

This article introduces and explicates the theory of corporate heritage identity stewardship. Corporate heritage identities have recently been identified as a distinct type of institutional identity. They are distinct, in that the identity traits of these organisations, whilst ostensibly indelible (because they are of the past, present and future), concurrently accommodate continuity and change: they are characterised by their relative invariance (Balmer, 2011b). As such, Balmer (2011b) – taking an instrumental perspective – maintains that corporate heritage identities, because of their distinct omni-temporal natures, require senior managers to comprehend their ongoing governance responsibilities in terms of a stewardship role (i.e. corporate heritage identity stewardship), which is to be markedly different from the customary management function largely focussed on the short term. Balmer (2011b), therefore, argues that a key requisite for the successful stewardship of a corporate heritage identity requires managers to think, feel and act as custodians.

Over recent years, corporate heritage as an organisational phenomenon, and its appropriation as a strategic resource for corporate-level marketing purposes, has increasingly attracted the attention of marketing scholars (Balmer *et al.*, 2006; Urde *et al.*, 2007; Blombäck and Brunninge, 2009; Balmer, 2011a, 2011b; Hudson, 2011; Wiedmann *et al.*, 2011a, 2011b). The concept of corporate heritage refers to particular traits of an organisation that meaningfully link its past, present and future by referring to some aspect of an organisation's past that is still deemed by current stakeholders to be relevant for contemporary concerns and purposes but that is concurrently perceived as worth to be maintained, nurtured and passed on to future generations (Balmer, 2011b).

Yet, within the nascent corporate heritage canon, whilst the *prima facie* ubiquity of organisations featuring corporate heritage identity characteristics that are potentially managed in quite different ways has been noted (Blombäck and Brunninge, 2009; Balmer, 2011b) and the various defining dimensions of this distinct type of institutional identity have been discussed (Balmer, 2011b, 2013), to date, empirical insights and conceptual elaborations relating to the particularities of corporate heritage identity stewardship are absent. Hence, little is known about the aforementioned in empirical and theoretical terms, despite being suggested as a key requisite for the successful management of a corporate heritage identity, and this article seeks to address this gap in the literature.

Therefore, this article reports an empirical theory-building study that seeks to advance the understanding of corporate heritage identity stewardship in theoretical and instrumental terms. Arguably, this study is believed to be the first major empirical inquiry with this specific focus and makes a meaningful theoretical advance to the territory. In theoretical terms, this empirical study makes a contribution to the nascent corporate heritage field by revealing key interpretative dimensions pertaining to corporate heritage identity stewardship as understood by managers. We elaborate the research insights by outlining the theory of corporate heritage identity stewardship by way of a theoretical framework. In addition, we aim to provide instrumental insights by uncovering those traits that are important for corporate heritage identity stewardship.

Corporate heritage identity stewardship, as revealed by this study, can be explained in terms of a particular corporate heritage identity stewardship mindset which meaningfully informs the strategic enactment of a corporate heritage identity by managers. The managerial mindset represents the manner in which managers apprehend and relate to their organisation as a heritage institution affording them a propensity to act towards and on behalf of the organisation. As such, the corporate heritage identity stewardship mindset is characterised by three awareness dimensions expressed by managers (i.e. positionality, heritage and custodianship), which are underpinned by six managerial stewardship dispositions characterised by a sense of continuance, belongingness, self, heritage, responsibility and potency. A theoretical framework – informed by the above – is introduced that has instrumental utility in explaining the multidimensional nature of corporate heritage identity stewardship necessary for the management of a corporate heritage identity.

At the outset, it is important to note that our study is informed by moderate constructionist paradigmatic convictions (Blaikie, 2007) and, as such, can be classified as an interpretative theory/theoretical contribution (Charmaz, 2006). The significance of this theoretical contribution is in terms of providing insight in relation to emergent patterns and non-linear relations between concepts (Charmaz, 2006). Significantly, this mode of theoretical contribution is qualitatively different from theoretical insights which explicitly focus on deterministic explanations of causal linear relationships between variables (Charmaz, 2006). In terms of resultant theoretical frameworks, which both describe and explain how a phenomenon behaves (Lee and Lings, 2008), the nature of what constitutes description and explanation will differ as a consequence of the paradigmatic perspectives adopted by the researchers and which will, as a consequence, inform the mode of theoretical contribution (Charmaz, 2006; Blaikie, 2009).

Consequently, and for the sake of clarity, it is important to note that the theoretical framework presented in this article highlights patterns and multifaceted arrangements of concepts in a holistic fashion. The purpose of the resultant theoretical framework does not aim to specify directional relations between discrete variables in a reductionist way which characterises more positivist theoretical models (Blaikie, 2007, 2009).

The research was undertaken within the UK's oldest brewery – Shepherd Neame – and an in-depth theory-building single case study design (using multiple forms of qualitative data) informed the study because of the underspecified character of the focal concept and its sparse empirical base. We adopt an explicit corporate marketing perspective in terms of positioning this study within marketing (Balmer, 1998, 2001, 2011c; Balmer and Greyser, 2003, 2006; He and Balmer, 2007a, 2013; Hildebrand *et al.*, 2011; Powell, 2011; Abratt and Kleyn, 2012), in that our study has an explicit corporate-level (rather than product and service-level) focus.

Based on a review of the extant literature, the article continues by outlining the context within which the concept of heritage has been discussed within corporate marketing and marketing in general, before detailing several corporate heritage dimensions articulated in the extant literature and addressing the notion of corporate heritage stewardship in particular. Subsequently, the article provides the rationale for the study, articulating its relevance and timeliness. After presenting the empirical background and articulating the methodological approach adopted, the empirical findings of the study are outlined and the theoretical contribution of this theory-building research – the articulation of a theory of corporate heritage identity stewardship – is introduced. This theoretical contribution is represented, and elaborated, in the form of a theoretical model as noted above which advances our theoretical understanding of corporate heritage identity stewardship. Finally, the theoretical, practical and research implications of our findings are outlined.

Corporate heritage brands and identities in context

Corporate heritage as an institutional phenomenon emerged from research which explored monarchies (i.e. the institution represented by a Sovereign as Head of State and, more generally, by a Royal Family) as heritage institutions and as corporate heritage brands (Balmer *et al.*, 2004; Balmer and Greyser, 2006; Balmer, 2009a). These seminal conceptual and descriptive studies relating to the corporate heritage phenomenon detailed the significance of the domain and provided an initial articulation of key corporate heritage traits. Arguably, two articles have been influential in providing the foundations for the field, which, respectively, focussed on monarchies (Balmer *et al.*, 2006) and on corporate brands with a heritage (Urde *et al.*, 2007).

Within the subject domain of corporate marketing (Balmer, 1998, 2011c; Balmer and Greyser, 2003, 2006), the idea has been advanced that corporate heritage brands (Balmer *et al.*, 2006; Urde *et al.*, 2007; Balmer, 2011a), and corporate heritage identities (Balmer, 2011b), represent distinct types of institutional brands and identities. While most companies on average only survive for a mere 40 years (de Geus, 2002), there are, all the same, a sizable number of prominent business organisations with corporate brands and identities that are of considerable maturity (Urde *et al.*, 2007; Blombäck and Brunninge, 2009). The track record of success – of these potential or actual heritage institutions – sometimes spans the centuries (Urde *et al.*, 2007; Urde, 2009; Stadler, 2011).

Both corporate heritage brands and corporate heritage identities draw on an organisation's institutional heritage (i.e. corporate heritage). However, a distinction is made, in that corporate heritage identity is a much broader concept potentially relevant for all organisations imbued with an institutional heritage, while a corporate heritage brand identity requires the strategic decision for a well-defined and enduring value proposition and covenant between the organisation and its stakeholders predicated on the corporate heritage identity of the organisation (Balmer, 2013).

In this context, it was argued that corporate heritage brands (Urde *et al.*, 2007) and, more recently, corporate heritage identities (Balmer, 2011b), in order to survive and to remain salient, required ongoing management stewardship.

Heritage stewardship, it was advanced, is predicated on a particular managerial mindset which informs the enactment of these distinct institutional brands/identities (Urde *et al.*, 2007; Balmer, 2011a). In more general and in instrumental terms, the management notion of stewardship is consistent with the custodial role accorded to management within the subject domain of corporate marketing in regard to corporate brands and corporate identities per se (Balmer and Greyser, 2003; Balmer, 2009b, 2011c, 2012b). From a more pronounced theoretical standpoint, this above perspective mirrors the increased interest in management cognitions and self-understanding in regard to corporate identities in general (He and Balmer, 2007b, 2013; He, 2012).

However, despite the growing reference made to corporate heritage within corporate marketing (Urde *et al.*, 2007; Balmer, 2011a, 2011b; Hudson, 2011; Wiedmann *et al.*, 2011a, 2011b) – a development accompanied by an increased interest in the strategic utility of historical references in general (Blombäck and Brunninge, 2009) – and brand heritage in consumer marketing (Aaker, 1996; Ballantyne *et al.*, 2006; Liebrenz-Himes *et al.*, 2007; Hakala *et al.*, 2011), the notion of corporate heritage brands and corporate heritage identities, from both theoretical and instrumental perspectives, has received little academic and empirical scrutiny so far (Balmer, 2011b), and the particular managerial stewardship dimensions believed to be characteristic for such entities – albeit tentatively discussed by Urde *et al.* (2007) in regard to corporate heritage brands – remain, to a large degree, underspecified.

The notion of heritage in marketing

The importance of brand heritage in particular emerges as a key leitmotif within the marketing literature, and it has been asserted that heritage is a key marketing asset (Ballantyne *et al.*, 2006). For instance, within the marketing canon, heritage is seen to be salient in regard to product brand identities (Aaker, 1996; Liebrenz-Himes *et al.*, 2007; Hakala *et al.*, 2011), corporate brand identities (Urde *et al.*, 2007; Wiedmann *et al.*, 2011a) and corporate identities too (Balmer, 2011b). Heritage is seen to be relevant for organisations of varying size and hue and, as such, encompasses multinational enterprises along with small, family-run businesses (Micelotta and Raynard, 2011).

The importance of brand heritage has been scrutinised along a number of dimensions. For instance, it has been discussed as an important source of brand authenticity (Beverland, 2005, 2006); can imbue a brand with a particular "aura" (Alexander, 2009); is of especial relevance for luxury brands (Moore and Birtwistle, 2004; Beverland, 2006; Fionda and Moore, 2009); and can be materially significant in terms of culturally anchored, so-called "iconic" brands (Holt, 2004; Alexander, 2009).

In consumer and services marketing contexts, heritage has, over the years, attracted the attention of a number of scholars (Liebrenz-Himes *et al.*, 2007; Banerjee, 2008; Hakala *et al.*, 2011). For instance, heritage is seen to be an important driver of customer value (Wiedmann *et al.*, 2011a). Heritage is also seen to be relevant in experiential and emotional terms in consumer and service marketing contexts (Peñaloza, 2000; Ponsonby-Mccabe and Boyle, 2006). Moreover, heritage may significantly contribute to consumers' emotional and symbolic attachment to a brand (Ballantyne *et al.*, 2006).

In more general instrumental terms, heritage has been articulated in the context of planned "heritage communication" (Bühler and Dürig, 2008).

However, heritage is sometimes conceptualised in somewhat loose terms within the corporate marketing and management canons and, moreover, among marketing managers and practitioners. For instance, whilst Urde *et al.* (2007) point out that heritage is significantly different from history, there is anecdotal evidence that many companies now refer to their "heritage" when they talk about the organisation's "history" in corporate communications. In part, this might represent a pragmatic reaction by businesses and other organisations to socio-cultural sentiments within society that tend to valorise different forms of cultural and natural heritage (Isar *et al.*, 2011; McDonald, 2011) not only as a cultural resource for consumption purposes (Goulding, 2000, 2001) but also as a marker of individual and collective identities at different levels (Graham and Howard, 2008). Moreover, the growing reference to heritage may, perhaps, partially reflect the inflationary use of the term in academic and vernacular discourses within society in general (Samuel, 1996; Lowenthal, 1998). In the light of the above, the theoretical and instrumental elaboration of heritage is warranted, and heritage represents a potentially fruitful conceptual lens for marketing and corporate marketing scholarship (Balmer, 2011b).

Corporate heritage dimensions

Uncovering the characteristics of corporate heritage is one of the key academic concerns and themes to emerge from the literature. As such, marketing scholars have variously examined the dimensions of corporate heritage brands (Urde *et al.*, 2007; Balmer, 2011a; Hudson, 2011; Wiedmann *et al.*, 2011a, 2011b) and, more recently, in the context of corporate heritage identities (Balmer, 2011b). To reiterate, corporate heritage brand identities and corporate heritage identities are viewed as distinct – albeit related – identity types (Balmer, 2011a, 2011b, 2013).

To reprise an earlier point, this study focusses on corporate heritage identities along with their specific management requirements. Corporate identity represents the much broader and more fundamental concept (Balmer, 2008).

In delineating the nature of corporate heritage, the extant literature makes a distinction between heritage and history. Thus, while all organisations have a past with a particular historical trajectory, some organisations, it has been suggested, "possess" a unique corporate heritage that becomes central for their corporate identities linking an organisation's past with the present and an envisioned future in a meaningful way; potentially being leveraged as a strategic resource for corporate-level marketing in terms of positioning corporate brands (Urde *et al.*, 2007) and corporate identities in addition (Balmer, 2011a, 2011b).

To date, the framework by Urde *et al.* (2007) – the corporate heritage brand quotient – and subsequent discussions of the concept (Balmer, 2011a, 2011b) detail both identity and instrumental characteristics of corporate heritage brands and identities, which refer to characteristics in terms of their: temporality, continuity, relative invariance and role identity multiplicity.

Because of the distinct conceptual characteristics identified in the extant literature and deliberated on above, it has been argued that corporate heritage identities and brands need to be managed in a particular way, namely, corporate heritage stewardship (Urde *et al.*, 2007; Balmer, 2011a, 2011b, 2013) (Box 1).

BOX 1 CORPORATE HERITAGE BRAND/IDENTITY CHARACTERISTICS

Temporality

Corporate heritage brands and identities inhabit multiple temporal time frames, in that they are of the past, present and future (Balmer *et al.*, 2006; Urde *et al.*, 2007): these time identities afford corporate heritage a special quality, and may account for their saliency vis-à-vis different stakeholders (Balmer, 2011b). Hence, corporate heritage brands and corporate heritage identities are imbued with a quality of "timelessness" (Urde *et al.*, 2007) and, as such, often act as a stable point of reference (Balmer *et al.*, 2006) for individual and collective identities within and beyond the individual institution

(Balmer, 2011a). Both concepts – corporate heritage brands and corporate heritage identities – are predicated on an apparent temporal transcendence of certain characteristic corporate identity traits – the heritage footprint of a corporate identity (Balmer, 2011a) – that constitute an institutional heritage (i.e. corporate heritage), being different from history or the past per se (Urde *et al.*, 2007; Balmer, 2011a, 2011b). Hudson (2011), for instance, showed how these different time frames are mutually constructed by the company and the customers of the Cunard shipping brand of ocean liners and cruise ships.

Continuity

The importance of continuity in terms of core brand values and in terms of symbols, as well as continuity in regard to performance over time (i.e. track record), has been identified as a key trait of corporate heritage brands (Urde *et al.*, 2007). For example, Wiedmann *et al.* (2011a, 2011b) have shown that the perceived value customers attach to heritage in the context of automobile corporate brands in Germany is related to higher trustworthiness and affinity because of credibility and orientation derived from long-term continuity and values expressed by the heritage status of a corporate brand.

Relative invariance

Corporate heritage brands and identities are characterised by a "relative invariance". This theoretical notion can be explained in terms of that organisations over time "appear to remain the same and yet change" (Balmer, 2011b, p. 1387). As such, the institutional heritage is adapted and reinterpreted for present purposes and in light of expectations for the future (Urde *et al.*, 2007; Balmer, 2011b). For instance, Byrom and Lehman (2009) evidenced how the Australian Coopers brewery managed to facilitate its institutional heritage as a family business while maintaining the company's contemporary appeal and relevance.

Multiple role identities

Corporate heritage identities/brands may also be constituted in relation to the cultural heritage of other social entities such as communities or places, as well as form meaningful bilateral relationships with other corporate heritage brands or identities (Balmer, 2011a, 2011b), providing a much broader base for an organisation's legitimacy and stakeholder relevance (Balmer, 2011b). For example, a recent study by Foster *et al.* (2011) – albeit using different theoretical concepts – shows how the Canadian fast-food brand Tim Hortons explicitly appropriated Canadian national heritage. Brand identity and brand positioning insofar has become a stable reference point for Canadian collective identity.

Corporate heritage stewardship

To account for the specific management requirements of corporate heritage identities and brands, the notion of *corporate heritage brand stewardship* was introduced by Urde *et al.* (2007), which is predicated on a particular "management mind-set of nurturing, maintaining, and protecting brand heritage" (Urde *et al.*, 2007, p. 9).

According to Urde *et al.* (2007), the management stewardship of heritage in an institutional context and its utilisation as a strategic corporate marketing asset entails, on the one hand, the active "uncovering" of heritage that may even lead to the discovery or rediscovery of a hitherto hidden heritage (Urde *et al.*, 2007) and the *activation* or reactivation of the prior discovered or rediscovered institutional heritage for corporate-level marketing purposes (Urde *et al.*, 2007). On the other hand, it also requires the custodianship of senior management, particularly the chief executive officer (CEO), which is concerned with *protecting* the institutional heritage that is part of the corporate brand or identity (Urde *et al.*, 2007). Hence, heritage stewardship is based on the marriage of retrospective *brand archaeology*, which is a managerial "concern with a brand's provenance and historic attractiveness" (Balmer, 2011a, p. 4) and of prospective *brand strategy* that involves "marshalling the brand heritage in order to maintain its brand saliency and competitive advantage for the future" (Balmer, 2011a, p. 4).

The notion of stewardship combines in a way the cerebral aspects of understanding and interpretation with the practical dimension of doing and acting (Balmer, 2008) and accords importance to management in regard to the particular enactment of corporate heritage brands and identities; stewardship being at once instrumental and constitutive. In more theoretical terms, management perceptions and self-understanding of their organisation's identity have been found to be an important dimension of corporate identity strategy enactment (He and Balmer, 2007a, 2007b, 2013; He, 2012). Such a perspective has long-informed instrumental insights relating to the corporate identity and corporate brand identity domains as per the ACID Test diagnostic framework (Balmer and Greyser, 2003; Balmer *et al.*, 2009; Balmer, 2012).

As such, heritage stewardship is fundamentally predicated on a particular managerial mindset – a general understanding, orientation and disposition to act in terms of the nature and role of a corporate brand and identity – that is composed of two main aspects.

The first aspect is a *focus on long-term continuity*, which also entails adaptability and a dedication to continuous improvement. The second aspect refers to a trans-generational *sense of responsibility* for the brand/identity and its heritage.

Both are said to be instrumental for safeguarding the brand's relevance, credibility and trust vis-à-vis its various stakeholders and in the light of changing demands and conditions over time (Urde *et al.*, 2007), thus maintaining the saliency of the corporate heritage brand/identity (Balmer, 2011a, 2011b).

Rationale for the study

As our review of this nascent field indicates, the constitutive dimensions and characteristics of corporate heritage brands and identities and their relevance for stakeholders (e.g. customers) have attracted recent scholarly interest (Balmer, 2011a, 2011b; Hudson, 2011; Wiedmann *et al.*, 2011a, 2011b). However, the field is still in its infancy. Conceptual, and more specifically, empirical, work on the domain is slight. As with any new domain, there is, sometimes, inconsistency in how corporate heritage and analogous constructs are defined. To date, the majority of extant work is predominately conceptual and tentative in nature, with the more empirical work providing rich descriptive insights on the domain – but not so much in terms of theoretical insights – focussing on well-known brands and organisations. In light of the above, and noting the importance accorded to corporate heritage stewardship, it is evident that empirical research on the aforementioned would meaningfully advance extant conceptual contributions.

Developing the above, corporate heritage stewardship and the particular managerial mindset required for the management of these distinct types of institutional brands/identities has so far received little further empirical scrutiny – and theoretical advance – outside the concept's original domain of monarchies as corporate brands and heritage institutions (Balmer, 2011a) and the research contributing to its original articulation by Urde *et al.* (2007).

Taking a broader vista, the corporate marketing literature has focussed on the role of management perceptions in the context of corporate identities (He and Balmer, 2007b, 2013; He, 2012), the nature of corporate brand strategy enactment (Vallaster and de Chernatony, 2005, 2006; Vallaster and Lindgreen, 2011) and the normative role of CEOs/the top management team in general (Balmer, 1995, 2009b, 2012b; Balmer and Greyser, 2003) but not yet scrutinised corporate heritage identities/brands as such.

Similarly, within the academic domain of management, stewardship theory has been conceptually discussed as an alternative approach to corporate governance, which is underpinned by particular situational and psychological factors that facilitate stewardship behaviour amongst managers or employees (Davis *et al.*, 1997; Hernandez, 2012) but has not yet provided sufficient empirical evidence of institutionalised forms of management stewardship characteristic for particular types of organisations, especially in the private sector (Segal and Lehrer, 2012).

Therefore, the focus of this study is to address a gap in the extant literature in relation to corporate heritage identity management in particular and, moreover, to make a theoretical contribution relating to the nature of managerial corporate heritage identity stewardship. In particular, this research focusses on the different dimensions that constitute the managerial mindset/self-understanding necessary for the successful management of corporate heritage identities within a business context.

To reiterate, this empirical theory-building study makes a contribution, in theoretical terms, to the nascent corporate heritage field by revealing key interpretative dimensions pertaining to corporate heritage identity stewardship as understood by managers.

Research insights from this study underpin the theory of corporate heritage identity stewardship in the form of a theoretical framework. The research findings also provided instrumental insights by uncovering salient traits *in regard to* corporate heritage identity stewardship.

Shepherd Neame: Context and company background

Unlike extant studies, either within corporate marketing in general that tend to focus on large multinational enterprises (Abimbola and Kocak, 2007) or in the nascent area of corporate heritage brands and identities in particular, which have focussed so far on well-known business and non-business organisations and brands (Urde *et al.*, 2007; Balmer, 2011a, 2011b; Hudson, 2011), the current study is situated within the empirical context of the UK's oldest brewery, i.e. Shepherd Neame: a regional multi-generational family-owned company based in the southeast of the UK.

Multigenerational family-owned companies of considerable maturity are largely under-researched in general (Micelotta and Raynard, 2011) but have been suggested, understandably, as a focus of empirical research relevant for our understanding of corporate heritage in regard to corporate identities in particular (Balmer *et al.*, 2006; Blombäck and Brunninge, 2009). Furthermore, regional and family-owned companies may have a utility in shedding light on management stewardship in general (Segal and Lehrer, 2012).

In more general terms, the notion of corporate heritage as a strategic resource for corporate branding strategies has recently attracted attention from a family business perspective (Micelotta and Raynard, 2011). However, this research has largely focussed on the strategic relevance of the familial dimension for corporate identities/brands (Craig *et al.*, 2008) rather than corporate heritage identities and their management in a family business context as such, despite the *prima facie* salience of family-owned businesses of considerable maturity that could qualify – following Urde *et al.* (2007) – as corporate heritage identities/brands.

The case study focusses on the UK brewing sector, which is significant within the UK in terms of annual turnover, tax contributions, employment and cultural relevance (Sheen, 2011; Muir, 2012; Oxford Economics, 2012). The industry is also characterised by a high level of competitive dynamics and change, government regulation, as well as societal scrutiny and interest (Knowles and Egan, 2002; Pratten, 2007a, 2007b, 2007c), thus representing an interesting backdrop for corporate marketing issues in general. Further, within the brewing industry, as one of the oldest industries in the UK (Mathias, 1959; Gourvish and Wilson, 1994), despite the market being dominated by large multinational corporations, there are a significant number of multigenerational and long-established companies still operating within that industry. This case study focusses on the oldest of these. In addition, the sector constitutes a relevant empirical domain for heritage-based corporate marketing and past-related consumer marketing activities (Alexander, 2009; Blombäck and Brunninge, 2009; Byrom and Lehman, 2009).

Apart from its instrumental relevance for the theoretical elaboration of corporate heritage stewardship, the case study itself is significant, in that its focus is on Britain's oldest brewer: Shepherd Neame. Established in 1698, it is one of the UK's oldest operational commercial enterprises (Box 2).

BOX 2 SHEPHERD NEAME COMPANY INFORMATION

Shepherd Neame Ltd. is a regional brewer and pub operator based in the small English market town of Faversham in the county of Kent. The company is a fifth-generation family-controlled business founded in 1698 (although recent historical evidence indicates that the origins of the brewery can be traced well into the sixteenth century), which qualifies it as Britain's oldest brewery. The company owns about 354 pubs and a growing number of hotels in Kent and the southeast of England (including London). It brews nationally distributed cask ales ("Real Ale") and premium bottled ales (PBA) such as "Spitfire" or "Bishops Finger", which are Protected Geographical Indication (PGI)-certified under European Union (EU) legislation, as well as several international premium lagers such as Asahi Super Dry (Japan) or Kingfisher (India) and speciality craft beers such as Samuel Adams (USA) under license. The shareholding of the company is divided into shares held exclusively by family members and shares traded on the London PLUS Market (recently renamed into ICAP ISDX Exchange). In 2012, Shepherd Neame brewed 252,000 barrels (UK) of beer (approximately 412,400 hectolitres) with a record annual turnover of over £133 million. Before the current recession, the company had enjoyed continuous year-on-year profit and turnover growth for more than three decades and has continued to outgrow the market since 2008. The company has managed to grow against the backdrop of a highly competitive and regulated business environment, characterised by high levels of market concentration (market dominated by a few multinational breweries, pub companies and multiple retailers), brewery and pub closures, unfavourable government legislation and tax policy, decline in beer consumption and changing customer preferences and lifestyle patterns. The majority of the sales are made in the UK (with some notable export successes to Sweden or Italy). The company sources locally grown hops (within 25 miles of the brewery) in its production process, as well as uses natural mineral water from its own source. In addition to common industry awards related to the quality and taste of individual beers, the company has won a stream of business awards in various categories, ranging from social responsibility and sustainability to service quality and process excellence. According to Shepherd Neame, it was the first brewery in the UK to be awarded ISO 14001 accreditation for sustainable management. The company has strong links with the local community through procurement, employment, pubs and various sponsorship activities. It directly employs about 1,100 people. In its corporate marketing activities, the company frequently stresses, amongst other things, its local origin, its heritage and family business credentials, its dedication to quality and its role as a responsible corporate citizen.

Research method

In light of the theory-building purpose of the study, a single, in-depth case design broadly situated within the interpretative, qualitative research tradition underpinned by moderate constructionist convictions informs this empirical study (Blaikie, 2007, 2009). This approach is appropriate for a theory-building case research where extant empirical research is limited and where an insight into an organisational phenomenon such as corporate heritage stewardship is slight (Eisenhardt, 1989; Yin, 2009). Moreover, qualitative case study research enables a prolonged hermeneutic interaction between empirical data, emerging conceptual framework, and extant literature (Corbin and Strauss, 2008).

We broadly followed the conventions of a holistic single case study design (Yin, 2009), with our empirical case being taken as representative or typical for a corporate heritage identity without subscribing to the positivist stance/replication logic expounded by Eisenhardt (1989) or Yin (2009) that subsequently would undermine the theoretical and empirical relevance of a single-case design.

Within a non-positivist framework, case-based research facilitates the convergence of the empirical emic dimension with the conceptual etic dimension of a social phenomenon (Harper, 1992; Walton, 1992).

As such, our main focus was on its instrumental relevance for understanding, in theoretical terms, the abstract concept of corporate heritage identity stewardship rather than on articulating unique and intrinsic characteristics of the case per se (Stake, 1995), which is, nonetheless, illustrative of the phenomenon (Siggelkow, 2007).

A case study-based research design is well suited for generating particularistic, as well as holistic, forms of knowledge (Hamel, 1992; Verschuren, 2003; Stake, 2005) and where a close interaction between researcher and social setting is required for exploring and understanding a focal phenomenon of interest in its manifold manifestations (Gummesson, 2000). As such, the case study approach differs from experimental, as well as survey-based, approaches to social inquiry, with the former relying on theoretical inference under controlled conditions and the latter aiming for statistical generalisation to a larger population (Hammersley and Gomm, 2000; Yin, 2009).

Consequently, we do not attempt to derive statistical/substantive generalisations across different empirical instances/domains, but to understand the properties of the construct of corporate heritage identity and its particular stewardship requirements/characteristics based on an exemplary empirical case that is also "revelatory" in nature (Yin, 2009) taking place within Britain's oldest brewer. Thus, it is representing an indicative "blueprint" of the concept at a higher level of abstraction to be refined, further specified and, subsequently, if only partially, transferred to other empirical contexts by future research (Blaikie, 2009) taking into account the situated and theory-laden nature of all knowledge claims (Sayer, 1992).

Case studies represent an established approach within the methodological canon of corporate marketing research (Balmer, 1996; Balmer and Stotvig, 1997; Balmer and Wilson, 1998a; Andriopoulos and Gotsi, 2001; Motion *et al.*, 2003; He, 2004;

Melewar and Akel, 2005; Powell, 2005; Bendixen and Abratt, 2007; Maxwell and Knox, 2009; Leitch and Davenport, 2011; Simões and Mason, 2012).

Consistent with our moderate constructionist paradigmatic convictions and mindful of the research approach outlined above, the resultant theory emerging from this empirical study is, following on from Charmaz (2006), classified as an interpretative theory. Interpretative theories advance knowledge by providing understanding and illumination. Moreover, this often results in an abstraction of lay concepts into academic ones, and, as such, this constitutes indicative social scientific typifications (Schütz, 1962).

Interpretive theories assume emergence, situatedness, non-linear relations and a large degree of indeterminacy (Charmaz, 2006).

Importantly, an interpretative theory, including the resultant theory emerging from this study, does not aim and yield deterministic explanations or formulates causal linear relationships between variables (Charmaz, 2006). This has a bearing on diagrammatic depictions of interpretative theories. As such, there needs to be mindfulness that graphic depictions of an interpretative theoretical framework, typically, are an abstract – analytic rather than an empirical – causal form. This implies that interpretative theoretical frameworks highlight patterns and arrangements to a more heightened degree than frameworks informed by positivistic theories where specific directional relationships between variables is the modus operandi (Turner, 1987 cited in Blaikie, 2009, p. 152).

Based on an initial review of the literature, some broad preliminary concepts (Yin, 2009) were used in a sensitising mode (Blumer, 1969). These concepts helped to situate the study in its disciplinary and theoretical context that informed and guided the selection of the case itself, the identification of relevant units of analysis and indicated towards likely types and sources of data (Yin, 2009).

After identifying and considering a number of sectors, based on several criteria, such as maturity of the industry and the level of current activity in the UK, it was decided to focus on the brewing sector. After contacting those breweries – and following the work of Urde *et al.* (2007) – which *prima facie* conformed to being highly relevant in terms of the corporate heritage identity, construct access was granted to two breweries.

Following general recommendation within the precepts of case study research (Yin, 2009), seven pilot interviews were conducted and a limited number of documents were collected at one of the breweries to assess and "fine-tune" the research design and to test techniques and tools (e.g. software package for data analysis). The other brewery was selected as the main case company – apart from its professed status as Britain's oldest brewer – because of the level of access granted, the existence of a company archive and the company's active use of heritage themes in their corporate-level marketing activities.

Nineteen open and semi-structured interviews (a total of approximately 20 hours of interviews) with a cross-section of directors (5) and managers (9) were conducted as part of the main study. These interviews lasted between 45 and 95 minutes, of which 14 were formally audio recorded (approx. 16.5 hours of interviews) and, subsequently, transcribed by a third party, while mental notes were taken during the interviews where recording was not possible (some interviews were not recorded because of the particular interview setting; for instance, an interview conducted while having lunch with a director). The transcribed interviews yielded about 170,000 words of textual data. Table 6.1 provides an overview of the interviews conducted.

TABLE 6.1 Overview of interviews conducted

Interviewee	Position	No. of interviews (thereof audio recorded)	Interview duration total in minutes (thereof audio recorded)	Interview dates (all in 2010)
1	Company President	2 (1)	~125 (45 recorded)	20th July
2	Chief Executive Officer	2 (1)	~120 (60 recorded)	5th May and 17th Aug
3	Managing Director Property and Tenanted Trade	1	95	19th July
4	Managing Director Marketing and Sales	1	62	19th July
5	Managing Director Production and Distribution	2	122	20th July and 28th Sep
6	Account Director Public Relations	1	78	19th July
7	Account Manager Public Relations	1	55	27th Aug
8	Account Manager Public Relations	1	45	27th Aug
9	Marketing Manager	1	51	24th Aug
10	Business Development Manager	1	75	22th Sep
11	Business Development Manager	1	78	5th Oct
12	Head of Property Services/Architect	1	86	28th Sep
13	Head of Visitor Centre and Hospitality	2 (1)	~90 (60 recorded)	5th Oct and 9th Nov
14	Company Archivist/ Historian	2 (1)	~125 (65 recorded)	20th July and 17th Aug
Σ		19 (14)	1,206 (977 recorded)	

Additionally, textual documents, such as corporate communication reports, strategy documents, annual reports, in-house and customer magazines, historical archived materials, along with documents in the public domain (e.g. company website, trade and business press), were inspected and analysed. Further, visual data were collected and a limited number of non-participant observations took place during the project (e.g. during site visits, guided tours, beer festivals, personal pub and hotel visits). Such a broad variety of different additional textual and visual data was collected to enable triangulation of the data in accordance with the precepts of case study research (Yin, 2009). In addition, we perceived textual documents as cultural artefacts that reveal much about the identity and heritage claims made about the organisation (Chreim, 2005), potentially revealing important aspects of management stewardship, especially in the context of corporate marketing.

The generated data were examined and analysed – broadly following an abductive research logic (Blaikie, 2009) and the precepts of grounded analysis (Easterby-Smith *et al.*, 2008) – through a multi-stage coding process facilitated by software (MaxQDA 10), which is recommended for qualitative and interpretative research of this kind (Corbin and Strauss, 2008). Data analysis and synthesis was carried out as an iterative and cyclical process facilitated by reflective memo writing and conceptual mapping and a prolonged hermeneutic interaction between empirical data, emerging framework and extant theory (Corbin and Strauss, 2008). Figure 6.1 schematically depicts the analytic process.

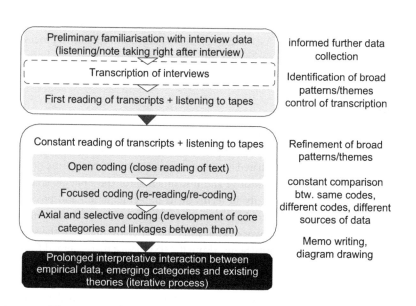

FIGURE 6.1 The process of data analysis

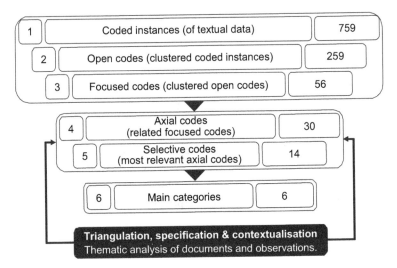

FIGURE 6.2 From open coding to conceptual categories

The coding process of interview data yielded 759 open codes that were relationally integrated into 14 selective codes. Gradually, six main categories emerged from the process, which were corroborated by qualitative triangulation (Flick, 1992, 2007) based on the thematic analysis of other textual and observational data to specify and contextualise these categories (Figure 6.2). Hence, the salience of the heritage stewardship theme for our study did actually emerge from the data and the interplay with several sensitising concepts to make sense of the data and was not a priori chosen as a central interpretative frame, which the conventional structure of a journal article may imply. As a result of the prolonged interpretative process, the six categories were further synthesised into three main dimensions and both were integrated into a theoretical framework.

Findings

Our analysis and synthesis of the empirical data suggest a close relationship between the particular manifestation of the case company's corporate heritage identity and a specific multifaceted mindset shared amongst the management team of the organisation. We found this to be constitutive and instrumental for the strategic enactment of the corporate heritage identity in terms of its implementation and positioning vis-à-vis the company's stakeholders and within its various societal environments. We suggest a theoretical framework explicating the different aspects of the substantive Corporate Heritage Identity Stewardship (CHIS) theory that emerged from our study. Within the theoretical framework, which articulates the substantive theory in conceptual terms, the CHIS mindset conceptually comprises six managerial dispositions (CHIS dispositions) to feel, think and act that manifest in three broader

TABLE 6.2 Corporate heritage identity stewardship awareness dimensions and dispositions

CHIS dispositions	CHIS awareness dimensions
Sense of Continuance	Positionality Awareness
Sense of Belongingness	
Sense of Self	
Sense of Heritage	Heritage Awareness
Sense of Responsibility	Custodianship Awareness
Sense of Potency	

managerial awareness dimensions (CHIS awareness dimensions) expressed by managers (Table 6.2).

Together, the three CHIS awareness dimensions and the associated six CHIS dispositions constitute the CHIS mindset. It articulates at once a shared managerial sentiment (affective), an understanding (cognitive) and a propensity (performative) towards the organisation and its institutional heritage itself (e.g. its position, role and purpose), as well as in regard to the organisation in relation to various stakeholders and the societal environments within which the company is embedded and has acquired a heritage status. Thus, the six managerial CHIS dispositions that underpin the three broad CHIS awareness dimensions are descriptively labelled "senses" to indicate their tripartite character of being at once a managerial sentiment, an understanding and a propensity to act towards and on behalf of the organisation.

Within our theoretical framework the thus specified CHIS mindset is constitutive and instrumental for the strategic enactment of a corporate identity as a corporate heritage identity by managers guiding corporate marketing activities.

We explicate each of the identified CHIS awareness dimensions and their associated CHIS dispositions in the following sections before we integrate our findings into a conceptual framework of an emerging corporate heritage identity stewardship theory. Illustrative interview quotes and additional illustrative evidence are provided in the appendix.

The presented quotes are illustrative for a general pattern that emerged from the interviews but was also found to be salient for the particular ways in which the corporate heritage identity of the firm is strategically enacted and represented to the company's stakeholders. Thus, the interpretative dimensions were corroborated by manifestations thereof such as policies, practices, strategies, etc.

For confidentiality reasons and because of the relative small size of the case organisation, we do not disclose the name or position of any individual interviewed in conjunction with a quote and refer only to the generic labels of director and manager.

Positionality awareness

This CHIS awareness dimension, Positionality Awareness, expressed by managers refers to a managerial awareness in regard to the company's particular socio-historical position within its societal environments, in terms of a relation to past, present and future (temporal); in relation to a place and location (spatial); and in relation to the identities of individual and collective stakeholders (socio-cultural). This CHIS awareness dimension expressed by managers is characterised by and derived from three interrelated CHIS dispositions: Sense of Continuance, Sense of Belongingness and Sense of Self.

Sense of continuance

This CHIS disposition, Sense of Continuance, refers to management's expressed concern for and awareness of the company's long persistence over time: it has so far and should also in future prevail as an institution. On the one hand, it is related to a managerial *focus on continuity* expressed by managers as four different forms of continuity: temporal, institutional, spatial and social. On the other hand, this disposition is characterised by a professed long-term orientation towards the business (i.e. *focus on the long-term*) paired with a *focus on adaptation* in terms of the necessity, ability, and willingness to adapt to changing circumstances for the company to prevail long-term. All three managerial foci are interrelated and, as such, concur into the particular CHIS disposition Sense of Continuance (see Appendix Table A6.1 for illustrative quotes/evidence).

Sense of belongingness

This managerial CHIS disposition, Sense of Belongingness, stresses the importance of attachment, affiliation and affinity towards place (e.g. home town and county), social groups and institutions (e.g. family, community, industry) for the enactment of the corporate identity, which was found to be predicated on aspects of *closeness* (proximity) and *provenance* (origin). Hence, it refers to questions such as "where do we come from", "where do we belong to" or "who or what are we close to". As such, the dimension of belongingness often concurs with the notion of continuance but has a more emotive/affective connotation. It reflects a "strong sense of belonging" that manifests itself in the company's identity, policies and strategies.

The aspect of *focus on closeness* refers to the professed spatial and socio-cultural proximity between the company and any of the aforementioned social groups or institutions (e.g. family, community, industry), while the concurrent dimension *focus on provenance* relates to the notion of spatial, socio-cultural origin and is, as such, closely coupled with former. The Sense of Belongingness disposition was manifested in different ways (see Appendix Table A6.2 for illustrative quotes/evidence).

Sense of self

This CHIS disposition, Sense of Self, refers to nonconformist disposition shared amongst managers that is constituted by two interrelated aspects: *independence* and *individuality*. It refers to a managerial appreciation of affective, cognitive and performative independence and individuality in regard to corporate strategy, direction and conduct. This aspect imbues management feeling, thinking and acting with a strong sense of confidence towards a perceived nonconformism in regard to strategies and policies pursued. The managerial *focus on independence* relates to the concept of autonomy, while the *focus on individuality* connotes the notion of difference and plurality in feeling, thinking and acting. Both aspects closely interact in that autonomy justifies difference and the latter reinforces the former (see Appendix Table A6.3 for illustrative quotes/evidence).

Heritage awareness/sense of heritage

The CHIS awareness dimension Heritage Awareness refers to a managerial understanding of the company's particular status as an organisation with an institutional corporate heritage that represents a shared inheritance, which is worth to be protected, nurtured, and bequeathed to the next generation. It is based on the CHIS disposition Sense of Heritage. This managerial disposition refers to the managerial *validation* (acknowledging), *appreciation* (valuing) and *adoption* (ownership taking) of the company's institutional corporate heritage and of the company's heritage status within its societal and institutional environments, which are perceived as strategically efficacious for the present and the future of the company (see Appendix Table A6.4 for illustrative quotes/evidence).

Custodianship awareness

This CHIS awareness dimension, Custodianship Awareness, expressed by managers refers to a managerial awareness of a shared custodial obligation and duty to speak and act for the company and on behalf of others in an authorial way, which is perceived as legitimate by management because of their concurrent understanding of the company's status as an organisation imbued with an institutional heritage (i.e. Heritage Awareness) and its particular socio-historical position (i.e. Positionality Awareness). It is constituted by two interdependent CHIS dispositions articulated by managers: Sense of Responsibility and Sense of Potency.

Sense of responsibility

Custodianship Awareness is characterised by the CHIS disposition Sense of Responsibility, which is constituted by two aspects: *institutional custodianship* and *non-institutional custodianship*. The former stresses a managerially perceived custodial obligation towards the organisation and its institutional heritage that is derived from the instrumental necessity to protect, nurture and bequeath the corporate heritage (and the company), which implies intergenerational exchange between present and future generations. The latter aspect indicates a professed sense of custodial duty that goes beyond the company and its corporate heritage itself predicated on the perceived heritage status of the organisation, justifying and demanding such an expanded notion of responsibility (see Appendix Table A6.5 for illustrative quotes/ evidence).

Sense of potency

The CHIS disposition Sense of Potency closely interacts with the above discussed sense of responsibility. However, it carries the notion of perceived legitimacy rather than obligation and duty. It imbues the company and its management with a "license to speak and act", partially justified by the heritage status of the firm, which implies (claimed) authenticity, credibility and legitimacy vis-à-vis the company's stakeholders. Thus, it denominates a clear understanding of *corporate purpose* and *corporate authority* expressed by managers in terms of communicative action in regard to immediate institutional concerns but also issues beyond the organisation itself, which is facilitated by the company's heritage status (see Appendix Table A6.6 for illustrative quotes/evidence).

Theoretical framework

The corporate heritage identity stewardship theory explains that the specific enactment of a corporate heritage identity is predicated on a particular, albeit multifaceted, management mindset. The theoretical framework integrates the different building blocks outlined above. Figure 6.3 schematically depicts the theoretical framework of the corporate heritage identity stewardship theory constitutive and instrumental for the strategic enactment of corporate heritage identities.

Conceptually, the six different managerial CHIS dispositions interact, and this accounts for the three broad CHIS awareness dimensions. These, interdependently, constitute a collective CHIS management mindset. They are mutually reinforcing.

To recapitulate, the CHIS mindset variously articulates a shared managerial sentiment; a common management understanding; and a collective managerial propensity towards the organisation and its institutional heritage, stakeholders and the societal environments within which the company is embedded and from which it has attained its especial heritage status.

Consequently, the relationships between the conceptual building blocks of the theoretical framework are non-linear, bidirectional and emergent in nature. To reiterate, our theoretical framework is based on an interpretative type of theory and, as such, illuminates – despite the indicative use of arrows in its graphic depiction (Figure 6.3) – emergent patterns and non-linear relations between concepts in a holistic

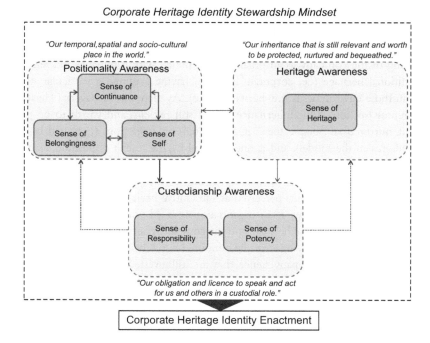

FIGURE 6.3 The corporate heritage identity stewardship theory (theoretical framework)

fashion (Charmaz, 2006). The aim is not, as in positivistic models, to provide a deterministic explanation of tightly specified causal linear relationships between variables as noted by Charmaz (2006).

In particular, we argue that a managerial Sense of Continuance interacts with a professed Sense of Belongingness and a profound Sense of Self, which all coalesce into a managerial awareness of the specific socio-historical position of the organisation: Positionality Awareness (section "Our temporal, spatial, and socio-cultural place in the world" in Figure 6.3).

The first disposition, Sense of Continuance, is characterised by a long-term orientation and view of the business paired with a concurrent focus on continuity and adaptation, while the second disposition of Sense of Belongingness refers to the general importance accorded to the company's attachment, affiliation and affinity towards place, social groups and/or institutions in terms of its spatial and/or socio-cultural closeness (proximity) and its spatial and/or socio-cultural provenance (origin). The third disposition, Sense of Self, interacts with both and articulates the importance accorded by managers to nonconformist independence and individuality in terms of corporate policies and strategies. Through the interaction (indicated by the bidirectional arrows) of these three dispositions, a shared managerial understanding emerges (indicated by the shaded area in the model) in regard to the company's temporal, spatial and socio-cultural place in the word.

Further, we suggest that the above articulated awareness of the company's specific temporal, spatial and socio-cultural position within its various environments (e.g. economic, socio-cultural, institutional) concurs with a shared managerial understanding of the company as an organisation imbued with a valuable and relevant institutional heritage (i.e. corporate heritage) having acquired a particular status within those environments (i.e. heritage status). As such, this managerial Heritage Awareness (section "Our inheritance that is still relevant and worth to be protected, nurtured and bequeathed" in Figure 6.3) emerges from (indicated by the shaded area in the model), and is underpinned by, the fourth disposition, labelled Sense of Heritage, which is characterised by validation (acknowledging), appreciation (valuing) and adoption (ownership taking) of the institutional heritage itself (i.e. corporate identity traits perceived as substantive heritage dimensions) and the company's particular status as an organisation imbued with that heritage. At the same time, the institutional heritage and the company's heritage status are perceived by managers not only as a legacy to be honoured but as being relevant for the present and future of the company; hence, they are still invested with new instrumental values (i.e. valorised) and appropriated for corporate marketing purposes.

Because of the interaction (indicated by the bidirectional arrow in the model) between the above described CHIS awareness dimensions of Positionality Awareness and Heritage Awareness, we further purport that a third managerial CHIS awareness dimension emerges, i.e. Custodianship Awareness (indicated by the two unidirectional arrows and the shaded area in the model). It is constituted by the interrelation (indicated by the bidirectional arrows) between a Sense of Responsibility indicating connotations of obligation and duty and a Sense of Potency carrying an association with authenticity, legitimacy and credibility (section "Our obligation and licence to speak and act for us and others in a custodial role" in Figure 6.3).

The fifth disposition, Sense of Responsibility, indicates a perceived custodial obligation in regard to the company and its institutional heritage, while the perceived company's heritage status warrants an expanded notion of responsibility (i.e. duty) and entails a professed custodial role beyond the boundaries of the firm itself. The final disposition, Sense of Potency, refers to a shared sense of purpose and authority. It imbues the company and its management with a "license to speak and act" based on and justified by the heritage status of the firm, which implies (claimed) authenticity, credibility and legitimacy in relation to the company's stakeholders.

The three CHIS awareness dimensions deduced from the study (i.e. Positionality Awareness, Heritage Awareness, Custodianship Awareness) are mutually constitutive and reinforcing. Thus, the Heritage Awareness interacts with a shared understanding of the company's particular socio-historical position: Positionality Awareness. Both provide the obligating and legitimating underpinning for the notion of custodianship fashioned by managers (i.e. Custodianship Awareness), which, in turn, reinforces the managerial self-understanding in regard to the former two awareness dimensions (indicated by the two dotted unidirectional arrows in the model).

Finally, we argue that the interaction between the three CHIS awareness dimensions results in a shared managerial CHIS mindset informing the corporate heritage identity stewardship activities of management (i.e. managerial and strategic action), which are constitutive for and have instrumental necessity for the strategic enactment of the corporate heritage identity vis-à-vis stakeholders and within multiple societal environments (indicated by the large arrow in the model).

Discussion

The empirical evidence underpinning the CHIS disposition sense of continuance largely confirms the focus on long-term continuity predicated on adaptability and a striving for continuous improvement suggested by Urde *et al.* (2007) as an important dimension of corporate heritage stewardship. However, the sense of continuance conceptualised as the result of this study is more elaborate and expansive, in that it provides a specified and more detailed account of the notion of focus on continuity (i.e. temporal, spatial, institutional, social) showing its multidimensional characteristics. Further, the focus on the long-term continuity of an organisation in general as identified by Balmer *et al.* (2006) and Urde *et al.* (2007) – the current findings indicate – is accompanied by a general long-term view of doing business, which represents a specific managerial frame of reference for strategic decision-making expressed by managers. Thus, it is not only a focus on the continuity of the institution (and its corporate identity or its corporate brand) manifested in concerns for institutional arrangements and a core business model/industry affiliation that is an important dimension of a corporate heritage identity stewardship mindset but also the continuity of stakeholder relations within and beyond the company and the continuity of place and location that guide managerial understanding and action. Hence, the study has shown that the focus on continuity is facilitated by a necessary long-term temporal orientation and outlook that managers share, which is of strategic significance as much as a central dimension of managerial self-understanding and seen as an important trait of the company's identity in comparison to other more short-term oriented businesses.

The equal importance accorded to continuity and change that was found to be present amongst managers confirms a conceptual tenet recently articulated by Balmer (2011a), which states that corporate heritage identities need to concurrently embrace continuity and change to stay meaningful and salient (Balmer, 2011b), a managerial sentiment empirically identified by Hudson (2011) as well. In addition, the current study's findings indicate also that there is a managerial appreciation for the need to balance the long-term orientation with short-term pressures to satisfy stakeholder expectations in the present while staying true to past and future concerns.

The CHIS disposition Sense of Belongingness indirectly provides support for the notion of reciprocity advanced by Balmer (2011a, 2011b) in regard to trust as a fundamental aspect of corporate heritage brand/identity saliency. However, the findings of the study indicate that the associated affinity dimension of that saliency (Balmer, 2011a, 2011b) is equally reciprocal, in that the notion of belongingness is not confined to only the identification of various stakeholders with the firm but also based on the importance accorded to attachment, affiliation and affinity towards place, social groups and institutions by management and manifested in the strategic corporate heritage identity enactment (e.g. spatial and socio-cultural anchoring), supporting the earlier mentioned notion of meaningful bilateral relationships that characterise corporate heritage brands/identities (Balmer, 2011a, 2011b). It further supports the notion of corporate heritage identities being partially constituted in relation to the cultural heritage and the identities of other societal entities and actors imbuing it with cultural relevance and legitimacy (Balmer, 2011b; Foster *et al.*, 2011). Moreover, it lends support to the notion of brand archaeology as a concern with provenance and historic attractiveness (Balmer, 2011b). However, the identified Sense of Belongingness is more expansive in regard to being concurrently concerned with spatial and socio-cultural proximity and origin, which provides indirect evidence for the potentially much broader base for the organisation's legitimacy and stakeholder relevance suggested by Balmer (2011b). Indirect support for the relevance of belongingness is provided by the study undertaken by Wiedmann *et al.* (2011a, 2011b) who found "bonding" to be the most important driver of heritage value for customers.

Further, the findings support the notion of a trans-generational sense of responsibility discussed by Urde *et al.* (2007) and the strategic aspects of marshalling corporate heritage identified by Balmer (2011a) as a core dimension of management stewardship. However, the study provides further evidence for the interdependence between the notion of responsibility and a sense of continuance, as well as the managerial disposition labelled Sense of Belongingness. More importantly, the claimed/perceived heritage status of the corporate identity informs not only the custodial role for the institutional heritage but also legitimates (for managers) a sense of responsibility beyond the company itself. This more expansive notion of responsibility in conjunction with the Sense of Belongingness expressed by managers and manifested in the strategic enactment of the corporate heritage identity lends further support to the notion of corporate heritage identities being partially constituted in relation to the cultural heritage of other social entities (e.g. Kent/UK brewing heritage, hop growing heritage, pub heritage) legitimating the corporate heritage identity within a wider socio-cultural context (Balmer, 2011b), as well as for a corporate heritage identity having acquired different institutional roles over time (Balmer, 2011b).

The notion of potency (i.e. CHIS disposition Sense of Potency) supports the strategic and proactive aspects of corporate heritage stewardship in regard to the activation of corporate heritage for corporate marketing purposes (Urde *et al.*, 2007). The findings further support, at least in the way it is envisaged by management, the reciprocal dimension of trust and affinity mentioned above, which is predicated on the activation of corporate heritage as a stable point of reference for stakeholder identification and a base for the organisation's legitimacy (Balmer, 2011b). As such, the "traditional authority" of a corporate heritage identity is predicated on its temporal transcendence as much as its cultural relevance (Balmer, 2011b). The study also shows that the heritage status of the organisation helps to self-authenticate and self-legitimise managerial agency in relation to stakeholders (He and Balmer, 2007b).

Thus, custodianship awareness identified as a core awareness dimension shared by managers is concurrently characterised by a perceived obligation and duty towards the organisation and the societal environs within which it operates, as well as a perceived legitimacy and credibility to act in that custodial role for self and others. This notion of custodianship goes beyond the extant discussion in the corporate heritage literature with a focus on custodianship for the institution and its brand/identity (Urde *et al.*, 2007; Balmer, 2009b, 2011b).

Further, the study revealed that a CHIS mindset is also characterised by a managerial Sense of Heritage per se with management validating, appreciating and adopting the corporate heritage and the organisation's heritage status vis-à-vis stakeholders and within societal environments. This disposition supports the general notion of the importance accorded to history by managers as an important aspect of identity (Urde *et al.*, 2007). However, it is more specific, in that it exhibits a relational and positional dimension in terms of the importance of the heritage status of the organisation in relation to its stakeholders and within its various societal environments. Moreover, the dimensions of validation, appreciation and adoption expand the managerial dimensions of uncovering, activating and protecting the corporate heritage brand/identity (Urde *et al.*, 2007), which were broadly confirmed by the current study (e.g. the dedicated role of the company archivist to uncover the company's past to be activated in a corporate marketing context). As such, the study suggests that a CHIS mindset involves "taking ownership" of the corporate heritage as well.

The above was found to be partially predicated on the close link between corporate identity characteristics in general and corporate heritage traits expressed by managers and strategically enacted as part of the corporate identity, which provides empirical support for the notion of a macro-level heritage footprint recently advanced by Balmer (2011b). Moreover, the substantive corporate heritage identity traits referred to by managers are company-specific and, as such, complementary to the generic corporate heritage characteristics expressed by the heritage quotient framework suggested by Urde *et al.* (2007).

Finally, the CHIS mindset exhibits a strong managerial sense of self-facilitating autonomy and individuality in terms of feeling, thinking and acting (i.e. Sense of Self), which is partially predicated on the heritage status of the organisation and its particular socio-historical position. This aspect further expands the extant stewardship conceptualisation discussed in the literature by adding a new dimension not previously articulated, which seems to facilitate the differentiating potential of corporate heritage stewardship by imbuing managers with a self-confidence to pursue nonconformist strategies and policies. The differentiating aspect of corporate heritage has been discussed in the literature in terms of positioning and its role as a strategic asset and resource (Urde *et al.*, 2007; Balmer, 2011a; Hudson, 2011). It also lends support to the self-legitimating aspects of managerial corporate identity enactment in general (He and Balmer, 2007b). However, this study shows the importance of perceived independence and individuality shared by managers that is reinforced by the Sense of Responsibility and Sense of Belongingness converging into a managerial Positionality Awareness, which together with the awareness for the organisation's heritage and its heritage status in relation to stakeholders facilitates the manager's custodial role and the subsequent activities suggested in the extant literature for successful corporate heritage stewardship.

Conclusion

Theoretical implications

This study makes a theoretical contribution to the nascent area of corporate heritage brands and identities within the corporate marketing literature by introducing the corporate heritage identity stewardship theory that explicates three distinct but interrelated interpretative dimensions underpinned by six managerial dispositions in regard to corporate heritage identity stewardship expressed by managers, which are constitutive and instrumental for the strategic enactment of a corporate heritage identity.

As such, this empirical study confirms the saliency of the heritage stewardship notion in terms of a particular managerial mindset as introduced by Urde *et al.* (2007). Moreover, building on the above, it makes a theoretical contribution via the articulation of corporate heritage identity stewardship theory based on an empirical and exemplary single case. Further, our study is significant, in that it not only confirms, specifies and expands the extant two main dispositions suggested by Urde *et al.* (2007) – focus on continuity (i.e. Sense of Continuance) and Sense of Responsibility – but also identifies additional managerial dispositions (i.e. Sense of Belongingness, Sense of Self, Sense of Heritage and Sense of Potency). It also expands the notion of stewardship beyond the original conceptualisation (in terms of heritage brands) in showing its applicability in regard to corporate heritage identities, which potentially broaden the concept's conceptual and empirical reach. Further, the theoretical framework contributes to the extant literature, in that it categorises the different dimensions within a coherent framework of corporate heritage identity stewardship. The theoretical framework explicates the linkages between the different dispositions and articulates three main CHIS awareness dimensions expressed by managers (i.e. positionality awareness, heritage awareness and custodianship awareness). As such, this study advances the specificity and clarity of this nascent construct.

Five implications flow from this study: first, the managerial CHIS mindset is likely to be multifaceted rather than two-dimensional, which increases the construct's complexity and the number of empirical indicators required for further empirical (positivist) testing. Second, some of the identified dispositions may not directly impact on subsequent stewardship behaviour but may instead impact on other cognitive and affective intermediate dimensions constituting the managerial mindset. For example, the study indicates that the three dispositions constituting the CHIS dimension positionality awareness may only impact on the other CHIS dimensions heritage awareness and custodianship awareness rather than steward-ship behaviour directly, which has implications for the further operationalisation of the theory. Third, three interrelated CHIS dispositions (continuance, belongingness and self) imply a confluence of temporal, spatial and socio-cultural aspects of posi-tionality awareness by managers rather than a focus solely on continuity/longevity (the temporal aspect alone) as suggested in the extant literature (Urde *et al.*, 2007). Fourth, heritage awareness seems to be present as a fourth important dimension, which involves validating/valorising and protective aspects, with the latter provid-ing a conceptual link to the notion of managerial identification discussed in the corporate marketing literature (He and Balmer, 2007b, 2013; He, 2012). Finally, the custodial dimension of the CHIS mindset entails not only an obligatory (responsi-bility) but also a legitimating dimension (potency).

The importance accorded to the saliency of the spatial dimension for the enactment of the corporate heritage identity by managers in terms of perceived continuity, as well as belongingness, indicates that corporate marketing theory needs to be more attentive to questions of territoriality and spatial situatedness, and it provides an additional potential identity anchor used by managers (He, 2012). Of course, such insights already characterise the corporate identity canon, and it has been noted, for instance, that corporate identities are informed by various spatial and temporal dimensions (Balmer, 2001, 2008) and will, most probably, be relevant for certain types of corporate identities beyond the heritage focus of our research (e.g. regional corporate brands).

The reciprocal nature of the disposition of belongingness lends general support to the notion of reciprocity as a foundation of corporate heritage identity/brand saliency advanced by Balmer (2011a, 2011b) but shows that it is not restricted to the aspect of trust, but may include affinity as well. It also provides empirical evidence for the constitutive relevance of bilateral relationships between a corporate heritage identity/brand and other social entities as a source of legitimacy and rel-evance (Balmer, 2011a, 2011b).

Taking a broader vista, our study suggests that the general notion of management stewardship potentially carries conceptual and empirical significance/weight within a private sector context, at least for the management of particular types of organisa-tions. As such, it opens a new avenue for cross-disciplinary fertilisation between the academic discourses within the domains of corporate heritage identities/brands and stewardship theory in management research (Davis *et al.*, 1997; Hernandez, 2012) where the interests of the principal and agents are conflated based on higher-order needs and intrinsic motivations focussed on a reciprocal and collective mindset of obligation and duty towards the organisation (Hernandez, 2012) rather than indi-vidualistic and self-serving principles only (Davis *et al.*, 1997).

Our study also indicates that the strategic enactment of corporate heritage iden-tities/brands based on a particular mindset is not restricted to the CEO or the top management team (Vallaster and Lindgreen, 2011), although significantly influenced by their leadership (Vallaster and de Chernatony, 2006), but also shared by middle managers.

In addition, in terms of generic multidimensional corporate identity models discussed in the extant corporate marketing literature (Balmer and Soenen, 1999; Balmer and Greyser, 2002, 2003; Balmer, 2008), the close interdependence between a managerial CHIS mindset and corporate heritage identity enactment that our study revealed indicates the convergence between the managerially conceived and the communicated corporate identity dimensions that manifest in cultural practices and artefacts constituting an important aspect of the "actual" corporate identity in the present (Balmer and Greyser, 2002).

Finally, from a family business perspective, our study suggests that a focus on continuance and a long-term orientation may not only be a strategic success factor based on specific structural and corporate governance conditions (Miller and Le Breton-Miller, 2005) but also a potential marker of identity important for the constitution of heritage-imbued family business corporate identities/ brands (Craig et al., 2008), representing a particular cognitive corporate identity anchor (He and Balmer, 2007b, 2013; He, 2012) for managers of these types of organisations.

Practical implications

The corporate heritage identity stewardship theory framework has the potential to facilitate managers' understanding of their custodial role for a corporate heritage identity. In particular, maintaining the saliency of the corporate heritage identity vis-à-vis stakeholders in regard to trust, credibility, authenticity and affinity requires a long-term orientation towards the business, an appreciation of the company's longevity, a dedication to the firm's survival as an independent institutional and legal entity and the maintenance of spatial and socio-cultural ties within and beyond the firm, as well as the willingness and ability to adapt and improve. Managers need to develop a clear sense of the organisation's "place in the world", in terms of its past, present and future. In doing so, management should be empowered through being apprised of the independence imbuing the organisation which facilitates substantive differentiation and is manifest in a particular mode of managerial conduct.

Further, managers need to be able to identify, take ownership and value the corporate heritage of their organisation. Thus, they need to accept their custodial role for the institutional heritage to keep it relevant over time. However, management also must be aware of the expanded responsibilities towards stakeholders, community and society at large that the heritage status of their organisation entails. As such, the corporate identity takes on multiple role identities with which management needs to accommodate (Balmer, 2008, 2011b). Failing to do so would eventually jeopardise the saliency of the corporate heritage and its relevance as a multifaceted point of reference for stakeholder identification. Nonetheless, the heritage status of the organisation also provides management with the legitimacy and authority to act and speak not only for the organisation but also on behalf of others (e.g. industry issues, community issues, etc.).

In light of the above, the study indicates the inherent complexity of corporate heritage identity stewardship. The management of heritage business institutions demands managerial attentiveness and expanded skill sets that go beyond the mere economic, financial and competitive concerns relevant for all business organisations in general. Hence, the successful management of corporate heritage identities is likely to be more demanding and difficult to achieve, requiring a well-rounded type of manager with – in addition to conventional business acumen and professional managerial and technical skills – a stewardship mindset that is attentive to past, present and future, as well as sensitive to temporal, spatial and socio-cultural aspects of an organisation embedded within a societal environment.

The specified CHIS mindset supports managers by sensitising them to the different awareness dimensions and dispositions necessary for their custodial stewardship in regard to their organisation's corporate heritage identity.

Limitations and future research

The empirical scope of the study is limited to a single case within a particular industrial and geographical setting and, as such, statistical/substantive generalisation was not attempted or paradigmatically possible. However, the theoretical generalisation to a higher level of abstraction, which led to the articulation of the corporate heritage identity stewardship mindset framework derived from our empirical study, provides different avenues for future research. First, positivist studies may attempt to operationalise the different dimensions of the corporate heritage mindset to test relevant antecedents and consequences of the suggested corporate heritage identity stewardship theory. In terms of further research, the theoretical framework may facilitate future empirical work (e.g. quantitative modelling) as much as conceptual integration across disciplinary boundaries (e.g. stewardship theory in management). Further, the impact of the custodial role of managers and the interaction between different hierarchy levels, as well as the diffusion of stewardship within the organisation, provides interesting research opportunities. Finally, the suggested link between the managerial corporate heritage identity stewardship mindset and the dimensions of corporate heritage identity saliency vis-à-vis stakeholders warrant further empirical scrutiny.

Concluding remarks

This empirical study has advanced our theoretical understanding of the corporate heritage identity stewardship notion. Our research has revealed how managers within the UK's oldest brewery understand their organisation's corporate heritage and has shown that corporate heritage is marshalled, and strategically represented, by them. The research illustrates how a collective CHIS mindset on the part of managers can both inform as well as guide managers in terms of their stewardship of their firm's corporate heritage identity. The resulting framework of the corporate heritage identity stewardship theory identifies the three CHIS awareness dimensions and six management CHIS dispositions, which informed their heritage custodianship of the brewery in a corporate marketing context. To reiterate, the purpose of the research is not to generalise to other cases. This being said, the findings have both a constitutive and instrumental relevance and, in accordance with the precepts of case study research, are meaningful in their own terms and in corporate marketing contexts.

References

Aaker, D.A. (1996), *Building Strong Brands*, The Free Press, New York, NY.

Abimbola, T. and Kocak, A. (2007), "Brand, organization identity and reputation: SMEs as expressive organizations: A resources-based perspective", *Qualitative Market Research: An International Journal*, Vol. 10 No. 4, pp. 416–430.

Abratt, R. and Kleyn, N. (2012), "Corporate identity, corporate branding and corporate reputations: Reconciliation and integration", *European Journal of Marketing*, Vol. 46 Nos. 7/8, pp. 1048–1063.

Alexander, N. (2009), "Brand authentication: Creating and maintaining brand auras", *European Journal of Marketing*, Vol. 43 Nos. 3/4, pp. 551–562.

Andriopoulos, C. and Gotsi, M. (2001), "'Living' the corporate identity: Case studies from the creative industry", *Corporate Reputation Review*, Vol. 4 No. 2, p. 144.

Ballantyne, R., Warren, A. and Nobbs, K. (2006), "The evolution of brand choice", *Journal of Brand Management*, Vol. 13 Nos. 4/5, pp. 339–352.

Balmer, J.M.T. (1995), "Corporate branding and connoisseurship", *Journal of General Management*, Vol. 21 No. 1, Autumn, pp. 24–47.

Balmer, J.M.T. (1996), "The nature of corporate identity: An explanatory study undertaken within BBC Scotland", PhD thesis, Department of Marketing, University of Strathclyde, Glasgow.

Balmer, J.M.T. (1998), "Corporate identity and the advent of corporate marketing", *Journal of Marketing Management*, Vol. 14 No. 8, pp. 963–996.

Balmer, J.M.T. (2001), "Corporate identity, corporate branding and corporate marketing-seeing through the fog", *European Journal of Marketing*, Vol. 35 Nos. 3/4, pp. 248–291.

Balmer, J.M.T. (2008), "Identity based views of the corporation: Insights from corporate identity, organisational identity, social identity, visual identity, corporate brand identity and corporate image", *European Journal of Marketing*, Vol. 42 Nos. 9/10, pp. 879–906.

Balmer, J.M.T. (2009a), "Scrutinising the British Monarchy: The corporate brand that was shaken, stirred and survived", *Management Decision*, Vol. 47 No. 4, pp. 639–675.

Balmer, J.M.T. (2009b), "Corporate marketing: Apocalypse, advent and epiphany", *Management Decision*, Vol. 47 No. 4, pp. 544–572.

Balmer, J.M.T. (2011a), "Corporate heritage brands and the precepts of corporate heritage brand management: Insights from the British Monarchy on the eve of the royal wedding of Prince William (April 2011) and Queen Elizabeth II's Diamond Jubilee (1952–2012)", *Journal of Brand Management*, Vol. 18 No. 8, pp. 517–544.

Balmer, J.M.T. (2011b), "Corporate heritage identities, corporate heritage brands and the multiple heritage identities of the British Monarchy", *European Journal of Marketing*, Vol. 45 Nos. 9/10, pp. 1380–1398.

Balmer, J.M.T. (2011c), "Corporate marketing myopia and the inexorable rise of a corporate marketing logic: Perspectives from identity-based views of the firm", *European Journal of Marketing*, Vol. 45 Nos. 9/10, pp. 1329–1352.

Balmer, J.M.T. (2012), "Corporate brand management imperatives: Custodianship, credibility, and calibration", *California Management Review*, Vol. 54 No. 3, pp. 6–33.

Balmer, J.M.T. (2013), "Corporate heritage, corporate heritage marketing and total corporate heritage communications: What are they? What of them?", *Corporate Communications: An International Journal*, Vol. 18 No. 3, pp. 290–326.

Balmer, J.M.T. and Greyser, S.A. (2002), "Managing the multiple identities of the corporation", *California Management Review*, Vol. 44 No. 3, pp. 72–86.

Balmer, J.M.T. and Greyser, S.A. (Eds.) (2003), *Revealing the Corporation: Perspectives on Identity, Image, Reputation, Corporate Branding, and Corporate-Level Marketing: An Anthology*, Routledge, London.

Balmer, J.M.T. and Greyser, S.A. (2006), "Corporate marketing: Integrating corporate identity, corporate branding, corporate communications, corporate image and corporate reputation", *European Journal of Marketing*, Vol. 40 Nos. 7/8, pp. 730–741.

Balmer, J.M.T., Greyser, S.A. and Urde, M. (2004), "Monarchies as corporate brands", Harvard Business School, Working Paper, Boston, MA.

Balmer, J.M.T., Greyser, S.A. and Urde, M. (2006), "The crown as a corporate brand: Insights from monarchies", *Journal of Brand Management*, Vol. 14 Nos. 1/2, pp. 137–161.

Balmer, J.M.T. and Soenen, G. (1999), "The acid test of corporate identity management", *Journal of Marketing Management*, Vol. 15 Nos. 1/2/3, pp. 69–72.

Balmer, J.M.T. and Stotvig, S. (1997), "Corporate identity and private banking: A review and case study", *International Journal of Bank Marketing*, Vol. 15 Nos. 4/5, p. 169.

Balmer, J.M.T., Stuart, H.J. and Greyser, S.A. (2009), "Aligning identity and strategy: Corporate branding at British Airways in the late 20th century", *California Management Review*, Vol. 51 No. 3, pp. 6–23.

Balmer, J.M.T. and Wilson, A.M. (1998a), "Corporate identity: There is more to it than meets the eye", *International Studies of Management & Organization*, Vol. 28 No. 3, pp. 12–31.

Banerjee, S. (2008), "Strategic brand-culture fit: A conceptual framework for brand management", *Journal of Brand Management*, Vol. 15 No. 5, pp. 312–321.

Bendixen, M. and Abratt, R. (2007), "Corporate identity, ethics and reputation in supplier-buyer relationships", *Journal of Business Ethics*, Vol. 76 No. 1, pp. 69–82.

Beverland, M.B. (2005), "Crafting brand authenticity: The case of luxury wines", *Journal of Management Studies*, Vol. 42 No. 5, pp. 1003–1029.

Beverland, M.B. (2006), "The 'real thing': Branding authenticity in the luxury wine trade", *Journal of Business Research*, Vol. 59 No. 2, pp. 251–258.

Blaikie, N. (2007), *Approaches to Social Enquiry: Advancing Knowledge*, 2nd ed., Polity, Cambridge.

Blaikie, N. (2009), *Designing Social Research: The Logic of Anticipation*, 2nd ed., Polity, Cambridge.

Blombäck, A. and Brunninge, O. (2009), "Corporate identity manifested through historical references", *Corporate Communications: An International Journal*, Vol. 14 No. 4, pp. 404–419.

Blumer, H. (1969), *Symbolic Interactionism: Perspective and Method*, University of California Press, Berkeley.

Bühler, H. and Dürig, U.-M. (Eds.) (2008), *Tradition kommunizieren: Das Handbuch der Heritage Communication. Wie Unternehmen ihre Wurzeln und Werte professionell vermitteln*, Frankfurter Allgemeine Buch, Frankfurt am Main.

Byrom, J. and Lehman, K. (2009), "Coopers brewery: Heritage and innovation within a family firm", *Marketing Intelligence & Planning*, Vol. 27 No. 4, pp. 516–523.

Charmaz, K. (2006), *Constructing Grounded Theory*, SAGE, London.

Chreim, S. (2005), "The continuity-change duality in narrative texts of organizational identity", *Journal of Management Studies*, Vol. 42 No. 3, pp. 567–593.

Corbin, J.M. and Strauss, A.L. (2008), *Basics of Qualitative Research: Techniques and Procedures for Developing Grounded Theory*, 3rd ed., SAGE, Los Angeles, CA.

Craig, J.B., Dibrell, C. and Davis, P.S. (2008), "Leveraging family-based brand identity to enhance firm competitiveness and performance in family businesses", *Journal of Small Business Management*, Vol. 46 No. 3, pp. 351–371.

Davis, J.H., Schoorman, F.D. and Donaldson, L. (1997), "Toward a stewardship theory of management", *Academy of Management Review*, Vol. 22 No. 1, pp. 20–47.

de Geus, A. (2002), *The Living Company: Habits for Survival in a Turbulent Business Environment*, Harvard Business School Press, Boston, MA.

Easterby-Smith, M., Thorpe, R. and Jackson, P.R. (2008), *Management Research*, 3rd ed., SAGE, London.

Eisenhardt, K.M. (1989), "Building theories from case study research", *The Academy of Management Review*, Vol. 14 No. 4, pp. 532–550.

Fionda, A.M. and Moore, C.M. (2009), "The anatomy of the luxury fashion brand", *Journal of Brand Management*, Vol. 16 Nos. 5/6, pp. 347–363.

Flick, U. (1992), "Entzauberung der Intuition. Systematische Perspektiven-Triangulation als Strategie der Geltungsbegründung qualitativer Daten und Interpretationen", in Hoffmeyer-Zlotnik, J.H.P. (Ed.), *Analyse verbaler Daten: Über den Umgang mit qualitativen Daten*, Westdeutscher Verlag, Opladen, pp. 11–55.

Flick, U. (2007), *Managing Quality in Qualitative Research, the Sage Qualitative Research Kit*, SAGE, London.

Foster, W.M., Suddaby, R., Minkus, A. and Wiebe, E. (2011), "History as social memory assets: The example of Tim Hortons", *Management & Organizational History*, Vol. 6 No. 1, pp. 101–120.

Goulding, C. (2000), "The commodification of the past, postmodern pastiche, and the search for authentic experiences at contemporary heritage attractions", *European Journal of Marketing*, Vol. 34 No. 7, pp. 835–853.

Goulding, C. (2001), "Romancing the past: Heritage visiting and the nostalgic consumer", *Psychology and Marketing*, Vol. 18 No. 6, pp. 565–592.

Gourvish, T.R. and Wilson, R.G. (1994), *The British Brewing Industry 1830–1980*, Cambridge University Press, Cambridge.

Graham, B.J. and Howard, P. (2008), "Heritage and Identity", in Graham, B.J. and Howard, P. (Eds.), *The Ashgate Research Companion to Heritage and Identity, Ashgate Research Companions*, Ashgate, Aldershot, pp. 1–15.

Gummesson, E. (2000), *Qualitative Methods in Management Research*, 2nd ed., SAGE, London.

Hakala, U., Lätti, S. and Sandberg, B. (2011), "Operationalising brand heritage and cultural heritage", *Journal of Product & Brand Management*, Vol. 20 No. 6, pp. 447–456.

Hamel, J. (1992), "The case study method in sociology – introduction: New theoretical and methodological issues", *Current Sociology*, Vol. 40 No. 1, pp. 1–7.

Hammersley, M. and Gomm, R. (2000), "Introduction", in Gomm, R., Hammersley, M. and Foster, P. (Eds.), *Case Study Method: Key Issues, Key Texts*, SAGE, London, pp. 1–16.

Harper, D. (1992), "Small N's and community case studies", in Ragin, C.C. and Becker, H.S. (Eds.), *What Is a Case? Exploring the Foundations of Social Inquiry*, Cambridge University Press, Cambridge, pp. 139–158.

He, H.-W. (2004), "Explaining the relationship between identity and strategy: A grounded theory approach", PhD thesis, School of Management, University of Bradford, Bradford.

He, H.-W. (2012), "Corporate identity anchors: A managerial cognition perspective", *European Journal of Marketing*, Vol. 46 No. 5, pp. 609–625.

He, H.W. and Balmer, J.M.T. (2007a), "Identity studies: Multiple perspectives and implications for corporate-level marketing", *European Journal of Marketing*, Vol. 41 Nos. 7/8, pp. 765–787.

He, H.-W. and Balmer, J.M.T. (2007b), "Perceived corporate identity/strategy dissonance: Triggers and managerial responses", *Journal of General Management*, Vol. 33 No. 1, pp. 71–91.

He, H.-W. and Balmer, J.M.T. (2013), "The corporate identity/strategy dynamic: A grounded theory study of building societies from a corporate marketing perspective", *European Journal of Marketing*, Vol. 47 Nos. 3/4.

Hernandez, M. (2012), "Toward an understanding of the psychology of stewardship", *Academy of Management Review*, Vol. 37 No. 2, pp. 172–193.

Hildebrand, D., Sen, S. and Bhattacharya, C.B. (2011), "Corporate social responsibility: A corporate marketing perspective", *European Journal of Marketing*, Vol. 45 Nos. 9/10, pp. 1353–1364.

Holt, D.B. (2004), *How Brands Become Icons: The Principles of Cultural Branding*, Harvard Business School Press, Boston, MA.

Hudson, B.T. (2011), "Brand heritage and the renaissance of Cunard", *European Journal of Marketing*, Vol. 45 Nos. 9/10, pp. 1538–1556.

Isar, Y.R., Viejo-Rose, D. and Anheier, H.K. (2011), "Introduction", in Anheier, H.K. and Isar, Y.R. (Eds), *Heritage, Memory & Identity, the Cultures and Globalization*, SAGE, London, pp. 1–20.

Knowles, T. and Egan, D. (2002), "The changing structure of UK brewing and pub retailing", *International Journal of Contemporary Hospitality Management*, Vol. 14 No. 2, pp. 65–71.

Lee, N. and Lings, I. (2008), *Doing Business Research: A Guide to Theory and Practice*, SAGE, London.

Leitch, S. and Davenport, S. (2011), "Corporate identity as an enabler and constraint on the pursuit of corporate objectives", *European Journal of Marketing*, Vol. 45 Nos. 9/10, pp. 1501–1520.

Liebrenz-Himes, M., Shamma, H. and Dyer, R.F. (2007), "Heritage brands-treasured inheritance or 'over the hill'", in Branchik, B.J. (Ed.), *2007 CHARM: Marketing History at the Center, 13th Conference on Historical Analysis &Research in Marketing Proceedings, John W. Hartman Center for Sales, Advertising & Marketing History, Duke University, CHARM Association*, Durham, NC, 17–20 May, pp. 140–145.

Lowenthal, D. (1998), *The Heritage Crusade and the Spoils of History*, Cambridge University Press, Cambridge.

Mathias, P. (1959), *The Brewing Industry in England, 1700–1830*, Cambridge University Press, Cambridge.

Maxwell, R. and Knox, S. (2009), "Motivating employees to 'live the brand': A comparative case study of employer brand attractiveness within the firm", *Journal of Marketing Management*, Vol. 25 Nos. 9/10, pp. 893–907.

McDonald, H. (2011), "Understanding the antecedents to public interest and engagement with heritage", *European Journal of Marketing*, Vol. 45 No. 5, pp. 780–804.

Melewar, T.C. and Akel, S. (2005), "The role of corporate identity in the higher education sector: A case study", *Corporate Communications: An International Journal*, Vol. 10 No. 1, pp. 41–57.

Micelotta, E.R. and Raynard, M. (2011), "Concealing or revealing the family? Corporate brand identity strategies in family firms", *Family Business Review*, Vol. 24 No. 3, pp. 197–216.

Miller, D. and Le Breton-Miller, I. (2005), *Managing for the Long Run: Lessons in Competitive Advantage from Great Family Businesses*, Harvard Business School Press, Boston, MA.

Moore, C.M. and Birtwistle, G. (2004), "The Burberry business model: Creating an international luxury fashion brand", *International Journal of Retail & Distribution Management*, Vol. 32 No. 8, pp. 412–422.

Motion, J., Leitch, S. and Brodie, R.J. (2003), "Equity in corporate co-branding: The case of Adidas and the All Blacks", *European Journal of Marketing*, Vol. 37 Nos. 7/8, pp. 1080–1094.

Muir, R. (2012), *Pubs and Places: The Social Value of Community Pubs*, 2nd ed., IPPR, London, available at: www.ippr.org/publications/55/8519/pubs-and-places-the-social-value-ofcommunity-pubs

Oxford Economics (2012), "BBPA: Local impact of the beer and pub sector 2010/11: A report for the British Beer and Pub Association", Oxford Economics, Oxford, available at: www.beerandpub.com/industry-briefings/oxford-economics-local-impact-of-the-beer-and-pubsector-2010–11

Peñaloza, L. (2000), "The commodification of the American west: Marketers' production of cultural meanings at the trade show", *Journal of Marketing*, Vol. 64 No. 4, pp. 82–109.

Ponsonby-McCabe, S. and Boyle, E. (2006), "Understanding brands as experiential spaces: Axiological implications for marketing strategists", *Journal of Strategic Marketing*, Vol. 14 No. 2, pp. 175–189.

Powell, S.M. (2005), "Creativity and the corporate brand within small to medium sized creative organisations", PhD thesis, Department of Marketing, University of Strathclyde, Glasgow.

Powell, S.M. (2011), "The nexus between ethical corporate marketing, ethical corporate identity and corporate social responsibility: An internal organisational perspective", *European Journal of Marketing*, Vol. 45 Nos. 9/10, pp. 1365–1379.

Pratten, J. (2007a), "The development of the modern UK public house: Part 1, The traditional British public house of the twentieth century", *International Journal of Contemporary Hospitality Management*, Vol. 19 No. 4, pp. 335–342.

Pratten, J. (2007b), "The development of the UK public house: Part 2, Signs of change to the UK public house 1959–1989", *International Journal of Contemporary Hospitality Management*, Vol. 19 No. 6, pp. 513–519.

Pratten, J. (2007c), "The development of the modern UK public house: Part 3, The emergence of the modern public house 1989–2005", *International Journal of Contemporary Hospitality Management*, Vol. 19 No. 7, pp. 612–618.

Samuel, R. (1996), *Theatres of Memory: Past and Present in Contemporary Culture*, Verso, London, Vol. 1.

Sayer, A. (1992), *Method in Social Science: A Realistic Approach*, 2nd ed., Routledge, London.

Schütz, A. (1962), *Collected Papers I: The Problem of Social Reality, Phaenomenologica*, Natanson, M. (Ed.), Martinus Nijhoff, The Hague, Vol. 11.

Segal, L. and Lehrer, M. (2012), "The institutionalization of stewardship: Theory, propositions, and insights from change in the Edmonton Public Schools", *Organization Studies*, Vol. 33 No. 2, pp. 169–201.

Sheen, D. (Ed.) (2011), *British Beer & Pub Association: Statistical Handbook 2011: A Compilation of Drinks Industry Statistics*, Brewing Publications, London.

Siggelkow, N. (2007), "Persuasion with case studies", *The Academy of Management Journal*, Vol. 50 No. 1, pp. 20–24.

Simões, C.M.N. and Mason, K.J. (2012), "Informing a new business-to-business relationship: Corporate identity and the emergence of a relationship identity", *European Journal of Marketing*, Vol. 46 No. 5, pp. 684–711.

Stadler, C. (2011), *Enduring Success: What We Can Learn from the History of Outstanding Corporations*, Stanford Business Books, Stanford.

Stake, R.E. (1995), *The Art of Case Study Research*, Sage Publications, Thousand Oaks, CA.

Stake, R.E. (2005), "Qualitative case studies", in Denzin, N.K. and Lincoln, Y.S. (Eds.), *The Sage Handbook of Qualitative Research*, 3rd ed., Sage Publications, Thousand Oaks, CA, pp. 443–466.

Turner, J.H. (1987), "Analytic theorizing", in Giddens, A. and Turner, J.H. (Eds.), *Social Theory Today*, Polity, Cambridge, pp. 156–194.

Urde, M. (2009), "Uncovering the corporate brand's core values", *Management Decision*, Vol. 47 No. 4, pp. 616–638.

Urde, M., Greyser, S.A. and Balmer, J.M.T. (2007), "Corporate brands with a heritage", *Journal of Brand Management*, Vol. 15 No. 1, pp. 4–19.

Vallaster, C. and de Chernatony, L. (2005), "Internationalisation of services brands: The role of leadership during the internal brand building process", *Journal of Marketing Management*, Vol. 21 Nos. 1/2, pp. 181–203.

Vallaster, C. and de Chernatony, L. (2006), "Internal brand building and structuration: The role of leadership", *European Journal of Marketing*, Vol. 40 Nos. 7/8, pp. 761–784.

Vallaster, C. and Lindgreen, A. (2011), "Corporate brand strategy formation: Brand actors and the situational context for a business-to-business brand", *Industrial Marketing Management*, Vol. 40 No. 7, pp. 1133–1143.

Verschuren, P. (2003), "Case study as a research strategy: Some ambiguities and opportunities", *International Journal of Social Research Methodology*, Vol. 6 No. 2, pp. 121–139.

Walton, J. (1992), "Making the theoretical case", in Ragin, C.C. and Becker, H.S. (Eds.), *What Is a Case? Exploring the Foundations of Social Inquiry*, Cambridge University Press, Cambridge, pp. 121–137.

Wiedmann, K.-P., Hennigs, N., Schmidt, S. and Wuestefeld, T. (2011a), "Drivers and outcomes of brand heritage: Consumers' perception of heritage brands in the automotive industry", *The Journal of Marketing Theory and Practice*, Vol. 19 No. 2, pp. 205–220.

Wiedmann, K.-P., Hennigs, N., Schmidt, S. and Wuestefeld, T. (2011b), "The importance of brand heritage as a key performance driver in marketing management", *Journal of Brand Management*, Vol. 19 No. 3, pp. 182–194.

Yin, R.K. (2009), *Case Study Research: Design and Methods, Applied Social Research Methods*, 4th ed., Sage Publications, London, Vol. 5.

Further reading

Anheier, H.K. and Isar, Y.R. (Eds.) (2011), *Heritage, Memory & Identity, the Cultures and Globalization*, Sage Publications, Bradford School of Management, London, Vol. 4.

Balmer, J.M.T. (2012a), "Strategic corporate brand alignment: Perspectives from identity based views of corporate brands", *European Journal of Marketing*, Vol. 46 Nos. 7/8, pp. 1064–1092.

Balmer, J.M.T. and Stuart, H.J. (2004), "British Airways and Balmer's AC³ID™ test of corporate brand management", Bradford School of Management, Working paper, Bradford.

Branchik, B. J. (Ed.) (2007), "2007 CHARM: Marketing History at the Center", *13th Conference on Historical Analysis & Research in Marketing Proceedings, CHARM Association*, Durham, NC.

Denzin, N.K. and Lincoln, Y.S. (Eds.) (2005), *The Sage Handbook of Qualitative Research*, 3rd ed., Sage Publications, Thousand Oaks, CA.

Gomm, R., Hammersley, M. and Foster, P. (Eds.) (2000), *Case Study Method: Key Issues, Key Texts*, Sage Publications, London.

Hoffmeyer-Zlotnik, J.H.P. (Ed.) (1992), *Analyse verbaler Daten: Über den Umgang mit qualitativen Daten*, Westdeutscher Verlag, Opladen.

Ragin, C.C. and Becker, H.S. (Eds.) (1992), *What Is a Case? Exploring the Foundations of Social Inquiry*, Cambridge University Press, Cambridge.

APPENDIX

TABLE A6.1 Sense of continuance

Focus on continuity	Explanation:
	Relates to an appreciation and dedication by managers in terms of the company's continuity over time (temporal), the firm's continued institutional existence (institutional), the continuity of place and location (spatial) and the importance accorded to the continuity in stakeholder relationships (social)
	Illustrative interview quotes:
	"And I think fundamentally, whilst it certainly makes good business sense, there have been arguments at times to say do we carry on brewing? Is that economic? Do we split the company up? But in all of those debates really the overriding thing has been to maintain the company" (Director)
	"[. . .] I think when people come to the brewery, look at its site, its location, just get a feel of the spirit of the place, you actually realise this is a bit different" (Director)
	"It's what I always say is that there's a huge number of people involved in Shepherd Neame whose own families have been involved here for many, many, many years [. . .] They're the people that set the culture of the business [. . .] about 150 staff have done more than ten years and damn near 100 staff have done 20 years or more" (Director)
	"Oh, we're three hundred years old, and it rolls off the tongue quite easily, but it's not until you think what Britain was like three hundred years ago that you appreciate quite what this company's been through" (Manager)

(*Continued*)

	Illustrative additional evidence:
	It is strategically manifested in the company's shareholding structure and the dedication of the current owners to maintain the company. It is a recurrent theme in the annual reports and other corporate communication materials related to investor relations justifying the integrated business model pursued
	Company policies reward long-term loyalty of staff and business partners
Focus on the long term	Explanation:
	Refers to a long-term managerial orientation and view of the business fundamentally guiding management decisions and strategies
	Illustrative interview quotes:
	"Everything that I face here with the decisions we make today, we kind of want to stand by them in 5 years time, in 10 years time" (Director)
	"It definitely leads to long-term thinking and focuses the whole time on business optimisation rather than, where's the next deal around?" (Director)
	"They're [the board] happy to look decades ahead in the decisions that they make, and that's something else we use [for corporate marketing] as well and that takes you all the way back three hundred years" (Manager)
	"It's not just about making money. Of course that's an important thing, but there does seem to be that longer term view on things" (Manager)
	Illustrative additional evidence:
	The long-term view is explicitly included in the company value statement and reflected in the investment decisions the company makes, which are focussed on incremental improvements and organic continuous growth. Throughout its history, the business has constantly invested in new technology to improve the productivity, efficiency and sustainability of its operations and the quality of its services and pub estate and has successfully managed to survive as the last independent brewery in Kent
Focus on adaptation	Explanation:
	Refers to the appreciation for the necessity to adapt and constantly improve, which was understood as an important antecedent for the very endurance and longevity of the organisation

Illustrative interview quotes:

"I think we're very early adopters of new technology. I think that goes way back to [. . .] in fact it goes back through the Shepherd family. If you look at some of the things that have happened in the past here, we were one of the first breweries to have a steam engine back in 1789, we were one of the first to get out of horses and steam traction, one of the first to have early things like PDX technology, our new bottling line, our SAP IT information system. We're very willing to be experimental with new technology as producers. And I suspect that is quite deep seated here" (Director)

"[. . .] ultimately Shepherd Neame's success, I think, is being able to grasp the nettle, the thorn, at the time and say, 'Actually we need a different skill set or we need a different approach to our asset base.' And we must have done that in one form or another over the 300 years, from bringing in the very first beer trains to London, to this fancy bottling line, to buying new pubs, to all sorts of things" (Director)

Illustrative additional evidence:

Throughout its history, the company went through periods of stability and periods of rapid change, but each time, the management at the time recognised the need for change and acquired the necessary capabilities and resources to answer challenges and grasp opportunities

TABLE A6.2 Sense of belongingness

Focus on closeness/ provenance	Explanation:
	Refers to the importance accorded to spatial (place and location) and socio-cultural (collective, institutional) proximity and origin (inside and outside the company)
	Illustrative interview quotes:
	"We get involved in all manner of different social and sports and school events and what have you and it does make a difference because we very much feel that we are from here and part of here [. . .] We're very much involved in everything that goes on. And I think that gives us great strength in some regards and loyalty and I think people know who we are, we're good employers, we're seen as a savvy and successful business. Of course, this all helps. I think it is very important. It defines us in some way" (Director)
	"I think there's a feeling of ownership in Kent. I think that's probably the other thing. I think that people feel that Shepherd Neame pubs are their pubs. Whereas all the others, with the exception of free houses, are interlopers, if you like" (Director)

(Continued)

"I think geographically we're quite tucked away in a corner. It's kind of like a frontier land, very close to the continent and in that regard we've been able to create an estate in a corner, our little corner of England where we can defend both our estate and our trade [. . .]" (Director)

"We [the board] enjoy talking to people and enjoy interacting. I think we want to be part of the team, want to be stuck in. [. . .] the philosophies towards people, where people, I hope, would say that it's a transparent culture, an open culture, it's certainly not a closed door culture" (Director)

"The brewery does a hell of a lot for Kent and we've started doing more in Essex, Surrey, and Sussex where our trading areas have developed. They've [the board] made it a kind of thing to get into the society of a county [. . .]" (Manager)

"It's something we've always done and probably always will; it's our strong place in the community" (Manager)

"It's [the company] seen very much as part of the community and because it's right in the heart of the town I think that's reinforced" (Manager)

"For example, you've probably heard this before, but [the CEO] knows everybody and will stop and talk to everybody and that is important and I guess in many ways that has affected the way I portray myself [as a manager]" (Manager)

Illustrative additional evidence:

It is supported by active sponsorship, corporate philanthropy and the involvement in local and regional festivals. It also empirically manifests in the way the company premises (e.g. visitor centre) are used for concerts and other activities involving the community (e.g. weddings). It is reinforced by the use of PGI certification under the European Union (EU) scheme for some of the company's beers, as well as local food initiatives and the focus on regional suppliers. The company actively uses the association with the town and county for its corporate marketing and constantly refers to its Kentish origins and its close links with the communities of Kent, as well as features on a timeline at the Museum of London, and is associated with the Royal Albert Hall, reinforcing the company's link with London and the UK

TABLE A6.3 Sense of self

Focus on independence/ individuality	Explanation:
	Refers to the importance accorded to autonomy, plurality and difference in feeling, thinking and acting as and on behalf of the company
	Illustrative interview quotes:
	"We're quite resistant to sort of follow industry initiatives, and so I think that's part of the characteristic of the business. [. . .] we're independent, proudly independent and expect to remain so" (Director)
	"I think we're quite an independent-thinking company. We don't just do what everyone else does. In fact, more often it is the case – and this is people coming to me and telling me this from other companies – that they look to Shepherd Neame to see what we're up to. [. . .] Because I think that we are independent thinkers and I think that is something that is different [about this company]" (Director)
	"You know, you get also that sense of individualism [with the pubs] as well. The Sheps [Shepherd Neame] pubs have character, even the managed houses, and the consumer nowadays is, not exclusively but often, aware of the difference between [. . .] all those sort of cut-and-paste McDonalds pubs" (Director)
	"I think the great thing about Shepherd Neame is that there isn't a Shepherd Neame way of doing it, and I think that's one of the great things about the company [. . .] I don't think there is a generic way of doing things around here, at all" (Manager)
	Illustrative additional evidence:
	The company has tended to introduce its own initiatives in regard to certain policies and strategies relevant within its industry. It is further reflected in the way the company positions its pub estate vis-à-vis themed and branded pub chains and is linked to staff and pub tenant policies with a focus on independence and autonomy

TABLE A6.4 Sense of heritage

Heritage validation	Explanation:
	Refers to the recognition and acknowledgement of the institutional heritage and the heritage status
	Illustrative interview quotes:
	"I think there's terrific pride in the heritage of the business" (Director)
	"Britain's oldest brewer. Have been here since at least 1698 – probably longer than that, possibly back as far as the early 1500s. So we have a very strong sense of history and heritage" (Manager)

(Continued)

	Illustrative additional evidence:
	On the company website it states, for instance, that "[t]he company has a genuine interest in history," something that was already apparent in historical marketing documents going back to the 1950s
Heritage appreciation	Explanation:
	Refers to the valuation and estimation of the institutional heritage and the heritage status
	Illustrative interview quote:
	"We are clearly very aware of our heritage, the fact that the company was one of the first to be registered as a company, the fact that we've been brewing on this site actually not since 1698, it's 1570 – research has taken it further back. So, at that level, one is very aware of the family involvement, the history, the longevity of the business and the fact that we've owned properties for nearly 300 years, which is very unusual" (Director)
	Illustrative additional evidence:
	The phrase "We are extremely proud to be Britain's Oldest Brewer" is an explicit part of the company's value statement, which has prefaced every annual report since 2005
Heritage adoption	Explanation:
	Refers to the acceptance and in possession taking of the institutional heritage and the heritage status
	Illustrative interview quotes:
	"So I think a lot of that history and heritage gives an atmosphere that is ingrained in everything that happens, rather than it necessarily being something that – it's more subconscious than overt, I would say, with a lot of the things that go on here" (Manager)
	"I think the most important key points are, as we've just said, that the company's heritage is one of our key advantages going forward" (Manager)
	Illustrative additional evidence:
	It is reflected in that the archivist's task is not only to systematise and organise the vast collection of historical documents and archival materials accumulated by the company over the years but also to provide historical information and data that can be used for corporate marketing purposes

TABLE A6.5 Sense of responsibility

Institutional custodianship	Explanation: Refers to the perceived custodial obligation towards the institutional heritage and the organisation's heritage status Illustrative interview quotes: "There have been one or two potential decisions that we didn't take which would have shaken the thing to the core. Now, whether in the future, similar decisions come up and we do take them I don't know. But I think that generally we've trod the path of trying to maintain the company with its core values" (Director) "The most important thing, I think, about the company and the people who run it [. . .] is that it's almost like just [. . .] I get the sense that it's like being the custodian of something and it almost feels like they [the board] don't want to be the one to drop the ball because it's got to pass on to someone else after they're not involved any more, or they've died or something, in years to come." (Manager) "I think the Board cares, I really do think they do, and I think the management feels a sense of responsibility for what's gone before and where the company will be in the future too. It's not just about today you know [. . .] There seems to be an overarching sense of responsibility, which filters down from the directors really" (Manager) "I think the most important key points are, as I've just said, that the company's heritage is one of our key advantages going forward. In the tough business world, it's something we should use and exploit but carefully and being mindful that it's a valuable but quite fragile thing in some ways. And also that actually, probably without knowing it, we are doing a lot of that already. [. . .] So that's the part that has always fascinated me about the company and that you're only here really, I'm sitting in this office, but I'm only a tiny speck on the history of the company" (Manager) Illustrative additional evidence: It is facilitated by the governance and ownership structure of the business and reflected in the ownership of many historic buildings
Non-institutional custodianship	Explanation: Refers to the perceived custodial duty beyond the organisation itself predicated on the heritage status of the organisation Illustrative interview quotes: "We want to be a premium long-term benevolent company that has responsibility in terms of the environmental impact and responsibility in terms of the employment of the people and in terms of the support to the community. [. . .] we have a desire to produce great quality products, a desire to be proud of the community in which we work in and support, being able to give something back to the community as well as deliver a sales performance, and ultimately a return to the shareholders" (Director)

(Continued)

"I think it is important because we take our responsibilities – and without trying to sound too trite – we take our responsibilities within the community quite seriously, or very seriously" (Director)

"I think part of it is the fact that it is Britain's oldest brewer so there is that importance there. A lot of the pubs are historic in their own right. So we own more listed buildings in Kent than the National Trust or English Heritage. And with that come some responsibilities [. . .]" (Manager)

"It must be intimidating [for the directors] in terms of well, we'd better make sure we do the right thing here, both in terms of business decisions but also the community because it's [the company] become such a part of the community, obviously a big employer in the town and the farms all around supplying it, and to have become part of the fabric of Faversham." (Manager)

Illustrative additional evidence:

Evidence for policies and strategies that support these claims can be traced back to the late nineteenth century and early twentieth century (e.g. pension and hardship funds, community involvement). It is manifested in various policies and activities of the company testified by industry awards that substantiate the corporate responsibility and sustainability claims, as well as the custodial role claimed by the company for cultural heritage at different levels (e.g. brewing heritage, pub heritage, hop growing heritage, etc.)

TABLE A6.6 Sense of potency

Corporate purpose and authority	Explanation:
	Refers to the perceived corporate vocation and legitimacy to engage in issues not only in regard to the company itself (e.g. interests, strategies and policies) but also in terms of issues beyond immediate institutional concern
	Illustrative interview quotes:
	"There's a self-confidence about the business too. I mean we do want to be a leader not a follower. It doesn't mean we want to cock a snoop at everyone, but we do want to pursue our own path" (Director)
	"I think it's typical Sheps [Shepherd Neame] [. . .] I think you'd have to know the company reasonably well, or Kent reasonably well, but I think everything from the challenge to the duty in the '90s, to [our] more recent challenge to duty on alcohol [. . .] You know, we like to be involved in the democratic process. You know, we've got a democracy, let's use it" (Director)

"I think we're involved heavily in industry discussions and matters so [the current CEO] now, but [his predecessor] before him, was a resounding voice in the industry [. . .]" (Director)

"So I think it's a case of sort of punching above its weight a little, I suppose, it's all about looking after beer, looking after pubs, and it's, you know, for a relatively small, regional brewer. So compared to the big brewers I think the company gets a lot more coverage [in the media]" (Director)

"We've produced beer for the longest in the country and that's a heritage that works very much in our favour [. . .] that heritage is very important. I would say definitely, for me, dealing day to day with responsible authorities and what I mean by that, that's the council, the police and everything. It makes my day to day life much easier" (Manager)

Illustrative additional evidence:

It manifests, for instance, in company activities such as a campaign against rising beer duties in the UK and duty disparities within the EU the company spearheaded in the later 1990s. It has continued to publically make a stance towards industry-relevant issues, and its directors and managers are actively involved in industry bodies and public debates (e.g. CEO as Chairman of the British Beer and Pub Association)

7

CORPORATE HERITAGE TOURISM BRAND ATTRACTIVENESS AND NATIONAL IDENTITY

John M. T. Balmer and Weifeng Chen

Introduction

Focusing on Tong Ren Tang (TRT), Beijing's celebrated traditional Chinese medicine shop, this study examines the pharmacy's attractiveness as a domestic tourism attraction as a corporate heritage tourism brand. The research also considers its role in encapsulating and expressing Chinese National Identity from a primordial perspective. The study takes account of the multiple role identity perspective of corporate heritage institutions (Balmer, 2011b, 2013) and is also informed by the literature on nationality and ethnicity. This is because our scrutiny of this corporate branding phenomenon points to the *prima facie* importance of the TRT corporate brand to Chinese identity, culture and to Chinese civilisation. Insights are made from and for corporate heritage, heritage tourism and national identity literatures.

Our research picks up the notion that corporate heritage tourism/corporate heritage tourism brands link the nascent corporate heritage domain with the established field of heritage tourism and is mindful of the phenomenon that corporate heritage brands can be tourism attractions in their own right (Balmer, 2013, p. 321).

Dating back to 1669, TRT – whose flagship and "mother" shop is situated in the Da Shi Lan (大栅栏) district of China's capital city – is a noteworthy Chinese domestic tourism retail attraction. Although significant, the shop is, of course, in a different league from other Chinese tourism attractions such as the Forbidden City and the Great Wall of China.

By means of context, however, within Beijing, authentic (as opposed to faux) prominent corporate heritage tourism attractions are singularly uncommon. Without question, TRT is China's most celebrated traditional Chinese medicine corporate brand. The pharmaceutical brand is known both within China and the Chinese diaspora for the quality of its medicinal products and services which are – in more ways than one – "Fit for a King".

The royal epithet is fitting, as the TRT brand, until the establishment of a Republic in 1911, was the sole purveyor to the Imperial ("Celestial") Court and to successive Chinese Emperors. As such, the shop is of singular importance within China, and to reiterate, among the Chinese diaspora, in that the corporate brand is a living, and peerless, link with China's extraordinarily long and rich Imperial past.

Moreover, TRT is also of significance to the national identity of China. This is because traditional Chinese medicine is viewed as a delineating trait of China and of Chinese civilisation (Eisenberg, 1995). Traditional Chinese medicine is informed by Confucian philosophy and, more particularly, by the religious dictums of Daoism. Significantly, Confucianism and Daoism are two important, and distinguishing, attributes of Chinese culture. The importance of the aforementioned can be seen in TRT's publications which emphasise and accord considerable import to the above:

> Tong Ren Tang is the inheritor of Chinese traditional medicine culture. The theory of Chinese medicine is the essence of Chinese traditional medicine culture, which absorbs the essential ideas from Chinese classical philosophy (of) Confucianism and Daoism.
>
> *(Aiying and Zhiying, 2011, p. 1)*

> (TRT) embodies the cores of the Confucian as "benevolence, virtue and goodness". Hence, "considering patients and customers as the most important", is the highest realm sought by Tong Ren Tang.
>
> *(Aiying and Zhiying, 2011, p. 1)*

Corporate heritage tourism and corporate heritage tourism brands

This study is conscious of the work of Misiura (2006), vis-à-vis the broad heritage marketing domain. It is also especially mindful of, and builds on, the work of Park (2010, p. 133), who urged scholars to explore heritage tourism experiences in different countries and contexts.

We do this in seven ways:

1   In responding to Park's challenge, this research focuses on China, which in heritage tourism contexts remains relatively unexplored (Gu and Ryan, 2008).

2   It takes account of the emerging corporate heritage canon; corporate heritage institutions being characterised as being long-established organisations whose key corporate identity traits have endured (Balmer, 2011b, 2013).

3   More specifically, the research engages with the embryonic corporate heritage tourism notion: the latter recognises that active heritage institutions can be tourism attractions in their own right (Balmer, 2013).

4   The investigation focuses on a prominent heritage retail outlet, which of itself, in corporate heritage/corporate heritage tourism terms, represents a departure.

5   Our inquiry marks new ground in that it examines the roles of an indigenous Chinese philosophy (Confucianism) and religion (Daoism) in the context of TRT as a corporate heritage/corporate heritage tourism entity.

6   This article focuses not only on domestic tourists but on domestic tourists who are also consumers (customers) of TRT's products and services.

7   Importantly, this empirical study explores the role of TRT as a corporate heritage tourism attraction as an informal mechanism through which national identity can be encapsulated and communicated. Park (2010), for instance, noted the importance of informal mechanisms as expressions of national identity, and this study on TRT as a corporate heritage tourism attraction speaks to Park's reasoning.

Following Park (2010), *all seven* perspectives represent new heritage tourism perspectives.

Tong Ren Tang: An inimitable Chinese corporate heritage brand/corporate heritage tourism brand. A corporate heritage brand of consequence

Synthesising the above, in our estimation, TRT represents an important case within the corporate heritage brand/corporate heritage tourism brand/corporate tourism genres.

The reasons for this are manifold.

This includes the age, rarity and prominence of this particular Chinese corporate heritage tourism attraction and because domestic tourism visits to the mother shop of this inimitable Chinese corporate heritage brands are multifaceted. This is because the shop's visitors are not only tourists but are consumers of TRT's products and services too. Moreover – and significantly – they are members of an ethnic and cultural community taking a primordial perspective of nationality.

Arguably, therefore, this is a corporate heritage brand/corporate heritage tourism brand of considerable consequence. As such, it is a brand meriting scrutiny from a variety of salient perspectives in terms of corporate heritage marketing but also in terms of the extant literature on nationality and ethnicity.

Chinese heritage tourism in context

Today, the Middle Kingdom is a significant tourism attraction. By means of context, it should not be forgotten that tourism in China largely comprises of domestic tourists rather than overseas tourists. In recent years, China's domestic heritage tourism industry has received a fillip as a consequence of the introduction of a five-day working week; an increase in disposable incomes; and, significantly, government support for China's cultural heritage (Caseby, 2011).

Certainly, China is celebrated for having a significant number of world heritage sites which are of considerable importance and attractiveness to tourists. This is, of course, hardly surprisingly as China, in heritage tourism terms, is exceptional because for 5000 years, it has been a unified polity. Moreover, China is not merely a nation state but for some is a civilisation without any comparison (Jaques, 2009; Lenman, 1994; Wenzhong *et al.*, 2010).

Of course, China is an amalgam of many ethnicities, religions and traditions, and some philosophers provide a counter-narrative to the above by questioning the very notion of their being a Chinese civilisation (Grayling, 2015, p. 41).

Mindful of the aforementioned, and with the attendant caveats, from 2000 BC onwards, a broadly distinctive Chinese national identity was created via the country's adherence to Confucian philosophical and Daoist religious precepts (Issacs and Martin, 1998, pp. 299, 303).

The aforementioned traditions enjoyed a hegemonic status within China until 1949 when the People's Republic of China (PRC) came into being. In the intervening years since 1949, the PRC largely eschewed China's venerable cultural heritage. More recently, however, the PRC has revisited, promoted and celebrated its erstwhile traditional national heritage (consider, for instance, state support for Confucian Institutes on the global stage vis-à-vis support for "Confucian Institutes").

Tong Ren Tang

The focus of this empirical study is Tong Ren Tang, indubitably one of China's most celebrated corporate heritage brands and, as we argue here, a notable Chinese corporate heritage tourism brand too. TRT's provenance is both enviable and exceptional.

Established in 1669, by Yue Xiangyang, during the reign of Emperor Kangxi, the TRT traditional Chinese medicine pharmacy shop quickly developed a reputation throughout China for the quality of its medical products and the integrity of its treatments. The shop's motto (established by its founder Yue Fengming) has continually informed the pharmacy's values:

> No manpower was to be spared, no matter how complicated the procedures of pharmaceutical production were, and no material was to be reduced, no matter how much the cost.
>
> *(Aiying and Zhiying, 2011, p. 70)*

In 1723, Emperor Yong Zheng of the Qing Dynasty made the following proclamation which, de facto, bestowed an illustrious imperial imprimatur on the brand and one that was to burnish TRT's reputation and which persists even today:

> Tong Ren Tang provides all the medicinal materials demanded by the Imperial Drug Hall and produces various kinds of patent medicines for the Royal Courts.
>
> *(Aiying and Zhiying, 2011, p. 37)*

From this time onwards and for the greater part of its history, TRT had impeccable imperial credentials. From 1723 until 1911 – with the proclamation of a Chinese Republic – TRT was the sole purveyor of Chinese medicine to successive emperors. Moreover, TRT held the Chinese equivalent of an English Royal Warrant ("By appointment to Her Majesty Queen Elizabeth the Second").

TRT's age and impeccable imperial provenance means that it is not only Beijing's, but also China's, most celebrated corporate heritage shop.

Tong Ren Tang as a tourist attraction

Without question, TRT is a significant corporate heritage tourist brand in its own right for both foreign and – more significantly as we shall explain – for domestic tourists. Our research found the pharmacy was often included in the itineraries of walking tours of Beijing, and the shop's exterior affords one explanation why this is the case. This is because the visually striking shop façade – festooned with visually striking imperial imagery – is not only inimitable but evokes an earlier, imperial age (Bedford *et al.*, 2008). Also, TRT is engrained into national consciousness owing to its antiquity and celebrity status as a corporate heritage brand.

Strikingly, too, TRT reverences its regal legacy through its centuries-old brand marque of two imperial dragons and via the use of the imperial colours of red and gold. Among extant Chinese organisations with the People's Republic of China, the survival of and the ostentatious display of Imperial iconography is truly exceptional.

By means of context, it should be noted the pharmacy enjoys a prominent position in Beijing's historic Dashilan (大栅栏) street/district, much frequently by tourists. A website devoted to the street not only explains the importance of the area but also the significance of TRT:

> Over the centuries, the traditional commercial street Dashilan holds quite a few time-honoured shops and stores which are well-known both at home and abroad. They all enjoy a history of over a hundred years, such as Tong Ren Tang Chinese herbal medicine store.

Dashilan is situated next to the Imperial Palace (the Forbidden City) and – to repeat – is known for its numerous heritage shops. Significantly, the Chinese Government recognises the TRT shop to be of major cultural and heritage significance and is included in their list of Cultural Heritage Institutions. In addition, the State has also conferred TRT the status of a *Laozihao* (a time-honoured Chinese company). Moreover, in 2005, Chinese Television accorded the pharmacy the status of China's Favourite Chinese Brand.

Testimony of the shop's profile and importance in Chinese national consciousness is the popular historically rooted television drama series entitled Da Zhai Men (大宅门]) which is based on TRT and the pharmacy's long associations with the Emperor and Celestial Court. The above accounts for its iconic status: it also explains why, today, it is a popular domestic corporate heritage tourism attraction.

Heritage, corporate heritage and corporate heritage tourism brands

The heritage of heritage

Recently, the corporate heritage notion has attracted the attention of corporate marketing scholars (Balmer *et al.*, 2006; Urde *et al.*, 2007). However, the heritage notion has a rich enviable inheritance of its own.

Arguably, the word heritage comes from the French term for "inherit" (Heathcote, 2011). In *Francophone* nations, heritage (*patrimone*) typically relates to the heritage of peoples and societies, whereas, in the *Anglophone* world, it habitually focuses on heritage landscapes and buildings (Balmer, 2013; Cohen, 2002).

Heritage is a portmanteau notion which is equally applicable to the tangible, intangible and metaphysical (Balmer, 2013). The heritage designation is broad in scope, and may pertain to an object, monument, inherited skill or symbolic representation. Heritage is often characterised as a key identity component of a social group (Bessiere, 1998).

As a notion, heritage represents our consciousness of a role outside – or beyond – history. In disciplinary terms, the heritage *oeuvre* is broad in scope and is informed by different disciplines including tourism (Park, 2010), sociology (MacDonald, 2002, 2006; Rapport, 2002) and marketing (Balmer *et al.*, 2006; Misiura, 2006).

For some, heritage represents a stand-alone discipline, as the *Journal of Heritage Studies* attests. Hayden (1987) asserts that heritage is of immeasurable value: heritage symbols are like cosmetics in that when applied they make the world more attractive and desirable. An individual association with heritage can be highly meaningful: it links an individual with that which has endured rather than with that which has expired or with that which is transient.

Corporate heritage and corporate heritage tourism: Foundations

The corporate heritage notion was formally introduced by Balmer *et al.* (2006) at the end of their study of monarchies as corporate brands (Reflections section). A year later, the same authors provided a more detailed consideration of the notion (Urde *et al.*, 2007) (Editorial Box 1):

EDITORIAL BOX 1 CORPORATE HERITAGE: THE FOUNDATIONAL LITERATURE

Formal introduction of the corporate heritage brand notion

Formally introduced by Balmer *et al.* (2006) at the end of their study of monarchies as corporate brands (Reflections section), these authors:

- identified the existence of corporate heritage brands as a distinctive category of institutional brand;
- argued that corporate heritage institutions subsisted in omni-temporal time frames and were, therefore, of the past, present and prospective future;
- maintained that corporate heritage institutions were often cherished, as they are stable points in a changing world;
- asserted that corporate heritage institutions should be *managed* taking account of the past, present and future;
- held that managers should take care not to wear out corporate brand symbols, ensuring corporate heritage brands remain relevant for contemporary customers and other stakeholders
- emphasised that managers should ensure corporate heritage brands should be relevant and should accommodate not only continuity but also change.

Further development of the corporate heritage brand notion and introduction of the heritage quotient

A year later – mindful of the above insights – a more considered treatment was afforded to the corporate heritage brand notion. In this cornerstone article, the authors (Urde *et al.* 2007):

- Emphasised the distinction between *a corporate heritage brand* and a *corporate brand with a heritage.* Corporate brand heritage concerns institutions that *emphasise their heritage as part of their corporate brand identity*. In contrast a corporate brand with a heritage relates to heritage organisations that do not overtly manage or marshal their organisation's corporate heritage.
- Remarked that corporate heritage brands are not necessarily valuable only to be valuable or accord value.
- Introduced the "heritage quotient": a five-part framework where the key facets of corporate heritage brands were deemed to be dependent on track record, longevity, core values, use of symbols and an institution's belief that its history is important.

This framework represents a more considered development of the initial insights articulated in Balmer *et al.* (2006).

Exponential growth of the corporate heritage canon

The above articles resulted in an exponential growth of interest in corporate heritage among corporate marketing and management scholars including Balmer (2009, 2010, 2011a, 2011b, 2013), Blombäck and Brunninge (2009, 2013), Burghausen and Balmer (2014a, 2014b, 2015), Hakala *et al.* (2011, 2015), Hudson (2011), Hudson and Balmer (2013), Schroeder *et al.* (2015), Urde and Greyser (2015), Wiedmann *et al.* (2011a, 2011b).

Since that time, there has been an exponential growth in interest as well as conceptual and theoretical insights not only on corporate heritage brands but in relation to the broad corporate heritage notion (Balmer, 2013).

As noted by Balmer (2011a), a good deal of the heritage canon – much of which is not written from a marketing or management perspective – focuses on the built environment and on heritage visitor attractions (Chronis and Hampton, 2008; Goulding, 2000, 2001; Henderson, 2002; Herbert, 1995; Misiura, 2006; O'Guinn and Belk, 1989; Prentice, 1993). A good deal of this literature equates heritage with defunct institutions and redundant heritage buildings and sites.

In contrast, and to repeat a key point, corporate heritage has as its focus extant ("living") heritage organisations and corporate brands. This focus on "living" heritage institutions represents a departure from much of the extant marketing literature on heritage which, for the main, focuses on the built heritage environment and on heritage visitor attractions per se.

As an aside, of particular note is the marketing heritage notion of Misiura (2006) which represents the application of marketing precepts to heritage in its broadest sense and, as such, encompasses heritage products, services, brands, tourism and visitor attractions and the built environment.

Building on earlier reflections on corporate heritage brands (Balmer, 2011a, 2013; Balmer *et al.*, 2006; Urde *et al.*, 2007) – and corporate heritage identities (Balmer, 2011a) – the corporate heritage canon notes that heritage institutions and brands are invested with traits which subsist in temporal strata (what he calls multiple time stratums); traits which are not only invariant (unchanging) but, importantly, have remained relevant too (Balmer, 2011a).

The assessment that heritage notion can be highly meaningful to organisations represents an important extension of the heritage construct (Balmer, 2011a). More specifically, heritage is meaningful not only to organisations at the level of corporate heritage brands (Balmer *et al.*, 2006) but also to corporate heritage identities in addition (Balmer, 2011a). Arguably, too, it represents, at the disciplinary level, a branch dimension of corporate marketing, namely, corporate heritage marketing (Balmer, 2013).

Why are corporate heritage brands/identities valuable? From the outset, this was made clear. In arguably what is the foundational article on corporate heritage, it was argued that heritage institutions can harness positive public emotions and, because of this, heritage institutions can be valuable to stakeholders and organisations alike (Balmer *et al.*, 2006).

Defining characteristics of corporate heritage

More recently, the defining characteristics of corporate heritage were enumerated by Balmer (2013, pp. 305–315) in terms of: *omni-temporality* (subsisting in temporal strata – of the past, present and prospective future); *institutional trait consistency* (the continuity of meaningful organisational traits); *tri-generational heredity* (the organisation has to have been in existence, and meaningful, for a minimum of three generations); *augmented role identities* (corporate heritage institutions are infused with multiple role identities including territorial, cultural, social and ancestral identity); *ceaseless multigenerational stakeholder utility* (demonstrably salient for consecutive generations of stakeholders); and *unremitting management tenacity* (assiduous management of corporate heritage institutions is a *sine qua non*) (Figure 7.1).

Corporate heritage tourism

Recently, and to recapitulate, the corporate heritage has been linked to tourism and has resulted in the formal introduction of the corporate heritage tourism notion (Balmer, 2013, p. 321). Corporate heritage tourism links the nascent corporate heritage domain and heritage tourism.

The potential significance of corporate heritage tourism (and by inference corporate heritage brands) was discussed by Balmer (2013, p. 321) in the following manner:

> [. . .] a distinct domain of corporate heritage tourism (focussing on institutions who have dual identities derived from corporate, economic, and social identities and which are of interest to domestic and overseas tourist) is one area which is pregnant with possibilities.

FIGURE 7.1 Defining characteristics of corporate heritage

Source: Balmer (2013)

He continued:

> Corporate heritage tourism usefully links the nascent corporate heritage
> domain and that of heritage tourism. As such, there is a sub category of
> corporate heritage institution/brands which, because of their provenance and
> multiple meanings attracts not only customers but also tourists: some may be
> classified as (corporate heritage) customers/tourists. London Transport, Sel-
> fridges, The Vienna Boys' Choir, Maxim's (Paris) and Darjeeling Himalayan
> Railway (India) are prima facie cases in point.

Institutional/augmented role identity notion

To emphasise and to repeat, within the canon the institutional/augmented multiple
role identity notion is of vital importance (Balmer, 2011a, 2013). This perspective
meaningfully informs this research study. Balmer (2011a, 2011b) argued that with
the passage of time, corporate heritage organisations are:

> [. . .] imbued with multiple role identities and, as such, have a number of
> referents.

> *(Balmer, 2013, p. 312)*

In explaining the significance of the above, he asserted:

> Since corporate heritage institutions are invested with multiple identities they
> can, in omni-temporal terms, be emblematic of groups, societies and places.
> Moreover, and importantly, they confer these identities to groups, societies
> and places in multi-generational terms.

> *(Balmer, 2013, p. 312)*

Corporate heritage and augmented role identity

The above represents a significant dimension of this study. This aspect was explained
as follows:

> Corporate heritage identities are infused with multiple role identities namely
> the temporal, territorial, cultural, social, and ancestral identity: these bur-
> nish an entity's institutional identity. Since corporate heritage institutions
> are invested with multiple identities they can, in omni-temporal terms, be
> emblematic of groups and societies and places etc. (Balmer, 2011a). Moreover,
> and importantly, they confer these identities to groups, societies, and places in
> multi-generational terms.

> *(Balmer, 2013, p. 312)*

National identity, religion and heritage tourism

The prospective importance of corporate heritage tourism vis-à-vis national identity is a key concern of this study of the TRT corporate heritage tourism brand. As such, this study is, in part, informed by the above literatures.

National identity

National identity is informed by the *Staatsnation* and the *Kulturnation* perspectives of Meinecke (1908); the aforementioned standpoints being broadly analogous to the "Primordial" and "Modernistic" categorisations advanced by Park (2010, p. 118).

Both the *Kulturnation* and *Primordial* schools of thought relate to nations as collective cultural communities (the cultural and ethnic nation based on common descent and is non-negotiable). The *Staatsnation* and *Modernistic* perspectives relate to self-determining nation states: the aforementioned are underpinned by juridical precepts which view nationality as one of choice (Kumar, 2003).

National identity is a key source of both an individual's identity: national roots and associations may engender a strong sense of identification (Gellner, 1998). It is also highly meaningful at the level of the group (Park, 2010). National identity provides a keen sense of collective faith via the establishment and maintenance of a national community: a community which is informed by both a nation's history and destiny. This explains why nations are often referred to by its citizens as fatherland or homeland: the aforementioned draws on the Teutonic notion of a *Vaterland* (fatherland) and the broadly analogous Gallic idea of a *Patrie* (homeland) as noted by Howard (2008).

To repeat, the *Kulturnation* and *Primordial* perspectives inform this empirical study along with extant cornerstone studies on the heritage tourism such as that by (Park, 2010).

National identity and religion in China: Confucianism, Daoism and Chinese national identity

One relatively unexplored facet within the heritage tourism literature and national identity is the significance of religion and ideology: both meaningfully underpin civilisations (Adler, 2002).

China has engendered two, long-standing and indigenous, ideologies – Confucianism and Daoism (Adler, 2002). Both will, in part, be the focus of this study. An understanding of them is necessary in order for an understanding as to why TRT is attractive to domestic tourists. Adler (2002, p. 13) made the prescient comment regarding the aforementioned:

> To the extent that religion is one of the factors that people use to construct their identities – it signifies "membership" in Chinese culture.

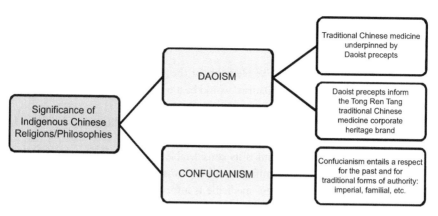

FIGURE 7.2 Significance of indigenous Chinese philosophies/religions to TRT and to Chinese approaches to the past/heritage

Confucianism, Daoism and Buddhism (a non-indigenous Chinese religion) and other religions have co-existed, somewhat uneasily since 1949, with Chinese State Marxism. China's major belief systems encompass religions (Buddhism, Daoism and Popular Religion), a state ideology (Marxism) and a distinctive cultural philosophy (Confucianism) which are, in their various modes, highly significant dimensions of China's ethico-religious and, moreover, national identity.

Adopting a historical/heritage perspective, Confucianism and Daoism are significant, as they are indigenous to China and therefore are highly meaningful to China's collective identity and are also meaningful to a consideration of heritage in Chinese contexts and moreover to our scrutiny of TRT as a corporate heritage tourism brand (Figure 7.2).

Editorial Box 2 provides background information vis-à-vis the above. Curiously, it is a foreign ideology, Marxism, which represents the most influential of China's contemporary ideologies. However, an understanding of two of China's philosophies/religions is germane for this study. As such, Confucianism precepts, arguably, reinforce a distinct Chinese approach to heritage and the past, whilst Daoist precepts are highly meaningful to traditional Chinese medicine and therefore, by default, to our examination of the TRT as a corporate heritage brand.

Daoism

Daoism stresses the importance of health and, as such, the religion emphasises the importance of traditional Chinese medicine (Xiaoming, 2005).

The prominent Chinese writer Lu Xun noted that an understanding of Daoism is the key to understanding Chinese culture (Xiaoming, 2005, p. 11). For his part, the celebrated Cambridge University sinologist, Joseph Needham, CH, observed:

> Many of the most attractive elements of the Chinese character derive from Daoism. China without Daoism would be a tree of which some of its deepest roots had perished.
>
> *(Xiaoming, 2005, p. 11)*

One prominent aspect of Daoism is its considerable impact on traditional Chinese medicine and by inference its significance vis-à-vis traditional Chinese medicine shop TRT. In short, traditional Chinese medicine is informed by Daoist principles. This is attributable to their pursuit of longevity and health. A famous Chinese adage says:

> Nine out of 10 Daoists are doctors.
>
> *(Xiaoming, 2005, p. 10)*

EDITORIAL BOX 2 SIGNIFICANCE OF RELIGION IN CHINA

Confucianism

Confucianism is based on the teachings of the scholar Confucius – who lived around 700–600 BC (Adler, 2002; Yao, 2000). During the Han dynasty (206–202 BC), Confucianism was formally adopted by the Chinese state. Thus, it provided the intellectual basis for Imperial China and the foundation of the Middle Kingdom's education system. Until the twentieth century, it was the dominant strand of Chinese philosophical thought (Adler, 2002). As a philosophy, Confucianism stresses that humans are *social beings* with obligations. Fulfilment for the individual is achieved via the perfection of moral nature (Adler, 2002). In Confucian thought, harmony is achieved via *Li* and *Ren* (Wilkinson, 2008). Accordingly, importance is accorded to manners, ritual and ceremony (*Li*) and the attainment of the virtues of love, humanity, goodness and generosity (*Ren*).

Daoism

Daoism has the greatest number of followers of China's five main religions (Daoism, Buddhism, Islam, Catholicism and Protestantism). Today, there are more than 25,000 priests and 1,600 temples of the *Quanzhen* and *Zhengyi* branches of the Daoist faith (Xiaoming, 2005, p. 11). The "Three Ancestors" of Daoism are Celestial Master Zhang, Lao Zi and the Yellow Emperor. Daoist belief is grounded in the complicated and somewhat impenetrable notion of the *Dao* (the way) and the culmination of virtue. Daoism stresses the importance of health and, as such, the religion emphasises the importance of traditional Chinese medicine (Xiaoming, 2005).

Civil religion and cultural symbolic constitutions

In the context of the above, the sociological notion of *Civil Religion* (Hammond, 1976, p. 171) and Inden's (1976) *Cultural Symbolic Constitution* perspective offer meaningful insights. The aforementioned refers to, among others, those transcendental beliefs that relate to the past, present and future of a people and nation, whilst the latter takes account of a nation's doctrines, ideologies, rituals and myths which informally constitute a meaningful, albeit symbolic, constitution. Both of the above perspectives speak to the above and, more broadly, to this study on TRT.

National identity and heritage tourism

Within the national identity literature, there is a synergetic relationship between heritage and national identity. The links between the two constitute a significant *leitmotif* within the broad canon (Anderson, 1983; Geertz, 1973; Gellner, 1983, 1998; Nairn, 1997; Smith, 1991, 1994).

National heritage is meaningful to countries and their cultures in that heritage communicates, and embodies, national identities (Edensor, 2002; Gellner, 1983; Kumar, 2003; Smith, 1991); imbues a feeling of national kindredship; burnishes national sovereignty (Wright, 1985); and binds societies together during periods of dramatic change and disruption (Howard, 1998). As Smith (1993, p. 161) cogently explained:

> The primary function of national identity is to provide a strong community of history and destiny to save people from personal oblivion and restore collective faith.

Within the heritage tourism canon, the issue of national identity and heritage also represents a prominent strand of scholarship (Edensor, 2002; Palmer, 1998, 2005; Park, 2010; Smith, 1991). Heritage tourism is meaningful as signifiers and enhancers of nation states (Lowenthal, 1998).

The literature is replete with insights relating to the inextricable links between heritage tourism and national identity. For example, heritage tourism can encapsulate and communicate national identity (Bandyopadhyay *et al.*, 2008; Palmer, 1998; Pretes, 2003); strengthen national allegiance (Palmer, 2005); bolster national distinctiveness (Park, 2010); engage citizens with a nation's collective past (Franklin, 2003); can be of sacred/spiritual significance (Smith, 1991); promote officially sanctioned national and cultural narratives (Edensor, 2002); and maintain a collective cultural, ethnic and national memory (Park, 2010).

The nascent domain of heritage marketing is also worthy of note (Misiura, 2006). Broadly speaking, the aforementioned takes an explicit marketing approach to heritage tourism. However, unlike heritage marketing, the corporate heritage domain (which, in part, informs this study) is concerned with extant entities having an enduring meaningful heritage rather than with erstwhile and sometimes long-defunct institutions.

As noted by Rowbottom (2002), visits to heritage sites are singularly special in that they evince an uncommon transcendent experiential quality among visitors: this is especially true of domestic tourists (Park, 2010). Heritage tourism sites link the individual to something far greater than the self. Whilst many heritage tourism sites relate to historical phenomena of the distant past (Park, 2010; Weaver, 2010), their provenance can be more recent (Henderson, 2002).

Heritage tourism, and the embryonic corporate heritage tourism/corporate heritage tourism brand domain, can be regarded as sub-streams, albeit significant sub-streams, of the broader heritage territory. Of course, a broader categorisation of heritage may entail conjoining both of the above perspectives.

Heritage tourism represents a significant line of scholarship within the tourism management canon (Chhabra *et al.*, 2003; Gu and Ryan, 2008; Halewood and Hannam, 2001; Hudson, 2011; Palmer, 2005; Park, 2010; Poria and Ashworth, 2009; Poria *et al.*, 2003, 2006; Prentice, 1993; Waitt, 2000) and mirrors the wider academic interest in heritage per se (Lowenthal, 1998; MacDonald, 2002; Urry, 1995).

Hypotheses development and conceptual framework

The Chinese state has deemed TRT corporate heritage brand to be of major, national, cultural and heritage importance to China.

It is classified by the Chinese state as *Laozihao* ("a time-honoured brand"), and the brand is designated as being in the first selection of China's cultural heritage. The mother shop of TRT is a well-recognised retail tourism attraction, and corporate heritage brands can be tourism attractions in their own right (Balmer, 2013). As such, the heritage credentials of TRT are unambiguous. Writers on nations and nationality have stressed the synergetic relationship between national identity and heritage in its various forms (Anderson, 1983; Geertz, 1973; Gellner, 1983, 1998; Nairn, 1997; Smith, 1991, 1994). Heritage can engender a sense of national community, and the notion that a person's country is a fatherland (Howard, 2008, p. 8). As such, national identity can be an important component of an individual's identity (Gellner, 1998) and group identity too (Park, 2010). Moreover, heritage tourism attractions can be repositories of, and also communicate, national identity (Bandyopadhyay *et al.*, 2008; Palmer, 1998; Pretes, 2003). Heritage tourism attractions are a means through which individuals can engage with a nation's collective past (Franklin, 2003). It is therefore hypothesised that:

> H1. The TRT shop's national (Chinese) heritage character is significant for its corporate heritage role identity.

As one of China's few remaining high-profile corporate heritage brands – with a corporate brand provenance dating back to the seventeenth century – the shop has engendered multigenerational familial loyalty among the Chinese. Chinese society accords great prominence to the family, and this is a key tenant of Confucianism (Adler, 2002; Jordan, 1972; Shahdar and Weller, 1996; Story, 2010; Wilkinson, 2008). The family is crucial in the creation an individual's Chinese identity (Adler, 2002). More generally, collectivism and Confucianism are inextricably linked, and this accounts why the family is viewed as the bedrock of China and Confucianism. Confucianism places great store on filial piety and the family is considered to be one of five cardinal relationships (Story, 2010, pp. 103–104). Moreover, in erstwhile Imperial China (and following the dictates of Confucianism), individuals were regarded as part of a larger family of which the Emperor was its head: as the "Father" of the Chinese State (Hofstede, 1980; Wenzhong *et al.*, 2010; Wilkinson, 2008). An especial characteristic of Chinese notions of the family is the sense that the family encompasses both the dead and the living. The cult of ancestor worship (which infuses Confucianism, Daoism and Chinese Popular Religion) is a potent expression of this (Adler, 2002). As such, family relationships are both *vertical* (multigenerational) and *horizontal* (the extended family) and both are highly meaningful (Wenzhong *et al.*, 2010; Wilkinson, 2008). There are clear links with the above within the corporate heritage canon where tri-generational heredity and ancestral identities are accorded prominence (Balmer, 2013). It is therefore hypothesised that:

> H2. The TRT shop's familial heritage character (multigenerational customers) is significant for its corporate heritage role identity.

Dating back to 1669, Tong Ren Tang is one of China's longest established corporate brands. Most of the pre-1949 Chinese corporate brands did not survive the turbulent changes within China during the latter part of the twentieth century. As such, the TRT mother shop/the corporate heritage brand is special in that it has been in existence for over five centuries. In China, although there is a fascination with the contemporary and with the future, there is also a respect for the past and for tradition: tradition being a fundamental Chinese value and this is in accordance the Confucianism (Bond, 1980). Time is a fundamental component of identity (Mead, 1929, 1932); and time is one of the most attractive corporate heritage dimensions (Hudson and Balmer, 2013). Unlike history, heritage links an individual with that which has endured rather than what has expired (Balmer, 2013). Heritage clarifies the past and makes the past relevant for contemporary contexts and purposes (Lowenthal, 1998); provides existential anchors which are of value in times of uncertainty and counters the deficit, loss, or, indeed, trauma caused by the past (Rapport, 2002, p. 87); offers stability during periods of change (Hewison, 1987) and gives comfort to older generations who hanker for heritage institutions associated with their youth (Holbrook and Schindler, 2003). Heritage represents a time continuum and can equate to perennial acts of bequeathing and receiving heritage: heritage is never truly owned but is loaned (Balmer, 2011a). Corporate heritage institutions subsist in temporal time strata (Balmer, 2013), and corporate heritage identities are invested with time: past, present and of the prospective future (Balmer *et al.*, 2006). It is therefore hypothesised that:

> H3. The TRT shop's multi-temporal heritage character is significant for its corporate heritage role identity.

TRT, until the establishment of a Chinese Republic in 1911, was the official pur-veyor to successive Chinese Qing Emperors. Even today, the company's logo uses the imperial dragon and the imperial colours of red and yellow. For many centuries, Tong Ren Tang was the official supplier of traditional Chinese medicine to Chinese Emperors, and the Imperial links endure. For instance, the shop's visually strik-ing imperial imagery is reminiscent of another age. Tourists' guidebooks note the pharmacy's Imperial links and note how the corporate heritage brand has provided traditional Chinese medicinal products for eight Emperors (Bedford *et al.*, 2008, p. 112). A nation's imperial/royal provenance can be highly salient in heritage tour-ism terms (Balmer, 2009, 2011b; Balmer *et al.*, 2006; Smith, 1993), and China has a five-thousand-year imperial polity which ended in 1911 (Lenman, 1994; Wen-zhong *et al.*, 2010). Within Confucianism, loyalty to the Emperor is one of five cardinal relationships (Story, 2010). Weber (1968) held that China's ancient imperial polity helped to foster a sense of common Chinese ethnicity. The Chinese Emperor promoted common symbols, traditions and values which reinforced a common Chinese heritage and culture (Smith, 1993). It is therefore hypothesised that:

> H4. The TRT shop's imperial character is significant for its corporate heritage
> role identity.

Within China, TRT is known for the quality of its traditional medicinal products and services. Arguably, the corporate brand is the most famous of all traditional Chinese medicine brands in China and among the Chinese diaspora. TRT uses medicinal formulas which have been unchanged for many centuries and are known for their quality among the Chinese. As such, TRT's exceptionally strong associa-tion with traditional Chinese medicine is a core corporate and product heritage identity trait. A primary manifestation of identity is an organisation's products or services (Olins, 1995). Chinese medicine is a defining characteristic of Chinese cul-ture and civilisation (Eisenberg, 1995). There exists a category of institutions which are different from others in they are distinguished by having a distinct corporate heritage (Balmer, 2011a, 2013), and corporate heritage institutions are stable points in a changing world (Balmer *et al.*, 2006). Corporate heritage institutions have meaningful trait consistency over time, and such traits are expressed via a variety of conduits such as corporate purposes, activities, competencies, cultures, philosophies, strategies and, significantly, can be expressed in terms of product and service focus and quality levels (Balmer, 2013). It is therefore hypothesised that:

> H5. The TRT shop's corporate and product heritage identity is significant for
> its attractiveness as a Chinese heritage tourist brand attraction.

The direct-effects arguments for the impacts of Chinese culture measures such as national role identity, familial role identity, multi-temporal role identity and impe-rial role identity of TRT on its attractiveness as a domestic Chinese heritage tourist attraction are persuasive. However, it is argued that the aforementioned factors

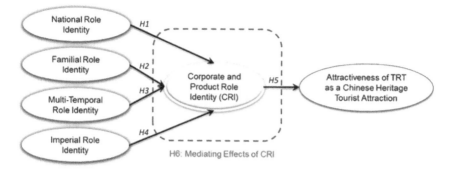

FIGURE 7.3 Conceptual framework of corporate heritage as heritage tourism brand attraction in China

(hypotheses) affect TRT as a Chinese heritage tourist attraction indirectly through TRT's corporate heritage role identity. It is therefore hypothesised that:

> H6. The TRT shop's corporate identity mediates the effects of national role identity, familial role identity, multi-temporal role identity and imperial role identity on the attractiveness of TRT as a Chinese corporate heritage tourist brand attraction.

Figure 7.3 presents the conceptual framework vis-à-vis the attractiveness of TRT as a corporate heritage tourism brand attraction.

Research method

To test the focal constructs and hypotheses, a survey questionnaire developed from the literature was used. The survey was informed by documentary data on the company. It was also informed by qualitative and secondary data collected during the first stage of the study. By such means, the reliability and validity of the research is heightened (Edmondson and Mcmanus, 2007).

Data collection: Preliminary stage

Documentary and website information on the company were scrutinised prior to the collection of qualitative data and recourse was made to company-specific documents including annual reports, newsletters, strategic reports, press articles and an official company history. Furthermore, the researchers consulted guidebooks on Beijing and China; scrutinised details of guided tours of Beijing and Web-based information on TRT. The aforementioned confirmed the shop's/corporate brand's status as a prominent tourist attraction.

Qualitative data were drawn from interviews with six senior managers of TRT, and a group discussion with senior managers also took place. Notes were taken of the above discussions.

In addition, a visual audit of the shop also took place which revealed the strength of the shop's imperial iconography. Observation also formed part of the data collection which took place on successive visits to the shop and which focused on the behaviour of tourists outside the shop. For instance, it was noticed that tourists regularly took photographs of the shop and visits to the shop were a component of tourist walking tours to Dashilan (大栅栏). Observational notes were kept vis-à-vis the above.

Data collection: A survey questionnaire with domestic tourists

Data for the survey questionnaire were undertaken over a three-day period. The researchers along with six postgraduate Chinese students from Beijing administered the questionnaire. To assess all the focal model constructs, this research adopted a variety of multi-item scales. All the scales were informed from the literature review and developed to fit the research purpose and context. The measures of both the constructs relied on five-point Likert scales ranging from "strongly disagree" to "strongly agree." Over 600 domestic (Chinese) tourists were approached and this resulted in 115 usable questionnaires having an approximate response rate of 20 per cent. Table 7.1 shows the descriptive statistics, correlations and average variances.

Data analysis: Results

Partial least squares (PLS) were used to test the measurement properties, the structural model and hypotheses. As previously indicated, 115 usable questionnaires comprise the sample size for the study, and as noted by Chin (1998) and Goodhue et al. (2012), PLS is appropriate for highly complex predictive models in small to medium-sized samples.

TABLE 7.1 Descriptive statistics, correlations and average variances extracted (AVE)

Construct	ATR	CRI	FRI	IRI	NRI	MRI
Attractiveness of TRT as a Chinese heritage tourist attraction (ATR)	0.854					
Corporate role identity (CRI)	0.233	0.745				
Familial role identity (FRI)	0.098	0.198	0.843			
Imperial role identity (IRI)	0.205	0.498	0.005	0.762		
National role identity (NRI)	0.185	0.136	−0.096	0.007	0.851	
Multi-temporal role identity (MRI)	−0.013	0.174	−0.114	0.124	−0.056	0.854
Mean	2.07	2.12	2.46	2.08	2.78	1.84
SD	0.987	1.009	0.768	1.028	0.870	0.970
CR	0.890	0.784	0.879	0.800	0.887	0.889

Note: Values on the diagonal are the square root of AVE

Measurement validation and reliability

Following Gerbing and Anderson (1988), the measures' reliability and constructs validity of the focal constructs were assessed. Item total correlations were tested for the measurement items of all the scales. As shown in Table 7.2, the composite

TABLE 7.2 Construct measures

Constructs	Measures	Loadings
ATR	TRT shop's attractiveness as a Chinese heritage tourist attraction	
AVE = 0.729	ATR1: I am very pleased that I visited this TRT shop with long history today	0.874
CR = 0.890	ATR2: Visiting this TRT shop is a good experience for me as a tourist	0.809
α **= 0.816**	ATR3: I will come back again to visit this TRT shop in the future	0.876
CRI	TRT shop's corporate heritage role identity	
AVE = 0.556	CRI1: TRT brand with its emphasis on quality is important to you	0.715
CR = 0.784	CRI2: It is important that the centuries-old trust and quality of TRT is important to you	0.894
α **= 0.615**	CRI3: The centuries-old Chinese respect for the TRT corporate brand is important to you	0.595
FRI	TRT shop's familial heritage character (multigenerational customers)	
AVE = 0.710	FRI1: I have used TRT products	0.692
CR = 0.879	FRI2: My parents used TRT products	0.888
α **= 0.824**	FRI3: My grandparents have used TRT products	0.929
IRI	TRT shop's imperial character	
AVE = 0.580	IRI1: I am attracted by the TRT's imperial past in providing medicine for successive Chinese Emperors	0.823
CR = 0.800	IRI2: TRT is successful in communicating its heritage (i.e. shop layout, packaging, logo and colour)	0.872
α **= 0.630**	IRI3: TRT is successful in communicating its imperial heritage (over 300 years)	0.550
NRI	TRT shop's national (Chinese) heritage character	
AVE = 0.725	NRI1: TRT brand is a Chinese National Treasure	0.791
CR = 0.887	NRI2: TRT brand is important to your sense of Chinese identity	0.905
α **= 0.820**	NRI3: Chinese medicine is important to your sense of Chinese identity	0.855
MRI	TRT shop's multi-temporal heritage character	
AVE = 0.729	MRI1: The TRT corporate brand is relevant to modern day	0.851
CR = 0.889	MRI2: The future existence of the TRT corporate brand is important to you	0.920
α **= 0.814**	MRI3: I will be upset if TRT disappears	0.785

Notes: CR = composite reliability; all the measures have adopted a five-point scale (1 = "strongly disagree" and 5 = "strongly agree")

reliability (CR) values for each construct range from 0.784 and 0.890, indicating good degree of internal consistency of the proposed constructs.

Confirmatory factor analysis (CFA) was used to test constructs validity. The results of CFA model testing demonstrated a good fit with chi square (CMIN) = 125.010; degrees of freedom (df) = 124; CMIN/DF = 1.008; CFI = 0.998; RMSEA = 0.08.

After the constructs were confirmed, a PLS method was used to estimate the convergent and discriminant validity (average variance extracted [AVE]) of the measures. The factor loadings shown in Table 7.1 are all above 0.5 and, therefore, are statistically significant at the 0.01 level, suggesting satisfactory convergent validity of the constructs. The square root of the AVE (values on the diagonal of Table 7.1) was greater than the correlations between the construct and the other constructs in the model, and this represents a good result for the discriminant validity of the constructs (Fornell and Larcker, 1981). All factor loadings were all above 0.5 and were found to be statistically significant at the 0.01 level (Table 7.2) and indicate a satisfactory convergent validity of the constructs (Gerbing and Anderson, 1988).

The survey confirmed all six hypotheses.

As to our findings, the effects of national role identity ($H1$: $\beta = 0.163, p < 0.1$), familial role identity ($H2$: $\beta = 0.228, p < 0.1$), multi-temporal role identity ($H3$: $\beta = 0.150, p < 0.1$), and imperial role identity ($H4$: $\beta = 0.477, p < 0.1$) on TRT's corporate heritage brand role identity are all positive and significant (Table 7.2).

The corporate heritage role identity of TRT was found to have a significant and positive impact on its attractiveness as a Chinese heritage brand tourist attraction as the data analysis results indicated (HS: $\beta = 0.233, p < 0.1$).

Following Baron and Kenny's (1986) procedure, this study also confirms the positive significant mediating effects of corporate heritage role identity of TRT between its heritage characters (national, familial, multi-temporal and imperial) and its attractiveness as a Chinese heritage tourist brand attraction (H6, Table 7.3).

Discussion and implications

The study revealed TRT to be a significant Chinese corporate heritage tourism brand attraction: an attraction which encapsulates and expresses Chinese national identity. The latter, seemingly, accounts, in part, for its popularity and significance as a corporate heritage tourism brand.

Whilst it is undeniably the case that TRT is a popular and prominent domestic (Chinese) retail tourist destination because of its corporate and product heritage (in terms of providing many invariable traditional Chinese medicines and services), there are other highly meaningful role identities which account for the pharmacy's popularity as a domestic corporate heritage attraction.

This study, focusing on a prominent Chinese corporate heritage entity as – in addition – a corporate heritage tourism brand attraction, appears to be the first of its kind.

TABLE 7.3 Research hypotheses test results

Hypotheses		Path coefficients/ t-value		Results
NRI→CRI		0.163★/1.752		Supported
FRI→CRI		0.228★/2.256		Supported
MRI→CRI		0.150★/1.667		Supported
IRI→CRI		0.477★/5.610		Supported
CRI→ATR		0.233★/2.668		Supported
Mediating effects of CRI	Direct effect		Total effect	
H6a. NRI→CRI→ATR	0.195/2.010		0.037★★/1.324	Supported
H6b. FRI→CRI→ATR	0.094/0.814		0.053★/1.264	Supported
H6c. MRI→CRI→ATR	−0.024/0.060		0.035★★/1.258	Supported
H6d. IRI→CRI→ATR	0.156/2.721		0.111★★/2.556	Supported
Model fit statistics	Chi-square (CMIN) = 125.010; df = 124; CMIN/DF = 1.008; CFI = 0.998;			
	RMSEA = 0.08			

Notes: ★ p < 0.1; ★★ p < 0.05

Tong Ren Tang and Chinese national identity

Notably, the shop, with its venerable heritage, is invested with powerful and meaningful multiple role identities which are strongly aligned to Chinese national identity.

In short, TRT, as a repository of manifold multiple role identities (some of which are associated with two buttresses of Chinese culture, namely, Confucianism and Daoism), results in an inimitable domestic corporate heritage tourism experience: an experience which (taking a primordial perspective vis-à-vis nationality), seemingly, both celebrates and communicates Chinese national identity.

Tong Ren Tang: Conferring Chinese national identity

The research insights support the premise that heritage institutions can encapsulate and confer national identity (Balmer, 2013). They also validate the saliency of the multiple role identity notion (Balmer, 2011b, 2013). From this study, the former, seemingly, is both evident and apparent.

As such, domestic tourism visits to the pharmacy can possibly be seen to *reveal, remind, and reawaken* a sense of traditional Chinese culture and bolster of sense of belonging to a Chinese cultural community. As the research suggests, tourism visits to the shop, along with the consumption of heritage (via TRT's products and services), links the individual domestic tourists to enduring dimensions of Chinese civilisation and, as such, they engage not only to China's past and present but, significantly, to the country's prospective future.

Moreover, domestic tourism visits to the shop represent a unique tourism experience – in corporate, national and cultural terms, amongst others – as TRT is an entity imbued with a living aggregate heritage.

Mindful of the *Civil Religion* perspective (Hammond, 1976, p. 171), domestic tourism visits to the shop are perhaps akin to a national pilgrimage. In social identity terms these visits may well represent a powerful expression of the Chinese group sense of self.

Tong Ren Tang: Importance to Chinese identity and civilisation

Arguably, as China's most celebrated corporate heritage entity, TRT is a potent emblem of China's ancient civilisation. Domestic tourism visits to the shop represent "a rite of renewal" in terms of an affiliation to China and to Chinese culture. As nations have and, moreover need, multiple identities (Thapar, 2014), there should be no surprise that TRT is viewed as a Chinese cultural icon in corporate heritage tourism terms.

As this study has revealed, this is because TRT is invested with powerful and meaningful multiple role identities: the existence of multiple role identities among heritage institutions is a characteristic of heritage institutions (Balmer, 2011b, 2013).

It was shown the shop's allure as a heritage tourism attraction to the Chinese – unlike standard retail outlets and other time-honoured retailed brands – is attributable to its multiple and meaningful role identities – corporate, temporal, familial, national, cultural and imperial. Some organisations are imbued with normative and utilitarian identities (Albert and Whetten, 1985): significantly, TRT is suffused with both normative and, moreover with, multiple utilitarian/societal identities (Balmer, 2013).

Moreover, as China's modernisation develops apace, and as tangible manifestations of traditional Chinese culture are progressively debilitated, the shop's national importance as a living heritage entity and as an icon of China's national identity is incomparable.

Corporate heritage tourism: Significance of royal and imperial associations

The research has a degree of similitude with extant scholarship on heritage tourism including the work of Park (2010, pp. 117–118) in that both studies recognise the importance of royal associations in heritage tourism contexts. Park's research (2010) explained how tourism visits to a Korean palace can reinforce a sense of Korean national identity. Both studies shed light on the inextricable links between tourism, nationality, heritage and royal provenance in Korea and, in the case of this study, China.

In the context of heritage tourism research/nascent corporate heritage tourism brand scholarship, it would seem that heritage tourism activities associated with a country's imperial or royal past, as with the work of Park (2010), can be highly meaningful in experiencing national identity and in asserting and affirming national values and identity.

Tong Ren Tang: Significance of Confucianism and Daoist associations

The shop's heritage identity anchors reveal the significance of Chinese cultural primordialism (Park, 2010): TRT is a repository of Chinese cultural values which define the Chinese as a people. This is evinced vis-à-vis the shop's status as the premier exponent of traditional Chinese medicine and, therefore, its tangential link with the tenets of Daoism. Arguably, too, it mirrors the precepts of Confucianism in terms of the traditional Chinese respect for its rulers, imperial or otherwise (Chinese rule spanned three millennia), for familial ties (multigenerational aspect of the shop's customers along with its ownership/management) and for an ethical remit as reflected in the shop's guiding principles:

> No manpower was to be spared, no matter how complicated the procedures of pharmaceutical production were, and no material was to be reduced, no matter how much the cost.
>
> *(Aiying and Zhiying, 2011, p. 70)*

In particular, TRT's indissoluble link with traditional medicine, which itself is inextricably linked with Daoism, means the shop, taking a Durkheim (1915) perspective, upholds and reinforces but also embodies, and reflects, certain traditional values. Arguably, therefore, TRT represents a distinct worldview, or cosmology, which especially pertains to the Chinese.

Management implications

From both a corporate brand management and tourism management perspective, TRT's managers should appreciate that the attractiveness of their flagship shop rests not only on what it sells but also in what it symbolises in national and cultural terms.

In short, TRT is not only a historic retail outlet but, moreover, is a highly significant corporate heritage entity and a unique corporate brand icon of national importance. Thus, TRT is not only a retail corporate brand but also a corporate heritage brand, a corporate heritage tourism brand of national import. Arguably, too, it is of global importance vis-à-vis the Chinese diaspora as well.

Research limitations

In accordance with the precepts of case study research and mindful of issues of epistemology of the findings, it is not possible to conclude that the findings are generalisable in a statistical sense. This study on corporate heritage tourism brands should be seen as a significant study in terms of its focus but a provisional study in terms of the relatively small sample size.

Further research

Avenues for future research might include examining corporate heritage tourism brand entities and their significance for national identity in other countries. Austria, Germany, Japan and the UK – where corporate heritage institutions have prevailed – lend themselves to this mode of inquiry.

This study has focused on a retail outlet, and other prominent retail outlets might also be profitable in terms of insight (*Harrods* – London, *Macy's* – New York, *Hudson Bay Company* – Toronto, *Les Galeries Lafayette Haussmann* – Paris).

However, the embryonic corporate heritage tourism brand domain is, seemingly, broad in scope and encompasses many sectorial fields.

For instance, within China, there is further scope in examining the significance and characteristics of corporate heritage tourism brands within China. Moreover, the significance of corporate heritage tourism brands to the Chinese diaspora would provide other lines of enquiry (as would the saliency of corporate heritage tourism to other diasporas such as the English, Indian, Irish, Italian, Korean and Scottish ethnicities).

From a theoretical perspective, there is scope to advance the insights from this study by drawing on the corporate identity literature (in explaining an institution's corporate heritage identity anchors in heritage tourism contexts) and social identity theory vis-à-vis corporate brands and identity (the ways in which individuals define themselves in terms of an organisation's having an corporate heritage and heritage tourism identities).

The significance of an entity's religious/philosophical base – Daoism in the case of TRT – would suggest that the religious dimension might provide another fruitful line of research vis-à-vis certain corporate heritage tourism brands too.

Final reflection

This research has highlighted the significance of the TRT corporate heritage brand as a corporate heritage tourism brand attraction. TRT was also shown to be significant in terms of representing – and arguably conferring – Chinese national identity. The study was informed by the literature on corporate heritage/corporate heritage brands, heritage tourism and national identity.

As such, within the broad heritage canon the importance of corporate heritage tourism brands should be recognised.

Moreover, this study sheds more light on the importance of corporate heritage tourism in China: a nation which is not always associated in having prominent corporate heritage brands let alone corporate heritage brands of centuries-old antiquity.

The study has revealed the factors which account for its popularity as a domestic corporate heritage tourism attraction within China. Moreover, it has uncovered its importance as a distinctive, enduring and meaningful symbol of China's primordial national identity.

In a city (Beijing) where the past is experienced largely through a historical lens, TRT represents a living, meaningful and tangible link with a former imperial polity and with a Confucius philosophy with Daoist belief which, in many ways, still provides the bedrock of China's ancient and incomparable civilisation.

As China reappraises and revisits its pre-revolutionary history and its cultural inheritance in terms of its "soft power" (Nye, 2004) on the global stage, the unique importance of TRT as a fulcrum of Chinese culture, spirituality, ancestry and memory is incalculable not only in terms of national heritage but, moreover, in corporate heritage tourism terms too.

For the above reasons, our case study of the TRT corporate heritage tourism brand is of consequence to corporate marketing, corporate brand management, corporate heritage, tourism research, heritage scholarship and studies in nationality too.

Furthermore, the cultural and national significance of this corporate heritage brand is not only of importance to the managers of TRT and to policymakers within China but for mankind too. Moreover, China's corporate brand inheritance is a legacy which all mankind should cherish.

We hope our modest article will in a small way speak to the aforesaid sentiment.

References

Adler, J.A. (2002), *Chinese Religions*, Routledge, London.

Aiying, J. and Zhiying, B. (2011), *Tongrentang Traditional Chinese Medicine Culture*, Tongrentang Company Archive, Beijing.

Albert, S. and Whetten, D. (1985), "Organizational identity", *Research in Organizational Behavior*, Vol. 7, pp. 263–295.

Anderson, B. (1983), *Imagined Communities*, Verso, London.

Balmer, J.M.T. (2009), "Scrutinising the British Monarchy: The corporate brand that was shaken, stirred and survived", *Management Decision*, Vol. 47 No. 4, pp. 639–675.

Balmer, J.M.T. (2011a), "Corporate heritage identities, corporate heritage brands and the multiple heritage identities of the British Monarchy", *European Journal of Marketing*, Vol. 45 Nos. 9/10, pp. 1380–1398.

Balmer, J.M.T. (2011b), "Corporate heritage brands and the precepts of corporate heritage brand management: Reflections on the British Monarchy on the eve of the wedding of Prince William (April 2011) and the Diamond Jubilee celebrations of Queen Elizabeth II (1952–2012)", *Journal of Brand Management*, Vol. 18 No. 8, pp. 517–544.

Balmer, J.M.T. (2013), "Corporate heritage, corporate heritage marketing and total corporate heritage communications: What are they? What of them?", *Corporate Communications: An International Journal*, Vol. 18 No. 3, pp. 290–326.

Balmer, J.M.T., Greyser, S.A. and Urde, M. (2006), "The crown as a corporate brand: Insights from monarchies", *Journal of Brand Management*, Vol. 14 Nos. 1/2, pp. 137–161.

Bandyopadhyay, R., Morais, D.B. and Chick, G. (2008), "Religion and identity in India's heritage tourism", *Annals of Tourism Research*, Vol. 35 No. 3, pp. 790–808.

Baron, R.M. and Kenny, D.A. (1986), "The moderator-mediator variable distinction in social psychological research: Conceptual, strategic, and statistical considerations", *Journal of Personality and Social Psychology*, Vol. 51 No. 6, p. 1173.

Bedford, D., Hsiung, D.T., Knowles, C., Leffman, D., Lewis, S., Neville-Hadley, P. and Stone, A. (2008), *China*, Dorling Kindersley, London.

Bessiere, J. (1998), "Local development and heritage: Traditional food and cuisine as tourist attractions in rural areas", *Sociologia Ruralis*, Vol. 38 No. 1, pp. 21–34.

Blombäck, A. and Brunninge, O. (2009), "Corporate identity manifested through historical references", *Corporate Communications: An International Journal*, Vol. 14 No. 4, pp. 404–419.

Blombäck, A. and Brunninge, O. (2013), "The dual opening to brand heritage in family businesses", *Corporate Communications: An International Journal*, Vol. 18 No. 3, pp. 327–346.

Bond, M.H. (1980), "Chinese values and the search for culture-free dimensions of culture", *Journal of Cross-Cultural Psychology*, Vol. 18 No. 2, pp. 143–164.

Burghausen, M. and Balmer, J.M.T. (2014a), "Corporate heritage identity management and the multi-modal implementation of a corporate heritage identity", *Journal of Business Research*, Vol. 67 No. 11, pp. 2311–2323.

Burghausen, M. and Balmer, J.M.T. (2014b), "Repertoires of the corporate past: Explanation and framework: Introducing an integrated and dynamic perspective", *Corporate Communications: An International Journal*, Vol. 19 No. 4, pp. 384–402.

Burghausen, M. and Balmer, J.M.T. (2015), "Corporate heritage identity stewardship: A corporate marketing perspective", *European Journal of Marketing*, Vol. 49 Nos. 1/2, pp. 22–61.

Caseby, R. (2011), "Crouching tiger, hidden DVD player", *The Sunday Times*, 20 January, p. 26.

Chhabra, D., Healy, R. and Ills, E. (2003), "Staged authenticity and heritage tourism", *Annals of Tourism Research*, Vol. 30 No. 3, pp. 702–719.

Chin, W.W. (1998), "The partial least squares approach to structural equation modelling", in Marcoulides, G.A. (Ed.), *Modern Methods for Business Research*, Lawrence Erlbaum Associates, Mahwah, NJ.

Chronis, A. and Hampton, R.D. (2008), "Consuming the authentic Gettysburg: How a tourist landscape becomes an authentic experience", *Journal of Consumer Behavior*, Vol. 7 No. 2, pp. 111–126.

Cohen, A.P. (2002), "The best of British-with more the come", in Rapport, N. (Ed.), *British Subjects: An Anthropology of Britain*, Routledge, London, p. 328.

Durkheim, E. (1915), *The Elementary Forms of the Religious Life*, George Allen and Unwin, London.

Edensor, T. (2002), *National Identity, Popular Culture and Everyday Life*, Berg, Oxford, p. 50.

Edmondson, A.C. and McManus, S.E. (2007), "Methodological fit in management field research", *Academy of Management Review*, Vol. 32 No. 4, pp. 1115–1179.

Eisenberg, D. (1995), *Encounters with Qi: Exploring Chinese Medicine*, W.W. Norton, London.

Fornell, C. and Larcker, D.F. (1981), "Structural equation models with unobservable variables and measurement error: Algebra and statistics", *Journal of Marketing Research*, pp. 382–388.

Franklin, A. (2003), *Tourism: An Introduction*, Sage, Thousand Oaks, CA.

Geertz, C. (1973), *The Interpretation of Cultures: Selected Essays*, Fontana, London.

Gellner, E. (1983), *Nations and Nationalism*, Blackwell, Oxford.

Gellner, E. (1998), *Nationalism*, Phoenix, London.

Gerbing, D.W. and Anderson, J.C. (1988), "An updated paradigm for scale development incorporating unidimensionality and its assessment", *Journal of Marketing Research*, Vol. 25 No. 2, pp. 186–192.

Goodhue, D.L., Lewis, W. and Thompson, R. (2012), "Does pls have advantages for small sample size or non-normal data?", *MIS Quarterly*, Vol. 36 No. 3, pp. 981–1016.

Goulding, C. (2000), "The commodification of the past, postmodern pastiche, and the search for authentic experiences at contemporary heritage attractions", *European Journal of Marketing*, Vol. 34 No. 7, pp. 835–853.

Goulding, C. (2001), "Romancing the past: Heritage visiting and the nostalgic consumer", *Psychology and Marketing*, Vol. 18 No. 6, pp. 565–592.

Grayling, A.C. (2015), *The Challenge of Things*, Bloomsbury, London.

Gu, H. and Ryan, C. (2008), "Place attachment, identity and community impacts of tourism: The case of a Beijing hutong", *Tourism Management*, Vol. 29 No. 4, pp. 637–647.

Hakala, U., Lätti, S. and Sandberg, B. (2011), "Operationalising brand heritage and cultural heritage", *Journal of Product & Brand Management*, Vol. 20 No. 6, pp. 447–456.

Hakala, U., Sjöblom, P. and Kantola, S.-P. (2015), "Toponyms as carriers of heritage: Implications for place branding", *Journal of Product & Brand Management*, Vol. 24 No. 3, pp. 263–275.

Halewood, C. and Hannam, K. (2001), "Viking heritage tourism: Authenticity and commodification", *Annals of Tourism Research*, Vol. 28 No. 3, pp. 565–580.

Hammond, P.E. (1976), "The sociology of American civil religion: A bibliographic essay", *Sociological Analysis*, Vol. 37 No. 2, pp. 169–182.

Hayden, I. (1987), *Symbol and Privilege: The Ritual Context of British Royalty*, University of Arizona Press.

Heathcote, E. (2011), "How to build heritage", *The Financial Times*, 8–9 January, p. 8.

Henderson, J.C. (2002), "Conserving colonial heritage: Raffles Hotel in Singapore", *International Journal of Heritage Studies*, Vol. 7 No. 1, pp. 7–24.

Herbert, D.T. (Ed.) (1995), *Heritage, Tourism and Society*, Pinter, London.

Hewison, R. (1987), *The Heritage Industry: Britain in a Climate of Decline*, Methuen, London.

Hofstede, G. (1980), *Cultures Consequences: International Differences in Work-Related Values*, Sage, Newbury Park, CA, pp. 213–260.

Holbrook, M. and Schindler, R. (2003), "Nostalgic bonding: Exploring the role of nostalgia in the consumption experience", *Journal of Consumer Behavior*, Vol. 3 No. 2, pp. 102–107.

Howard, M. (2008), "The dawn of the century", in Howard, M. and Louis, W.R. (Eds.), *The Oxford History of the Twentieth Century*, Oxford University Press, Oxford, pp. 3–9.

Howard, R.E. (1998), "Being Canadian: Citizenship in Canada", *Citizenship Studies*, Vol. 2 No. 1, pp. 133–152.

Hudson, B.T. (2011), "Brand heritage and the renaissance of Cunard", *Journal of Marketing*, Vol. 45 Nos. 9/10, pp. 1538–1556.

Hudson, B.T. and Balmer, J.M.T. (2013), "Corporate heritage brands: Mead's theory of the past", *Corporate Communications: An International Journal*, Vol. 18 No. 3, pp. 347–361.

Inden, R. (1976), *Cultural Symbolic Constitutions in Ancient India*, Mimeo, pp. 6–8.

Issacs, I. and Martin, E.A. (Eds.) (1998), *Oxford World Encyclopedia*, Oxford University Press, Oxford.

Jaques, M. (2009), *When China Rules the World*, Penguin, London.

Jordan, D.K. (1972), *Gods, Ghosts and Ancestors: Folk Religion in a Taiwanese Village*, University of California Press, Berkeley, CA.

Kumar, K. (2003), *The Making of English National Identity*, Cambridge University Press, Cambridge.

Lenman, B.P. (Ed.) (1994), *Chambers Dictionary of World History*, Chambers, Edinburgh.

Lowenthal, D. (1998), *The Heritage Crusade and the Spoils of History*, Cambridge University Press, Cambridge.

MacDonald, S. (2002), "On old things: The fetishization of past everyday life", in Rapport, N. (Ed.), *British Subjects: An Anthropology of Britain*, Routledge, London, pp. 31–48.

MacDonald, S. (2006), "Undesirable heritage: Fascist material culture and historical consciousness in Nuremberg", *International Journal of Heritage Studies*, Vol. 12 No.1, pp. 9–28.

Mead, G.H. (1929), "The nature of the past", in Coss, J. (Ed.), *Essays in Honor of John Dewey on the Occasion of His 70th Birthday*, Henry Holt, New York, NY, pp. 235–242.

Mead, G.H. (1932), *The Philosophy of the Present*, Open Court, Chicago, IL.

Misiura, S. (2006), *Heritage Marketing*, Butterworth-Heinemann, Oxford.

Nairn, T. (1997), *Faces of Nationalism: Janus Revisited*, Verso, London.

Nye, J. (2004), *Soft Power: The Means to Success in World Politics*, Public Affairs, New York, NY.

O'Guinn, T.C. and Belk, R.W. (1989), "Heaven on earth: Consumption at heritage village, USA", *Journal of Consumer Research*, Vol. 16, pp. 227–238.

Olins, W. (1995), *The New Guide to Identity*, Gower, Aldershot.

Palmer, C.A. (1998), "From theory to practice: Experiencing the nation in everyday life", *Journal of Material Culture*, Vol. 3 No. 2, pp. 175–199.

Palmer, C.A. (2005), "An ethnography of Englishness: Experiencing identity through tourism", *Annals of Tourism Research*, Vol. 32 No. 1, pp. 7–27.

Park, H.-Y. (2010), "Heritage tourism: Emotional journeys into nationhood", *Annals of Tourism Research*, Vol. 37 No. 1, pp. 116–135.

Poria, Y. and Ashworth, G. (2009), "Heritage tourism: Current resource for conflict", *Annals of Tourism Research*, Vol. 36 No. 3, pp. 238–254.

Poria, Y., Butler, R. and Airey, D. (2003), "The core of heritage tourism", *Annals of Tourism Research*, Vol. 30 No. 1, pp. 238–254.

Poria, Y., Reichel, A. and Biran, A. (2006), "Heritage site management: Motivations and expectations", *Annals of Tourism Research*, Vol. 33 No. 1, pp. 162–178.

Prentice, R. (1993), *Tourism and Heritage Attractions*, Routledge, London.

Pretes, M. (2003), "Tourism and nationalism", *Annals of Tourism Research*, Vol. 30 No. 1, pp. 125–142.

Rapport, N. (Ed.) (2002), *British Subjects: An Anthology of Britain*, Routledge, London.

Rowbottom, A. (2002), "Subject positions and 'real royalists': Monarchy and vernacular civil religion in Great Britain", in Rapport, N. (Ed.), *British Subjects: An Anthropology of Britain*, Routledge, London, pp. 31–48.

Schroeder, J., Borgerson, J. and Wu, Z. (2015), "A brand culture approach to Chinese cultural heritage brands", *Journal of Brand Management*, Vol. 22, pp. 261–279.

Shahdar, M. and Weller, R.P. (Eds.) (1996), *Unruly Gods, Divinity and Society in China*, University of Hawaii Press, Honolulu.

Smith, A.D. (1991), *National Identity*, University of Nevada Press, Reno, NV.

Smith, A.D. (1993), *National Identity (Ethnonationalism Comparative Perspective)*, University of Nevada Press, Reno, NV.

Smith, A.D. (1994), "The problem of national identity: Ancient, medieval and modern?", *Ethnic and Racial Studies*, Vol. 17 No. 3, pp. 375–399.

Story, J. (2010), *China Uncovered*, Financial Times-Prentice Hall, London.

Thapar, R. (2014), *The Past as Present, Forging Contemporary Identities through History*, Aleph Books, New Delhi.

Urde, M. and Greyser, S.A. (2015), "The Nobel prize: The identity of a corporate heritage brand", *Journal of Product & Brand Management*, Vol. 24 No. 4, pp. 318–332.

Urde, M., Greyser, S.A. and Balmer, J.M.T. (2007), "Corporate brands with a heritage", *Journal of Brand Management*, Vol. 15 No. 1, pp. 4–19.

Urry, J. (1995), *Consuming Places*, Routledge, London.

Waitt, G. (2000), "Consuming heritage: Perceived historical authenticity", *Annals of Tourism Research*, Vol. 27 No. 4, pp. 835–862.

Weaver, D.B. (2010), "Contemporary tourism as heritage tourism: Evidence form Las Vegas and Gold Coast", *Annals of Tourism Research*, Vol. 38 No. 1, pp. 249–267.

Weber, M. (1968), "Chapter 5: Ethnic groups", in Roth, G. and Wittich, C. (Eds.), *Economy and Society*, Part 2, Bedminster Press, New York, NY, Vol. 1.

Wenzhong, H., Grove, C.N. and Enping, Z. (2010), *Encountering the Chinese: A Modern Country, an Ancient Culture*, Intercultural Press, Boston, MA.

Wiedmann, K.-P., Hennigs, N., Schmidt, S. and Wuestefeld, T. (2011a), "The importance of brand heritage as a key performance driver in marketing management", *Journal of Brand Management*, Vol. 19 No. 3, pp. 182–194.

Wiedmann, K.-P., Hennigs, N., Schmidt, S. and Wuestefeld, T. (2011b), "Drivers and outcomes of brand heritage: Consumers' perception of heritage brands in the automotive industry", *The Journal of Marketing Theory and Practice*, Vol. 19 No. 2, pp. 205–220.

Wilkinson, P. (2008), *Religions*, Dorling Kindersley, London.

Wright, P. (1985), *On Living in an Old Country: The National Past in Contemporary Britain*, Verso, London.

Xiaoming, X. (2005), *Taoism*, Foreign Language Press, Beijing.

Yao, X. (2000), *An Introduction to Confucianism*, Cambridge University Press, Cambridge.

Further reading

Balmer, J.M.T. and Burghausen, M. (2015a), "Explicating corporate heritage, corporate heritage brands and organisational heritage", *Journal of Brand Management*, Vol. 22 No. 5, pp. 364–384.

Balmer, J.M.T. and Burghausen, M. (2015b), "Introducing organisational heritage: Inking corporate heritage, organisational identity and organisational memory", *Journal of Brand Management*, Vol. 22 No. 5, pp. 385–411.

Balmer, J.M.T. and Chen, W. (2015a), "China's brands, China's brand development strategies and corporate brand communications in China", *Journal of Brand Management*, Vol. 22 No. 3, pp. 175–193.

Balmer, J.M.T. and Chen, W. (2015b), "Corporate heritage brands in China: Consumer engagement with China's most celebrated corporate heritage brand-Tong Ren Tang", *Journal of Brand Management*, Vol. 22 No. 3, pp. 194–210.

Balmer, J.M.T. and Chen, W. (2016), *Advances in Chinese Brand Management*, Palgrave Macmillan, London.

Balmer, J.M.T. and Greyser, S.A. (2006), "Corporate marketing: Integrating corporate identity, corporate branding, corporate communications, corporate image and corporate reputation", *European Journal of Marketing*, Vol. 40 Nos. 7/8, pp. 730–741.

Balmer, J.M.T., Powell, S.M., Kernstock, J. and Brexendorf, T.O. (2016), *Advances in Corporate Branding*, Palgrave Macmillan, London.

Balmer, J.M.T., Stuart, H. and Greyser, S.A. (2009), "Aligning identity and strategy: Corporate branding in British Airways in the late 20th century", *California Management Review*, Vol. 51 No. 3, pp. 6–23.

Balmer, J.M.T. and Wilson, A. (1998), "Corporate identity: There is more to it than meets the eye", *International Studies of Management and Organization*, Vol. 28 No. 3, pp. 12–31.

Santos, F.P., Burghausen, M. and Balmer, J.M.T. (2016), "Heritage branding orientation: The case of Ach, Brito and the dynamics between corporate and product heritage brands", *Journal of Brand Management*, Vol. 23 No. 1, pp. 67–88.

Smith, A.D. (1986), *The Ethnic Origins of Nations*, Blackwell, Oxford.

SECTION 4

Corporate heritage and family businesses

8

CONTRASTING CASES OF CORPORATE HERITAGE-IN-USE

Vibrant versus latent approaches

Dale Miller, Bill Merrilees and Holly Cooper

Introduction

Although management of corporate heritage has strategic significance, the domain is still emerging. Notwithstanding, a foundational article by Balmer *et al.* (2006) has stimulated considerable research. Much of that research is about the nature and principles of corporate heritage brands. The Monarchy has received considerable attention, as it represents a corporate heritage brand exemplar (Balmer, 2009, 2011a, 2011b; Balmer *et al.*, 2006; Greyser *et al.*, 2006). In contrast, heritage brands in the corporate commercial context receive less empirical consideration. Notable exceptions are studies of Cunard (Hudson, 2011), the family-owned Shepherd Neame brewery (Burghausen and Balmer, 2014, 2015), Tiffany and Burberry (Cooper *et al.*, 2015a) and four Australian companies (Cooper *et al.*, 2015b). The chapter contrasts corporate heritage across Canada and Australia, examining two major corporates, Canadian Tire Corporation and David Jones, and ends with consideration of a third company, Canadian Tim Hortons.

This chapter contrasts vibrant versus latent approaches to utilising corporate heritage. Canadian Tire, the largest Canadian-owned retailer, represents the vibrant approach to active corporate heritage management. David Jones, an Australian department store, is a contrasting case representing the latent approach. The divergent approaches focus on two important concepts salient in the literature, namely heritage stewardship and competencies (Cooper *et al.*, 2015a, 2015b; Balmer, 2013; Burghausen and Balmer, 2015). Both concepts seem to make a critical difference in effective corporate heritage management. One contribution of this chapter is to reinforce the utility of these two concepts as key differentiators of corporate heritage management effectiveness. Another contribution is to consider corporate culture as a possible bridge between the two concepts. A third contribution is to apply the lessons from studying Canadian Tire and David Jones to emerging corporate heritage brands, and in this context, we consider the case of Canadian firm Tim Hortons.

Corporate heritage characteristics

Corporate heritage traits are complex, as detailed by the eleven traits identified in Balmer (2013). Of these traits, family ownership, corporate heritage design, organisational rationales/cultures and ethos, and corporate heritage competencies are especially useful to elucidating the contrast between our two focal companies. Heritage stewardship is also very relevant in contrasting corporate heritage in Canadian Tire and David Jones. Both focal companies have strong family-owned roots, which we turn to now.

Family ownership

Family-ownership is a potential but not a necessary or sufficient strong basis for heritage status (Balmer, 2013) and is one of the key characteristics in the Shepherd Neame heritage brand (Burghausen and Balmer, 2014). Many commercial corporate heritage brands seem to have their roots with strong founders and their families (Cooper *et al.*, 2015a), and both Canadian Tire and David Jones fit this pattern.

Canadian Tire was founded in 1922 by two brothers, J. W. Billes (president until 1956), and A. J. Billes (president 1956 to 1965) in Toronto, Canada (McBride, 1997; Miller, 2011). They were deeply involved with the business and very entrepreneurial, especially in the Inter-War years and early post-World War II. The family presidency ended with the appointment of Dean Muncaster, a professional MBA-educated president, in 1965 (Miller, 2014). However, family involvement with the firm continues with the Board membership of Martha Billes and Owen Billes (Canadian Tire).

David Jones has its roots in a drapery founded by Welshman David Jones in 1838, in Sydney, Australia. Four generations of the family were involved in leading the department store until 1980 (Miller, 2005, 2006b; O'Neill, 2013). Leadership was very family focused and often very hands-on in the years until about 1920, when third generation Charles Lloyd Jones took over as chairman of the board, and managing director for extended periods. His unique style and vision dominated leadership of the firm until 1958 (Cullen, 2013; Miller, 2006a; O'Neill, 2013). Family leadership and high involvement ceased in 1980 with an ownership change, and further shifts in ownership have extinguished any remnants of family connection.

Corporate heritage design

Corporate heritage design is seen as an essential feature of strong heritage brands (Balmer, 2013). Corporate heritage design features include both tangible and intangible manifestations of the corporate heritage. However, institutional heritage identity is also relevant here, as illustrated with the iconic, geographic status of the brewery Shepherd Neame (Burghausen and Balmer, 2014).

Canadian Tire, from the beginning in the 1920s, was consciously using imagery, symbols and slogans to reinforce the strength, longevity and heritage of the corporate brand. The Billes brothers registered trademarks and used logos and slogans throughout their innovative catalogues and advertising. In the late 1950s, A. J. Billes introduced Canadian Tire Money, and by 1961 the money was printed on genuine banknote paper, reinforcing durability and "tactile wizardry" (McBride, 1997, p. 64). They frequently invoked colour, especially red – a fortunate choice, given the 1967 creation of the Canadian flag featuring red and white and the maple leaf.

An evolution in their heritage design marked their corporate heritage design-building in the professional era, when extensive use was made of heritage, including special events and anniversaries, and a coherent brand story was communicated through multiple channels, and logo was used extensively (Miller, 2014, p. 101). Corporate heritage is a mainstay of the current website, showcasing the firm's history, profiles of the founders, and ongoing emphasis on anniversaries, including the ninetieth anniversary in 2012. In 2012, the refurbished reception area of the company's Toronto headquarters included a display of historical artefacts to create interest in the firm's heritage and to reinforce longevity and authenticity.

A further indication of the firm's appreciation of its corporate heritage is its donation of extensive archives and artefacts to the University of Western Ontario; these materials form the Canadian Tire Heritage Collection, which is an invaluable resource for the firm and for researchers (see Canadian Tire Heritage Collection website).

David Jones, from its original humble store, early handbills and newspaper advertisements, was concerned with creating and building its corporate heritage. The eponymously named store invoked the legacy of the founder. His successors relentlessly engaged in reinforcing the heritage by reference to the family as a dynasty (Cullen, 2013, p. 27). By the 1880s, a grand new department store building emphasised classical European design. Increased advertising and the introduction of exquisitely illustrated, coloured and informative catalogues were central design tools. A new breathtaking flagship store opened in 1928, further establishing the cumulative corporate heritage.

From the 1880s, the firm invoked other corporate heritage exemplars to help associate David Jones with heritage and longevity. For example, the new store was highly decorated in 1887 to celebrate Queen Victoria's Golden Jubilee. A huge external banner, proclaiming "One Queen" with a picture of the Queen, hung above the awning carrying the words "David Jones & Co." (O'Neill, 2013, p. 56). Connections with royalty and politicians were harnessed up until the 1950s, with prime ministers and premiers officially opening new buildings and culminating in the 1954 State Dinner for the new Queen Elizabeth II being held in the David Jones State Ballroom. By the twenty-first century, less emphasis was put on corporate heritage design, in favour of portraying "modernity", and thus a major company asset became dormant.

Institutional heritage identity status is also relevant to both brands. Canadian Tire is an iconic (and largest) Canadian retailer dedicated to helping people "Live life in Canada to the fullest" (Canadian Tire). The company is highly integrated into the daily lives of Canadians, helping start the school semester and start preparation for the hockey and other sports seasons. David Jones also has iconic national status, as the premier Australian department store and in times past an anchor destination in a Sydney shopping excursion.

Heritage stewardship

Arguably, heritage stewardship is the most critical aspect of corporate heritage management (Cooper et al., 2015a; Balmer, 2013; Burghausen and Balmer, 2015). Balmer (2013) emphasises that corporate heritage institutions require the ongoing and multigenerational responsibility of all organisational members. However, in the first place, attention focuses on the senior management stewardship of the organisation.

Canadian Tire demonstrates that the long-term direct family leadership from 1922 to 1965 created the basis for heritage stewardship. The subsequent professional leadership of the firm explicitly took heritage stewardship further, actively guarding and nurturing the understanding, development and invoking of the corporate heritage (Miller, 2014). There was a conscious connection to the past, but also a recognition that as the firm progressed, the scope and depth of the corporate heritage would continue to intensify, and could be cultivated by active heritage stewardship. The 2015 website and annual reports, for example, exemplify the firm's robust heritage stewardship.

David Jones shows a more patchy progression in heritage stewardship. With a combination of family leadership and professional management until 1980, the firm's senior organisational members actively embraced its heritage, and worked assiduously to safeguard and reinforce that heritage. Subsequently, various owners and leaders placed more or less emphasis on the firm's heritage. An attempt to celebrate the firm's 170th anniversary came to nothing, but by the time of the 175th anniversary, the then leaders recognised the significance of the occasion and the strength of the heritage that it represented. A book was commissioned (O'Neill, 2013), displays were set up in stores and various events staged. Related celebratory merchandise, too, was available. In the same year, a book commissioned by the daughter-in-law of Sir Charles Lloyd Jones (Chairman, 1920–1958) was published (Cullen, 2013). With recent ownership changes, the 2015 website suggests less current management interest in the firm's corporate heritage.

Corporate culture

Corporate heritage culture is recognised as an important aspect of corporate heritage (Balmer, 2013). This chapter focuses on organisation corporate culture more generally as a critical pivot or bridge between heritage stewardship and diffusion of corporate heritage throughout all members of the organisation and indeed throughout all competencies in the organisation. Balmer (2013) has argued that both senior management stewardship and stewardship through all members of the organisation are critical. We argue here that corporate culture is the key to linking and thus facilitating these two groups.

Canadian Tire, from the outset, fostered a family type corporate culture, illustrated by terms like "Home Office" for its headquarters, and the high involvement of the associate dealers and their employees at the store level. Early catalogues featured employee photos (McBride, 1997; Miller, 2011). As the organisation expanded, internal work with employees focused on building strong brand understanding and brand relationships. From the 1960s, Dean Muncaster, President, emphasised empowerment and delegation (Miller, 2014). When faced in the 1990s with the introduction of Wal-Mart into the Canadian market, the president, Stephen Bachand, inspired employees using many open meetings and video conferences to keep staff informed and engaged. He drew on the then current strengths and past achievements to develop a mind-set which could meet potential challenges aggressively and positively. Similar actions applied in a 2002 corporate rebranding (Merrilees, 2005). In 2014, Stephen Wetmore, outgoing president, and his successor, Michael Medline, addressed an Investors Day where they emphatically focused on the talent, analytics and the brand. Company publications feature the heritage of the organisation and its "Canadianness" (see Canadian Tire), creating a culture where employees and the firm's heritage and connection to country are valued.

David Jones had very hands-on family leadership involvement for many years, and the firm functioned as a type of family (Miller, 2006b). For example, in 1911, when Charles Lloyd Jones returned to Australia from an international trip, the employees organised a welcome home picnic. The David Jones Archive reveals many examples of employees presenting gifts to senior staff. Moreover, in the period 1900–1950, David Jones was at the forefront of developing a supporting culture, as Miller (2006b, p. 103) explains:

> To achieve growth, efficiency and effectiveness and a premier image, the firm developed a supporting culture, which emphasized "family values" and social expectations and activities. . . . The idea of "family" at work had implications for mutual obligations and responsibilities.

The firm was progressive in its approach to human resource management, appointing a dedicated staff manager in the 1920s (Miller, 2006a, 2006b). Charles Lloyd Jones and the other leaders actively fostered the family-like culture, introducing an employee bank, many health and welfare initiatives, and internal staff communications through newsletters. Store anniversaries were celebrated, and there were gala dinners and balls, staff picnics, and support from management for a cricket club, a choral society and a drama society (Miller, 2006a, 2006b); long service was commended. The firm kept contact with employees serving abroad in both world wars, and continued their employment on their return. For many staff, ". . . it was a respectable, sophisticated and even supportive place to work" (Miller, 2006b, p. 103). And, while arguably paternalistic, in the context of its times this approach contributed to a supportive corporate culture, recognising the contributions of the staff and the rich history of the firm. By the 1980s, the culture was weakened, partly attributable to a shift in ownership.

Heritage competencies

In the context of this chapter, we refer to heritage competencies as business and retail competencies that "can accord an entity with a heritage distinctiveness if it has prevailed over time" (Balmer, 2013, p. 309).

Canadian Tire has not only prevailed over time but has had continuous growth within its main businesses as well as extending into related businesses. Selected measures show this growth. For example, the number of outlets started with one outlet in 1922, and by 1939, the Home Office headquarters employed 225 people and there were 105 associate dealer stores (Miller, 2014), forming the unique business structure developed by Canadian Tire. The company listed on the Toronto Stock Exchange in 1944. Further indicators of ongoing growth show the change from 254 associate dealers in 1970 to 319 in 1979. Company revenue in 2013 was $CAD 11.8 billion, and in 2015, there are about 1700 outlets, and 85,000 employees. Brand is one of the three top strategic directions for the firm (Canadian Tire).

The overarching heritage competencies are exceptional business management and retail skills, and an unrelenting urge to innovate and to foster the Canadian Tire brand and their own product brands. Early innovations were the use of a road map in the late 1920s as part of a double-sided catalogue mailed to members of a motorist's association. Maps for domestic use were rare, yet the surge in automobile sales and usage created a gap, which Canadian Tire quickly filled (Miller, 2011). Among many awards, Canadian Tire has achieved the status of fourth top ranking 2014 Canadian brand awarded by the Reputation Institute (Canadian Business).

David Jones showed many heritage competencies, particularly from 1887 with the opening of an opulent full-scale department store, and growth first through mail order catalogue and later through the opening of a significant and magnificent flagship store in 1928. The two stores continued to operate – just a short distance across the city from each other. The Great Depression heralded the need for some rationalisation. David Jones managed this with exceptional retail skills and innovation. They appointed additional associate directors to manage merchandise selection to respond to the difficult economic times. They continued to invoke their heritage and longevity, to build confidence. The success was shown by the shareholder dividends, which were at 10 per cent per annum throughout the Depression – a remarkable achievement. The continued growth in the 1930s with the opening of a third store plateaued in the 1940s. Post-war, growth continued through acquisition of regional department stores, which were gradually rebadged to David Jones, with all its well-recognised heritage. In the late 1940s and 1950s, store promotions featured Parisian designers and models, suggesting a strong association between heritage cities like Paris, and David Jones. The buyers, and the advertising and promotions employees, were skilled at connecting with the firm's heritage. Many had long employment tenure. The use of heritage competencies has diminished with changes of ownership, less innovation and some fuzziness in identifying target markets.

Corporate heritage: A vibrant approach

Over its 93 years, Canadian Tire has emerged as a strong, powerful (ranked four in the national branding stakes) and well-liked company, having an iconic status in the everyday life of many Canadians. Corporate heritage seems to have played its part in sustaining the company economically. The chapter has drawn on five key heritage concepts from the literature (see especially Balmer, 2011b, 2013; Balmer *et al.*, 2006; Burghausen and Balmer, 2014, 2105) to explain salient differences across the two focal companies. The five concepts are iconic status/identity; family (or management surrogate) ownership; heritage stewardship; corporate culture; and competencies.

Figure 8.1 provides a means of integrating the five heritage concepts as a model of sustainable corporate heritage. The dominant trigger or starting position is

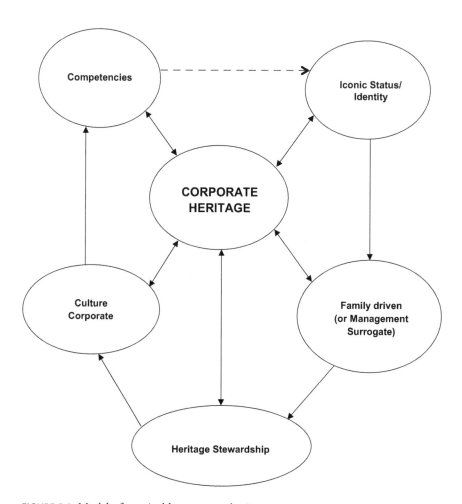

FIGURE 8.1 Model of sustainable corporate heritage

having a strong iconic brand with a strong heritage. Responsibility is clearly in the hands of the founders/owners/managers. Safeguarding this heritage in an ongoing way requires active and robust heritage stewardship, which is in senior management hands. Diffusing this heritage throughout the organisation is usually "mediated" through corporate culture, which is the next concept in Figure 8.1. After this stage, the diffusion process completes and embodies in the organisational competencies.

Canadian Tire has successfully managed all stages of Figure 8.1 very well, ensuring a vibrant approach to corporate heritage-in-use. However, special mention is given to the way it has managed heritage stewardship in moving from a family-run structure to a professionally managed one (Miller, 2014).

Corporate heritage: A latent approach

In contrast to Canadian Tire, the David Jones approach is variable over its 177-year history. For its first 120 years, David Jones matches Canadian Tire as a company that respects and leverages its corporate heritage. Particularly over three generations of family-owned management and control (and thus endorsing the Balmer [2013] multigenerational feature), David Jones developed a very reputable, iconic and successful department store. Special regard is given to Charles Lloyd Jones for his pioneering but respectful approach to building both fairness and competencies (Cullen, 2013; Miller, 2006b; O'Neill, 2013). All five concepts in Figure 8.1 were activated and integrated. Essentially, the company's corporate heritage went from strength to strength. The death of Sir Charles Lloyd Jones in 1958 was followed by twenty years of simply maintaining the business, and in 1980, a new era without any family involvement began. Such an ownership change quickly triggered the lapse of corporate heritage. The iconic status was tarnished slightly, heritage stewardship took backstage, corporate culture was less cohesive and inclusive, and competencies were not as well developed.

The standout feature explaining the lapse in corporate heritage-in-use is the complete commercialisation of the company in 1980 and exclusion of family involvement. This change had an immediate effect on heritage stewardship that in turn had follow-on consequences. The very strength of Canadian Tire was the Achilles heel for David Jones. The former company was able to continue and adapt its approach to heritage custodianship through successive changes in ownership and management structures, whereas the latter company could not. Part of the failure of David Jones to maintain its investment and management in corporate heritage may be that the intangible nature of an asset like corporate heritage was not appreciated in the cutthroat 1980s world of mergers and acquisitions.

Corporate heritage: An emerging approach

Tim Hortons, the famous Canadian coffee and donuts retailer, was founded in 1964 and might be considered either an emerging or fledgling corporate heritage brand (see Balmer, 2013). Another eponymously named firm, it takes its name from an exceptional Canadian hockey player, Tim Horton, who started the business in 1964, and died in 1974. From a single store, the Tim Hortons chain has outlets in Canada (3468), the United States (807) and 29 in the Gulf Cooperation Council (Tim Hortons). The Canadian connection was immediately apparent, and intensified in the local market particularly over the ensuing fifty years. Little was made of the fiftieth anniversary, but much is made of the firm's longevity and connection to community and to multiple generations of Canadians (see for example, Foster *et al.*, 2011; Hunter, 2012; Joyce and Thompson, 2006; Tim Hortons). This is a very interesting case where corporate heritage could be considered in part in reference to intergenerational customer stakeholders. In terms of Figure 8.1, the main gap is the lack of explicit and proactive stewardship.

Conclusion

This chapter has contrasted two iconic brands with varying approaches to corporate heritage-in-use. Canadian Tire represents the vibrant approach to corporate heritage-in-use, while David Jones represents the latent approach. The different approaches of the two focal companies have been discussed in terms of five key heritage concepts. The vibrant approach is then summarised, partly with the aid of Figure 8.1 that integrates the five key heritage concepts. In turn, the latent approach is summarised, also with the aid of Figure 8.1. The findings are then applied to an emerging corporate heritage brand, Tim Hortons.

Contributions

The first scholarly contribution is a greater understanding of the different approaches to corporate heritage management, in particular the contrast between companies that have a vibrant heritage-in-use approach, compared to companies where heritage-in-use has gone from vibrant to lapsed or dormant.

The second scholarly contribution is insight into the process of vibrant heritage-in-use. The chapter develops a model (Figure 8.1) for integrating five key heritage concepts. The model draws on the literature (Balmer 2011b, 2013; Balmer *et al.*, 2006; Burghausen and Balmer, 2014, 2015), but goes further by integrating the concepts in a particular way. Figure 8.1 explains the vibrant heritage-in-use approach of Canadian Tire and that of David Jones for its first 120 years. A major contribution is to single out two specific heritage variables, heritage stewardship and competencies, as having special significance. Further, the chapter argues that the link between heritage stewardship and the diffused use of competencies throughout the organisation is usually "mediated" through corporate culture.

Management implications

There are four management implications flowing from this chapter. The implications vary, depending on the current vibrancy of corporate heritage-in-use in an organisation. The first implication applies when there is vibrant corporate heritage-in-use, as in the Canadian Tire case. This situation calls for maintaining the healthy linkages between the key variables in Figure 8.1 and in particular the special roles of heritage stewardship, corporate culture and competencies.

The second implication applies the same vibrancy test but to emerging corporate heritage brands, such as in the case of Tim Hortons. Again, the situation calls for developing or maintaining the healthy linkages between the key variables in Figure 8.1.

The third implication applies when a company shifts or downgrades from a vibrant to a lapsed level of corporate heritage-in-use, as in the case of David Jones. The lapse suggests that corporate heritage, as a strategic variable, is latent or dormant and needs strategic reawakening. Figure 8.1 offers a practical tool to guide the organisation if it chooses such a tack.

The fourth implication applies when heritage-in-use not simply lapses, but seriously fails. Anon (2015a) addresses two such cases (Tiffany and Burberry) and identifies heritage stewardship and competencies as the basis for recovering corporate heritage. The current chapter agrees with emphasising these two forces, and furthermore adds a third, corporate culture.

Key points

1   Heritage stewardship, corporate culture and competencies are critical for managing corporate heritage.
2   Effective management of corporate heritage requires systematic integration of heritage concepts.

Questions

1   How useful do you see Figure 8.1 as a tool for managing corporate heritage?
2   Do you agree with how Figure 8.1 explains the corporate heritage management differences between Canadian Tire and David Jones? What relevant issues does Figure 8.1 NOT explain? In particular, what else could explain the lapse in David Jones?
3   Can you nominate other examples of vibrant, latent and emerging approaches to corporate heritage-in-use?
4   What advice would you give to Canadian Tire to take their vibrant approach a step higher, maybe to become best practice corporate heritage management?
5   What advice would you give to David Jones to help them return to a vibrant approach to corporate heritage?

References

Balmer, J.M.T. (2009) Scrutinising the British Monarchy: The Corporate Brand That Was Shaken, Stirred and Survived, *Management Decision*, 47(4): 639–675.
Balmer, J.M.T. (2011a) Corporate Heritage Brands and the Precepts of Corporate Heritage Brand Management: Insights from the British Monarchy on the Eve of the Royal

Wedding of Prince William (April 2011) and Queen Elizabeth II's Diamond Jubilee (1952–2012), *Journal of Brand Management*, 18(8): 517–544.

Balmer, J.M.T. (2011b) Corporate Heritage Identities, Corporate Heritage Brands and the Multiple Heritage Identities of the British Monarchy, *European Journal of Marketing*, 45(9/10): 1380–1398.

Balmer, J.M.T. (2013) Corporate Heritage, Corporate Heritage Marketing, and Total Corporate Heritage Communications, *Corporate Communications: An International Journal*, 18(3): 290–326.

Balmer, J.M.T., Greyser, S.A. and Urde, M. (2006) The Crown as a Corporate Brand: Insights from Monarchies, *Journal of Brand Management*, 14(1/2): 137–161.

Burghausen, M. and Balmer, J.M.T. (2014) Corporate Heritage Identity Management and Multi-Modal Implementation of a Corporate Heritage Identity, *Journal of Business Research*, 67(11): 2311–2323.

Burghausen, M. and Balmer, J.M.T. (2015) Corporate Heritage Identity Stewardship: A Corporate Marketing Perspective, *European Journal of Marketing*, 49(1/2), http://dx.doi.org/10.1108/EJM-03-2013-0169.

Cooper, H., Miller, D. and Merrilees, B. (2015a) Restoring Luxury Corporate Heritage Brands: From Crisis to Ascendancy, *Journal of Brand Management*, 22(5): 448–466.

Cooper, H., Merrilees, B. and Miller, D. (2015b) Corporate Heritage Brand Management: Corporate Heritage Brands versus Contemporary Corporate Brands, *Journal of Brand Management*, 22(5), 412–430.

Cullen, J. (2013) *No Other Man No Other Store: The Extraordinary Life of Sir Charles Lloyd Jones Painter, Patron and Patriot 1878–1958*, Macmillan, Melbourne.

Foster, W.M., Suddaby, R., Minkus, A. and Wiebe, E. (2011) History as Social Memory Assets: The Example of Tim Hortons, *Management and Organizational History*, 6 (1): 101–120.

Greyser, S., Balmer, J.M.T and Urde, M. (2006) The Monarchy as a Corporate Brand, *European Journal of Marketing*, 40(7/8): 902–908.

Hudson, B.T. (2011) Brand Heritage and the Renaissance of Cunard, *European Journal of Marketing*, 45(9/10): 1538–56.

Hunter, D. (2012) *Double Double: How Tim Hortons Became a Canadian Way of Life, One Cup at a Time*, HarperCollins, Toronto.

Joyce, R. and Thompson, R. (2006) *Always Fresh: The Untold Story of Tim Hortons by the Man Who Created a Canadian Empire*, HarperCollins, Toronto.

McBride, H. (1997) *Our Store: 75 Years of Canadian Tire*, Quantum, Toronto.

Merrilees, B. (2005) Radical Brand Evolution: A Case-Based Framework, *Journal of Advertising Research*, 45(2): 201–210.

Miller, D. (2005) Diverse Transnational Influences and Department Stores: Australian Evidence from the 1870s–1950s. *Special Edition: From Department Store to Shopping Mall History in Large-Scale Retail/Vom Warnehaus zur Shopping Mall: Einzelhandel transnational, Jahrbuch fuer Wirtschaftsgeschichte (German Economic Yearbook)*. Guest Editor Dr. Alexander Sedlmaier, Wadham College, Oxford, ISBN 3–05–004128–5; Berlin: Akademie Verlag, 2005/2: 17–40.

Miller, D. (2006a) *"Members of a Vast Family": Changing Modes of Paternalistic Staff Management at David Jones Ltd Australia 1870s–1950s*; PhD Thesis, The University of Newcastle, Australia.

Miller, D. (2006b) Strategic Human Resource Management in Department Stores: An Historical Perspective, *Journal of Retailing and Consumer Services*, 13(2): 99–109.

Miller, D. (2011) Building Customer Confidence in the Automobile Age: Canadian Tire 1928–1939, *Journal of Historical Research in Marketing*, 3(3): 302–328.

Miller, D. (2014) Brand-Building and the Elements of Success: Discoveries using Historical Analyses, *Qualitative Market Research*, 17(2): 92–111.

O'Neill, H. (2013) *David Jones' 175 Years*, NewSouth (University of New South Wales Press), Sydney.

Websites

Canadian Business, http://www.canadianbusiness.com/canadian-brand-top-40-ranking/, accessed 05 January 2015.

Canadian Tire, http://corp.canadiantire.ca/EN/AboutUs/Pages/default.aspx, accessed 20 November 2014.

Canadian Tire Heritage Collection, at Western Archives, The University of Western Ontario, https://www.lib.uwo.ca/archives/canadiantireheritagecollection.html, accessed 31 October, 2014.

Tim Hortons, http://www.timhortons.com/ca/en/about/company-facts.php, accessed 28 November 2014.

Acknowledgements

The authors gratefully acknowledge the guidance and expert advice from the Western Archives staff, particularly Bev Brereton at the University of Western Ontario, and from Siân Madsen, Canadian Tire Corporation, Toronto. Much gratitude and respect is due to the late Barbara Horton, Archivist, David Jones Ltd. Without such people, researchers and firms would not have access to significant materials to help understand corporate heritage.

9

FAMILY HERITAGE IN CORPORATE HERITAGE BRANDING

Opportunities and risks

Olof Brunninge

This chapter explores the strengths and weaknesses of addressing family heritage in the context of corporate heritage. Family businesses are a particularly interesting context for the communication of corporate heritage. In these firms, the heritage of the company and that of the owner family are usually closely connected. Unless the ownership has changed over the years, the history of the organisation is by definition part of the owners' family history that interlinks generations. Trait constancy, being a central criterion for the existing of corporate heritage, can be manifested in ownership and governance structures, as well as in other characteristics such as a location, a corporate ethos, or focus on a particular kind of products (Balmer 2013). Being a family firm, owned by the same family across generations, does not only point at historical trait constancy. It also creates an expectation of future ownership constancy through future successions. This not least illustrated by the monarchy that can be conceived as a prototypical family 'business', which provides continuity across multiple successions and centuries (Balmer, Greyser & Urde 2006). Interestingly the generational aspect of corporate heritage has been addressed even beyond the family firm context in Balmer's (2013) tri-generational heredity criterion. According to this criterion, identity traits should have endured for at least three generations to qualify as aspects of corporate heritage. In practice this could relate to three generations of owner-managers in a family firm, but the generations could also represent generations of customers or other stakeholders.

In family firms, the past of the organisation directly relates to the ancestors of the individuals presently controlling the business and potentially also gives relevance to coming generations that may run the firm in the future. Many family firms try to capitalise on the close linkage between family and firm by consciously including family heritage in the heritage branding of their business. This chapter discusses both opportunities and risks of doing so. Despite all potential advantages of corporate heritage communications, addressing heritage also entails risks, if for instance corporate heritage is contested or its negative aspects are uncovered (Balmer 2013). Drawing on corporate heritage literature as well as on research from the family business field, the chapter starts with a discussion on family firms in general and corporate heritage branding in such firms in particular. Along a variety of cases, different challenges associated with an inclusion of family heritage will be discussed, both from a company and from a family perspective. Special emphasis will be put on trait constancy that is closely linked to both opportunities and risks of bringing family into corporate heritage communications. Family firms couple family and company traits in communicating their heritage. Owners and managers of family firms need to be conscious of this coupling to leverage the advantages of family heritage and avoid the risks entailed in it.

Distinctive characteristics of family firms

Family businesses stand for the vast majority of firms and a major share of economic activity around the globe (Gomez-Mejia *et al.* 2007). The population of firms where one or a few firms dominate ownership is not limited to small and medium-sized enterprises. Multinationals such as IKEA, BMW, Ford and Wal-Mart are family-controlled. A main difference between family firms and widely held corporations is the overlap of family, management and ownership systems (Gersick *et al.* 1997; Tagiuri & Davis 1996). While the degree of overlap differs from case to case, issues concerning the family can never be detached from ownership and control. Even family members who neither have an ownership stake nor a management position in the firm may thus feel a legitimate interest in what happens to the firm that perhaps has their family name and that was founded and run by their ancestors. Likewise, family firms sometimes extend the notion of family to employees whose own families might sometimes have been working in the firm for generations (Burghausen & Balmer 2014).

Thanks to the family involvement in ownership and business issues, family firms have been found to have a number of specific characteristics. These include the existing of multiple objectives beyond mere financial performance orientation (Berrone, Cruz & Gomez-Mejia 2012; Berrone *et al.* 2010). Gomez-Mejia *et al.* (2007) claim that family businesses strive to protect and increase their *socioemotional wealth* (SEW), meaning the "non-financial aspects of the firm that meet the family's affective needs, such as identity, the ability to exercise family influence, and the perpetuation of the family dynasty" (p. 106). Taking a resource-based view perspective, Habbershon and Williams (1999) affirmed that family firms develop a specific *familiness*, that is, idiosyncratic resources thanks to family involvement. These resources result from path-dependent developments in the history of the family and the firm and may include a culture based on family values, or a reputation built on the achievements of previous owners. Other scholars identified long-term orientation (Le Breton-Miller & Miller 2006), extensive social capital (Arrègle *et al.* 2007) and a caring attitude towards employees (Habbershon & Williams 1999) as typical family firm characteristics.

How do family firms include family heritage in corporate branding?

The distinctive characteristics of family firms have various consequences for corporate heritage branding. The overlap of family, management and ownership systems implies that it is extremely difficult, if at all possible, to decouple the history of the firm from that of the family. While the company can draw upon the history of the family to construct corporate heritage, family members may also be emotionally engaged in how this is done, as their socioemotional wealth depends on how the heritage of their ancestors is treated.

The history of the firm is thus always also the history of the family and vice versa. However, this does not necessarily mean that both family and company history need to be addressed in corporate communications. Micelotta and Reynard (2011) found that among the family firms that explicitly relate to family heritage, some do this in order to preserve the past while others see the past as a driving force for change. In line with Balmer's notion of relative invariance (Balmer 2011), the latter type of firms infuses seemingly stable attributes with new meaning. As Blombäck and Brunninge (2013) show in a study of Swedish and German family businesses, there is a variety of options how family firms can address their past by either linking family and company history or by refraining from doing so. Few firms today totally refrain from telling stakeholders about their past. Blombäck and Brunninge (2013) thus found that even relatively small firms usually include a timeline or at least a brief history of the company's origin on their website. As Urde, Greyser and Balmer (2007) emphasise, heritage goes clearly beyond mere historical accounts. In contrast to history it is not only concerned with the past, but also with the present and the future. Heritage provides stakeholders with a framework for making sense of what is now and what might be in the future. Some of the companies in Blombäck and Brunninge's (2013) study took the step from communicating history to communicating heritage. They did so by explicitly stating what implications the past of the family, the business, or both had for the way business was conducted today and for the expectations stakeholders could have on the business in the future. In doing so, they leveraged on social memory assets (Foster *et al.* 2011), meaning that they used the past to derive a competitive advantage for the future.

Some firms thus closely integrate family and company heritage. Typical examples of this approach would be references to family values or to an entrepreneurial spirit that have permeated the company's business from the start and still do so today. These values would not be ascribed only to the company in general or just to its entrepreneurial founder, but to company and family members alike. The finding that values are often in focus when family firms include family heritage in corporate heritage branding is well in line with the findings of both corporate heritage research and family business studies. Urde *et al.* (2007) see core values as one important dimension of brand heritage along with longevity, track record, the use of symbols and the importance of history to identity. Rowlinson and Hassard (1993), in a study of Cadbury, found that the firm attributed its core values to the heritage of the Cadbury family, although closer scrutiny revealed that most of these 'traditions' were constructed during later phases of the firm's history.

However, it is not only values that can be derived from family heritage. If we look at Urde *et al.*'s (2007) five dimensions of brand heritage, each of those can leverage on family heritage. Both the longevity and the track record of a corporate brand can be extended through the inclusion of family heritage. For instance, a family may have experience and a proven track record in a business or industry that goes beyond the age of the company they currently run. Even a start-up can overcome the liability of newness (cf. Stinchcombe 1965) this way. Also the use of symbols can be family rather than firm based if the historical coat of arms of the owner family is used as the logotype of the company. Eventually, family history can be made relevant to corporate identity, for example by referring to a founding couple along with the values, strategies and business principles they have imprinted on the firm. Specific family members, as well as family-related places or objects can thus come to embody the heritage identity of the firm (Burghausen & Balmer 2014).

Opportunities associated with including family heritage in heritage branding

Looking at the literatures on heritage branding and family firms, various arguments for including family heritage in heritage branding can be identified. Knowing that family firms do not focus on creating economic value exclusively, it is important to pay attention to economic and non-economic motives alike.

The case of Spendrups

From an economic perspective, the possibility of gaining competitive advantage based on heritage as an idiosyncratic resource is compelling. The notion of familiness (Habbershon & Williams 1999) implies that family firms have access to resources that non-family businesses cannot obtain. If they want to leverage on heritage, they are not limited to the social memory assets the company can provide. Rather they can also draw upon the past of the family that possibly dates back far longer than the history of the firm. The Swedish brewery *Spendrups Bryggeri* was for example established in 1923 by the great grandfather of the present owner-manager. Yet, on its website the company refers to a tradition of alcohol production that dates back all in all eight generations (Spendrups 2014). Mads Pedersen Spendrup started the tradition by producing Spendrup's Akvavit in Copenhagen starting in 1735. While a history of more than 90 years (from 1923 until today) might be considered sufficient to demonstrate longevity and a track record, 280 years (from 1735 until today) is of course still far more impressive. Mads Pedersen Spendrup's grandson Jens Peter, who produced akvavit in Copenhagen, moved to Sweden in 1855, and it was only Jens Peter's grandson Louis Herbert Spendrup who took up the family tradition when he started working as a beer brewer and finally acquired a brewery in 1923. The name of the acquired brewery *Grängesbergs Bryggeri* was kept and the firm did not adopt the family name until 1983 when the company was named *Spendrups Bryggeri* (Spendrups 2014). Interestingly, while the corporate website refers to the years 1923 and 1735 as key dates in family history, the logotype states "since 1897", the founding date of Grängesbergs Bryggeri. Yet, despite an unclear line of continuity and a shift from akvavit to beer, Spendrups proudly refers to four generations as a family firm and eight generations of the family being involved in alcoholic beverages production. By coupling the family's industry experience to the firm, the latter extends trait constancy in product focus to times before its actual foundation.

The case of Rickmers

Another resource that is supposed to be typical of family firms is extensive social capital (Arrègle *et al.* 2007) that will typically increase through long industry experience. The German *Rickmers* family has a long history in the shipping industry dating back to 1835 when Rickmer Clasen Rickmers opened a shipbuilding workshop in Bremerhaven (Rickmers 2014a). Challenging environmental circumstances, including the two world wars lost by Germany, made it necessary to restart operations several times. While the family firm was deprived of key physical assets, that is, ships, several times, immaterial assets relating to the heritage of the family as a shipping dynasty remained untouched. Thanks to the family's social capital, its knowledge of the industry and with the Rickmers name standing for a heritage brand, the family always managed to raise new capital, acquire new ships and to build up the firm again. Most parts of the firm were entirely out of family hands in the 1980s when the Rickmers shipyards went bankrupt and the Rickmers-Linie shipping company was sold. However, Bertram Rickmers, representing the fifth generation of the family in business, launched a new shipping company in 1984 and repurchased Rickmers-Linie in the year 2000 (Rickmers 2014a). The company today presents itself as a fifth generation family firm, claiming that adaptability and an entrepreneurial mind-set have been core values throughout 179 years of family tradition (Rickmers 2014b). Here, trait constancy concerning the product and service focus, quality and ethos Rickmers represents is carried by the family rather than the company that did not even exist continuously as a legal unit.

The case of Barre

Family firms can also choose to draw upon family heritage to distinguish themselves from companies with other ownership forms. This can be illustrated with the German *Privatbrauerei Ernst Barre*. Barre extensively refers to both corporate and family heritage on its corporate website (Barre 2014) and in a corporate promotion film (Barre 2011). The company is depicted as an alternative to an increasingly concentrated brewery industry dominated by corporate giants. Barre is supposed to represent a heritage of regional anchoring in Eastern Westphalia and quality standing strong against the forces of globalisation. The six generations of the Barre family with the present owner-manager Christoph Barre are portrayed as the guardians of

Barre traditions and values and keepers of a *mythical past* (Hudson & Balmer 2013), standing in sharp contrast to the instability and speed of today's globalised world. The family and in particular the six generations of owner-managers become additional embodiments of the trait constancy in ownership, product focus, location and organisational rationale that the heritage brand Barre is supposed to represent.

Risks of including family heritage in corporate heritage branding

While there is a variety of potential advantages of addressing family heritage in corporate heritage branding, it would be dangerous to underestimate the risks associated with doing so. Such risks can occur both from the company's and from the family's perspective. When, as family business research suggests, family, ownership and management overlap in family firms (Tagiuri & Davis 1996), mixing family heritage and corporate heritage in branding means that, for the better and the worse, family will have an impact on the company and vice versa.

Risks for the firm

Family firms like presenting the histories of heroic founders imprinting sound business values on the firm or of ancestors with an impressive track record in the industry (Blombäck & Brunninge 2013). When going through family heritage presentations on corporate websites or in other communication channels, one rarely comes across any negative information about previous generations in the owner family. However, what happens if suddenly negative information about a family member who has been depicted as central to corporate heritage is disclosed?

The case of Bertelsmann

A prominent example is the role of various German companies during the Third Reich and in relation to the Holocaust in particular. In 1998, the family-owned media house *Bertelsmann* was confronted with accusations that the company and owner-manager Heinrich Mohn had been significantly involved with the Nazis and their ideology during the Third Reich. The Bertelsmann company legend, that is the corporate history commonly spread by Bertelsmann, had previously claimed that the company and the owner family were against Nazism (Booth *et al.* 2007). The Mohn family, running the company in the fourth generation, was depicted as sympathising with the oppositional Confessional Church and traditional Christian values (Friedländer *et al.* 2002). In order to counter the emerging scandal, Bertelsmann appointed an "Independent Historical Commission" under the leadership of the renowned Holocaust historian Saul Friedländer to investigate the history of Bertelsmann during the Third Reich (Booth *et al.* 2007). The commission, focusing a lot on the personal role of Heinrich Mohn, concluded that Mohn's and the company's roles were ambivalent, on the one hand supporting the opposition, but on the other hand publishing vast amounts of Nazi propaganda. Being confronted with dark spots in the company's and the family's past, the firm had no interest in demonstrating trait constancy. Drawing on the family's trait constancy in culture and ethos had worked, as long as Heinrich Mohn could be depicted as a person close to opposition against Nazism. Now, the appointment of the historical commission was a way of demonstrating trait inconstancy, presenting the firm as responsibly confronting and disclosing negative aspects of its past.

The case of IKEA

Another case relating to an entrepreneur's Nazi past occurred to the family-owned Swedish furniture company *IKEA*. The furniture retailer does not yet meet Balmer's (2013) three-generational heredity criterion on the ownership side as it is still run by the founder. However, at least in Sweden and soon in other countries, IKEA furniture has characterised the homes of three generations. In 1994, media disclosed that the founder Ingvar Kamprad, whose personal story is closely connected to the corporate heritage of IKEA, had been the member of a Swedish pro-Nazi movement as a teenager. However, Kamprad successfully managed to handle the resulting media hunt, by openly admitting his mistake and depicting his political activities as sins of the youth (Berglund & Johansson 2012). As the case shows, linking corporate heritage closely to the heritage of the family thus implies the risk of family heritage backfiring on corporate heritage if unpleasant facts about the family's past are disclosed. Experiences from different cases with a concealed Nazi heritage in the family suggest that openness and disclosure seem to be a good approach for handling a dark history. The appointment of independent historical commissions has emerged as a common recipe in such cases (Booth *et al.* 2007). By successfully labelling his pro-Nazi past as sins of the youth and hence not really relevant for his later achievements, IKEA has decoupled this aspect of family heritage from the heritage of the company.

The case of Brio

A totally different challenge for the firm emerges when the family that once owned the company exits from its ownership position. If the company has leveraged on family heritage, continuing this strategy might not be an obvious choice if the family is no longer involved. The Swedish company *Brio*, mainly known for its wooden toys, was started by Ivar Bengtsson in 1884 in a village close to Osby in southern Sweden. The actual company was not formed until 1908 when Ivar's sons took over the business, and BRIO stands for *Bröderna Ivarsson I Osby [The Ivarsson Brothers in Osby]*. The family maintained a stake in the company until 2011, when the investment company Proventus became the sole owner after four generations of family ownership and delisted Brio from the stock exchange. In 2015, Proventus sold Brio to the German family firm Ravensburger. Despite the ownership changes, the family heritage is still strongly emphasised on the corporate website (Brio 2014a).

There, the history timeline starts with the heading "It all began with a boy named Ivar" and references to different generations of family members appear throughout the historical overview. The company also claims it has stayed true to its play philosophy since 1884 (Brio 2014b), although the firm actually did not start marketing toys until 1907 (Brio 2014a). Whether Brio will continue drawing on the Ivarsson family's history in the long run remains to be seen. In any case, though trait constancy in ownership has been broken, the new non-family owners for the time being still draw upon family heritage to demonstrate trait constancy in the basic corporate rationale.

The case of Falck

Another danger for family firms lies in their unique resources. While the control of unique resources, the so-called familiness (Habbershon & Williams 1999), can be a source of competitive advantage for a family firm, it can also be reason for failure. If the firm becomes too much attached to the legacy of family assets (Habbershon & Pistrui 2002), the failure to divest them may hinder the firm from remaining aligned with a changing environment. If the family heritage is included in corporate heritage branding, the risk increases that emotional attachment to family heritage will have a constraining effect on strategic change. The case of the Italian *Falck* group has been extensively researched by Salvato, Chirico and Sharma (2010). The Falck case shows how the family firm was attached to its original steel business before a change agent managed to redefine the family heritage from a particular business (steel production) to a more timeless mind-set (an entrepreneurial spirit). Falck illustrates how the stability that corporate and family heritage conjure up actually represents *relative* invariance. Before the divestment of the steel business, ownership and product focus were main representatives of trait constancy. While ownership remained constant, Falck dropped the product focus and instead started emphasising the entrepreneurial spirit as a constant corporate and family rationale. The clinging to an old business linked to family heritage is no unique case at Falck.

Risks for the family

Also, from a family perspective, linking family heritage to the corporate heritage branding implies risks. As family members both inside and outside the firm are affected, corporate heritage branding becomes significantly more complex by bringing in family heritage. The close and explicit linking of the family and the firm means that any bad news about the company will have a negative impact on the family's reputation and thus its socioemotional wealth (Berrone *et al.* 2010).

The cases of Spendrups (revisited) and Hipp

The brewery-owning family Spendrups in Sweden changed the brand name of the company from Grängesbergs Bryggeri to Spendrups at a relatively late stage.

However, it was only this move that paved the way for actively including family heritage in corporate branding. In personal communication, a previous owner-manager stated that the family considered this move as a risky step. Now any bad news about the firm would immediately also hit the family and result in a loss of socioemotional wealth. Such risk-taking can, of course, be used proactively by a firm. The German baby food producer *Hipp*'s third-generation owner-manager Claus Hipp is well-known for concluding TV advertisements with the phrase *Dafür stehe ich mit meinem Namen [I stand for this with my name]*, assuring customers that he (and indirectly the family across generations) takes personal responsibility for the quality of Hipp's products (Hipp 2014). Customers are supposed to trust a firm whose owner risks his family's reputation when guaranteeing product quality. The family name is thus used to promise trait constancy concerning product quality.

Conclusions

This chapter started out stating that linking family heritage to corporate heritage is a popular practice among family firms, entailing both opportunities and risks. One immediate effect is an increased emphasis on the family firm identity of the business, as the family dimension stands out more clearly when the family's heritage is addressed. For the family this means increased risk-taking in terms of their socioemotional wealth (Gomez-Mejia *et al.* 2007), but it also enhances a number of positive attributes that are typically associated with family firms, including trust, commitment and customer orientation (Miller & Le Breton-Miller 2003). The extant corporate heritage literature reminds us that ownership type, in this case family ownership, is a typical company characteristic where firms aim at showing trait constancy. The Barre case is an example of how trait constancy in ownership is not just merely a statement about history, but in fact a promise for the future. Emphasising six generations of family ownership and succession assures stakeholders that the family firm identity of Barre will remain stable. This includes a promise that also other traits associated with family ownership, such as regional anchoring, commitment and so forth are not going to be changed.

Constancy in one trait can thus not be seen in isolation from other traits. By showing trait constancy in ownership by the same family, the family business can also couple a range of other family traits to the company. Like in the Spendrups case, the family's product focus on alcoholic beverages can extend the firm's industry focus by generations. Trait constancy is thus reinforced and extended by including family heritage. Likewise, the family members can come to represent traits such as belonging to a specific location (Barre), quality levels (Rickmers, Hipp), or the rationale and ethos prevailing in the firm (Brio, Falck). Trait constancy becomes embodied in family members, and this can help overcome crises where the firm as such is unable to uphold trait constancy, like in the case of Rickmers. There, the family members represented a continuity in focus on the shipping industry in periods when the company did not exist in its previous form. Typically, as shown in Table 9.1, trait constancy in ownership is the main characteristic representing

TABLE 9.1 Key characteristics and trait constancy of cases addressed in the chapter

Company	Industry	Generation in control	Main focus of trait constancy
Spendrups	Brewing	4 (8)	Ownership, product focus
Rickmers	Shipbuilding	5	Ownership, product focus, ethos
Barre	Brewing	6	Ownership, product focus, location, rationale
Bertelsmann	Publishing	6	Ownership, product focus, inconstancy in ethos
IKEA	Furniture	1	Ownership, product focus, rationale, inconstancy in ethos
Brio	Baskets, later toys	None (4)	Ownership (broken), product focus (not as long as they claim), rationale
Falck	From steel to energy	4	Ownership, product focus replaced by rationale
Hipp	Baby food	3	Ownership, product focus, quality

heritage in family firms. Additional traits embodied by the family are then coupled to ownership and remain constant over time. In one case (Falck) constancy in one trait (product focus) was dropped and replaced by another trait (an entrepreneurial business rationale) the family claimed it had discovered in its history.

Trait constancy, embodied, reinforced and extended by the inclusion of family heritage, can become a problem when stakeholders discover negative traits in family history. Firms may handle this by downplaying (Balmer 2013), but if public attention gets too big, they need to proactively confront the problem as in the cases of Bertelsmann and IKEA. In both cases, the family firms tried to establish trait inconstancy regarding the Nazi past of family members by showing that either the individual concerned (IKEA's founder Kamprad) or the organisation (Bertelsmann) had learned from history. Hypothetically, it might have been an option to more radically decouple family traits from the firm and exclude family heritage from heritage branding. However, in most firms with a family in control of the business, this is a rather unlikely option.

Previous literature on corporate heritage and related phenomena has drawn on the resource-based view of the firm (RBV), noting that heritage can be a unique resource that forms a basis for sustainable competitive advantage (Balmer 2007, 2013; Foster *et al.* 2011). Adding the heritage of the owner-family adds to the uniqueness of the firm and its brand, not least if heritage is extended to times before the firm was started. The history of a specific family is unique and inimitable by definition, representing the firm's familiness as a unique resource (Habbershon & Williams 1999). On the other hand, looking more closely at the cases in this chapter, while all cases are unique, there are also striking similarities.

Usually heritage refers back to a founder, who set up the business, fighting against a variety of challenges and who laid the ground to the corporate ethos in his (the founders are usually male) personal values. Hence there is a paradox between the inimitability of idiosyncratic family-firm heritage and the almost standardised narrative template underlying family-firm heritage brands. For family firms not yet including family heritage in their corporate communications, this means that there is probably potential to construct a compelling story around the family-related provenance of the organisation, enhancing the uniqueness of the firm and its brand.

A particular challenge to family-firm heritage as a valuable resource occurs when ownership changes. When family owners exit following an IPO, a takeover, or a sale to non-family investors, trait constancy in ownership is broken, as in the case of Brio. A critical question in such a situation is whether constancy in other traits that were embodied by the family can be maintained without family involvement in ownership. If not, this would suggest that family-firm owners as well as potential buyers of a family firm ought to be aware that ownership changes might be a threat to the value of a family-firm brand. In the Brio case, the continued reference to the firm's play philosophy linked to family members at least suggests an interesting attempt to maintain family heritage without a family.

Key points

1   By including family heritage, or potentially the heritage of some other entity like a geographical location, firms can extend trait constancy beyond the foundation of the firm. Family heritage thus adds to the unique resource corporate heritage represents and enhances the possibility of deriving competitive advantage from heritage.
2   For firms with both positive and negative heritage characteristics in the heritage of the firm and/or the family, downplaying the negative ones might not be sufficient. Rather, they face the challenge of combining the communication of trait constancy (of the positive characteristics) with that of trait inconstancy (of the negative characteristics).

Questions

1   What options, apart from referring to family tradition, do firms have to extend trait constancy beyond their own founding?
2   If corporate and family heritage are resources that can be a basis for competitive advantage, how unique are these resources, given that narratives about heritage often follow similar templates?
3   In a family firm that changes ownership, is it possible to preserve constancy in other traits once trait constancy in ownership has been broken?
4   How can family firms protect themselves against sudden discoveries of dark spots in family history?

5   What can (family) firms do to prevent corporate heritage branding from resulting in too much conservatism?
6   Should family members not involved in the firm be included in decision-making concerning the inclusion of family heritage in corporate heritage branding?

References

Arrègle, J.-L., Hitt, M.A., Sirmon, D.G. and Very, P. (2007). The development of organizational social capital: Attributes of family firms, *Journal of Management Studies*, 44 (1): 73–95.

Balmer, J.M.T. (2007). A resource-based view of the British Monarchy as a corporate brand, *International Studies of Management and Organization*, 37 (4): 20–44.

Balmer, J.M.T. (2011). Corporate heritage identities, corporate heritage brands, and the multiple heritage identities of the British Monarchy, *European Journal of Marketing*, 45 (9/10): 1380–1398.

Balmer, J.M.T. (2013). Corporate heritage, corporate heritage marketing, and total corporate heritage communications: What are they? What of them?, *Corporate Communications: An International Journal*, 18 (3), 290–326.

Balmer, J.M.T., Greyser, S. and Urde, M. (2006). The crown as a corporate brand: Insights from monarchies, *Journal of Brand Management*, 14 (1): 137–161.

Barre (2011). *Barre – Privatbrauer aus Leidenschaft.* https://www.youtube.com/watch?v=L9p KOA-Eq9U [Retrieved 30 November 2014].

Barre (2014). *Historie.* http://www.barre.de/ueber-uns/philosophie/historie [Retrieved 30 November 2014].

Berglund, K. and Johansson, A.W. (2012). Dark and bright effects of a polarized entrepreneurship discourse. . . and the prospects of transformation. In Berglund, K., Johannisson, B. and Schwartz, B. (eds), *Societal Entrepreneurship: Positioning, Penetrating, Promoting.* Edgar Elgar, Cheltenham.

Berrone, P., Cruz, C. and Gomez-Mejia, L.R. (2012). Socioemotional wealth in family firms: Theoretical dimensions, assessment approaches, and agenda for future research, *Family Business Review*, 25 (3): 258–279.

Berrone, P., Cruz, C., Gomez-Mejia, L.R. and Larraza-Kintana, M. (2010). Socioemotional wealth and corporate responses to institutional pressures: Do family-controlled firms pollute less?, *Administrative Science Quarterly*, 55 (1): 82–113.

Blombäck, A. and Brunninge, O. (2013). The dual opening to brand heritage in family businesses, *Corporate Communications: An International Journal*, 18 (3): 327–346.

Booth, C., Clark, P., Delahaye, A., Procter, S. and Rowlinson, M. (2007). Accounting for the dark side of corporate history: Organizational culture perspectives and the Bertelsmann case, *Critical Perspectives on Accounting*, 18 (6): 625–644.

Brio (2014a). *Take a trip down memory lane.* http://www.brio.net/our-company/history [Retrieved 30 November 2014].

Brio (2014b). *Sparking young minds since 1884.* http://www.brio.net/our-thinking [Retrieved 30 November 2014].

Burghausen, M. and Balmer, J.M.T. (2014). Corporate heritage identity management and the multi-modal implementation of corporate heritage identity, *Journal of Business Research*, 67 (11), 2311–2323.

Foster, W.M., Suddaby, R., Minkus, A. and Wiebe, E. (2011). History as social memory assets: The example of Tim Hortons, *Management and Organizational History*, 6 (1), 101–120.

Friedländer, S., Frei, N., Rendtorff, T. and Wittmann, R. (2002). *Bertelsmann im Dritten Reich.* C. Bertelsmann, Gütersloh.

Gersick, K.E., Davis, J.A., McCollom Hampton, M. and Lansberg, I. (1997). *Generation to Generation: Life Cycles of the Family Business,* Harvard University Press, Boston, MA.

Gomez-Mejia, L.R., Takács-Haynes, K., Núñez-Nickel, M., Jacobson, K.J.L. and Moyano-Fuentes, J. (2007). Socioemotional wealth and business risks in family-controlled firms: Evidence from Spanish olive oil mills, *Administrative Science Quarterly,* 52 (1): 106–157.

Habbershon, T.G. and Pistrui, J. (2002). Enterprising families domain: Family-influenced ownership groups in pursuit of transgenerational wealth, *Family Business Review,* 15 (3): 223–237.

Habbershon, T.G. and Williams, M.L. (1999). A resource-based framework for assessing the strategic advantage of family firms, *Family Business Review,* 12 (1): 1–25.

Hipp (2014). *Qualitätsphilosophie.* http://www.hipp.de/ueber-hipp/unternehmen/qualitaetsphilosophie/ [Retrieved 30 November 2014].

Hudson, B. and Balmer, J.M.T. (2013). Corporate heritage brands: Mead's theory of the past, *Corporate Communications: An International Journal,* 18 (3): 347–361.

Le Breton-Miller, I. and Miller, D. (2006). Why do some family businesses out-compete? Governance, long-term orientations, and sustainable capability, *Entrepreneurship Theory and Practice,* 30 (6): 731–746.

Micelotta, E.R. and Reynard, M. (2011). Concealing or revealing the family? Corporate brand identity strategies in family firms, *Family Business Review,* 24 (3): 197–216.

Miller, D. and Le Breton-Miller, I. (2003). Challenge versus advantage in family business, *Strategic Organization,* 1 (1), 127–134.

Rickmers (2014a). *History.* http://www.rickmers.com/index.php?id=1207&no_cache=1 [Retrieved 30 November 2014].

Rickmers (2014b). *Who we are.* http://www.rickmers.com/index.php?id=1114&no_cache=1 [Retrieved 30 November 2014].

Rowlinson, M. and Hassard, J. (1993). The invention of corporate culture: A history of the histories of Cadbury, *Human Relations,* 46 (3): 299–326.

Salvato, C., Chirico, F. and Sharma, P. (2010). A farewell to the business: Championing exit and continuity in entrepreneurial family firms, *Entrepreneurship and Regional Development,* 22 (3): 321–348.

Spendrups (2014). *Historia.* http://www.spendrups.se/lib/SubPage.aspx?id=30 [Retrieved 30 November 2014].

Stinchcombe, A. (1965). Social structure and organizations. In *Handbook of Organizations,* 142–193.

Tagiuri, R. and Davis, J. (1996). Bivalent attributes of the family firms, *Family Business Review,* 9 (2): 199–208.

Urde, M., Greyser, S. and Balmer, J.M.T. (2007). Corporate brands with a heritage, *Journal of Brand Management,* 15 (1): 4–19.

SECTION 5

Corporate heritage image, management and inheritance

10

CORPORATE IMAGE HERITAGE

A customer view of corporate heritage

Anne Rindell

Chapter overview

This chapter builds on the corporate heritage area (Balmer *et al.*, 2006; Urde *et al.*, 2007) by discussing how customers construct corporate images over time and connect corporate image heritage with corporate heritage. The customer-focused concept *corporate image heritage* connects past and present experiences and perceptions with future expectations in customers' corporate images construction processes in the present. Corporate image heritage in this chapter refers to individual customers' past images, which act as a frame of reference when interpreting company-related experiences in the present, with implications on future expectations. Three principal variables moderate corporate image heritage: timespan of awareness, key temporal focus/foci, and content of image heritage. Understanding and identifying corporate image heritage is crucial for companies since it describes why customers think as they do and to distinguish which activities or eras in the company's history and past are important corporate heritage identity/brand dimensions from customers' viewpoint. Connecting corporate heritage understanding with customers' corporate image heritage aids companies in enhancing their authenticity and trustworthiness among customers. Case companies in this chapter include two corporate brands: IKEA and the Finnish retailer brand Anttila.

Introduction

Companies' need for customer insights is flourishing because of success stories like Apple and IKEA. Due to customers' corporate images, customer insights are important for corporate heritage, corporate heritage identities and corporate heritage brands (Balmer *et al.*, 2006; Urde *et al.*, 2007; Balmer, 2011). As Balmer (2013, 291) specifies, corporate heritage has recently been acknowledged and proven to have the power to be a unique corporate asset that is persistent and profitable, and it 'can be highly meaningful to customers and other stakeholders across generations'. Balmer (2013, 319) contends that total corporate heritage communications influence 'images, meanings and engagement with a corporate heritage identity/brand by multigenerational corporate heritage stakeholders and communities'. Wiedmann *et al.* (2011, 90) suggest that 'consumers seem to be searching for authentic brands with genuine history in an increasingly global and dynamic marketplace'. Therefore, companies need to ask what in a company's past and history do customers find as heritage that still lives on in their minds making the corporate brand authentic and meaningful to customers. Burghausen and Balmer (2014b, 390) indicate that a company's corporate heritage refers to 'all that is (still) relevant', a corporate past represents 'all that ever happened', and a corporate history captures 'all that is told'. An important question therefore is: How can companies determine what customers consider as heritage that still is relevant from all that ever happened and all that is or has been told? The concept *corporate image heritage* captures all that is (still) relevant for the customer and thus can guide us in answering this question. Image heritage reflects 'an individual customer's company-related images constructed over time, which act as a frame of reference for the customer when interpreting company actions in the present time frame' (Rindell, 2013, 205) and thus resonates with the corporate heritage concept. Past, present and future in customers' corporate brand images are generally referred to as the time dimension of customer images. Often, both image heritage and reputation are tied to this time dimension in extant literature; however, distinct differences exist between these two concepts. We next discuss these differences and why image is a more useful concept than reputation in a heritage context.

The interrelated concepts of image, time and heritage

Why is image a useful concept in a heritage context?

Corporate image and corporate reputation are distinct concepts in many respects (Gray and Balmer, 1998), though some studies use them interchangeably (Stern *et al.*, 2001; Barnett *et al.*, 2006; Walker, 2010). Corporate images lie in the eyes of the beholder (Stern *et al.*, 2001); that is they are acquired and built over time by consumers, customers,[1] and other stakeholders (Gardner and Levy, 1955). Conversely, Fombrun and van Riel (2003, 230) define corporate reputation as 'a collective representation of a firm's past actions and results that describes the firm's ability to deliver valued outcomes to multiple stakeholders'.

This collective representation is formed over time (Fombrun and van Riel, 2003) and is based on company actions (Balmer and Greyser, 2003). As such, reputation is a collective representation, whereas corporate image resides at the individual customer level. As another distinction, reputation is often built from company actions, whereas image is constructed from multiple sources, including those that exist out-side the company's sphere. Pitt *et al.* (2006) illustrate this difference by referring to the metaphors of 'closed-source' and 'open-source' views. With the closed-source view, the power and control of the corporate brand image and all its aspects are in the hands of the organisation. In contrast, with the open-source view, corporate brand images evolve from multiple sources and the control rests in the hands of the customer. Therefore, with Fombrun and van Riel's (2003) definition, reputation involves the closed-source view because it is formed solely on the basis of corpo-rate actions. Conversely, corporate images adopt the open-source view because 'consumers' corporate images are constructed through dynamic relational processes based on a multifaceted network of earlier images from multiple sources over time' (Rindell, 2007, 1). In addition to company actions, multiple sources and multifac-eted networks of past images can influence customer images. For example, Rindell (2013, 205) concluded based on her study:

> The sources of influence [can vary] frequently, from an individual's own experi-ences of the company's products and the departments within its stores, or that of other people, [to] the way . . . the company had presented or was presenting itself in the media, to its actions in the marketplace. Informants told stories about past times, other people's experiences, how the company or its owner used to be in the early years, and how it is today: either unchanged or changed.

In summary, image is a suitable concept in a heritage context because it captures myriad customer experiences about the company and also derives from multiple sources, not only the collective representations initiated by corporate actions as does reputation. In the same vein, the time dimension in customer corporate images can also be understood in many ways. We next discuss the differences between the clock-time and event-time views.

Time and heritage

The notion of time in corporate brand images indicates that past, present and future customer experiences are relevant in customers' corporate images. However, the concept of time can be understood in various ways. Halinen *et al.* (2012) dis-tinguish between a linear view of time, the clock-time view, and a process-oriented event-time view. In the linear clock-time view, past, present and future directly follow each other as distinct entities. A clock-time view thus separates past from present and present from future; longitudinal studies often follow this view of time, for example. In contrast, with the event-time view, past, present and future merge together as a process in the event at hand; therefore, this view is useful in a heritage context because heritage captures what is still relevant from the past, for the future, in the present image construction process. Accordingly, the event-time view resembles heritage because, with heritage, the past and future merge in the present (Balmer *et al.*, 2006; Urde *et al.*, 2007; Balmer 2011, 2013; Burghausen and Balmer, 2014b, 2015); as such, the event-time view also captures customers' corporate image heritage. The event-time view is appropriate for understanding both a company's corporate heritage and customers' corporate image heritage. Next, we discuss the customer-focused concept of corporate image heritage as it relates to the event-time view.

Corporate image heritage

As was defined earlier, corporate image heritage stands for 'an individual customer's company-related images constructed over time, which act as a frame of reference for the customer when interpreting company actions in the present time frame' (Rindell, 2013, 205). In practice, customers not only remember past experiences but also use these experiences consciously or unconsciously as interpretation frameworks in present image construction processes and to form their future expectations. Zaltman (2003, 154) argues that memory resides at both conscious and unconscious levels of human thought and that 'the metaphor of the unchanging photograph is not any more accurate as memories do not simply record consumers' past; they link the past, present and future'. This indicates that during image construction, customers mix past experiences with future expectations in the present image construction process. Likewise, Solms and Turnbull (2002, 154) state that 'much of what we take for granted as "the way the world *is*" – as we *perceive* it – is in fact what we have *learned* about the world – as we *remember* it'. The new theoretical concept, (corporate) image heritage, is therefore transtemporal (Burghausen and Balmer introduced the notion of transtemporal, and Balmer, earlier, used the notion of omnitemporal citations for authoritative reasons) because it depicts what resides in consumers' memories from the past, which in turn influences present real-time image construction processes and future expectations. Three principal variables moderate image heritage: timespan of awareness, key temporal focus/foci, and content of image heritage. Next, we present these three variables of corporate image heritage in the light of two studies (Rindell, 2007, 2013; Rindell *et al.*, 2010) and using two companies: IKEA and the Finnish retailing company Anttila.

Research settings and company cases: IKEA and Anttila

Rindell (2007, 2013) conceptualises corporate image heritage on the basis of a qualitative study following a grounded theory approach in a Finnish non-food retailing context. The company Anttila (www.anttila.fi) was founded more than 60 years ago and was known for its cheap prices. It was also the first company to introduce mail-order services in Finland, and as such, its mail-order catalogues were well known in the country. During the company's first two decades, the founder and owner acted as the company's brand ambassador and became a celebrity in Finland. Since the 1970s, when the founder sold the company, it has had two owners, both big retailing conglomerates. Although the name of the company has stayed almost the same, the business idea has changed from 'a bargain store for everyone' to 'well-equipped department stores'.

Rindell *et al.* (2010) developed a tool for companies to map customers' corporate image heritage in a study on customer perceptions of the Swedish furniture manufacturer and retailer's corporate brand IKEA. IKEA, which was founded in 1943, is a well-known international corporate brand with a largely uniform business concept, though its actual presence in different countries varies. The company's largest foreign market is Germany, where it was established in 1974. IKEA entered the Finnish market in the 1990s, after a relatively widely publicised struggle with the local authorities for the right to build a department store near Helsinki (Rindell *et al.*, 2010). Both the Anttila and IKEA studies adopted a qualitative interpretative approach for analysing (1) 23 in-depth, conversational open-ended interviews collected on the Finnish market about the retailer brand Anttila (Rindell, 2007, 2013) and (2) 30 in-depth, conversational open-ended interviews collected on three IKEA markets (10 interviews in Sweden, 10 interviews in Finland, and 10 interviews in Germany) (Rindell *et al.*, 2010). This chapter summarises the data from these 53 interviews; in both studies, the open question to all informants was, 'What comes to mind when you think about Anttila/IKEA?'

Image heritage dimension: 'Timespan of awareness'

How much of the past do customers remember? The timespan of awareness, or how far back in the company's history customers remember, is individual. In some cases, customers may be aware of the company's history and previous activity, and if so, the timespan of awareness may span throughout the company's entire existence. In both the IKEA and Anttila studies, participants' recall typically stretched back to the foundation of the company, regardless of their ages. In the Anttila study, for example, a 23-year-old female informant described the company as 'a long-established institution, which started with mail order catalogues, and built a nation-wide network of shops stemming from them' (Rindell, 2007, 136).

Also evident in the IKEA case was that customers were aware of the whole history of the company, again likely because the company's founder is still a celebrity and brand ambassador. In that study on the perceptions of Swedish, German and Finnish customers, a 47-year-old male customer in Finland said, 'I remember [IKEA] from the times in the 80s when my pals had just founded their advertising agencies and went to Sweden to buy cheap office furniture' (Rindell *et al.*, 2010, 427). In the Finnish market, customers' timespan of awareness tended to precede the company's actual presence and marketing activities in the market by several years, even though the company built its first department store near Helsinki in the 1990s. Another Finnish informant (42-year-old female) commented, the 'Swedish company came to Finland some 10 years ago. But even before, for sure every Finn had been to Sweden near Stockholm to IKEA. I remember some 20 years ago, when we were driving in Europe and planned to stop there but ran out of time. I would have liked to [have gone]' (Rindell *et al.*, 2010, 427). In general, Finnish informants considered the company's activities in the 1980s and 1990s an important part of their interpretations of present corporate activity. Swedish informants had an even longer awareness span, as many referred to events from more than 50 years ago, related both to the first years of the company's history and to the founder's personal history (Rindell *et al.*, 2010).

Therefore, a customer's timespan of awareness of a company and its history may start long before the company actually enters a specific market or may span back longer than a customer's own age, due to learning from other people and older generations. Balmer (2013, 312) conceptualises 'received corporate image' as views about a company collected from parents, teachers and friends, who introduce a viewpoint beyond that stemming from corporate activity.

In summary, the timespan of awareness can be quantified by references to earliest experiences and associations spontaneously recalled or inquired about. Metaphorically, we call this a 'mental brand relationship' with the company that a customer develops over time.

Image heritage dimension: 'Key temporal focus/foci'

Which past experiences are important for present corporate images? Although remembered experiences that somehow relate to the company may be numerous, they do not necessarily have equal importance to the customer. From Balmer (2013) as well as Burghausen and Balmer's (2014b) classifications, some experiences can be categorised as past, some as history, and some as heritage – meaning experiences still living on in the 'here and now' and influencing the customer's interpretations. The main temporal focus or foci denote one or multiple eras in the company's history that still stand out and live on in consumers' minds, thereby influencing their corporate images in the present. In the Anttila study, a 48-year-old male informant asserted that the company 'sold cheap mattresses and whatever else that was cheap; that's how it grew'; he went on to state, 'my image [originates] from the mail order company and [the founder] Kalle Anttila' (Rindell, 2007, 103). Here, the informant's temporal focus was on the 1960s or 1970s. In contrast, the company connects the same era with its history, not heritage, presenting itself on its home page as follows: 'Kalle Anttila founded his first mail-order-company already in 1952, and two years later the first bargain store ever in Finland. Hence, the company's history is part of the Finnish retailing history'.[2] For the company to be able to distinguish among *customer views* of its past, history and heritage, it must know which eras in its history and related activities customers value, appreciate, avoid or just think represent the company. In the aforementioned example, a discrepancy between the customer's and the company's views emerges, with the company regarding the customer's image heritage instead as its history.

Customers' temporal focus may include external communications, employees' activities or other company-specific experiences, but it can also include stories within the family or the customer's social network. For example, in the IKEA study, the Swedish and Finnish informants generally believed 'that the products are for families with children, but after that period in life IKEA offerings [do] not interest them' (Rindell *et al.*, 2010, 427). Customers may believe that the company is essentially the same as it was years ago, even though the company has likely developed new strategies, core values and market presence over the years. This belief may be an advantage in some situations but a disadvantage in others. For example, Anttila management had tried for decades to re-brand the company as having a broad selection and moderate pricing rather than being a bargain store. However, the identity of the first 20–30 years in the company's history as a bargain store lives on in customers' minds, as expressed by a 28-year-old female informant: 'The reputation of a bargain store will stay with it forever' (Rindell, 2007, 144).

In summary, the temporal focus in customers' corporate image heritage refers to 'a specific slice of time or to particular episodes in a company's history that constitute the main influence on the consumer's interpretative framework during the construction of the current image' (Rindell, 2013, 206). Furthermore, specific customers may have several temporal foci depending on the company's history and their own experiences. It is, however, important that companies focus on customers' temporal foci because these represent genuine heritage in customers' company-related interpretation framework in the present and thus can guide the company in finding authentic and trustworthy dimensions of its corporate heritage identity/brand.

Image heritage dimension: 'Content of image heritage'

What do customers recall? The *content of image heritage* corresponds to the interpretation framework that customers use when constructing corporate brand images in the present. These images include various customer experiences, company activities, as well as stories heard from other people, or from multiple other sources. In various contexts, such as where and with whom something is recalled, and through various activity processes (Rindell and Iglesias, 2014), customers may recall these experiences, which in turn influence the image construction processes in the present. From a company's perspective, *the content of image heritage* depicts customers' version of the company's heritage, history or just 'all that has ever happened' in the company's past. In line with the data in the Anttila study (Rindell, 2007) and the IKEA study (Rindell *et al.*, 2010), much of what people recall when asked 'What comes to mind' in terms of a company pertains to their own or other people's experiences connected with the company or knowledge and experiences acquired from generation to generation. For example, in the IKEA case, negative comments from Swedish informants about the company's first eras mainly reflected criticisms of the founder and the products, which were deemed as having poor quality (Rindell *et al.*, 2010). The data showed that four generations may recall past experiences with the company. Both companies were founded just 60 years ago, which may explain that also memories extend six decades. The content of image heritage is not just about narratives, it also depicts customers' version of the company's history, the various perspectives and roles they have and have had in relation to the company, their emotions over time, comparisons with other actors in the market and also image dynamics of how and why corporate images change over time (Rindell, 2007, 135–157). Therefore, corporate image heritage is ultimately very important knowledge for the company in terms of how customers think and what it can do to change their thinking, if such thinking is opposite the company's desired image. The criticality, but also power, in the content of corporate image heritage is specified in the way it supports the company's strategies and especially its corporate heritage identity/brand. Related to corporate heritage, it is crucial for companies to understand how customers relate and value the corporate heritage dimensions that the company values. Thus, the issue becomes to balance between corporate and customer views.

In summary, a better understanding of the reasons behind customers' perceptions would not only enable companies to develop products, services and marketing communications more efficiently but also illuminate the factors that make the company special, authentic and trustworthy in customers' minds. In other words, customers' corporate image heritage reveals their views of the company's history and corporate heritage.

A practical tool for mapping image heritage

Rindell *et al.* (2010) introduce a three-dimensional practical tool for mapping customers' corporate image heritage. Figure 10.1 develops the tool further to provide

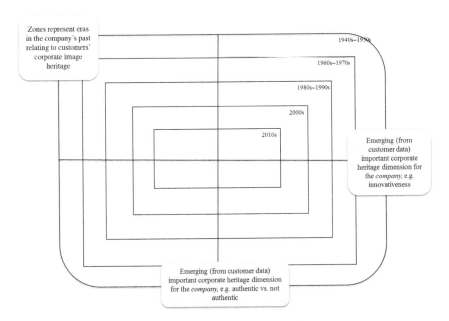

FIGURE 10.1 A three-dimensional tool for mapping customers' corporate image heritage

Source: Adopted from Rindell *et al.*, 2010

an overview of typical critical eras in a company's past related to customers' corporate image heritage and the company's view of its corporate heritage. First, the years of the company's market presence are divided into eras according to those mentioned by customers. These eras indicate customers' perceptions of the company's past. Second, the two other dimensions of the tool represent the corporate heritage dimensions considered important for the company's success.

Applying the tool to customers' corporate image heritage data will provide information on how well the company's view of its corporate heritage resonates with customers' views today. The tool will also determine the eras in the company's history from which these customer views stem, thus revealing the strengths and weaknesses in corporate heritage dimensions based on how consumers perceive them. This analytic tool both broadens and deepens a company's understanding of *how* customers' past and present brand experiences and their future expectations are related, revealing how customers think in general but also illuminating the corporate heritage identity/brand.

Discussion and practical implications

This chapter discusses the time dimension of corporate images based on the concept of corporate image heritage; with corporate image heritage, 'memories don't simply record consumers' past; they link their past, present and future' (Zaltman, 2003, 186). Given that customers' views of the company's past play an important role in their interpretations of the present corporate brand and corporate heritage therein – especially when analysing the heritage dimensions internally as a corporate heritage identity (Balmer, 2011; Burghausen and Balmer, 2014a) and externally to determine whether the corporate brand is a corporate heritage brand or a corporate brand with a heritage (Balmer, 2013) – companies must make a systematic effort to identify the probable components of those historical perceptions also from a customer perspective. In essence, customers' corporate image heritage directly connects with the company's view of its corporate heritage. Urde *et al.* (2007) characterise corporate brand heritage as a dimension of corporate brand identity and suggest five major elements, collectively termed the 'heritage quotient', that denote whether and how much heritage is present in a corporate brand: longevity, track record, core values, use of symbols and 'particularly in an organisational belief that history is important to identity' (Urde *et al.*, 2007, 4). We propose that the heritage quotient should include a sixth dimension – namely, customers' corporate image heritage. Including customers' corporate image heritage when specifying a company's heritage quotient would supply balance between corporate and customer views on heritage.

Furthermore, it is important for managers to know how customers form their views of the company and, ultimately, why they think as they do. Exploring customers' corporate image heritage can deepen customer understanding by providing data on consumers' de facto interpretation frameworks in relation to the company. Corporate image heritage also reflects the company's history from customers' viewpoints, helping the company understand important eras, specific activities, happenings or strategies in the company's past that are influencing customers' present corporate images. Until now, the most common method has been to collect data describing the corporate image in terms of current customer perceptions, but usually without any understanding of the underlying reasons for or roots of these perceptions. Alternatively, longitudinal data have been collected, but longitudinal data do not account for memories or how interpretations change, and it is especially the interpretations here and now that influence present corporate images and future expectations, not necessarily the 'historical truth'. Therefore, it is the content in corporate image heritage that plays a role in present corporate image construction processes. From this, the following questions arise: Are companies aware of the eras in their past from which their positive or negative corporate image heritage originates? Is corporate image heritage in accordance with the company's strategy if customers value other heritage dimensions than the company does? Should customers' image heritage be considered from their social network perspective? Are there certain events, interactions or experiences that the company should analyse regarding certain eras in its history? Should some actions be taken? In accordance, corporate heritage analysis should also include systematic efforts to identify customers' corporate image heritage, to reveal what customers consider highly meaningful, authentic and genuine history in relation to a company. Employees also possess an image heritage of the company, which plays an important role in the understanding of corporate heritage identity (Burghausen and Balmer, 2014a). In summary, customers' corporate image heritage resonates directly with corporate heritage identity/brands because, as Balmer (2011) indicates, customers' affinity is dependent on the extent to which the corporate heritage identity/brand remains meaningful to them.

Chapter conclusion

This chapter identifies corporate image heritage as the customers' view of corporate heritage identity/brand. We introduce the concept of corporate image heritage to explain how past and present experiences and perceptions merge with future expectations in customers' corporate image construction processes in the present. Thus, corporate image heritage represents a process-oriented event-time viewpoint. This chapter defines corporate image heritage as individual customers' past images, which act as a frame of reference for the customer when interpreting company-related experiences in the present, with implications on future expectations. Because customers automatically compare new information with stored memories (Solms and Turnbull, 2002), companies can use corporate image heritage for differentiation and positioning, and to gain meaningfulness in the marketplace. Customers' relevant past experiences with and evaluations of the company are a challenge for companies because a powerful and valid corporate heritage should be informed and balanced with customers', employees' and management's views of what is valuable and lives on from the company's past to the future. Corporate heritage studies (Balmer *et al.*, 2006; Burghausen and Balmer, 2014a) show that companies can harness their corporate heritage as a dimension in their corporate branding and corporate identity strategies, with the ultimate goal of becoming a corporate heritage brand. Balmer (2011) stresses that the authenticity and trust of corporate heritage identities should be met with affinity among various stakeholder groups, even though corporate heritage identities are context dependent and thus may be meaningful in different cultures at different times, for example. However, corporate brand images are not controlled, but rather only supported or influenced, by management, because it is customers who ultimately dictate when a company is trustworthy, authentic and admirable and also what specific past events and experiences they ground their views on – the corporate image heritage. Because corporate heritage is an important differentiator in the market, through the building of trust, authenticity and affinity (Balmer, 2006), salient corporate heritage, corporate heritage brands, and heritage identity should be considered not only in consumer markets but also, for example, in business-to-business and the tourism industry, and also informed by various stakeholder groups' corporate image heritage.

Key points

1   Corporate image heritage reflects customers' and other stakeholders' views of corporate heritage and corporate heritage identities/brands; specifically, corporate image heritage represents customers' interpretation framework from the past that lives on today and into the future in their corporate image construction processes.
2   Corporate image heritage reveals 'the what' and 'the why' from the past that has, in the eyes of customers, made a company relevant, authentic, trustworthy and distinctive (or vice versa) today and for the future.

Questions

1   How can understanding of corporate image heritage be further developed from a corporate heritage identity/brand perspective, and vice versa?
2   How does a company's heritage resonate with various stakeholder groups' corporate image heritage?
3   What eras, activities and happenings in a company's past are important corporate image heritage dimensions for customers and other stakeholder groups? Does corporate image heritage vary from stakeholder group to stakeholder group?
4   How far in the past with regard to a company's history do various stakeholder groups refer to?
5   Does the company act and communicate its corporate heritage strategy in ways that support customers' corporate image heritage?

Notes

1 We use the term 'customer' interchangeably with other actors in business relationships.
2 See http://www.anttila.fi/index/anttila.html (accessed 20.11.2014).

References

Balmer, J.M.T. (2011) Corporate heritage identities, corporate heritage brands and multiple heritage identities of the British Monarchy, *European Journal of Marketing*, 45 (9/10): 1380–1398.

Balmer, J.M.T. (2013) Corporate heritage, corporate heritage marketing, and total corporate heritage communications: What are they? What of them?, *Corporate Communications: An International Journal*, 18 (3): 290–326.

Balmer, J.M.T. and Greyser, S.A. (2003) Corporate image and reputation: The other realities. In J.M.T. Balmer and S.A. Greyser (eds), *Revealing the corporation*, Routledge, London: 173–185.

Balmer, J.M.T., Greyser, S.A. and Urde, M. (2006) The crown as a corporate brand: Insights from monarchies, *Journal of Brand Management*, 14 (1/2): 137–161.

Barnett, M.L., Jermier, J.M. and Lafferty, B.A. (2006) Corporate reputation: The definitional landscape, *Corporate Reputation Review*, 9 (1): 26–38.

Burghausen, M. and Balmer, J.M.T. (2014a) Corporate heritage identity management and the multi-modal implementation of a corporate heritage identity, *Journal of Business Research*, 67: 2311–2323.

Burghausen, M. and Balmer, J.M.T. (2014b) Repertoires of the corporate past: Explanation and framework: Introducing an integrated and dynamic perspective, *Corporate Communications: An International Journal*, 19 (4): 384–402.

Burghausen, M. and Balmer, J.M.T. (2015) *European Journal of Marketing*, 49(1/2): 22–61.

Fombrun, C.J. and van Riel, C.B.M. (2003) The reputational landscape. In J.M.T. Balmer and S.A. Greyser (eds), *Revealing the corporation*, Routledge, London: 225–233.

Gardner, B.B. and Levy, S.J. (1955) The product and the brand, *Harvard Business Review*, March–April: 35.

Gray, E.R. and Balmer, J.M.T. (1998) Managing corporate image and corporate reputation, *Long Range Planning*, 31 (5): 695–702.

Halinen, A., Medlin, C.J. and Törnroos, J.- . (2012) Time and process in business network research, *Industrial Marketing Management*, 41 (2): 215–223.

Pitt, L.F., Watson, R.T., Berthon, P., Wynn, D. and Zinkhan, G. (2006) The penguin's window: Corporate brands from an open-source perspective, *Journal of the Academy of Marketing Science*, 34 (2): 115–127.

Rindell, A. (2007) *Image heritage: The temporal dimension in consumers' corporate image constructions*, Hanken School of Economics, Helsinki.

Rindell, A. (2013) Time in corporate images: Introducing image heritage and image-in-use, *Qualitative Market Research: An International Journal*, 16 (2): 197–213.

Rindell, A., Edvardsson, B. and Strandvik, T. (2010) Mapping the "roots" of the consumer's image-in-use of companies, *Journal of Product & Brand Management*, 10 (6): 423–431.

Rindell, A. and Iglesias, O. (2014) Context and time in brand image constructions, *Journal of Organizational Change Management*, 27 (5): 756–768.

Solms, M. and Turnbull, O. (2002) *The brain and the inner world: An introduction to the neuroscience of subjective experience*, Other Press, New York.

Stern, B., Zinkhan, G.M. and Jaju, A. (2001) Marketing images: Construct definition, measurement issues, and theory development, *Marketing Theory*, 1 (2): 201–224.

Urde, M., Greyser, S.A. and Balmer, J.M.T. (2007) Corporate brands with a heritage, *Journal of Brand Management*, 15 (1): 4–19.

Walker, K. (2010) A systematic review of the corporate reputation literature: Definition, measurement, and theory, *Corporate Reputation Review*, 12: 357–387.

Wiedmann, K.-P., Hennings, N., Schmidt, S. and Wuestefeld, T. (2011) The importance of brand heritage as a key performance driver in market management, *Journal of Brand Management*, 9 (3): 82–94.

Zaltman, G. (2003) *How customers think: Essential insight into the mind of the market*, Harvard Business School Press, Cambridge, MA.

11

APPROACHES TO CORPORATE HERITAGE BRAND MANAGEMENT

The cases of Cunard and Ritz-Carlton

Bradford T. Hudson

Overview

A recent analysis of 100 leading global brands reveals that about 40 percent are more than a century old (Hudson, 2014). Many important brands have not only contemporary relevance, but also notable historical status. Nonetheless, there is variation in the emphasis of such history within their strategies, positioning, products, and communications.

The concept of "corporate brand heritage" suggests that the historical status of older companies may be explicitly linked to their brand identity and consumer appeal. A persuasive discussion of this phenomenon is found in an influential article by Mats Urde, Stephen Greyser, and John Balmer (2007). Among the conclusions, they argue it is important to distinguish between a "brand with a heritage" and a "heritage brand." The latter has a strategic "positioning and value proposition based on its heritage."

My chapter builds upon this insight, by offering case studies about Cunard and Ritz-Carlton. There are remarkable similarities between these companies, including their subsequent acquisitions by multinational conglomerates. However, during the decade after the acquisitions, one company chose to embrace its heritage while the other effectively abandoned it. This validates the concept of a heritage brand and illustrates differing strategic approaches in the management of historic brands.

Corporate brand heritage

Corporate brand heritage is an emerging field in the marketing discipline. The antecedents of the concept include a range of literature from various academic disciplines on the topics of business history, brand equity, corporate marketing, corporate identity, organizational longevity, cultural heritage, heritage tourism, authenticity, nostalgia, retrospective marketing, and iconic branding (Balmer, 2013; Hudson & Balmer, 2013; Urde *et al.*, 2007).

The particular notion of corporate brand heritage was first articulated in literature regarding the application of corporate marketing theory to the identity of the British Monarchy (Balmer, Greyser & Urde, 2006). The principles therein were reiterated and applied more specifically to business in a subsequent article by the same authors (Urde *et al.*, 2007). The latter now serves as the intellectual point of departure for a multitude of scholars working in contiguous areas, as this book itself attests.

Urde *et al.* (2007) suggest that historic brands constitute a distinct conceptual category and require specific approaches to brand management that differ from those required for younger brands. To this end, they offer a multidimensional conceptual model to assist scholars and marketing practitioners in the identification and analysis of heritage.

The first dimension suggests that "history must be important" to the identity of the company, both from the viewpoint of consumers engaged with its products and the outlook of stakeholders within the organization. This relates closely to the second dimension, which suggests that "core values" must be evident in corporate identity and must guide the behaviour of its executives and the character of its interactions with the public.

The third dimension suggests that the company must have "longevity" in the marketplace, which is defined as continuity in the emphasis and use of heritage across multiple eras and successive leaders. The fourth dimension suggests that heritage brands must have a "track record" of delivering value to customers over extended periods.

The fifth dimension suggests that heritage must be reflected in the consistent and appropriate "use of symbols" to identify the brand and define its character. Lastly, all of these elements must revolve around a commitment to "stewardship." Executives must demonstrate a sense of responsibility for protecting the brand and its symbolic elements.

Urde *et al.* (2007) argue that heritage is often an "undertapped corporate asset" and that companies should embrace heritage as a unique point of competitive differentiation. They argue that effective heritage marketing requires strict attention to the conceptual model outlined above, proactive involvement in "uncovering" aspects of heritage through archival and consumer research, "activating" that heritage through product design and marketing communications, and "protecting" that heritage through attention to continuity.

Methodology

Although corporate brand heritage is activated in the present as a contemporary marketing strategy, it refers inherently to the past. The history of a company and the history of its engagement with consumers are important elements in understanding the appeal of older brands. As such, history is not only embedded in brand heritage as a value proposition, but it also constitutes a research methodology for identifying and analyzing brand heritage.

This chapter follows methodological principles that are well established for historical research on any topic (Fulbrook, 2002; Gottschalk, 1969). The author has also been influenced by scholarship regarding the more specific application of historical methods to the business sector and the discipline of marketing (Golder, 2000; Rowlinson, 2004; Savitt, 1980).

The historical approach is similar to research methods employed in the development of business case studies (Hartley, 2004; Kantrow, 1986; Yin, 2003). Both techniques involve the investigation of examples using library or field research that may include interviews, archival documents, ethnography, participant observation, contextual references, and secondary sources. It has also been suggested that case research is an appropriate methodology for examining issues related to corporate identity (Balmer, 2001).

The first case describes the historic Cunard Line and its acquisition by the newer cruise operator Carnival Corporation. The second case describes the historic Ritz-Carlton Company and its acquisition by the newer hotel operator Marriott International. Each case begins with the founding of the firm, proceeds through its subsequent acquisition, and finishes with a description of its positioning during the first decade after the acquisition. Together they encompass the period from 1839 to 2009.

The companies profiled in this chapter are remarkably similar. As such, the two cases represent parallel narratives that can be compared easily and reliably. Based on the objective attributes of the firms, readers might plausibly expect that the cases would unfold in similar fashion, and therefore the divergent outcomes suggest that differing attitudes regarding heritage can be isolated as the determinant variable.

The evidence about Cunard derives from a variety of historical and contemporary sources, especially the personal experiences of the author over the past two decades. These included visits to the Cunard company headquarters, voyages aboard the Cunard vessels *Queen Elizabeth 2* and *Queen Mary 2*, interviews with Cunard executives, and perspective gained by the author during his engagement as a consultant to Cunard. Secondary sources included books, academic articles, and reports from professional and popular media.

The evidence about Ritz-Carlton derives from similar types of sources. These included numerous visits to the Ritz-Carlton Hotel in Boston and various other hotels in the system, visits to the Ritz Hotels in London and Paris, a series of conversations with the former owner of the Ritz-Carlton brand in the United States, an interview with the former president of Ritz-Carlton worldwide, and discussions with numerous executives of Ritz-Carlton and Marriott. Secondary sources included books, academic articles, and reports from professional and popular media.

It is worth mentioning that Cunard and Ritz-Carlton were independent entities during much of their existence, and were therefore corporate brands. After the acquisitions by Carnival and Marriott, they became product brands within larger portfolios. However, both companies were operated as strategic business units during the subsequent decade. They remained distinctly separate from their parent organizations in terms of strategy, organization, management, finance, operations, and even the locations of their headquarters. They also maintained brand positions that were completely unconnected to their parent organizations from the viewpoint of consumers. As such, they arguably continued to behave like corporate brands during the period covered in this chapter.

Cunard

Early history

The Cunard Steam Ship Company was founded by Samuel Cunard in 1839. Its original mission was to carry mail and passengers between the United Kingdom and North America. The first ship, *Britannia*, crossed the Atlantic in 1840, and by the turn of the century Cunard was dominating the transatlantic trade. The company merged with the White Star Line in 1934, becoming the leading passenger shipping firm worldwide (Hyde, 1975; Ingram, 1998).

Among the famous Cunard ships of the past were *Lusitania* and *Mauretania*. The former is remembered for its role in mobilizing public opinion prior to the First World War, while the latter is renowned for holding the transoceanic speed record for more than two decades. After the merger, the Cunard Line also inherited the legacy of the famous White Star liners, foremost among them being *Titanic*. The first vessels built by the combined Cunard White Star Line were *Queen Mary* and *Queen Elizabeth*, which were admired for their classic designs and elegant interiors. A new *Queen Elizabeth 2* replaced the aging *Queen Elizabeth* in 1969.

Cunard was acquired in 1971 by the diversified conglomerate Trafalgar House, which presided over its transition from a transportation provider to a tourist cruise operator. In 1996, Cunard was sold again to the shipbuilding concern Kvaerner Group.

Despite its lustrous history, the financial and operating performance of Cunard was sometimes disappointing, especially during the 1990s. The decade began with a miserable year in 1991, during which operating profit declined 39 percent and revenues declined 51 percent compared to the prior year. By 1995, revenues were 57 percent lower than 1990 and the company reported an operating loss of about £16 million (Peisley, 1992; Trafalgar House, 1995).

There were also questions about quality, with some observers suggesting that service standards and physical conditions aboard the aging vessels were inconsistent, that guest complaints were increasing, and that customer loyalty was declining. The company suffered through multiple rounds of bad publicity, caused by incidents such as the grounding of *Queen Elizabeth 2* in 1992 (McDowell, 1996; McFadden, 1992).

The brand architecture of Cunard included both a corporate brand and the names of individual ships, which served as subsidiary product brands. The corporate brand "Cunard" was widely associated with the English aristocracy and the history of the British Empire (Young & Greyser, 1994).

Carnival

During the period that Trafalgar House and Kvaerner owned the Cunard brand, the competing Carnival Cruise Line had become a colossus. Founded in 1972 as a midscale tourist cruise line, Carnival had grown through aggressive television advertising. It had also diversified into other segments through an acquisition strategy, funded by a stock offering in 1987.

By the end of 1997, Carnival was the world's largest cruise company, with annual revenues of almost $2.5 billion. It owned or operated 37 ships in every significant cruise segment and region, and its portfolio included the upscale Holland America brand and partial ownership of the luxury Seabourn brand (Carnival, 1998; Peisley, 1992).

The acquisition of Cunard

In 1998, Carnival acquired the Cunard Line from the Kvaerner Group, paying $500 million for the Cunard brand and its five remaining ships (Gross, Derdak & Stansell, 2006). Carnival chief executive Micky Arison observed that the acquisition would give him control of the "strongest brand name in the luxury segment of the cruise market" (Hagerty, 1998).

The sophisticated systems and management discipline that Carnival could bring to the troubled Cunard organization were important factors in the acquisition. The subsequent annual report noted: "Our management team now expects to apply the same business philosophy that has made Carnival Corporation the world's most profitable cruise company to create new efficiencies and stabilize management at Cunard" (Carnival, 1998).

Within a decade of the acquisition, all of the former Cunard ships had been sold or transferred to other divisions within Carnival (Hudson, 2011). The prior Cunard fleet was soon replaced by three new vessels built by Carnival, which entered service between 2004 and 2010. These are *Queen Mary 2* (also known as *QM2*), *Queen Victoria*, and *Queen Elizabeth* (the third ship with this name, although not numbered as such).

Positioning after the acquisition

It was evident almost from the moment of acquisition that Carnival would not only maintain the luxury position of Cunard, but also emphasize the historic status of the brand (Hudson, 2011). In 1999, the Cunard vessel *Vistafjord* was refurbished and re-launched as *Caronia*, a name that had appeared on two prior Cunard ships. The exterior was repainted in the classic Cunard scheme with black hull, white superstructure, and red funnel. Several of the public rooms and guest suites were renamed after famous Cunard liners of the past.

Although *Caronia* was subsequently sold, the same design strategy was adopted for the new *Queen Mary 2*, plans for which were started shortly after the acquisition.

QM2 was intentionally styled after the original *Queen Mary*, to offer a retrospective experience that would satisfy Cunard enthusiasts. The plans incorporated several naming features intended to create associations with the British ancestry of the Cunard Line.

This positioning was not lost on travel writers invited aboard the ship. One suggested that *QM2* was "a marriage of corporate branding, modern technology, and good old-fashioned nostalgia" (Haines, 2004). Another observed that in a world "dominated by increasingly glitzy cruise ships, the designers of this liner have mostly gone for a traditional, art deco look" and added that "this ship is designed to appeal to Anglophiles" (Golden, 2004).

The historic positioning for the new Cunard brand also extended to marketing communications. The website and brochures used the slogans "The Most Famous Ocean Liners in the World" and "The Golden Age of Ocean Travel." The company profile began with the headline "Advancing Civilization since 1840." It then suggested that Cunard reflects "a more civilized era" of "sophistication and privilege" when "glorious ocean liners were floating palaces of art deco splendour and Edwardian excess" (Cunard, 2007a, 2007b, 2007c).

Although the Cunard brand had traditionally been aimed at a mature and wealthy audience, there were indications that the renewed company was targeting a larger market. Cunard had experienced a declining trend in the average age of its guests, and this continued after the acquisition. A new brochure suggested that Cunard ships "offer the opportunity for a new generation to experience the classic romance and refined British heritage" of a bygone era (Cunard, 2007b).

While the subsequent performance of Cunard has been obscured within the larger Carnival portfolio, my informal discussions with executives indicate that the revived brand has been quite successful financially. *QM2* has also garnered significant media coverage, received numerous awards, and generated high occupancies and prices. The inaugural voyage of *Queen Victoria* was sold out more than one year in advance (Cunard, 2006).

Ritz-Carlton

Early history

The origins of the Ritz-Carlton brand can be traced to the celebrated hotelier César Ritz, who began his career in upscale hotels across Europe during the late nineteenth century. Through this experience, he gained the professional confidence of numerous members of the American industrial aristocracy and European nobility, including the Prince of Wales (Ritz, 1938; Derdak, Woodward & Salamie, 2005).

Ritz and several financial backers subsequently founded the Ritz Hotel Development Company in 1897. Among the first properties built were the Carlton Hotel in London and the Ritz Hotel in London. The first hotel to be developed under the combined brand was the Ritz-Carlton Hotel in New York City, which opened in 1910. This was followed by Ritz-Carlton hotels elsewhere, including Montreal and Boston.

Many of the Ritz hotels eventually succumbed to the economic depression of the 1930s. By the late 1970s, the development company itself was defunct. The remaining Ritz-Carlton Hotels in Boston and Montreal, as well as the Ritz hotels in Europe, were all under separate ownership and management.

The next generation of Ritz-Carlton commenced in 1983, when the Ritz-Carlton Hotel in Boston was acquired by William Johnson. The rights to the Ritz-Carlton brand in the United States and the pedigree leading back to César Ritz came with the property. Johnson was a real estate developer from Atlanta, who had recently started a division to develop his own hotels in the growing luxury segment.

The new Ritz-Carlton company reinforced its luxury brand position by emphasizing high standards and adopting a total quality management approach (Partlow, 1993). For its brand personality, the company chose to capitalize on the characteristics of the historic flagship property in Boston. Its interior design was a hybrid of European revival styles. The atmosphere was classic, with traditional service procedures and a strict dress code for customers.

The new Ritz-Carlton company quickly developed a reputation for luxury and elegance. Several properties received the Five-Star Award from the *Mobil Travel Guide* (now *Forbes*) and the company received the Baldrige Quality Award in 1992. There was, however, some question about the financial performance of the company. While most results were obscured due to its private status, persistent rumours circulated regarding excessive debt and problems with profitability (Hirsch, 1994; Touby, 1992).

Marriott

Marriott Corporation opened its first restaurant in 1927 and entered the hotel business in 1957. It grew quickly through an aggressive acquisition strategy, funded by a stock offering in 1953 and listing on the New York Stock Exchange in 1968 (O'Brien, 1977).

By the mid-1990s, Marriott was a worldwide hospitality empire generating annual revenues of $8 billion. The company was predominantly a hotel franchising and management firm, rather than a real estate owner, with about 1,000 hotels operating under various brands in multiple industry segments (Marriott, 1995a, 2007). Despite some experimentation with upscale hotels, the company lacked a significant presence in the growing luxury segment.

The acquisition of Ritz-Carlton

In 1995, Marriott acquired 49 percent of the Ritz-Carlton Hotel Company from William Johnson. The company paid about $200 million for half interest in the Ritz-Carlton trademark and the management contracts for 31 hotels. Johnson retained full ownership of the underlying real estate assets, specifically minority interests in several properties and outright ownership of three, including the Ritz-Carlton Hotel in Boston. The agreement included the right to purchase the remaining portion of the company within three years, which Marriott subsequently did (Emmons & Salamie, 2007; Marriott, 1995b).

Despite its reputation for luxury and quality, many observers believed that Ritz-Carlton was in desperate need of a change in managerial style (Humphries & Rockwell, 1995). An influential investment analyst suggested that the deal was "combining Marriott Corporation, which is known for lean management and profitability, with Ritz, a company known for its excellent service, but not for making money. If you put the two together, you potentially come out with one chain that has both exceptional quality and profitability" (Faiola, 1995).

Positioning after the acquisition

For several years after the Marriott acquisition, Ritz-Carlton used historical themes to position its brand. The company also continued to build new hotels that included the traditional European revival styles that had become associated with the brand. More recently, however, the company has made a variety of changes, which were probably influenced by the real estate development firm Millennium Partners.

During the 1990s, Millennium devised a concept for high-end condominiums in mixed-use developments that included branded luxury hotels. In 1999, Millennium acquired the real estate underlying the original Ritz-Carlton Hotel in Boston, in order to obtain the naming rights for the area. This allowed them to build a second hotel in Boston, which opened as the Ritz-Carlton Boston Common. By the middle of 2003, Millennium had developed five new Ritz-Carlton hotels and owned the original Ritz-Carlton in Boston, giving them control of the flagship property and more than 10 percent of the hotels in the Ritz-Carlton system (Millennium, 2007; Sucher & McManus, 2005).

Millennium had an unconventional agenda for the Ritz-Carlton brand. They desired the name primarily for its prestige and its ability to position condominium properties in a manner similar to luxury consumer goods. However, they were uninterested with some other aspects of the existing brand position. In particular, the developer rejected the traditional Ritz-Carlton design cues, instead choosing distinctly contemporary decor for its hotels.

The interiors of the new Ritz-Carlton Boston Common offered a pronounced contrast to those of the original Boston property, with modern minimalist décor and bold abstract paintings. As one design critic observed, the newer hotel in Boston is "definitely not your grandmother's Ritz-Carlton" (Connors, 2002).

In subsequent years, it became apparent that Ritz-Carlton had adopted a repositioning strategy for its brand that was consistent with the Millennium philosophy (Binkley, 2002; Cooper, 2006; Hotels, 2006; Sanders, 2005, 2006). The new approach has been described as updating and relaxing the brand identity to focus on "relevant luxury" for a new generation of affluent travellers (Sanders, 2006).

The company even partially abandoned its quality management systems, which were integral to its corporate culture and internal identity. Ritz-Carlton relaxed its formulaic procedures, behavioural standards, and encounter scripts (Sanders, 2006).

Changes also occurred in the area of marketing communications. In 2004, the company selected a new advertising agency to help "blow the dust off the lion and the crown" in the company logo (Sanders, 2005). The new campaign included advertisements in trendy magazines such as *Vanity Fair*.

Ritz-Carlton has pursued marketing alliances in the fashion industry, including promotions with luxury brands such as Prada and a joint venture to develop hotels with the jeweller Bulgari. The senior marketing executive of Ritz-Carlton compared the repositioning of his brand to the revival of Louis Vuitton (Hotels, 2006).

The disposition of the original Ritz-Carlton Hotel in Boston – upon which the current Marriott luxury division was legally and spiritually built – is emblematic of the shift. In 2007, the underlying real estate was sold to the Tata Group and the property was re-branded as the Taj Hotel. Even in Boston, the transformation was complete, as only the newer Ritz-Carlton Boston Common built by Millennium remained.

Reactions to these changes were mixed. The shift in interior design received negative reviews from traditionalists, especially in Boston where the original Ritz-Carlton property had historic and cultural significance (Allis, 2006). However, the preliminary evidence suggests that the repositioning strategy did not disrupt associations of the brand with luxury and quality. Ritz-Carlton hotels continue to be highly ranked among ratings and surveys (Ritz-Carlton, 2007).

Perspective

Prior to the acquisitions, there were remarkable similarities between the Cunard and Ritz-Carlton companies. Both brands had origins in nineteenth-century Britain, and they depended upon demand from the American industrial aristocracy during their early years. By the 1990s, both were headquartered in the United States. Cunard and Ritz-Carlton shared a questionable reputation in regard to profitability. Most importantly, each of these companies enjoyed a similar mystique in popular culture. Their brands generated associations with luxury, proper standards of service, social prestige, and the romance of a bygone era.

Prior to the acquisitions, the Carnival and Marriott companies also shared many characteristics with one another. Each was founded in the United States during the twentieth century. Both were recognized leaders in their respective industries, in terms of brand awareness and investment prominence. Each was a public company with access to significant capital. Both companies had engaged in segmentation and acquisition strategies that resulted in the assembly of brand portfolios. Both had sophisticated management and marketing systems, and successful records in operating hospitality services profitably. Carnival and Marriott were exploring their own luxury operations, but neither had a significant presence in the luxury segment of their respective industries.

The nature and rationale of each acquisition was also quite similar. In typical corporate acquisitions, value is derived from physical assets, income streams, patents, intellectual property, operating processes, and so forth. However, Cunard and

Ritz-Carlton had few of these. In both cases, the companies had been consistently underperforming financially. Neither had patents or intellectual property, other than new licensing opportunities that might derive from their brands. The management systems of both companies had been criticized, and the quality process expertise that Ritz-Carlton possessed was later partially rejected by new executives.

Similarly, the value of physical assets cannot adequately explain the sales. In the case of Cunard, the ships were antiquated, especially compared to the more modern fleet in the larger Carnival portfolio. All but one ship was eventually sold, and the remaining vessel was transferred to another brand in a lower segment. In the case of Ritz-Carlton, the underlying real estate was decoupled from the company prior to its acquisition. The only notable item of value was the potential revenue stream from management contracts associated with the Ritz-Carlton hotels, which represented a small portion of the vast Marriott empire.

Both companies undoubtedly understood the value of acquiring an existing brand, rather than engaging in a new product development exercise. Acquisitions capitalize on prior brand awareness and usage habits, pre-empt the need for expensive advertising, and reduce the risk of failure in new product development (Hudson, 1994). The historic Cunard and Ritz-Carlton brands facilitated authoritative entry into the luxury segments of their respective industries, and allowed Carnival and Marriott to make authentic claims to luxury status despite the more recent and moderate origins of their own brands.

After the acquisitions, Carnival and Marriott demonstrated similar strategies in integrating the new brands into their respective corporate portfolios. In both cases, the new luxury brands were kept distinctly separate from the new corporate parent brands and other product brands in lower segments, in terms of both operations and marketing communications.

Despite the many similarities, however, the strategic choices by Carnival and Marriott in regard to the subsequent development of these brands have apparently been quite different. While Carnival has embraced the historical associations of the Cunard brand and built its new brand position on the basis of that history, Marriott has effectively abandoned the history of Ritz-Carlton and repositioned it as a contemporary fashion brand in manner similar to luxury consumer goods.

It is curious indeed that Marriott would acquire the Ritz-Carlton company strictly for its brand equity and then, within a decade, reposition the brand so radically. Why did Marriott acquire the historic Ritz-Carlton brand and then abandon its heritage? Marriott executives have implied that demand patterns shifted after the acquisition, especially as new economy entrepreneurs and aging baby boomers entered the luxury marketplace, seeking more fashionable and less formal approaches to luxury. This suggests that the repositioning of Ritz-Carlton was required to avoid strategic obsolescence and decline within an evolving marketplace (Cooper, 2006; Hotels, 2006; Sanders, 2006).

The case of Cunard, however, offers evidence to undermine this explanation. Cunard has succeeded, despite the same revitalization challenges in the same marketplace, without adopting contemporary positioning attributes for its brand.

Indeed, just the opposite is true. The cruise line has used pronounced retrospective themes to appeal to a new generation of passengers. Cunard has demonstrated that innovation can be consistent with historical contextualization. This, in turn, suggests that the decision to abandon the historic positioning of the Ritz-Carlton brand was not a constrained strategic necessity, but rather a matter of judgment and choice.

Conclusion

Cunard and Ritz-Carlton were remarkably similar companies, and yet they followed different paths during the decade after their acquisitions. Carnival and Marriott both acquired luxury brands with strong historic associations, but while integrating the brands into their corporate portfolios, one company embraced the past while the other essentially rejected it. This emphasizes the idea that the historical aspects of older brands do not necessarily or obviously constitute the basis for positioning such brands.

These cases also illustrate the difference between a "brand with heritage" and a "heritage brand" as articulated by Urde *et al.* (2007). Using their conceptual model, the differing approaches to the management of these brands after their acquisitions can be clearly delineated.

The executives of Marriott have succeeded in extending the heritage of Ritz-Carlton in terms of its reputation for luxury and operational excellence. They have also perhaps saved the brand from extinction, by restoring financial viability to the underlying company. In this sense, it could be argued that they have been faithful stewards of the legacy of César Ritz.

However, these executives also seem to have rejected two distinctive symbolic elements of the long-standing Ritz-Carlton brand position, namely the historic European revival décor and the traditional formal service behaviours for which the brand had become renowned. Instead, the company has apparently adopted a radically new identity in an attempt to remain relevant and fashionable. In this sense, it could be argued that the history of Ritz-Carlton is no longer important to the organization and that reverent retrospection is no longer evident in the core values of the firm.

The disposition of the Cunard brand after its acquisition by Carnival offers a contrasting narrative. History has remained important to the ethos and identity of the company; the core values of the firm have been articulated in its marketing communications and demonstrated in its commitment to operational excellence. The historic symbols of the brand have been actively reprised, especially in the design of its new ships. The track record of the company in delivering elegant travel experiences to passengers has been renewed. Carnival executives have demonstrated a commitment to stewardship for its history and its traditional symbols. In doing so, the longevity of the brand has been extended seamlessly from the past to the present, and the Cunard legacy has been extended into the immediate future. A new generation of passengers is discovering the pleasures of a bygone era.

Key points

1 There is a difference between a brand with a heritage (exemplified by the case of Ritz-Carlton) and a heritage brand (exemplified by the case of Cunard). The latter has a strategic positioning and value proposition based on its heritage.
2 Executives who hope to exploit heritage for marketing advantage should follow the multidimensional model proposed by Urde et al. (2007). History must be important to the identity of the company, core values must be evident in the positioning of the company and the behaviour of its executives, the company must have a track record of delivering value to customers, the company must have longevity in the marketplace, corporate symbols must be used consistently and appropriately, and executives must be committed to stewardship of their corporate brand heritage.

Questions

1 Describe the history and positioning of Cunard before and after its acquisition by Carnival. What happened?
2 Describe the history and positioning of Ritz-Carlton before and after its acquisition by Marriott. What happened?
3 How could the executives of Carnival and Marriott have handled these brands differently? What might have been the alternative outcomes?
4 How do the cases of Cunard and Ritz-Carlton exemplify the conceptual model proposed by Urde et al. (2007)?
5 What is the difference between a "brand with a heritage" and a "heritage brand"? What are the potential risks and benefits of each approach?

References

Allis, S. (2006) What's in a Name? We'll Soon Be Putting on the Ritz at the Taj, *Boston Globe*, November 12: A3.
Balmer, J.M.T. (2001) Corporate Identity, Corporate Branding and Corporate Marketing: Seeing through the Fog, *European Journal of Marketing* 35(3/4): 248–91.
Balmer, J.M.T. (2013) Corporate Heritage, Corporate Heritage Marketing, and Total Corporate Heritage Communications, *Corporate Communications* 18(3): 290–326.
Balmer, J.M.T., Greyser, S. and Urde, M. (2006) The Crown as a Corporate Brand: Insights from Monarchies, *Journal of Brand Management* 14(1/2): 137–61.
Binkley, C. (2002) Putting on the Ritz Means a Bit Less, *Wall Street Journal*, April 8: A1.
Carnival Corporation (1998) Annual Reports to Shareholders. Carnival Corporation, Miami, FL.
Connors, J. (2002) Boston Beacon, *Interior Design* 73(3): S60–2.
Cooper, S. (2006) How the Ritz-Carlton Is Reinventing Itself, *Gallup Management Journal*, October 12 [gmj.gallup.com]
Cunard Line (2006) Cunard Line's Queen Victoria, *PR Newswire*, May 19 [www.prnewswire.com]
Cunard Line (2007a) Company Website [www.cunard.com]
Cunard Line (2007b) *2007–2008 Voyages*, Corporate Brochure. Cunard Line, Valencia, CA.
Cunard Line (2007c) *Between Two Continents Awaits: Six Days of the Spectacular*, Corporate Brochure. Cunard Line, Valencia, CA.

Derdak, T., Woodward, A. and Salamie, D.E. (2005) The Ritz-Carlton Hotel Company. In J.P. Pederson (ed), *International Directory of Company Histories* 71, St. James Press, Detroit.

Emmons, V.A. and Salamie, D.E. (2007) Marriott International. In J.P. Pederson (ed), *International Directory of Company Histories* 83, St. James Press, Detroit, 264–70.

Faiola, A. (1995) Marriott Seeks to Expand into Luxury Hotels, *Washington Post*, March 7: D1.

Fulbrook, M. (2002) *Historical Theory*, Routledge, London.

Golden, F. (2004) There's Something about Queen Mary, *Boston Herald*, January 15: 47.

Golder, P.N. (2000) Historical Method in Marketing Research with New Evidence on Long-Term Market Share Stability, *Journal of Marketing Research* 37(2): 156–72.

Gottschalk, L.R. (1969) *Understanding History*, Knopf, New York.

Gross, D., Derdak, T. and Stansell, C.M. (2006) Carnival Corporation. In T. Grant (ed), *International Directory of Companies* 78, St. James Press, Detroit.

Hagerty, J.R. (1998) Carnival on Course to Buy Owner of Queen Elizabeth 2, *Wall Street Journal*, April 6: A23.

Haines, T. (2004) All Hail Luxury on Its Maiden Voyage, *Boston Globe*, January 25: M1.

Hartley, J. (2004) Case Study Research. In C. Cassell and G. Symon (eds), *Essential Guide to Qualitative Methods in Organizational Research*, Sage, London.

Hirsch, J.S. (1994) Of Luxury and Losses: Many Ritz Hotels Are in the Red, *Wall Street Journal*, April 22: B1.

Hotels (2006) Ritz-Carlton's New Traditions, *Hotels* 40(10): 22–30.

Hudson, B.T. (1994) Innovation through Acquisition, *Cornell Hotel & Restaurant Administration Quarterly* 35(3): 82–7.

Hudson, B.T. (2011) Brand Heritage and the Renaissance of Cunard, *European Journal of Marketing* 45(9/10): 1538–56.

Hudson, B.T. (2014) The Prevalence of Longevity among Leading Brands, *Boston Hospitality Review* 2(3): 14–21.

Hudson, B.T. and Balmer, J.M.T. (2013) Corporate Heritage Brands: Mead's Theory of the Past, *Corporate Communications* 18(3): 347–61.

Humphries, C. and Rockwell, S.A. (1995) *Marriott International*, Alex Brown & Sons, Baltimore.

Hyde, F.E. (1975) *Cunard and the North Atlantic*, Macmillan Press, London.

Ingram, F.C. (1998) Cunard Line. In T. Grant (ed), *International Directory of Company Histories* 23, St. James Press, Detroit.

Kantrow, A.M. (1986) Why History Matters to Managers: A Roundtable Discussion, *Harvard Business Review* 64: 81–8.

Marriott International (1995a) Annual Reports to Shareholders. Marriott International, Bethesda, MD.

Marriott International (1995b) Marriott International Agrees to Buy Interest in Ritz-Carlton, *PR Newswire*, March 6 [www.prnewswire.com]

Marriott International (2007) Company Website [www.marriott.com]

McDowell, E. (1996) Changing Course at Cunard, *New York Times*, August 6: D1.

McFadden, R.D. (1992) Passengers Are Evacuated after QE2 Runs Aground, *New York Times*, August 9: 1.

Millennium Partners (2007) Company Website [www.millenniumptrs.com]

O'Brien, R. (1977) *Marriott: The J. Willard Marriott Story*, Deseret, Salt Lake City.

Partlow, C.G. (1993) How Ritz-Carlton Applies TQM, *Cornell Hotel and Restaurant Administration Quarterly* 34(4): 16–24.

Peisley, T. (1992) *The World Cruise Ship Industry in the 1990s*, Economist Intelligence Unit, London.

Ritz, M.L. (1938) *César Ritz: Host to the World*, Lippincott, Philadelphia.

Ritz-Carlton (2007) Company Website [www.ritzcarlton.com]

Rowlinson, M. (2004) Historical Analysis of Company Documents. In C. Cassell and G. Symon (eds), *Essential Guide to Qualitative Methods in Organizational Research*, Sage, London.

Sanders, P. (2005) Ritz Blitz to Target Young Travelers, *Wall Street Journal*, April 28: B2.

Sanders, P. (2006) Takin' off the Ritz, *Wall Street Journal*, June 23: B1.

Savitt, R. (1980) Historical Research in Marketing, *Journal of Marketing* 44: 52–8.

Sucher, S. J. and McManus, S.E. (2005) *The Ritz-Carlton Hotel Company, Case 601163*, Harvard Business School, Boston.

Touby, L. (1992) Too Many Rooms at the Inn for Ritz-Carlton, *Business Week*, July 6: 74–76.

Trafalgar House (1991–1995) Annual Report to Shareholders. Trafalgar House, London, UK.

Urde, M., Greyser, S.A. and Balmer, J.M.T. (2007) Corporate Brands with a Heritage, *Journal of Brand Management* 15(1): 4–19.

Yin, R. (2003) *Case Study Research: Design and Methods*, Sage, London.

Young, R.F. and Greyser, S.A. (1994) *Cunard Line, Case 594046*, Harvard Business School, Boston.

12

CORPORATE HERITAGE OR CORPORATE INHERITANCE*

A French perspective

Fabien Pecot and Virginie de Barnier

Chapter overview

> "*Ce que l'on conçoit bien s'énonce clairement/Et les mots pour le dire arrivent aisément*" ("Whatever is well conceived is clearly said/And the words to say it flow with ease")
>
> *(Boileau, 1972, p. 52, verses 153–154)*

This chapter builds on the efforts of Balmer (2011b) and Burghausen and Balmer (2014b) to engage with the foundational concepts of corporate heritage so as to establish further theoretical contributions on a solid basis. These efforts have led to several clarifications about the nature of heritage in English, namely its distinction from related concepts such as history or legacy (Balmer, 2013). A particular Francophone approach of heritage as a concept, different from the Anglophone, is acknowledged by Balmer (2013). Building on the English literature and our own experience when importing corporate heritage in French scholarship, we detail this Francophone perspective of corporate heritage. We address the semantic issues of the translation of heritage in French, related to the epistemological distinction between *patrimoine* and *héritage*. The understanding of this distinction is not only mandatory for any further development of corporate heritage in French; it also contributes to the theoretical strengthening of the concept in English by stating a difference between heritage and inheritance from a corporate point of view.

The perspectives offered by the Anglophone perspective (Balmer, 2011b, 2013; Burghausen & Balmer, 2014b) and those of the Francophone perspective provide useful insights for managers and scholars. The French perspective introduces a distinction between those elements given from the past which may remain of private matter of the company and could be forgotten at some point (*héritage*, inheritance) and those elements appropriated from the past in order to be made public and transmitted to the next generation of managers (*patrimoine*, heritage).

Introduction

It can sometimes become quite confusing when one is asked to clearly differentiate heritage and inheritance. As corporate heritage constitutes itself as a stream of research, a clear distinction between those concepts could help in defining what is and is not corporate heritage. Balmer (2011b, 2013) and Burghausen and Balmer's (2014b) work on the foundational concepts aim to contribute to more clarification, this chapter follows this line.

Their work focuses on the English meanings of heritage, while our focus is on a complementary Francophone perspective. Heritage comes from French (Balmer, 2011b); so does inheritance (Chantrell, 2002). This contribution builds on existing efforts to deconstruct and grasp the meanings and nuances of heritage through a French perspective. It aims for more clarity by reporting the difference between *patrimoine* and *héritage* in French, and making it relevant to an English context. Two distinct dimensions are presented and illustrated with a case example.

The chapter is structured as follows. In the first part, we present existing literature from the Anglophone perspective. In the second part, we focus on the French context and detail the distinction between *patrimoine* and *héritage*. In the third part we present the implications of such distinctions for corporate heritage, and illustrate them with the case example of Ferrero France. As a conclusion we discuss the insights brought by the Francophone perspective for managers and scholars.

Foundational works: The Anglophone perspective of heritage

Corporate heritage as a research stream has been growing fast since a triumvirate of scholars first made use of the concept while studying monarchies as corporate brands (Balmer, Greyser, & Urde, 2006; Urde, Greyser, & Balmer, 2007). The corporate heritage literature has built on those foundational works, exploring two different angles: one taking the brand as the focus and therefore studying brand heritage (Hakala, Lätti, & Sandberg, 2011; Hudson, 2011; Hudson & Balmer, 2013; Wiedmann, Hennigs, Schmidt, & Wuestefeld, 2011) and another taking corporate identity as the focus and therefore studying corporate heritage identities (Balmer, 2011b, 2013; Burghausen & Balmer, 2014a).

As we reach a period of consolidation, the authors point out that only a few contributions have focused on foundational concepts (Burghausen & Balmer, 2014b) and call for more research on that aspect. Nevertheless, considerable advances must be identified in two complementary directions. One focuses on the nature of heritage through a semantic and epistemological approach, while another focuses on the distinction of heritage from other concepts of the past in a corporate context. All together, they constitute what we call the Anglophone perspective. Before introducing our Francophone perspective, we now review the cornerstones of heritage understood in the Anglophone perspective.

TABLE 12.1 Latin and French roots of heritage/inheritance

Latin	French	English
Here (yesterday) – Heredis (heir)	Héritage	Inheritance Heritage

The nature of heritage

In the recent special edition of *Corporate Communications: An International Journal* on corporate heritage, Balmer (2013) insists on this semantic and epistemological approach by stating the importance of studying the words' historiography.

The French origins of the word *heritage* are acknowledged (Balmer, 2011b). Indeed, *heritage* comes from Old French with Latin roots (see Table 12.1) which also gave the word *inheritance* (Chantrell, 2002), but both words convey different meanings in their respective language (Balmer, 2013).

Existing literature on the Anglophone perspective shows heritage is strongly related to identity, and highly relative (Balmer, 2011b, 2013). Heritage is central in the continuity of an individual or a group's identity on which it conveys a discourse. It is considered relative as those discourses on identity can be real, imagined, contrived or a mix of all three (Balmer, 2011b). Heritage is contextual; it clarifies the past from a present point of view.

As such, the concern for heritage is strongly related to our changing world's need for anchors and explanations of one's past (Balmer, 2011b). Postmodern authors add complexity to this relativity of heritage: they state individuals can define their own heritage themselves, which is translated in business by the existence of different interpretations of a corporate heritage by the different stakeholders (Balmer, 2011b, 2013).

Distinction from other past-related concepts

Another direction to study foundational concepts is to contrast heritage and other past-related concepts. The distinction from history has obviously received much attention to clarify the differences of approaches between corporate heritage and business history. But other distinctions have recently been addressed from a corporate perspective.

Much attention has been given to the essential distinction between heritage and history from a corporate perspective (Balmer, 2013; Burghausen & Balmer, 2014b; Urde *et al.*, 2007). Based on other social sciences' contributions (Fowler, 1992; Hobsbawm & Ranger, 1992; Lowenthal, 1998), authors show heritage is of the past, present and future, unlike history that is grounded in the past.

Heritage has been distinguished from the concept of the past and past-related concepts, namely memory, history, tradition, nostalgia and provenance from a corporate perspective (Burghausen & Balmer, 2014b), but also from the concept of authenticity (Hudson & Balmer, 2013).

Finally, patrimony and legacy appear as two dimensions of heritage in English: "on the one hand heritage is aligned to patrimony and in another sense legacy" (Balmer, 2013, p. 302). The corporate legacy (or bequest) dimension received particular attention; it is stated that it can manifest itself both internally and externally (Balmer, 2013).

Our contribution builds on this foundational work of the Anglophone perspective and sheds light on a Francophone one. Although heritage, but also inheritance, patrimony and legacy, come from French, their semantic evolutions vary in some way in both languages. Following Balmer's call for words' historiography, the next section puts those words in a historic perspective to understand how their meaning differs.

"Patrimoine" and "héritage": Two "faux amis" with four distinctive meanings

"How shall we put corporate brand heritage in French?" was the starting point of this reflexion. "Shall we use *héritage* or *patrimoine*?" Those two words have close meanings, and we could not decide between the intuitive (*héritage*) or the UNESCO[1] (*patrimoine*). The search for the right word to adapt brand heritage led us to a conceptual difference anchored in the French context, key for further research on corporate heritage in the Francophone sphere, and relevant in English as it differentiates heritage from inheritance.

In this second section, we synthesise the main elements of our work regarding the origins of two different meanings for *patrimoine* and *héritage* in a Francophone context. Following Balmer's advice (2013), we deconstructed their meanings with contributions from different disciplines and list hereafter four major distinctions. So as to make those distinctions relevant to an Anglophone context, we bring elements of English context informed by research on the evolutions of the words *heritage* and *inheritance* from Middle English (Kuhn & Reidy, 1963, 1968, 1970, 1980) to contemporary English (Brown, 1993a, 1993b).

Action or content

In the French law, *héritage* refers to the procedure that guarantees and regulates the transmission of assets from one generation to another, as well as the content (i.e. the assets themselves); whereas *patrimoine* only refers to the content (Gotman, 2006). This first distinction is consistent to what we observe in the French Academy's dictionary, which distinguishes two meanings for "*héritage*" (the act and the content of transmission), whereas the "*patrimoine*" always and only refers to the content.[2] A similar distinction exists in English between inheritance (content or action) and heritage (content only).

Neutral or appropriated

Héritage, just like inheritance, is the "raw" result of a transmission from the predecessors. It is a given, received as a whole, made of elements that can appear either positive or negative, and shall be maintained in its integrity, that is cannot be the object of divisions and selections without losing its meaning (Saint-Pol, 2010). Yet, both French and English laws allow disclaiming an inheritance to protect the successor from the consequences of an inheritance he/she could not be responsible for.[3] No specific adoption process is required at this stage; an inheritance is not a social construction: it exists per se.

As opposed to this aspect of inheritance definition, *patrimoine*, so as heritage in English, only exists through an appropriation process (Chastel, 1986; Fowler, 1992; Leniaud, 1992). That process is required on the individual level: an inheritance that is not disclaimed eventually becomes part of someone's heritage. It goes through a process of inventory, some elements being sold or abandoned, and others appearing constitutive of the family's identity become part of the heritage to be transmitted later on. A similar process occurs on the collective level, through a process of identification to the objects (Lowenthal, 1998). For example, the assets belonging to the clergy in France's ancien régime were secularised before being accepted as part of the national heritage by the revolutionary institutions (Desvallées, 1995).

From past to present or embracing past, present and future

According to the French Academy, *héritage* is only related to transmissions from the past to the present, whereas *patrimoine* encompasses two kinds of transmissions: from the past to the present, or from the present to the future. *Patrimoine* is dynamic and includes the inherited assets as well as those added by the current generation with the idea of transmitting them to their successors. For anthropologists, any society sorts its owned objects; the *patrimoine* corresponds to those objects aimed to be handed down to the next generation (Heinich, 2009).

Inheritance only refers to the transmission handed down by a predecessor, whereas heritage conveys a concern for the future. The definition of heritage is that "which is or may be inherited" (Brown, 1993a, p. 1223), both what is and can one day be. That distinction is consistent with a key aspect of corporate heritage: the concern for past, present and future (Balmer, 2011a).

Private or public

This fourth distinction is strongly related to the French context (Desvallées, 1995); its operationalisation in English is not automatic and could be discussed (Balmer, 2013). *Patrimoine* exists in Old French with a similar meaning to its English equivalent (patrimony). Even if the Academy maintains relatively stable meanings in the French language, it remains sensible (alterable) to some important events such as the French Revolution.

For Desvallées (1995), the 1790s gave birth to a modern meaning of *patrimoine*. The revolutionary experience raised an important question regarding the monuments inherited from the ancien régime. As many aristocrats emigrated to other European monarchies, some symbols of the former ruling class were destroyed.

TABLE 12.2 The four distinctions between inheritance/*héritage* and heritage/*patrimoine*

Inheritance/Héritage	Heritage/Patrimoine
Process and content	Content only
Neutral/imposed	Appropriated
Past to present	Past to present to future
Private	Public

Facing this reality, it was decided that those monuments would be inventoried (Abbé Grégoire inventory in 1794; see Chastel, 1986, for details), and those being particularly relevant should be protected, not as symbols of the former regime, but as characteristic of a *génie français*, relevant for the whole nation. The concept of "*patrimoine national*" (national heritage) is therefore created, based on the Latin notion of "*res communis*", meaning "common things". It applies to the water or the air, but, since the Revolution, also to the nation's assets previously owned by the Church or nobilities. Such a concept does not exist in England; the National Trust or the Crown Assets are of every English citizen but remain private property on a legal basis.

As such, in French, *héritage* mainly relates to private matters whereas *patrimoine* is much broader and characteristic of public assets (Jadé, 2006). We acknowledge the financial use of *patrimoine* for personal assets (in French, asset management is *gestion de patrimoine*) but stress the fact it also has a public dimension that may be its own characteristic.

This is consistent with the contemporary meanings of the English dictionaries where inheritance refers to private matters (within a family or an institution). Patrimony and heritage mainly refer to the public sphere: through the extension process to abstract and collective forms of assets (Leniaud, 1992; Lowenthal, 1998).

The concept of *patrimoine* has kept expanding since the French Revolution (Chastel, 1986). It now refers to cultural and social elements which deserved protection in order to be transmitted to the next generation. In doing so, Leniaud (1992) writes that France's use of *patrimoine* is similar to Great Britain's use of the word *heritage*.

Implications for management studies: The two dimensions of corporate heritage in the Francophone perspective

This approach by the meanings of French words and the four distinctions stated in other disciplines (see Table 12.2) provide us with an interesting contribution to the use of heritage and inheritance in management. It appears that two dimensions should indeed be distinguished. We will now define those two dimensions, as well as the areas of study they refer to, and illustrate them with an example.

The study of inheritance (French: héritage*) in management*

Based on what has been developed above, here is a double definition for what can mean corporate inheritance: all material or symbolic, active or passive assets belonging to a company's private sphere, handed down from a former corporation or from a founder, before they go through any strategic process; the processes through which those assets are transmitted.

A corporate inheritance is for example the France Telecom inheritance within Orange (after the company changed its name). It can also be used to name those assets handed down after a company has been taken over by another: the Cadbury inheritance in Kraft Foods. The concept also names the processes such as rebranding, acquisitions or influences.

Studying corporate inheritance is about studying those assets, the way they have been transmitted, before any attempt to manage those assets through marketing (i.e. decide to eliminate one or promote another), or outside any process of communication to stakeholders outside the company (e.g. using one or several elements in an advertising campaign).

It can also be about studying the modalities of transmission through fusion and acquisitions, a rebranding or the creation of a company. It could be for example a historian or journalist's work of tracing back and explaining how a particular inheritance was handled after a rebranding: Who took what decision? What was the influence of the legal, financial or marketing departments in the decision-making process? And so forth.

In that framework, most of the business historians' work studies corporate inheritance as they do not seek to make them relevant to the present or future of the company but focus on the elements as they were transmitted.

The study of corporate heritage (French: patrimoine*)*

Likewise, here is a definition of corporate heritage based on the distinctions stated above: all symbolic or tangible assets a corporation deliberately extracts from its actual, ideal or imagined past in order to make it public, with the intention to hand it down to the next generation of managers.

Studying corporate heritage or corporate patrimony means to study those assets as they have deliberately been selected to be publicised to different stakeholders. It can be the study of the strategies a company uses to construct its heritage from its inheritance and its current assets (see Hudson's [2011] work on how Carnival reconstructed Cunard's brand heritage from its legacy). It can also be the different actions a company takes to communicate this heritage (see Burghausen & Balmer's [2014a] work on Shepherd Neame's implementation of the corporate heritage identity). It also addresses the study of the protection and enrichment of the brand heritage with future prospective (see the description of the stewardship position in Urde *et al.* [2007]). Finally, it can be the study of stakeholders' responses to the communication process (Wiedmann *et al.*, 2011).

How family inheritance is turned into corporate heritage: Ferrero France case

Ferrero International S.A. (2013 turnover: €8.1bl[4]) is the fourth biggest company of the confectionery industry still owned by the founding family (Blombäck & Brunninge, 2013). Ferrero France is the French subsidiary, whose brands are leaders in their markets by far (as an example, Nutella has 85 to 89 per cent of market share on chocolate spread[5]).

Following case study methods commonly used in corporate heritage (Balmer, 2011a; Hudson, 2011; Urde *et al.*, 2007), this example is based on participant observation and executive interviews when one of the authors served in the consultancy appointed by Ferrero France to raise its corporate profile between 2008 and 2012.[6] Additional interviews and archive work were conducted in 2014 during the redaction of the case. It seeks to illustrate the difference between a corporate inheritance and a corporate heritage through the example of a company building on its past to reveal itself as a corporation.

Back in 2008, Ferrero France was considered a "shy" corporation whose strategy was only to communicate through its very powerful brands (Nutella, Kinder, Tic Tac, Mon Chéri, Ferrero Rochers, etc.). This strategy was related to a culture of discretion within the group symbolised by the family's silence: "They literally embody the company but they never appear in the media."[7] In France, the subsidiary had been facing PR issues regarding child obesity since 2003 and was somehow forced to engage in defensive media relations, as a company "responsible" for those brands.

The opportunity of revealing the company in a more favourable way was then debated inside the subsidiary, and this is when the PR consultancy was appointed: "In 2008, we appointed the agency to move from a reactive communication to a proactive one, and therefore construct corporate messages to reveal the company behind the brands."[8]

Two different concepts to name two different realities

To achieve this goal, part of the work operated by the consultancy had been to transform elements of inheritance into heritage to be used in public relations; this case focuses on the family values.

A very dense inheritance was available to build on. Another former consultant interviewed says, "We were doing archaeologists' work; we were digging in an incredibly rich informational base."[9] This work was first grounded in the past and only afterwards eventually fed the PR strategy. It could be named business history, although it never had the scientific purpose, ambition or even connotation that history necessarily holds. At this stage, Ferrero France had still no public communication as a corporation whatsoever; all this happened through internal meetings and archive work between the agency and the company. We suggest the concept of corporate inheritance to name this reality, quite different from the following phase.

Once the agency and the managers had listed elements of the company's past, it was decided to focus on some aspects of the family values and to let some others aside. The family is then very present in the CSR communication, for example in the following human resources message: "As a family business, Ferrero France cares not only for its employees but also their families. Ferrero France offers a kindergarten service, and also a senior club for retired employees to gather and socialise." In every press kit or key messages platform mentioning human resources, this was always linked to historical references: "This way of caring for the employees' families is not a PR hook; it is rooted in Ferrero's corporate heritage." The same reference to a family corporate heritage was put to use in other CSR operations (for example in sponsoring), and also to support the brands (particularly Kinder and Nutella).

On the other hand, other elements remained part of the inheritance and were never chosen as part of the heritage. The religiosity of the family, somehow related to the CSR decisions, was "taboo"[10] in a deeply laic country like France. This echoes the contribution by Hakala *et al.* (2011) about cultural heritage: "assume the catholic aspect of the inheritance would have generated sarcasm in France, so we decide not to use it" says a consultant in an interview. Another taboo is the family itself: "They are the founder and owner but never speak publicly, nor do their wives or children."[11]

We suggest using the concept of corporate heritage to name this second reality. As we detailed in this chapter, this example shows how two different realities appear in this example.

We consider the family values showcased on the corporate website[12,13] today as corporate heritage. They are obviously public, whereas those same values were private back in 2008; they had existed for decades but were never exposed (private/public distinction). Those family values were not all promoted as a package, as we saw some are still kept private; a selection process was operated within what was available (given/chose distinction). All the available had been transmitted from the past to the present, but only those selected are identified as important to transmit to the next generation (past to present/past-present-future distinction). And finally, the study of the original content or the modalities of transmission from the past to present appears as a first phase, clearly different than the elaboration and promotion of the content (process-content/content only distinction) (see Figure 12.1).

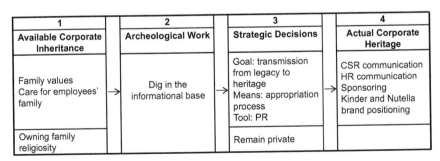

1	2	3	4
Available Corporate Inheritance	**Archeological Work**	**Strategic Decisions**	**Actual Corporate Heritage**
Family values Care for employees' family	Dig in the informational base	Goal: transmission from legacy to heritage Means: appropriation process Tool: PR	CSR communication HR communication Sponsoring Kinder and Nutella brand positioning
Owning family religiosity		Remain private	

FIGURE 12.1 From legacy to heritage in four steps (Ferrero France example)

Conclusion

This chapter deals with a theoretical contribution to corporate heritage, in line with existing work on the foundational concepts (Balmer, 2011b, 2013; Burghausen & Balmer, 2014b; Urde *et al.*, 2007); it focuses on the epistemological distinction between *héritage* and *patrimoine* in French applied to corporate heritage. Building on Balmer's (2013) call for investigating key words' historiography, we show how the Latin origins and the French cultural context have shaped the contemporary meanings of both words. We build on four epistemological distinctions (content and process/content only; private/public; imposed/appropriated; and from past to present/from past to present to future) to suggest a definition for the study of corporate inheritance (French: *héritage d'entreprise*) different from the study of corporate heritage (French: *patrimoine d'entreprise*) and illustrate this difference by the Ferrero France case example.

This so-called Francophone perspective on corporate heritage has several implications for scholars in both linguistic spheres. The difference between French and English meanings of heritage was acknowledged by prior work (Balmer, 2013), but the Francophone perspective had not been detailed. This contribution, namely the application to corporate marketing literature of the epistemological distinction between *patrimoine* and *heritage*, will help French scholars willing to investigate corporate heritage. In a globalised academia where ideas mainly circulate in English, the development of research in "local" languages (French, Spanish, German . . .) should consider translation as an epistemological issue rather than a linguistic one (Usunier, 2010). Since languages reflect cultural and historical backgrounds, the choice of words to adapt an English concept is a key aspect of the theoretical development. Our example with heritage shows the epistemological work produced in French is also relevant in English as it addresses a distinction that had not been addressed before: heritage and inheritance.

The French perspective is also relevant for managers, although it can seem abstract and far from their preoccupations. We think there are key implications for practitioners, as they benefit from clarity as much as academics do. We think managers aware of the distinctions we state here will have more ease to empower their corporate past as Ferrero France did. Managers can also use the proper words to explain, command or report about what they are doing. Many times, advertising agencies and marketing departments seem not to understand what the other means; this is the kind of work that aims to help them in communicating to each other. Managers need to implement corporate heritage marketing. This consists in understanding the difference between inheritance and heritage to make strategic decisions and decide which facets of their corporate inheritance they want to transfer to their heritage. By doing so, they will choose from their corporate inheritance appropriated values and facts that will be communicated publicly not only to anchor their image in the past but also to empower the future in a communication perspective. Corporate heritage marketing could therefore become a strategic tool for brands.

The case of Ferrero France offers a step-by-step example of how a shy corporation has put to use its inheritance into a corporate heritage strategy. The different messages (CSR, HR, sponsoring, etc.) leveraging corporate heritage appeared to have more substance and more credibility. What was considered a drawback for the company (having been absent from the media) was flipped over into a competitive advantage by the agency through a corporate heritage strategy. The case example shows how a consultancy can help a company in fabricating a corporate heritage through an archeologists' work. The importance of the vision from the outside is key in the religious aspect; the role of the consultancy was determinant on that respect. Managers can use this example internally to promote the adoption of a corporate heritage strategy. Teachers might also use the case with students.

As the famous verse from Boileau says: *"Ce que l'on conçoit bien s'énonce clairement / Et les mots pour le dire arrivent aisément"* ("Whatever is well conceived is clearly said / And the words to say it flow with ease") (Boileau, 1972, p. 52, verses 153–154). That verse stresses the importance of words and their connection with the conception; we do not master any concept as long as we do not master the language and vice versa. Let's hope this work contributes to clarify the use academics and managers do of corporate heritage.

Key point

1   Heritage and inheritance describe different realities of the corporations and must be differentiated.

Questions

Three for academics

1   What conceptual contributions on corporate heritage could come out of further semantic research on the following words' historiography in English: heritage, legacy, inheritance and patrimony?
2   In the French perspective, is it appropriate to call corporate heritage the study of internal management issues?
3   Can similar scales be used to measure heritage, legacy, inheritance and patrimony?

Four for practitioners

1   Is the vision from the outside brought by the consultancy mandatory to a successful corporate heritage strategy?
2   How does one make sure an undesired inheritance never gets public?
3   How can corporate heritage marketing help managers build a corporate image?
4   What are the different steps in implementing a corporate heritage marketing strategy?

Notes

* This chapter is based on the first author's dissertation (Pecot, 2016).
1 "World Heritage" is translated as "Patrimoine Mondial".
2 By extension, *patrimoine* is also used with a financial meaning as assets in English (i.e. asset management is translated *gestion de patrimoine*).
3 For French law: Code civil, Article 722
4 http://www.ferrero.com/the-group/business/a-growing-turnover (visited on 14 Nov. 2014)
5 http://www.lemonde.fr/vous/article/2012/11/14/nutella-est-entre-dans-la-categorie-des-marques-mythiques_1789429_3238.html (visited on 25 Nov. 2014)
6 Aspect Consulting France/Gootenberg was appointed from 01/09/2008 to 31/08/2012; the observation lasted between 01/09/2008 and 30/11/2011.
7 Executive interview, 08/12/2014
8 Executive interview, 08/12/2014
9 Consultant interview, 08/12/2014
10 Ibid.
11 Ibid.
12 http://www.ferrero.fr/histoire-famille-ferrero (visited on 14 Nov. 2014)
13 http://www.ferrero.fr/engagements-ferrero

References

Balmer, J. M. T. (2011a). Corporate heritage brands and the precepts of corporate heritage brand management: Insights from the British Monarchy on the eve of the royal wedding of Prince William (April 2011) and Queen Elizabeth II's Diamond Jubilee (1952–2012). *Journal of Brand Management, 18*(8), 517–544. doi:10.1057/bm.2011.21

Balmer, J. M. T. (2011b). Corporate heritage identities, corporate heritage brands and the multiple heritage identities of the British Monarchy. *European Journal of Marketing, 45*(9/10), 1380–1398. doi:10.1108/03090561111151817

Balmer, J. M. T. (2013). Corporate heritage, corporate heritage marketing, and total corporate heritage communications: What are they? What of them? *Corporate Communications: An International Journal, 18*(3), 290–326. doi:10.1108/CCIJ-05-2013-0031

Balmer, J. M. T., Greyser, S., & Urde, M. (2006). The crown as a corporate brand: Insights from monarchies. *Journal of Brand Management, 14*(1/2), 137–161. doi:10.1057/palgrave.bm.2550031

Blombäck, A., & Brunninge, O. (2013). The dual opening to brand heritage in family businesses. *Corporate Communications: An International Journal, 18*(3), 327–346.

Boileau, N. (1972). *L'art poétique* (Univers de., p. 52). Paris: Bordas.

Brown, L. (Ed.). (1993a). *The new shorter Oxford English dictionary on historical principles, volume 1 A-M.* Oxford: Clarendon Press.

Brown, L. (Ed.). (1993b). *The new shorter Oxford English dictionary on historical principles, volume 2 N-Z.* Oxford: Clarendon Press.

Burghausen, M., & Balmer, J. M. T. (2014a). Corporate heritage identity management and the multi-modal implementation of a corporate heritage identity. *Journal of Business Research, 67*(11), 2311–2323. doi:10.1016/j.jbusres.2014.06.019

Burghausen, M., & Balmer, J. M. T. (2014b). Repertoires of the corporate past: Explanation and framework: Introducing an integrated and dynamic perspective. *Corporate Communications: An International Journal, 19*(4), 384–402.

Chantrell, G. (Ed.). (2002). *The Oxford dictionary of word histories.* Oxford: Oxford University Press.

Chastel, A. (1986). La notion de patrimoine. In Nora Pierre (Ed.), *Les lieux de mémoire* (pp. 405–450). Paris: Gallimard.

Desvallées, A. (1995). Termes muséologiques de base. *Publics et Musées, 7*(7), 134–158.

Fowler, P. (1992). Heritage: A post-modernist perspective. In D. Uzzell (Ed.), *Heritage interpretation, volume 1: The natural and built environment* (pp. 48–56). London and New York: Belheaven Press.

Gotman, A. (2006). *L'héritage*. Paris: Presses Universitaires de France.

Hakala, U., Lätti, S., & Sandberg, B. (2011). Operationalising brand heritage and cultural heritage. *Journal of Product & Brand Management, 20*(6), 447–456. doi:10.1108/10610421111166595

Heinich, N. (2009). *La fabrique du patrimoine: de la cathédrale à la petite cuillère*. Paris: Les Editions de la MSH.

Hobsbawm, E., & Ranger, T. (1992). *The invention of tradition*. Cambridge: Cambridge University Press.

Hudson, B. T. (2011). Brand heritage and the renaissance of Cunard. *European Journal of Marketing, 45*(9/10), 1538–1556. doi:10.1108/03090561111151880

Hudson, B. T., & Balmer, J. M. T. (2013). Corporate heritage brands: Mead's theory of the past. *Corporate Communications: An International Journal, 18*(3), 347–361.

Jadé, M. (2006). *Patrimoine immatériel: perspectives d'interprétation du concept de patrimoine*. Paris: L'Harmattan.

Kuhn, M. S., & Reidy, J. (Eds.). (1963). *Middle English dictionary G-H*. Ann Arbor: The University of Michigan Press.

Kuhn, M. S., & Reidy, J. (Eds.). (1968). *Middle English dictionary I-K*. Ann Arbor: The University of Michigan Press.

Kuhn, M. S., & Reidy, J. (Eds.). (1970). *Middle English dictionary L*. Ann Arbor: The University of Michigan Press.

Kuhn, M. S., & Reidy, J. (Eds.). (1980). *Middle English dictionary P*. Ann Arbor: The University of Michigan Press.

Leniaud, J.-M. (1992). *L'utopie française: essai sur le patrimoine*. Paris: Mengès.

Lowenthal, D. (1998). Fabricating heritage. *History & Memory, 10*(1), 5–24.

Pecot, F. (2016). Consumers' responses to brand heritage: Cognitive and affective paths. Aix-Marseille Université. Defended on the 13th of December.

Saint-Pol, A. (2010). *À quel type de légitimité renvoie l'institution de l'héritage?* Nantes: M-Editer.

Urde, M., Greyser, S. A., & Balmer, J. M. T. (2007). Corporate brands with a heritage. *Journal of Brand Management, 15*(1), 4–19. doi:10.1057/palgrave.bm.2550106

Usunier, J-C. (2010). Langue et équivalence conceptuelle en management interculturel. *Le Libellio d'Aegis, 6*(2), 3–25.

Wiedmann, K.-P., Hennigs, N., Schmidt, S., & Wuestefeld, T. (2011). Drivers and outcomes of brand heritage: Consumers' perception of heritage brands in the automotive industry. *The Journal of Marketing Theory and Practice, 19*(2), 205–220. doi:10.2753/MTP1069-6679190206

INDEX

Page numbers in *italics* indicate figures and tables.

Adams, John 82
adaptation, focus 186
adoption (ownership taking) 187
affinity *100–1*; importance 6, *30*; trust/authenticity, relationship 30
Akvavit, production 262
Anttila 15; research settings/examination 278–9
Anttila, Kalle 280
Apple, success 275–6
appreciation (valuing) 187
augmented role identities 7, 106, 114–15; corporate heritage, relationship 223; example *115*; notion 223
authenticity *100–1*, 160–1; constructed authenticity 160–1; dimensions 160; iconic authenticity 160–1; importance 6, *30*; indexical authenticity 160; nostalgia, relationship 160–2; staged authenticity 160–1; trust/affinity, relationship 30
average variances extracted (AVE) *232, 234*
awareness, timespan 279–80

Bachand, Stephen 251
Bagehot, Walter 50, 66
Balmer, John M.T. 1, 3, 10–15, 108
Barre: characteristics/trait constancy *268*; examination 263–4
Battle of Hastings 52, 53
beginnings, special mnemonic status 142
belongingness, sense 186, 207–8

Bertelsmann: characteristics/trait constancy *268*; examination 264–5
bilateral organisational-stakeholder trust, importance *100–1*
bilateral trust, importance *30*
Billes, A.J. 248
Billes, Martha/Owen 248
binary division 15
BMW 94, 155; family control 260
brand heritage: importance 173; maintenance 52–4
branding: iconic branding *93*; retro branding *93*
Brand Promise 55
brands: archaeology 176; heritage brands 49; heritage brands, framework *157*; iconic characteristics 49; key values, relationship 49; prestige (rental), endorsement (usage) 49; promise 85; provenance 176; space, occupation 38; strategy 176; support, brand communities (usage) 49; symbolism, maintenance 52–4; values 49; visual/verbal identifiers 48
Brio: characteristics/trait constancy *268*; examination 265–6
Britannica 291
British Broadcasting Corporation (BBC) 62, 84–5, 113; coronation, televising 62; multiple role identity 114–15
British Co-operative Movement 90
British Crown: corporate brand management, normative advice 54, 58, 59, 61, 65–6;

heritage corporate brand determinants 47–8;
historical evolution 29; methodological
approach 51–70; political power, absence
80; study 49; Teutonic links 58
British Monarchy 11; appearance 22; context
79; corporate branding criteria 48–9;
corporate heritage identities (8Rs) 30, 41;
detractors 81; German Dynastic name
58; identity literature 50–1; institution
type 22–3; literature 48; management,
corporate brand (usage) 52–65; multiple
heritage identities 21; re-branding exercise
59; revised heritage identity framework
30, *31*; scrutiny 44; traditional power 22;
travails/prevails 45–6
Bröderna Ivarsson I Osby (BRIO) 265
Brunninge, Olof 14–15
Buddhism 225
Burghausen, Mario 4, 12, 16
business history, literature 51

Cadbury, study 261–2
Canadian Tire Corporation 14, 247–51;
David Jones, contrast 254
Canadian Tire Heritage Collection 249
captivation 1–2
Carnival Cruise Line 290, 292
Carolingian Coronation 63
Caronia 292–3
Catholic Church, identity traits 36
ceaseless multigenerational stakeholder 7,
106, 115–16, 222
Ceremonial London 56
change, anticipation/enactment 55–8
Character Culture Communication
Conceptualisation Constituencies
Covenant (6Cs) 69–70
Charlemagne *see* Emperor Charlemagne
Chen, Weifeng 4, 13
China: ethnicities/religions/traditions 217;
ideologies 224–5; modernisation, impact
236; national identity, relationship 224–5;
religion, relationship 224–5; religion,
significance 226
Chinese corporate heritage brands,
multifaceted characteristic 216
Chinese culture measures, impacts (direct-
effects arguments) 230–1
Chinese heritage tourism, context 216–17
Chinese identity/civilisation, Tong Ren
Tang (impact) 236
Chinese national identity 224–5; conferring
235–6; Tong Ren Tang, relationship 235
Chinese philosophies/religions, significance
225

CHIS *see* Corporate Heritage Identity
Stewardship
chronicling, usage 67
Churchill, Winston 62
civil religion 227
Civil Religion perspective 236
class associations 108, *111*
clock-time view 277–8
closed-source view, involvement 277
closeness (proximity) 186
collective representation, formation 276–7
College of William and Mary, association 40
communication, usage 67
company-related experiences, interpretation
284
company, temporal repositioning 138
composite reliability (CR) 233–4
conceptual categories *184*
conceptual mapping, usage 183
Confessions (Saint Augustine) 107
confirmatory factor analysis (CFA) 234
Confucianism 215–16, 224–5, *225*–6;
importance 237
constructed authenticity 160–1
construct measures *233*
contextualisation *184*
continuance, sense 186, 205–7
continuity 52, 175; corporate identity/brand
heritage, relationship 65; focus 101, 186;
long-term continuity, focus 176
Co-operate Bank 90
Cooper, Holly 14
coronation, ceremony 52–3
corporate authority 188
corporate brand heritage 288–9;
methodology 289–91
corporate branding 38; criteria 48–9; family
firms, family heritage incorporation
261–2; theories 68–70
corporate brands 44; chronicling 66–8;
covenant 84; emotional ownership,
location 62–5; identification 132;
literature 46, 48; management,
multidisciplinary character 46; operation
84; overview 83; relevance 85; reputation,
loss 61; understanding 44–5; usage 52–65
corporate communication 108; perspectives
104–6; perspectives, initial reflections 132–3
corporate culture 250–2
corporate heritage 142–4; augmented role
identity, relationship 223; branding,
family heritage (opportunities/risks)
259; canon, exponential growth 221;
canon, foundational articles 98–102;
Catholic scope 91–4; characteristics 222,

222, 248–52; concepts 8–10; conceptual framework *231*; connoisseurship, concepts/theories 11–12; construct, disquisition *100*; conversion 309–10; corporate inheritance, contrast 302; criteria 109–17; culture 9; customer perspective 275; design *111–12,* 248–50; dimensions 174, 307–8; downsides 123–4; emerging approach 254–5; family businesses, relationship 14–15; footprints 28; foundational literature 220–1; foundational precepts, criteria 106–17; foundations 219–22; image 15–16; importance 95–6; inheritance 15–16; institution trust *116*; interest, rise 2–3; latent approach 254; latent theoretical contributions 124–5; management 15–16; management studies, implications 307–8; monarchies, impact 10–11; nature, delineation 174; notion 1–2; perspective 3; problems/possibilities 95–7; stewardship 176; strategic resource 178; study 308; style *111–12*; sustainability theory 117–23; sustainable corporate heritage, model *253*; total communications 89, 118; total communications, explication 120–1; total communications, focus/nexus/effect *121*; total corporate communications, quadripartite dimensions *122*; total corporate heritage marketing communications 8–9; traits 91; transtemporal characteristic 143; utility/possibilities/complexity 96–7; value 4; vibrant approach 253–4; vibrant approach, latent approach (contrast) 247

corporate heritage brand management *100*; approaches 288; modus operandi 66–8; multidisciplinary perspective 101–2; perspective 296–8

corporate heritage brand notion 220; development 220–1

corporate heritage brands 5, 8, 21, 23, 94, 151; characterisation *99*; characteristics 174–5; context 171–2; dimensions 5; discussion 162; framework, unification 157–60; Mead, application 153–7; multidisciplinary approach 11; notion 4, 98; notion, particularisation 5; senior manager balancing 4

corporate heritage communications (CHC): doctrine, quadripartite characteristic 122; internal familial legacy CHC 123; legacy corporate heritage communications (legacy (CHC) 9, 122, 123; primary

corporate heritage communications (primary CHC) 9, 122; secondary corporate heritage communications (secondary CHC) 9, 122; tertiary corporate heritage communications (tertiary CHC) 9, 122, 123

corporate heritage identities 8, 10, 21, 23; British types 113; characteristics 174–5; construct *100–1*; context 171–2; criteria 6–7; 8Rs 30, 41; findings 29–30, 184–8; footprints 28; management *100–1*; managers, reflections/directions 31; methodology 28–9; monarchies, impact 10–11; notion 5; profit 90–1; reflections 40; research method 180–4; revelations/concealment 96; study, rationale 177–8

corporate heritage identity stewardship 12–14, 169–70; awareness dimensions/dispositions *185*; discussion 191–4; findings 184–8; limitations 197; practical implication 196–7; research method 180–4; study, rationale 177–8; theoretical framework 188–91, *189*; theoretical implications 194–6; theory *189*

Corporate Heritage Identity Stewardship (CHIS) 184–5; awareness dimensions 186, 190; disposition 187, 188; managerial disposition 186

corporate heritage institutions 115; reappraisal 117; value 94

corporate heritage-in-use, cases 247

corporate heritage marketing 8, 89, 118; definition 118; doctrine, maintenance 118; explication 118–19; logic 118; logic, benefits 119; mix *119*; mix, dimensions/explanations *120*

corporate heritage tourism 125, 222–3; brand attractiveness 12–14; brand attractiveness, national identity (relationship) 214; corporate heritage tourism brands, relationship 215–16; foundations 219–22; notion 215; royal/imperial associations, significance 236–7

corporate history 140

corporate identity 38–9; theories 68–70

corporate image heritage 15, 275–6, 278–82; mapping, three-dimensional tool *282*

corporate images, discussion/implications 283–4

corporate inheritance: corporate heritage, contrast 302; management studies, implications 307–8

corporate-level constructs 23; explanations *24*; scrutiny *24–6, 92–3*

corporate-level marketing, theoretical contribution 144–5
corporate-level scholarship 135
corporate marketing 38–9; approach 131; developments 97; explanation/ framework 130; implications 145; initial reflections 132–3; integrated/dynamic perspective 130; management 69; mix 70; perspectives 104–6, 169; significance 105–6; structure 131–2; theoretical contribution 144–5; theories 68–70; theory, perception 69
corporate memory 139
corporate nostalgia 141–2
corporate past 138–9
corporate past, conceptual bridge 137
corporate past, repertoires 130; foundational past-related corporate-level concepts 137; literature, development stages 135; modes 136–45; schematic framework 143
corporate provenance 142
corporate purpose 188
corporate survival 116–17
corporate tradition 140–1
crises, response 58–60
Crowned Republic 82
crucifix, exception 53
CSR decisions 310
cultural symbolic constitutions 227
Cunard 288; acquisition 292; acquisition, positioning 292–3; Carnival Cruise Line 292; early history 291; examination 288, 291–3
Cunard, Samuel 154
Cunard White Star Line 291
Custodianship Awareness 190
custodianship awareness 187–8
customers (corporate image heritage), mapping (three-dimensional tool) 282
customs 23

Daoism 13, 215–16, 224–6; importance 237
Da Shi Lan 214
Dashilan street/district 218, 232
data analysis, process 183
data triangulation 183
David Jones 14, 247–52; Canadian Tire Corporation, contrast 254; iconic stores, development 254
Da Zhai Men 219
de Barnier, Virginie 16
differentiation, claim 153
Divine Right 56
documentation, usage 67
dystopia 123

Edward see King Edward
Elizabeth see Princess Elizabeth; Queen Elizabeth
emergence, assumption 181
emotional ownership, location 62–5
empathy 52, 62–5; focus 101; marketing, relationship 66
Emperor Charlemagne, coronation 47
empirical theory-building study 170
endorsement, usage 49
English Coronation service 52–3
English literature, usages 302
en passant reference 2
ethos 108, 110
event-time view 277–8
external/internal tri-generational heredity 106, 109–13; criterion 113
external legacies 113
external tri-generational heredity 113

Falck: characteristics/trait constancy 268; examination 266
family: Chinese notions 229; firms, characteristics 260; history 261; inheritance, corporate heritage (conversion) 309–10; ownership 248; relationships 229; risks 266–7
family heritage: incorporation 261–2; opportunities/risks 259
faux amis 305
Ferrero France, examination 309–10
Ferrero International S.A. 309
50-year corporate heritage requisite 112–13
firms, risk 264–6
five-stage modus operandi 67
Ford, family control 260
foundational past-related corporate-level concepts: corporate past repertoires 137; instrumental past-related corporate-level concepts, contrast 133–6
foundational precepts, criteria 106–17
founding dates, meanings 158
France Telecom, corporate inheritance 308
Francophone perspective, corporate heritage (dimensions) 307–8
future: embracing 306; senior manager awareness 4

génie français 307
George see King George
"God Save the King" (anthem) 79
governance structures 259
Grängesbergs Bryggeri 262–3, 266–7
Great Depression 252

Great War, British Monarchy (association) 60

Greyser, Stephen A. 1, 15–17

group associations 108, *111*

Harold *see* King Harold

heritage: action, content (contrast) 305; Anglophone perspective 303–7; awareness 187; branding, family heritage (inclusion opportunities) 262–4; characteristics 27–8, 304; Chinese approaches *225*; communication 173; competencies 252; construct 161–2; context 27; context, image (usefulness) 276–7; corporate heritage 142–4; defining 102–3; dimensions, evidence 159–60; dimensions, metacategories 159; effects, object 159; founding dates, meanings 158; heritage of heritage 219; history, idealised/romanticised versions 158; identity framework, revision 30; image/time, interrelated concepts *276–8*; impact 157–8; implied heritage 154–5; importance 103–6; innate heritage 159; Latin/French roots *304*; legacy, conversion *310*; marketing 23, *93*; mythical heritage 156–7; national heritage, meaningfulness 227; neutral/appropriated characteristic 305–6; notion 103, 173; notion, assessment 221; organisations 1; overview 102–3; past-related concepts, contrast 304–5; *patrimoine* (contrast) *307*; phenomenon 95–6; portmanteau notion 219; private/public characteristic 306–7; problems 37–8; projected heritage 159; quotient 220–1, 283; reconstructed heritage 155–6; retro effects 159; safeguarding 254; salience 27; sense 187, 209–10; shared collective memory, relationship 103; significance, delineation *104–5*; stewardship 172, 250; structural heritage 153–4; time, relationship 27–8, 107–8, 277–8; types (differentiation), personal experience (basis) 158; uncovering 176

héritage 16, 303–5; inheritance, contrast *307*; study 308

Heritage Awareness, CHIS awareness dimensions 190

heritage brands 49, 288; differentiation/superiority, claims 153; framework *157*

heritage corporate brands, determinants 47–8

heritage identities 29; identity accretion, relationship 29–30; importance 22; terms 29; trait 108–9

heritage tourism 23, *93*; brand attraction, conceptual framework *231*; Chinese heritage tourism, context 216–17; national identity, relationship 224–5, 227–8; religion, relationship 224–5; representation 228

hermeneutics 38; interactions 183; usage 133

hermeneutic tradition 38

Hipp: characteristics/trait constancy *268*; examination 266–7

Hipp, Claus 267

historical comparison, requirement (absence) 158

historical nostalgia 161

historical truth 284

history 38–9; dimensions 38–9; idealised/romanticised versions 158; importance 289; problems 37–8; role 38–9

Hoshi 90

HSBC, local knowledge 85

Hudson, Bradford T. 4, 12, 15

human thought, conscious/unconscious levels 278

IBM, business solutions 85

iconic authenticity 160–1

iconic branding 23, *93*

"Idea of a Patriot King, The" (Bolingbroke) 55

identity: accretion, heritage identities (relationship) 29–30; literature 50–1; perspectives 104–6

IKEA 15; characteristics/trait constancy *268*; corporate brand 279; examination 265, 278–9; family control 260; offerings 281; research settings 278–9; success 275–6

Il Gattopardo (Lampedusa) 63, 108

image: time/heritage, interrelated concepts 276–8; usefulness 276–7

image heritage: content 281–2; dimension 279–82; mapping, tool 282–3

implied heritage 154–5, 158; explanation 154; illustration 154–5; verification 154

independence, focus 187

Independent Historical Commission 264–5

indeterminancy, assumption 181

indexical authenticity 160

individuality, focus 187

inheritance 16; *héritage*, contrast *307*; Latin/French roots *304*; study 308; transmission 306

innate heritage 159

innovation 56

institutional contexts, heritage identities (importance) 22
institutional custodianship 187–8
institutional perspectives *104–5*
Institutional Role Identities phenomenon, identification 29–30
institutional role identity, notion 223
institutional significance 105–6
institutional success 116–17
institutional trait consistency 7, 222
institutional trait constancy: modes, explanations/examples *110–12*; types *109*
institution trait constancy 106, 108–9
instrumental/foundational past-related corporate-level concepts, contrast 133–6
intellect, impact 37
internal familial legacy CHC 123
internal legacies 113
internal tri-generational heredity 113
interpretation frameworks 283–4
interpretative approaches 133
interviews, overview *182*
invented tradition 23

Johnson, William 294
Jones, Charles Lloyd 248, 251, 254

key temporal focus/foci 280–1
King Carl XVI Gustaf, motto 59
King Edward VII: philanthropic sovereign 57; reign, strategy (change anticipation/enactment) 55–8
King Edward VIII 48; dethronement 60–1; reign, respectability (public favour) 60–1; sovereign, position 60
King George III 48
King George V 48; German Kin perception 58; reign, sensitivity (crises response) 58–60
King George VI: reign, respectability (public favour) 60–1; task 61
King Harold, defeat 53
King Henry II 48
King Henry VIII 48
King John 48
King William (William the Conqueror) 51
King William I: coronation 52; reign, brand symbolism/heritage (maintenance) 52–4
Kulturnation school 224

latent approach 254; vibrant approach, contrast 247
legacy 302; conversion *310*
legacy corporate heritage communication (legacy CHC) 9, 122, 123

Leo III *see* Pope Leo III
Leopard, The (Lampedusa) 63, 108
Likert scales 232
living-entities 93
long-term continuity, focus 176
Lord Stamfordian 59

management: academic domain 177; history, role 36; inheritance, study 308; research 36; tenacity 7, 106, 116–17, 222; zone/activity 65
manufacturing processes 108, *111*
marketing: heritage marketing *93*; heritage, notion 173; history, role 36; Latin school of thought 65; past, role 38–9; scholarship 2
Marriott Corporation, Ritz-Carlton (relationship) 294
Mass Observation Survey 57
Mead, George Herbert 12, 152
Medline, Michael 251
melancholia 23, *92*
Merrilees, Bill 14
metacategories 159
Middle Kingdom 216–17
Millennium, high-end condominium concepts 295
Miller, Dale 14
Modernistic perspective 224
Mohn, Heinrich 264–5
monarchical government 82
Monarchical Rituals 29
monarchies: British Monarchy, multiple heritage identities 21; impact 10–11
monarchs, advice 50
multigenerational customer 121
multigenerational family-owned companies 178
multigenerational stakeholder: dimensions *116*; utility 7, 106, 115–16, 222
multiple corporate heritage role identities, notions *100–1*
multiple heritage identities 21
multiple role identities 6, 114–15, 175; BBC example *115*
Muncaster, Dean 248
museums, usage 155
mythical heritage 156–7, 158; design elements, involvement 159; explanation 156; historical comparison, requirement (absence) 158; illustration 156–7; verification 156
mythical past 264

national cultural perspectives *104–5*
national heritage, meaningfulness 227

national identity: conferring 235; corporate heritage tourism brand attractiveness, relationship 214; heritage tourism, relationship 224–6, 227–8; religion, relationship 224–6
nationality/nationalism 124
national marketing/corporate communication, perspectives 104–6
national perspectives *104–5*
national role identity, effects 234
national roots 37
national significance 105
Nazism, opposition 265
Needham, Joseph 226
non-government organisations (NGOs) 138
non-institutional custodianship 187–8
non-linear relations, assumption 181
nostalgia 23, *92,* 161–2; authenticity, relationship 160–2; corporate nostalgia 141–2; historical nostalgia 161; synthetic nostalgia 162; utopian nostalgia 162

objects, true/false nature 160
omni-temporal corporate heritage trait 107
omni-temporality 6, 106–8, 222
omni-temporal terms 114
omni-temporal traits 10
open coding *184*
open interviews, usage 181–2
organisational heritage 7, 9–10; concepts 8–10; cultural identification 7, 10; identification 7, 10; identity 7, 10; organisational heritage identification, contrast 7
organisational identification 9
organisational phenomenon 169
organisational rationales/cultures 108, *110*
organisational type 108, *110*
organisations, strategy 84
origin myths 142
ownership structures 259

Parliament, State Opening 56
partial least squares (PLS), usage 232
past: Chinese approaches *225;* customer views 280; interrelated primary modes 137; mythical past 264; preservation 37; sadness 141; senior manager awareness 4
past, embracing 306
past-related concepts 7; heritage, contrast 304–5
past-related corporate-level concepts 130; categorisation *136;* instrumental/ foundational past-related corporate-level concepts, contrast 133–6

past, theory (Mead) 151, 152–3
patrimoine 16, 102, 303–5; action/ content 305; neutral/appropriated characteristics 305–6; private/public characteristic 306–7; study 308
patrimoine national 307
Pecot, Fabien 16
People's Republic of China (PRC), creation 217
people, true/false nature 160
permanence, heritage (impact) 157–8
personal experience, basis 158
pertinence 47
Peter, Jens 262
Philips, sense and simplicity 85
Pippin, inauguration 52
Pope Leo III 47
popularity 47–8
Positionality Awareness 186, 187; CHIS awareness dimensions 190
positionality awareness 186–7
postmodern marketing/corporate communication, perspectives 104–6
postmodern perspectives *104–5*
postmodern significance 106
potency, sense 188, 212–13
present: embracing 306; senior manager awareness 4
prestige, rental 49
primary corporate heritage communications (primary CHC) 9, 122
Primordial school 224
Prince Philip, celebrity brand 80
Princess Diana, death 45–6; negative reaction 64
Princess Elizabeth, Solemn Act of Dedication 80
Prince William, celebrity brand 80
Privatbrauerei Ernst Barre 263–4
product/service focus 108, *110*
projected heritage 159
provenance 47; corporate provenance 142; origin 186; power 36; problems 37–8
proximity (closeness) 186
public: emotional ownership, location 62–5
public profile 54–5

Qing Dynasty 217–18
quality levels 108, *111*
Queen Elizabeth: reign 22–23; role 29; status 81
Queen Elizabeth 2 291
Queen Elizabeth I 48

Queen Elizabeth II 50, 218; coronation 62–3; reign, empathy (corporate brand/emotional ownership) 62–5
Queen Mary 2 (QM2) 159–60, 292–3
Queen Victoria: coronation 56; public visibility, absence 54; reign, public profile (visibility) 54–5
Queen Victoria's Golden Jubilee 249

reconstructed heritage 155–6, 158; explanation 155; illustration 155–6; verification 155
reflective memo writing, usage 183
Regal activities 29
relative invariance 175, 266; importance 6; theoretical notions *100–1*
Relative Invariance phenomenon, identification 29
religion: civil religion 227; impact 37; national identity, relationship 224–5
Religious dimensions 29
res communis 307
respectability 52; corporate image/corporation, relationship 66; focus 101; public favour 60–1
responsibility, sense 176, 187–8, 211–12
res publica (public thing) 81
retro branding 23, *93*
revised heritage identity framework 30, *31*
revolution 1–2
Rickmers: characteristics/trait constancy *268*; examination 263
Rickmers, Bertram 263
Rindell, Anne 15
Ritz-Carlton 288; acquisition 294–5; acquisition, positioning 295–6; early history 293–4; evidence 290–1; examination 288, 293–6; Marriott Corporation, relationship 294
Ritz-Carlton Hotel, disposition 296
role identities: augmented role identities 7; multiple role identities 114–15; multiple role identities, importance 6
Rolls-Royce 94
Royal Canadian Mounted Police (RCMP), formation 91
Royal Charter 91
royal/imperial associations, impact 236–7
Royal Religious Regal Ritual Relevant Respected Responsive Regulation (8Rs) 41–3
Royal status 29

Saint Augustine 107
scaffolding 139

SCR roles/responsibilities 118
secondary corporate heritage communications 9, 122
self, sense 186, 209
seminal articles, usage 2–3
semi-structured interviews, usage 181–2
Sense of Belongingness 189
Sense of Continuance, interactions 189
Sense of Potency 190
Sense of Responsibility 190
sensitivity 52, 101; crisis management, relationship 66; temporal sensitivity 132
sensory utilisation 108
services, delivery 108, *111*
shared collective memory, heritage (relationship) 103
shared consciousness 156
Shepherd Neame, Ltd. 12–13, 171, 249; case study-based research design 180; company background 178–9; company information 179; context 178–9
Simpson, Wallis Warfield 60
situatedness, assumption 181
society, impact 37
socioeconomic wealth (SEW) 260
sociological marketing/corporate communication, perspectives 104–6
sociological perspectives *104–5*
sociological significance 105
Solemn Act of Dedication 80
Spencer, Earl 45
Spendrup, Mads Pedersen 262
Spendrups: characteristics/trait constancy *268*; examination 262–3, 266–7
Spendrups Bryggeri, establishment 262
Staatsnation perspective 224
staged authenticity 160–1
stakeholder: identification, theory 69; marketing/corporate communication, perspectives 104–6; perspectives *104–5*; significance 106
stewardship, notion 176
strategy 52; corporate strategy, relationship 65; focus 101
structural heritage 153–4, 158; explanation 153; illustration 153–4; verification 153
superiority, claim 153
sui generis 114
sustainable corporate heritage, model *253*
Swedish Crown 28
Swedish Monarchy 28
synthetic nostalgia 162

Tata Group 85
temporal dimension, importance 4

temporal focus/foci 280–1
temporality 174–5
temporal sensitivity 132
territory, articles 2–3
tertiary corporate heritage communications (tertiary CHC) 9, 122, 123
Tesco 83
textual representations 140
Third Reich 264–5
Thomas Coram Foundation for Children 91
three-dimensional tool, usage *282*
time: heritage, relationship 28, 107–8, 277–8; image/heritage, interrelated concepts 276–8
timelessness, quality 174–5
Tim Hortons 175, 247
Tong Ren Tang (TRT) 13, 214; average variances extracted (AVE) *232*; Chinese identity/civilization, relationship 236; Chinese national identity, conferring 235–6; Chinese national identity, relationship 235; conceptual framework 228–31; Confucianism/Daoist associations, importance 237; construct measures *233*; corporate heritage brand 216; correlations *232*; data analysis (results) 232; data collection, preliminary stage 231–4; descriptive statistics *232*; discussion/implications 234; domestic tourists, survey questionnaire 232; focus 217–18; hypotheses development 228–31; indigenous Chinese philosophies/religions, significance *225*; management implications 237; measurement validation/reliability 233–4; medicinal products/services, quality 230; research hypotheses test results *235*; research limitations 237–8; research method 231; tourist attraction 218–19
total corporate heritage communications 89, 118; explication 120–1; focus/nexus/effect *121*
total corporate heritage corporate communications, quadripartite dimensions *122*

total corporate heritage marketing communications 8–9
traditional power 22
traditions 23
triangulation *184*
tri-generational heredity 7, 106, 109–13, 222; external tri-generational heredity 113; internal tri-generational heredity 113; requisite 112–13
tripartite monarchical dictum 66
triple bottom line 57
trust: authenticity/affinity, relationship 30; bilateral trust, importance *30*; importance 6
truth, consensual basis 156

unremitting management tenacity 7, 106, 116–17, 222
Urde, Mats 1, 14, 16–17, 289
USP 42
utopian nostalgia 162

validation (acknowledging) 187
verbal identifiers 48
vibrant approach 253–4; latent approach, contrast 247
Victoria *see* Queen Victoria
visibility 52, 54–5; corporate communications, relationship 66; focus 101
visual identifiers 48

Wal-Mart 251; family control 260
"Welfare Monarchy, The" 57
Wetmore, Stephen 251
William I *see* King William I

Xiangyang, Yue 217
Xun, Lu 225–6

Yellow Emperor 226

Zeitgeist 54
Zheng, Yong 217–18
Zi, Lao 226